To Connie:

Thanks for support!

Keep Moving Forward!

# Compulsion

Dr. Mark Svetcos

Compulsion



Address all inquiries to:
Dr. Mark Svetcos
P.O. Box 5293
Glacier, WA 98244
www.marksvetcos.com
mark@marksvetcos.com

ISBN: 978-1-890427-09-2

Library of Congress Control Number: 2009933616

Editor: Tyler Tichelaar
Cover Painting: Mark Svetcos
Author Photo: Susan Marsidi Photography
Cover Layout: Fusion Creative Works, www.fusioncw.com
Typesetting: Fusion Creative Works, www.fusioncw.com

Printed in the United States of America

For additional copies, visit:
www.MarkSvetcos.com

# Acknowledgements

I would like to present my sincerest gratitude to all of those who have directly and indirectly helped me to create Compulsion, the Responsibility Movement™, and the Common Sense Evolution System™. There are no chance encounters. And every one of you has profoundly impacted my life and work in a significant and positive way. I thank you.

Dalton Akkerman, John and Lee Allerton, Lance Armstrong, Robert Beccue, Don Beyer, Zac Bingham, Erik Biscoe, John and Gail Biscoe, Dr. Andy Boesky, Cynthia Breza, Jamie Butler, Mark Caldwell, Brad Case, Christine Chandler, Cynthia Chomos, Deepak Chopra, Gary Churchill, Winston Churchill, Frederick Coe, Alana and Mark Collins, Willie Cove, Dr. Jeffrey Cronk, Susan Cross, Richard and Muriel Cross, Neil Curry, James Daalke, Ryan and Elizabeth Dean, Ms. DeLuca, Susan Driscoll, Pamela Dundas, Dr. Wayne Dyer, Patrick and Jackie Eelnurme, T. Harv Eker, Darren Ernst, Rudy and Jo Finne, Susan Friedmann, Susan Garbarino, Doug and Joan Gehrke, Walter Gerber, John Goodman, Burke and Inarvis Greene, Javier Gumucio, Mark Victor Hansen, Robert Hayes, Irv Hoch, Darryl Hool, Lisa Hoonan, Jennifer Hoskinson, Gordie Howe, Marty Howie, Doris Huntman, Chad Huntman, Chris Jaeger, Michelle Jenkins, Kristen Johnson, Dr. Joseph Kauffman, Dr. Robert Kelder, Katie Kelley, Fred Kennedy, John F. Kennedy, Sr., Joseph and Sylvia Kessler, Martin Luther King, Jr., James Knight, Arvel and Daisy Koon, David Koons, Kacey Kroeger, Patricia Krown, Michael Kubicek, Katie Kurtain, Pamela L'Esperance, Tara

Larsen-Carter, Nicole, Wesley, and Lauren Lew, Seth Lewis, Ryan Lockmundy, James Malinchak, Jennifer Manlowe, Matt McAlpine, Helen McCarthy, Charles Meyer, James Montgomery, Courean Napolitano, Brian O'Hara, Gary Oldham, Nehal Patel, Dr. Scott Peseau, Dan Pesko, Davey Peterson, Dr. Stan Pierce, Sr., Joe and Cathy Prevost, Coach Putnam, Anthony Robbins, Christopher Rooseboom, Theodore Roosevelt, Matt Rosa, Dr. Anthony Salamony, Casey Scheopflin, Michael Scherner, David Schmidt, Adam Shehan, Shiloh Shroeder, Mike Siegel, Blair Singer, Patrick Snow, Kevin Svetcos, Jerry Svetcos, Krista Svetcos, Katherine Svetcos, Dimitri Svetcos, Daniel Svetcos, Alex Svetcos, Chris and Rebecca Sweeney, Tyler Tichelaar, Jack Toepfer, Michael and Nancy Townsend, Brian Tracy, Jerry Turner, Terry Twilley, Bryan Ubaghs, Kim Vaughn, Aditi Vidyasagar, Debi Waldeck, Steve Watkins, Priscilla Weber, Angela and Vance Weedon, Wesley Werich, Shannon Wicks, Carla Williams, Doug Wilson, Morgan Wolfe, Marc and Tianna Yates, Michael Yoder, Steve Yzerman, Robert Zielke, and Zig Ziglar.

I offer my biggest thanks to my wife, Denise. Your grace, understanding and love are all-empowering. Every day, I resonate in the calm and clarity allowed by the union of our souls.

# Contents

Introduction

# How This Book Will Help You to Liberate Your One True Life

I'm Dr. Mark Svetcos, and I've made some bad decisions. In this book, I will tell the story of my compulsion, the dysfunctional life I led, the mistakes I made, and how I was punished for them by losing everything I had. But this book is more than a tell-all confession. I'm not seeking to make a hit with a sensational story. My purpose is to share what I've learned to help others end their own compulsive behaviors or poor decision-making, so they may lead positive, fulfilling lives of responsibility. This book is for those who have the power within to change and are willing to do whatever is necessary to make that change possible. I hope my personal story will be a guide and an inspiration to help you make that change a reality.

Initially, I perceived my compulsive behaviors as mundane, seemingly inconsequential actions and part of what at the time I considered normal life. I surrounded myself with people who reinforced negative behavior. My daily routine was based solely on accumulation, and I lived inside my head when not in the immediate presence of others, all the while playing negative reels of tape in my mind, ad nauseam. My ego had become prolific and unbalanced, and it caused me to act out, often sexually, while unconscious that my behaviors were largely based in chronic fear and anxiety and in reaction to events from my past that had made me unable to define my boundaries. My relationships suffered from my own indifference and my life quickly spiraled into a one-track mode of work and the incessant need for more—more money, more production, more efficiency, more control, more escapism and more women. The more I fed my ego, the more insatiable it became.

I soared further and further from my truest ideals, and the anxiety caused by that rift allowed for the introduction and proliferation of compulsive thoughts and subsequent behaviors.

I became a shell of a person as my initially idiosyncratic thoughts evolved into compulsions, and those compulsions became the new me. Within a few short months, my mistakes were uncovered and plastered all over the national media for everyone to see. My privacy was invaded, my name dragged through the mud, my reputation forever soiled. My medical license was revoked, my homes went into foreclosure and were auctioned off, and my ill-perceived financial stability quickly eroded from underneath me. As the events of my downfall unfolded before the public's eyes, vultures swarmed, attorneys fought, extremists bantered, and angry women stirred the pot. My family and friends were unable to help. I became isolated and exhausted, shrouded in a blanket of shame and guilt. Nothing could save me, except myself.

As I dealt with injustice, unfair practices and judgment by the self-righteous, a power I'd never acknowledged was activated within me. I made the commanding decision to live my life differently, from the inside out. It was time for me to step up to the plate and accept full responsibility for every single thing in my life. Finally, I came to understand that I truly have the power within myself to create and maintain the life of my dreams. And because I actively chose to deal head-on with all the tumult that surrounded me, I was rewarded with the ability to make conscious, purpose-driven choices that inherently gave me the strength to live through the greatest of all personal injustices, lack of self-responsibility.

The lessons I learned are not mine alone. I believe my journey resembles the lives of many people caught in vicious cycles of dysfunction; my story is relevant, directly or indirectly, to everyone. Most of us, at one point or another, walk around in a fog of uncertainty and apathy. Some even make such behavior a daily routine. We make passive decisions and allow life to happen around us instead of creating the life we desire. We allow the government and media to infuse our thoughts with fear and scarcity; we seek endless hours of entertainment, gossip about the relationships of movie stars, and allow our children's minds to melt in front of video games and televisions. We live inside our heads most of every day as we constantly maneuver to avoid the imaginary eight ball that looms just out of sight. We're poisoned with drugs, addicted to emotions, while offered few practical action steps by which to change our lives.

Within these pages, you will find not just a riveting story, but a proactive and real-life approach to creating the life you've been afraid to live. By example, I will teach you how to eliminate destructive thoughts before you allow them to control and ruin your life. By the time you've finished reading this book, you won't even be able to think within the negative feedback loops that riddled your past. You will be different. You will have proactively changed your life for the better.

Throughout this book, specific action steps will help you to become more conscious about everything you do. You will be more productive, more efficient, and you will challenge your emotions. Balance, focus, and a clearer mind will become your norm, rather than the exception. You will learn easy ways to eliminate life-stifling fear and worry, as well as techniques to uncover your passions and become healthier physically, mentally and spiritually.

My story will serve as an example of how change is possible. Parts of my story will resonate with you while other parts may not. Use what you find valuable as I demonstrate how I systematically re-organized my life by using the myriad information and practices I'd learned as a medical practitioner, business coach, counselor, and friend. I replaced what had formerly filled the gaps in my life—compulsive thoughts and overindulgent destructive behaviors—with focused meditation, gentle exercise, good nutrition and active thought creation. I began to smile more with each passing day and to allow good people into my life. Connecting with others became easier as I became stronger from within. My relationships became much more loving and held more meaning. The needless banter that had once consumed my existence was replaced by stimulating conversation. All these lessons culminated into a program I created called The Responsibility Movement, with The Seven Pillars of Responsibility at its core.

Self-responsibility, and how I became responsible, is at the center of this book. Responsibility is the common thread that binds all of us as humans. It supersedes all other individualistic and humanistic beliefs. Morals are passive and oftentimes relative to a given situation, but responsibility is the lowest common denominator. It's the closest representation of your connection with the infinite. If you are still blaming others, you still haven't entered fully into the game of life. You've relinquished all responsibility, not understanding that everything that happens in your life is all your own doing, whether directly or indirectly. For one reason or another, you have relinquished your own independence of thought, and subsequently, your responsibility to self and to those around you.

The lack of self-responsibility is one of the major ingredients in America's current social recipe for disaster. In order to create a productive America, we must, as rational, proactive beings, be in a position to experience a self-created abundance. We mustn't get stuck in positions we don't like, either at work or at home. We must prepare ourselves to live responsibly and with integrity, not allowing the propagation of escapism and fear that hovers over so many of us. Uncover and follow your passion so you're not caught recreating your same unhappy existence in the future. Balance work and play, work on your relationships and practice living a purpose-driven life.

There's only one way to change the world, and that is to change ourselves. We must practice living consciously and with integrity with primary focus on the self. This process inherently improves the world around us. This book will teach you how to bridge the gap between your ideals and your every day existence. It will help you to uncover your essence, that part of you needed as a contribution to this world. It is time to come back into balance, to live in abundance with responsibility, and to heal your relationships. That healing process starts with you.

As you read the following pages, I implore you not to judge, but to use my story to catalyze the healing in your own life. I challenge you to take the opportunity to step back and deeply inspect your own situation and how the Points of Responsibility in this book might help you actively to evolve. By being introspective, you will come out on the other side a leader, an innovator and the creator of your one true life. Accept mediocrity no longer. Become part of the responsibility movement. Be responsible for your behaviors and experience the life you truly desire.

Dr. Mark Svetcos
Glacier, Washington
May 28, 2009

# Part One:

# The Downward Spiral

Chapter One:

# The Drive

I roared down the smooth, gently curved residential street at a speed of 145 mph. I'd taken that stretch of pavement many times before, but never so fast. The multimillion-dollar homes were a blur to my right, and the Olympic Mountains stood tall and proud to my left. The classic rosewood Porsche and I recklessly hurled ourselves forward. Natasha was sleek, sexy and was being tested to her limits. We were definitely going too fast for the conditions.

I paid no attention to the mothers and children on the sidewalks. If someone were to pull out in front of me, catastrophe would ensue. It was common knowledge that one shouldn't drive emotionally, but I had to get away, to escape.

As I powered through the gears, I wondered how my life had become such a mottled chaos. I had always been a good person and done good things for people. I was a natural healer and never intentionally hurt anyone. Things like what I was now up against only happened to others who deserved them, not to people like me. My hopes, dreams, fears and anxieties began to flash through my mind's eye, increasing with each upward tick of the speedometer.

As I reviewed the mess that surrounded my life, I pushed the gas pedal further to the floor. She actually had more, and invited me to dip my toe further into the water. As I obliged her, emotions rushed in and I began to weep. I was losing my mind.

Through the tears, I saw the yellow caution sign to my right whiz by; 1000 feet to the S-curves ahead; first right, then left.

I shook off the emotion and thrust my left foot hard to the floorboard, downshifted into third gear and let the clutch out completely. The powerful engine whined ferociously as I approached the first curve. The tires melted slightly under the strain, like hot tar on a tarmac. I sped toward the banked ninety-degree turn at somewhere around 110 mph. I wasn't really sure, as the needle of the speedometer shook so violently. At about 200 feet, I slammed on the brakes and released, downshifted into second gear and pounded on the gas to put weight into the back of the car. The speedometer hovered around 80 as I leaned to the right, practically putting my head on the passenger seat. I could feel the tires slide slightly, as they melted and became one with the road. Everything to the sides of the car was a blur. Tunnel vision. To the front, I could see infinitely. Time stood still. There were no problems, no issues, and no malice or misunderstanding.

I roared out of the first curve, unscathed and momentarily enlightened. The smell of rubber and unburned fuel infused the cockpit. The car had lost some speed, so I up-shifted to third gear to pick it back up. As I approached the second curve, I repeated the sequence yet again: clutch, downshift to second, off clutch, gas. I was again speeding into the turn at around 80, and crossed the centerline to my left to get as much pavement as I could. Cool tears dried on my face as I leaned my head close to the cold driver's side window. In that instant, as I exited the turn, I saw it: The unmistakable gleam of a chrome bumper coming straight at my head.

Without thought, my body immediately struggled to keep the vehicle on course. I violently swerved to the right, then back to the left. Bits of rubber and road rocks sprayed from the tires as I teetered on the edge of control. In the eternity of that split second, I waited for a horrific crash, but it never came. I had cheated death yet again.

As Natasha and I hurtled out of the second turn, I wondered why I had been forsaken. The frustration from merely asking the question caused me forcefully to ram my foot back onto the gas, and in no time at all, we were approaching 120 mph again. The turn-off was just up to the right about a half-mile. As the red reflectors marking the driveway became visible, I released the gas pedal and pounded on the brakes. With hands cold and trembling, I gripped the wheel tighter and swerved the car onto the one lane road.

I quickly drove through the park and ended up on a little-known dirt utility track that lead to The Cliffs. It was the place where so many others had begun their ethereal search away from the physical plane.

The path was long and rough. About a mile into it, I was concerned it might be too much for Natasha. The slow negotiation of the relentless potholes was killing me slowly. I couldn't take the drudgery. It was like walking through quicksand, and I needed speed.

My mind was confused and my body strangely numb. An increasingly gnawing, burning feeling filled the pit of my stomach. I was like a rat in a cage. I wanted to scream as loud as I could to drown out the songs of the past. I was about to do so when I noticed the road up ahead was washed out. The powers that be weren't making it easy for me.

I shut down the car, opened the door, peeled myself from the leather seat and crawled out. I looked at the keys dangling, still in the ignition. I thought to myself, "I won't be needing them where I'm going," and closed the door.

I seemed to be running on autopilot as I waded across the overrun creek and freshly unearthed boulders in my business attire. I ripped off my tie and threw it onto the ground as I looked back over the creek at Natasha. Thirty minutes before, I had been having a wonderful lunch with my new fiancée as we discussed our upcoming nuptials. I turned quickly and ran as fast as I could toward The Cliffs.

As I ran down the dark path, I recounted all the events that had led up to this moment. I tried to contrive ways of denying the allegations. I rationalized and justified that I was the real victim. I tried to figure out who knew the facts, and whether each of them would talk to the investigators.

But there was no denying the obvious. I was going to pay. People in my position never won.

The question presented itself, "Why is this happening now?" I had committed some time ago to living with truth, integrity and purpose. I was living consciously. I had everything going for me—plenty of money, toys, houses and a loving wife-to-be. Why this? Why now?

I ran for about a mile and finally came to the clearing that overlooked The Puget Sound and the snowy Olympic Mountain Range. The first time I saw that majestic view three and a half years earlier, it had cemented my decision to move from Colorado to Seattle. I remembered thinking, "This is where I want to live and thrive." And now? It was where I wanted to wither up and die. The midday sun beat down on me. I took a deep breath, but couldn't seem to inhale fully. I couldn't catch my breath. The recent months of waiting and being in shock trained my spine and rib cage to bear down, to protect me. I felt as if I had a tortoise shell on my back and shoulders, and I was afraid to peer out. I was caged. Despair had surrounded me; it was too much for me to suffer.

As I walked to the edge of the sandy, limestone cliff, a deluge of tears accompanied tremendous sorrow for the things I had done. I stepped up onto the old growth log one never should pass. I looked down at the cold, rocky surf below and outstretched my arms.

***Secure a blank notebook and utilize it while progressing through the steps within this book. Use paper, not a computer. Studies show that the physical act of writing completes your thoughts and precipitates a finalized understanding of those thoughts. Words on paper become an end-point, and they facilitate action. YOU have created them. YOU have written them. They are YOUR thoughts and ideas. This is the first step in creating self-esteem. If you do this program with a computer, your words, thoughts and ideas remain in the mind and are not manifested into the physical world. They are, in effect, in the mind of the computer. Don't cheat yourself; write everything down.*

*Answer all questions and complete all the steps fully. Dump everything down onto the paper, even if it doesn't make any sense while you're writing it. Don't leave anything left behind in your mind. Through the process of introspection and writing, be honest with yourself and get to the bottom of the more challenging parts of your life. Some of the questions and action steps might seem simple to you; others will certainly challenge the very nature of your relationships, your mind and your soul.*

*When prompted by each question or action step, raise your head, take a few deep breaths and then begin to think about not just the answer you want to apply to your notebook, but also the process by which you've come to your answer. Where do your ideas come from? Are they learned; are they inherited; or are they your own?*

*Understanding, acknowledging and then verbalizing one's processes of reason and emotion is sure to elicit moments of frustration, and possibly even confusion. Those particular emotions and sensations are from the ego. It wants you to remain in your comfort zone. Realize that those are the times when you've struck a resonating chord within yourself. That is a 'trigger' to something you haven't yet acknowledged. When a strong emotion or confusion arises, simply say aloud, "Thank you for sharing," and then move quickly into the action of reason. Acknowledging and then moving past the emotion while becoming more objective is at the center of self-responsibility.*

*When confronted with challenging questions and action steps, the easy thing to do would be to put this book down and never pick it back up, or to become absorbed only in the stories of this book. I challenge you to take the lessons from the stories, and then rigorously apply the relative points to your own life. Now is the time. To put off this gift any further is to be irresponsible to yourself, your family and to humanity. This book and the processes within it will allow you the wonderful opportunity to step up to the plate, and to make YOUR life a purpose-driven, conscious representation of your ideals. The most powerful way to change the world is truly to understand ourselves, and to act first from responsibility. This is your chance to become everything that you know you are. We need your shining light. The following quote, by Oscar Wilde, says it all:*

"Be yourself. Everybody else is taken."

## Points of Responsibility

*1. Scour your past for three prominent events that have taken place where you've let your emotions get the best of you, or when you felt out of control. Describe in your notebook, in great detail, your emotional state during such occurrences. Don't focus on the 'why,' or the story of any specific event(s), but on your internal environment. What did your body feel like? How was your breathing, your posture, and your voice? What was going on in your head? Were you absent of thought? Did you think of the consequences of your words and actions? Be excruciatingly specific. This step is designed to begin the process of self-awareness. Do not be ashamed of or feel guilty for your past reactions. They're in the past. Simply acknowledge them so you know where you stand. We'll talk later about how to change any negative behavior.*

*2. Write in your notebook the answers to the following introspections. How do you handle your positive and negative emotions? What types of emotions do you find repeating, like little reels of tape within your head? Are these emotions adopted from others, or are they your own? Do you voice your opinions in a healthy way, or do you tend to stuff your feelings down deep, bottling them up for no one to see? Do you carry shame or guilt with you regularly? Do you share a healthy affection for your friends and family every day? How often do you smile?*

*3. Have you ever perceived yourself as being manipulated or backed into a corner? Write in your notebook how you feel when such events occur.*

*4. Know this: No person can MAKE you feel an emotion. YOUR feelings and emotions are YOUR choice. You CHOOSE to be emotional. Or you CHOOSE to take your power back. And the two events are not synchronous.*

Chapter Two:

# New Beginnings

**Three years earlier…**

Crack! The thunder boomed! Archie jumped out of bed and bolted around the apartment barking his head off. Half asleep, I yelled at him to stop, but, as usual, he kept on. I peered over to the nightstand. The clock read 5:30 a.m., another short night. I lay there for a few seconds as the lunatic pug bounded up and down the stairs and throughout the small studio apartment. I tried to peel my eyelids open. They were sticky and hot. They were more comfortable closed.

Slowly, the day's activity list crept into my mind. Adrenaline started to flow…I was up for the day. I groaned a little and turned my head to the right to see whether Natalie was up, but she only lay there gently next to me. The girl would probably sleep through the apocalypse.

I jumped out of bed and drew the shades to reveal yet another day of heavy spring rain in Seattle. I was getting used to it. I hadn't seen Mount Rainier since the first day we moved here, some eight weeks previously.

Even so, I was definitely falling in love with the city and its surroundings. It was cleaner, greener and quieter than any other metropolitan area I had ever visited. Just an hour out of town in any direction were rainforests, mountains, hot springs and the ocean. Around every other corner one could find these quaint little neighborhoods teeming with coffee shops and eateries of all types. The place was truly wonderful.

The constant parade of storms propagated a calm, introspective and creative feeling from within. Most streets were dark, even in the middle of the day. Streetlights shimmered off wet pavement, which seemed to put me into a slow, comfortable trance. My senses and awareness were heightened. I felt more at home in Seattle than anywhere in my life. It reminded me of my college days in Kalamazoo, but with rocky mountains and salty sea air. I also kept hearing from patients that if one could make it through the nine months of rain, you would be rewarded with the best three months of summer one could imagine. Sun would certainly be welcomed. But for the time being, it was the rain on which I thrived.

I walked carefully down the unlit, carpeted stairs, through the living room and into the tiny kitchen. The only thing I ever ate in the morning was generic crisp rice with rice milk. I poured myself a bowl, went back to the living room and ate in the dark while I looked out over the dark city. The pug was settled down and started eating his own breakfast; I couldn't help but notice. Ever since he was a pup, he had this funny habit with eating. He'd go to his bowl, squirrel a few kibbles into his mouth, run to wherever I was, and drop the morsels on the floor. He would then proceed to eat them one by one. I'd tried on numerous occasions to teach him how to eat at his bowl, but he would just stare at me and immediately return to his habit. I loved his fortitude; it was endearing.

After breakfast, we sat there on the couch, covered with the afghan my grandmother crocheted for me twenty years prior. I leaned back, took a deep breath and began to recount many of the hurdles I'd had to jump over the past years. I thought about all the stress, worry and hard work it took to get where I was.

I started my journey almost twelve years prior in Kalamazoo, Michigan. First there was aviation school, then pre-med, followed by doctorate school in Atlanta, Georgia.

I hadn't always wanted to be a chiropractor. I didn't have a life-changing story like so many others did. In fact, I was in my second year of pre-med when it found me.

I was at the library studying for a Biochemistry II exam and needed a little break. Being a Type A personality, I was stressed not to know what I was going to do with the rest of my life. Research? Physical therapy? Private practice of some type? I simply wasn't sure. I didn't want to dole out drugs every day, which made me shy away from the MD route. I wanted to be around people, which steered me away from research. I liked the idea of physical therapy, but it was based around a cold, rigid medical model, and physical therapists were usually required to do what physicians told them, leaving little freedom. I knew the only way I would ever be happy was to be my own boss, in whatever capacity that might be.

I had recently heard from a friend about a book called *The Job Outlook Handbook*. So I jumped up from my chair and hunted it down. When I threw the book on the table, it opened to "*Chiropractor*." I gave a little chuckle, and thought to myself, "I'm not going to be some quack." But I was curious, so I read the full job description. I was absolutely blown away by what I read. The characteristics were quite magnetic. Most chiropractors were in private practice. They primarily utilized mechanical methods to relieve mechanical stressors on the nervous system. Approximately one hundred different techniques ranged from manual manipulation to more specific and gentler machine-aided adjusting. Chiropractors rated very high on the "job happiness" scale, and made piles of money. It was the real deal. I got a feeling of glitter inside me. It was warm, fuzzy, and I knew to follow it. I was going to be a chiropractor.

From that point on, my life was simply mechanics. I went to school year-round to finish my undergraduate studies as quickly as possible. In the afternoons and evenings, I worked landscaping and serving jobs to pay the bills. When I had spare time, I involved myself in various volunteer and social organizations.

When I moved to Atlanta, the routine continued. I went to school full time and worked my way through the doctorate program. I excelled in academics and had a voracious appetite to become proficient in as many techniques as possible. In my last year of study, I discovered the specialty within chiropractic called Atlas Orthogonality (AO). That particular technique was highly specific, which drew me closer immediately. Only a few doctors were providing it to their patients because it required a sizable investment to acquire all the proprietary equipment, it was difficult to learn, and even more difficult to reproduce objectively repeatable results. It was exactly what I wanted, a challenge and a chance to create a niche within my profession.

In my last year of study, I checked out the top AO clinics in the region, and I was lucky enough to get invited to participate in an elite internship at the most innovative clinic in the country for upper cervical chiropractic study. Upon graduating with the doctorate, I left my girlfriend Natalie and Archie for three months to pursue the endeavor.

While interning, I decided I was going to start my own clinic. It was typical protocol for most doctors to work for someone else for years before ever thinking about venturing out on their own. But I knew from the beginning that route wasn't for me. I felt I would soon be in possession of the tools, both as a doctor and a businessman, to make a serious go of it. Each patient I saw and every encounter I dealt with helped me to gain the knowledge and confidence.

I continued the internship; I fine-tuned my doctoring skills while envisioning myself having my own practice. I visualized a large clinic with many patients coming and going. The atmosphere was light and happy. I was both a doctor and an educator. I presented powerful health and wellness seminars, which sold out every week. Natalie ran the office and Archie shared snot with all the little kids running around. It was a beautiful sight. Only one big question remained—where would this clinic be?

After the first month of interning, I went home for a visit. Natalie and I discussed where we wanted to take up residence for the next five years or so. Among the front-runners were Michigan, New York, Colorado, Washington and California. Although all had advantages and disadvantages, Colorado quickly stood out. Natalie had family there, and I had always shared an affinity for the mountains and snow. So we planned a trip for Christmas to check things out.

The trip was still six weeks away, so in the meantime, I battled on with the internship and started to accumulate the equipment to start my first practice. I had very little working capital, so I decided to lease the larger ticket items and leave the minimal cash reserve to purchase office supplies and smaller furnishings. By the end of the internship, I had a whole room in our apartment full of odds and ends I'd picked up along the way.

Christmas in Colorado was beautiful. Snow quietly blanketed the land each night as we strolled around, checking out the neighborhoods. We fell in love with the area almost immediately. The vistas overlooking the foothills and Flatirons were simply majestic. I wondered how I had survived for so many years in the Midwest and South without such scenery. I'd seen mountains before, but the West was so much more grandiose and magnificent. The air was crisp and clean. The people were progressive, active and fun. There were things to do every day and night. We decided, without even looking at another location, that it was where we wanted to live. It was perfect for us.

Before we left for Colorado, I'd pre-arranged to meet with three different doctors who were looking to rent out some space. The first two situations didn't fit, but the third was perfect. The doctor and I hit it off instantly. He was a younger guy with a moderately sized practice who had some space and wanted to lower his overhead. His wife ran the office, and she offered to check in my patients and take day-to-day payments for me. The office was brand new and faced to the West, overlooking Long's Peak and the Continental Divide. It was a dream come true. I negotiated terms with the doctor and his lawyer and completed the deal before we left. I had a home for my practice!

After the deal was struck, Natalie and I went searching for an apartment. We found a new complex that had all the amenities one could want: pools, hot tubs, large fitness center, squash, racquetball and tennis courts. The development stood atop one of the rolling foothills that led up to the mountains. From the front door one could see for miles with no obstructions. To the north were two small lakes fed by the winter snow pack. To the west were the snow-covered Rockies. And to the south, wide-open ranch lands. It was close to shopping, cinemas and great boutique restaurants. We were so excited for our new start.

We flew back to Atlanta the next day and immediately started preparing for the move to Colorado. The next three months were a blur. I had to coordinate both the move and the delivery and installation of my equipment in the Colorado clinic. I also created a system for operating my practice. Many things like patient flow, care plans, marketing and advertising all had to be shaped and produced from the ideas in my head. I had no paperwork for patients to fill out, so I prepared it all from scratch. I had no software for patient charting, coding and billing, so I bought a program that was popular in the industry and practiced every chance I got. By the time we rolled into Colorado, I was chomping at the bit to get my practice going. When we finally arrived, I hit the ground running.

I created a grass-roots approach to marketing and advertising. I pounded the pavement to meet as many people as I could. I joined clubs and groups, went to networking meetings and talks. I was literally working sixteen-hour days. The patients slowly trickled in, and before I knew it, I had a presence in the community. I started making enough money to cover expenses within two months. Finally, my life and finances had some momentum; what a tremendous relief that was.

It soon became obvious that the room I had rented wasn't big enough for my growing practice, so I started searching for a larger space. Just a mile down the street, I found an 1800 square foot medical office that had been vacant for about a year. The doctor whose office I was currently sharing was fine with letting me move on as he admittedly didn't like all the noisy traffic in his new office. I appreciated his candor and flexibility. Better yet, I would be paying $400 less per month for ten times the space I currently rented.

Over the next week, I built a beautiful little X-ray room, and painted and furnished the new space. That following weekend, I moved my practice down the street and opened up shop on Monday morning. It all happened so quickly.

I was responsible for all the marketing, advertising, scheduling, phone calls, receivables, payables, billing, coding, charting, book keeping, oh, and even a little doctoring in between. Times were interesting and incredibly busy, but I thrived on it. I continued becoming part of the community and attended as many events as possible.

Natalie, my girlfriend of five years, wasn't doing so well. She was stressed out all the time, and for no apparent reason. I agreed that our situation wasn't the most stable, but she had the opportunity to do anything she wanted: go to school, work in a field she liked, something, anything! She simply couldn't find her purpose or happiness. I asked her repeatedly to come to events with me and to spend some time at the clinic. I could have definitely used the help. But she said she didn't really fit in there. I always wondered what that meant because I was usually the only one there.

After a few months, I began to resent Natalie for spending her days at the bookstores and coffee shops around town while I was out busting my hump every day to pay the bills. I became frustrated that she didn't seem to give a darn, and she wasn't trying to make it work as diligently as me. It finally got to the point where we didn't talk much, and when we did, it was short. This went on for about a year.

### *Point of Responsibility*

*5. In my case, I was quite unhappy in my personal life for over a year. In fact, neither Natalie nor I were very happy. Our relationship was stagnant, and even though we declared to the outside world that we were together, we were really living two separate lives. We didn't acknowledge that we needed help. Have you ever pretended things in a relationship were okay, even when you knew they weren't? Have you, in your past, tended just to let things go, hoping they'll get better in the future? Think back to all your relationships, including family. In your notebook, write down one recurring negative activity from each relationship. A few examples of such activities are lack of communication, indifference, procrastination, lack of affection and showing anger. Did that activity change over time without your active input? Is it still happening? This activity is one of the first steps in self-awareness and creating consciousness in your life.*

One random evening, over a glass of wine, Natalie and I had a long, calm discussion about our hopes and dreams, something we hadn't done in a long time. She described how she just didn't fit in anywhere, and that she didn't really know what she wanted to do with her life. The only thing that inspired her was the possibility of going to acupuncture school. No schools were nearby that provided such an education. But I truly wanted her to be happy. So I encouraged her to do some research to come up with a plan of attack to become an acupuncturist.

The discussion of goals that night also inspired me to action. I was interested in parlaying my practice experience and equipment into a larger opportunity. I wanted a bigger space in a bigger market. I jumped online to check out some practice listings in the Colorado area. Unfortunately, absolutely none were available. Apparently when doctors practiced in Colorado, they stayed for a long time.

Amidst my hunt for an opportunity, I came across an interesting article that declared Boulder County, Colorado, as the single most difficult market to start one's own healthcare practice. There were around 150 people per practitioner. When I was in school, the business professors declared that one should never start a practice with anything less than 3,500 people per practitioner. I sat back and pondered the fact that I had built a successful, albeit small, practice in an extremely difficult environment. It was gratifying to know I had created a niche for myself in such a tough place to start up. The moment was both humbling and gratifying.

I expanded my search to San Francisco, Portland, Seattle and Alaska. I'd always had an interest in living along the rocky Northwest coast. San Francisco had a few larger clinics, but nothing really hit home for me. Absolutely nothing was available in Portland. In Seattle, I noticed a bunch of small clinics for sale, and then I saw it: the most perfect practice I could imagine. It was a family oriented practice in a well-to-do residential community called Atherton. The income was ten times what I was currently making. The practice had been established and in the same place for thirteen years. And the doctor wanted to retire. "Ask and ye shall receive," I thought to myself. When I showed Natalie the listing, she became genuinely excited about the potential because Seattle had a great acupuncture school. We decided to fly to Seattle to check it out the next week.

On the plane ride to Seattle, I felt a little disappointed about possibly leaving my practice and Colorado altogether. But if the practice in Seattle were everything it professed to be, I would jump in with both feet. It was the kind of opportunity that came along only once in a great while. If it were a good fit, I wasn't going to let it slip by.

## *Point of Responsibility*

*6. Is there a pattern in your life of incessantly searching for the Next Big Thing? Throughout my college career and into the beginning of my professional career, I was willing to leverage my happiness and my relationships to achieve success. But I had almost no appreciation for what I had already achieved or had in my life. In hindsight, I could have had happiness, positive relationships and success all at the same time.*

*Nothing is wrong with achievement. But achievement just for the sake of achievement is, at best, worthless; and at the very least, it's soul robbing. To be happy is to be successful, and vice versa. The tie that binds these two is balance.*

*When happy, you're more passionate, trustworthy and responsible; it's the most powerful and easiest way to create abundance. Think back to your business and professional relationships. Has there been a pattern of searching for something better without the appreciation of what already exists? The grass may look greener on the other side of the hill. But if and when you get there, are you going to look at the hill beyond with the same thoughts? Are you just biding your time in your relationships until something better comes along? Do you tell yourself that it's better than nothing? This type of thought and self-trickery will keep you unhappy until you become grateful for the people and things in your life, no matter how successful you become. Anything less is disrespectful to yourself and everyone around you.*

*In your notebook, evaluate separately your business relationships and your personal relationships. With regard to business, do you have a well-thought-out plan to work within your ideals in a passionate way? Or are you trying to get to the next level of achievement because that's what you're "supposed" to do? The main point is that achievement can and does happen in both ways. But you'll be so much happier with the former. With regard to your personal relationships, be honest as you evaluate each one. If you're not happy in your relationships, but genuinely want them to continue and to be better, begin to think of ways to appreciate them more and act on them.*

*Write in your notebook the things you don't like about your relationships. Then think about how each of those things is manifested in your own language and activity. Always remember, people mirror your emotions. If you're constantly confronted with angry people, you're the angry one. This is true for all emotions, including love. This understanding is at the heart of claiming both the positive and negative sides of your personality. I remember reading an old quote,*

"If you're bored in your relationship, you're probably boring."

*Change yourself before you ask others to change.*

*If, after deep introspection, you know your relationship will not be successful or doesn't fit your ideals, stop being selfish and let your partner know what's really going on inside you. But remember, this should happen only after the two of you have discussed the relationship and tried to make it work. Everything must be laid out on the table. It's important not to feel guilty for bringing things up. You're probably doing your partner a favor as well. If any of these actions scare you or bring up anxiety, that's okay. Again, that's a trigger that's telling you something must be done for you to move forward.*

*I'll discuss more later about specific action steps to become a better partner and how to recapture or recreate your relationships.*

As the plane landed and we taxied in the rain, I heard someone say it had been raining for thirty days straight. We grabbed our baggage and walked out of the airport; I took a deep breath of the clean, crisp, evergreen air. It was like the first time I had ever taken in a full breath.

We caught a shuttle to the rental car booth and were quickly off to see the practice. The thirty-minute drive showed us some of the most beautiful scenery in the world. We saw Mount Rainier and the Northern Cascades. We drove the clean streets of downtown Seattle and finally went up a large bridge that overlooked a marina full of multimillion-dollar yachts. To the west were Elliott Bay, Puget Sound and the freshly snow-covered Olympic Mountain Range. In the rearview mirror was the famous city skyline with the Space Needle and Mount Rainier. We had been in town for less than an hour, but we were already in love with it.

We took a little drive around the posh residential neighborhood before meeting with the doctor. When we finally meandered our way to the clinic, he greeted us at the door. The staff was gone until after lunch, which gave us a great opportunity to talk business. We stayed until all questions were answered and we were satisfied with everything.

As we got into the car, Natalie asked me what I thought. To me, the whole situation was a dream come true. I'd already gone over the financials and sifted through the mountains of documented statistical trends associated with the clinic and the community, and the timing was perfect for us.

Natalie and I continued to talk further about everything late into the night and agreed that a new start would do us some good. She was excited because Seattle was home to one of the best acupuncture programs in the country. And I was excited to take over what could potentially be my dream practice.

All in all, we spent nine days in Seattle learning the ins and outs of the city, sipping coffee, and trying to figure out the best place to live. We noticed that, in every neighborhood, a lot of babies were being pushed around in strollers, which was always good for business. Mothers weren't the easiest on their backs. They had to lift, carry and push baby strollers and all the paraphernalia associated every day—a well-proven recipe for neck and back pain, sciatica and most types of headaches. And those ailments responded well to my specialty.

On one particularly day, the sun broke free of the clouds and beamed down onto the city below. Natalie and I decided to go to the top of the Space Needle to do the tourist thing. The view was breathtaking. The snow-covered Cascade and Olympic Mountains jutted up on either side of us. Puget Sound trafficked big ships and small sailboats below. The sky was crystal blue and the sun kept the bite of the cold away. I turned to Natalie, pulled from my pocket a ring, and asked her to marry me. She just looked at it for a few seconds, took it out of the box, and said, "Sure, I'd like that." I didn't really have any expectations around the event, but I was surprised she didn't express more excitement or give me a long embrace. I was somewhat disappointed. I remember thinking to myself, "I guess this is just how it is; how it's supposed to be." We quietly celebrated that night before returning to Colorado the next day.

When we got back to Boulder, my only focus was figuring out whether I could buy the practice in Seattle. I quickly analyzed my financial situation and concluded it would take 90% of the cash I had to put down on the practice. It was a ton of money, but my motto had always been, "No Risk, No Return."

Within days of our return to Colorado, I contacted the broker who listed the Seattle practice and informed him of my plans to seek financing to purchase it. Over the next few months, we negotiated terms; I easily found financing, and I quickly sold the Boulder practice to a local doctor. Then we were off to Seattle for yet another new beginning.

Transitioning the practice from the previous doctor to myself was definitely a challenge, but we made it as smooth as possible. He would go in alone with the patient and render treatment, and then I would come in after a few minutes to be introduced as the next owner and clinic doctor. Most patients were fine with having a new doctor. It was clear to them that I was more than proficient, and it helped that I was a likable guy. The patients made it easy on me; they just wanted to know they were going to receive quality care.

The staff was extremely helpful. In fact, they were rock stars. Interestingly enough, they consisted of three young, extremely religious women. At first, I was a little skittish about having my office run by them, as I had always been a more spiritual than religious person. But there was no guarantee any of them would stay with the clinic after the other doctor was gone, and I definitely couldn't run that practice on my own, so I needed to keep that team together at all costs. I made sure we experienced as little friction as possible. It took me some time to adjust to seeing eighty patients in a day, but with tons of help from those three ladies, the practice quickly became seamless.

The days were very long and tiring as the outgoing doctor and I discussed patients, went over X-rays and talked about everything else involved in running a successful large practice.

The first two weeks went by without a hitch. Then one night when the doctor and I were locking up, he asked, "Are you ready to rip the Band-Aid off and run it without me?" I immediately agreed it was a good idea. We both noticed that patients seemed a bit confused about whether to consult with the old doctor or the new doctor. We obviously saw the issue and determined if I were the only one there, patients would be clear on who would be continuing their care.

After that decision, the days seemed to fly by. I found it much easier running the practice on my own. As I came to understand fully in the next couple of months how the practice could function optimally, the worry and anxiety associated with the change began to dissolve.

I still had lots of work to do, but I felt I had arrived to a small degree. Times were busy, but good. Money started to flow in for a change, which was nice, since I had recently accumulated a mountain of debt to buy the practice. On one hand, I had genuine gratitude for the income, and on the other, I expected it. It was nice to see a reward, and dreams were coming to fruition. I perceived things as a natural upward progression.

Natalie seemed to be doing better as well. She enjoyed school and was less stressed. We didn't get a lot of time to talk or hang out, but it was okay with both of us. We were fine.

## Chapter Three:

# The Routine

Each morning I had a ten to fifteen minute commute to Atherton. Natalie and I got lucky when we initially came across our cool rooftop apartment. Someone vacated the place only days before our inquiry, and although a handful of people were interested, I bullied my way into seeing the manager and told him we'd take it before we were even on the list to view it.

After seeing three other joints, I was determined to live in that particular place. All the others were questionable at best. We really liked the funky little neighborhood, and it was relatively close to almost everything. We were only a ten to fifteen minute drive from anywhere in Seattle including Downtown, Atherton, the East side, and both North and West Seattle. That's why it was dubbed "The Center of the Universe."

Our apartment was a bit more expensive than we had planned, but unlike the others we checked out, it was clean, quiet and had plenty of natural light. Rumor had it that only a few years prior, our little neighborhood had been a seedy industrial warehouse area full of old dive bars and the scowling wretches who patronized them. Over the past five years, however, it had changed rapidly from a dumpy, run-down, inexpensive haunt to a yuppie-filled hangout with coffee shops, sushi joints and second-hand bookstores. The sheer number of people flocking to the city to support the IT industry apparently forced the transition. And with them came more expensive food, higher rent and more BMW's per block than one could count on both hands. But even with its close proximity to downtown and all the new money, it was still one of the least expensive places to live in Seattle. It was a good place to start.

My drive to Atherton in the morning was usually uplifting and exciting. The early morning summer sun shimmered off dew kissed leaves, grasses and plants. I would usually listen to some ambient dance music as I happily weaved through the horrible city traffic. Each morning, I would stop at the local coffee shop for a little jump-start. The lines were always long, but I never spent more than five minutes waiting for my highly caffeinated beverage. I was amazed at the efficiency of the whole process. The Seattle coffee craze was for real. After paying with a generous tip, I would quickly hop back into the car and be on my way.

The only tedious part of my daily trip was a tremendously crowded intersection I had to cross to go toward Atherton and Downtown. There were no short cuts as every single car had to pass over a drawbridge to get to its destination. But once on the bridge, one could see over the Puget Sound to the snow-covered Olympics on the right. And on the left was the sun rising in the East over Lake Union and the city. This part of the day was my most coveted. I oftentimes found myself smeared with one of those little smiles we give when we don't even know we're smiling.

Immediately following the bridge was my turnoff into Atherton, where one could take in the most beautiful views of and from Seattle. Everything can be seen from this highly desirable real estate: the cityscape, Elliott Bay, the Sound, both mountain ranges, and all the surrounding neighborhoods. It was one of the few places to see a completely unobstructed view of the sunset. It sat up high, about six hundred feet above the rest of the city. Originally, Atherton was an island. Many years previously, the powers that be filled in most of the waterway between it and Downtown, making it easier to access. They also built three small bridges that still served as the only access points; the limited access was desirable to the inhabitants of the small neighborhood. Unless one had specific business on the rock, there was no need to be there. It was a destination point, which limited riff raff and kept crime to an extreme minimum.

The fact that Atherton was only a few minutes from Downtown Seattle helped its desirability factor as well. It was highly sought-after real estate. Home values were higher than I'd ever personally experienced. Atherton was filled with well-to-do folks of various types from rich, old businessmen, to young professionals and business owners. It was where Seattle's elite lived, and where many of Seattle's professional athletes took up residence. An interesting mix existed of both old and new money, and I enjoyed immensely getting to know the place and the people who made it to thrive.

I had only a two-minute drive from the bridge to the clinic. I carefully meandered through the residential streets, went through the quaint Village of Atherton, and on to the clinic. Every day as I turned the key to shut off the engine, I took a few deep breaths, collected my thoughts, and put on my game face. I knew as soon as I walked through that door, my day would be nonstop until seven o'clock that night.

I typically started the day running. As soon as I walked through the door, I had a line that was four patients deep in the reception area. Once the staff heard me enter the building, patients were escorted to their respective rooms, and we were off. I would enter Room 1, discuss the pertinent information with the patient, provide the necessary treatment, use the percussion instrument to relax the musculature, and write notes as we talked and finished up. After a brief prognosis, I would release the patient for the day. Then I'd open the door and scoot into Room 2 to repeat the program. That was how it went until lunch. Visits were relatively short and incredibly efficient. Surprisingly, most patients liked it that way. They didn't like waiting, ever. Any time I was with someone who required more time, I would be greeted in the next room with a hurried atmosphere. Everyone was always late for whatever was next on his or her to-do list. It was trial under fire, as I was forced quickly to cultivate the art of successful healthcare in America.

Running that clinic wasn't as easy as just treating people all day. I was ultimately responsible for everything. I not only had to negotiate peoples' physical pain, but the anger and frustration around the injury, the psychology around that pain, and the specific role of each patient's internal and external daily environments. I had to tackle reservations and concerns about treatment and discuss policies and payment options for services rendered.

People didn't typically understand what chiropractic was. It was up to me to educate each of them. But that was where I thrived. Patients were typically amazed with how much could be affected by properly administered chiropractic care. Via specific and gentle mechanical adjustments, mobility was greatly improved; headaches, pain and poor immune function were things of the past. The overall improved functionality of the nervous and circulatory systems was profound. The whole process invigorated me, and I was excited to tackle any and all deficiencies and questions.

Being a doctor was absolutely wonderful. I originally had no expectations around it, but I was pleasantly surprised with the trust my patients gave me. I felt like a functional, helpful part of society. I was finally giving back, after all the years of study and hard work. All the failed relationships, the turmoil, the difficulties and giving without receiving seemed to be fading into my past. I thoroughly enjoyed helping people from a very fundamental level. My approach was unique and gentle and my focus was conservative and swam in common sense. I believed in a mechanical approach to aid mechanical problems, and most pain-related issues were mechanical in nature. I believed drugs and surgery were a last resort for such issues. Everyone seemed to agree America was over-drugged and undernourished. This straightforward approach was refreshing and new to many. I was getting back to the basics of non-extreme healthcare.

One thing paramount to a successful practice, in my opinion, was listening to every word every patient said. I encouraged patients to talk about their lives and inspired them to become better from the inside out. I created personalized plans for everyone including adjustments, massage, acupuncture, meditation, specific readings and nutrition. It was a well-rounded approach. People enjoyed coming into the office and having great conversations while being healed in a wonderfully low-stress atmosphere.

After the first few months, the hectic nature of the business transition started to slow a bit. I was becoming familiar with most of the returning patients, and the staff and I ran like a well-oiled machine. I had adopted some of the ideas and procedures from the previous doctor and created a systematic, objective and educational method to help patients not only to improve their physical health, but also improve the understanding of health itself. I was coming into my own, and it felt good.

While seeing patients, I felt I was in my zone. I noticed I was exceptionally gifted with the ability to allow people to calm down, to be quiet, and to relax. People trusted me with their deepest secrets, worries and fears. I wasn't just their chiropractor, but their confidant. Diagnosis and treatment quickly became second nature for me. Everything seemed to flow very easily.

After one memorable treatment, a patient jumped up and asked me, "Are your hands always that hot?" I didn't exactly know how to answer her, so she continued, "Your hands feel like they're on fire when you adjust my neck and back. It's like they have electricity running through them!"

Over that first summer, I had quite a few patients tell me how hot my hands were during treatment. I noticed when I was focused, quiet and listened to the patient's body, my hands became hottest; they seemed to know, before my mind could diagnose, where the problem areas were in each patient. It was like the heat was the connection, or the conduit of communication between our bioenergetic fields. I could actually feel heat emanating from inflammations associated with misaligned spinal joints and other injured areas. At first, I thought my mind was playing tricks on me, but after talking with a few of my mentors, I learned that heat emanating from the hands during treatment was a manifestation of pure focus.

I had a gift that was very exciting to cultivate. As the months went by, I learned to use this additional means of communication more effectively. In fact, it became the first mechanism by which I scanned the body of each patient to determine where to look further for mechanical deficiencies. On countless occasions, I found an aberrance or stagnation point in a patient's body that was actually much more important than the musculoskeletal condition for which he or she was being treated.

Near the end of one patient's treatment, I sensed I had missed something, even though I addressed everything with which she was concerned. As she lay on her back and told me about her plans for the day, I gained her consent to try an additional energy therapy I'd recently learned. I went to the head of the table and put one hand on either side of her head, near her ears but not touching her. Without being prompted, she immediately stopped talking and closed her eyes. Within seconds, her eyes were darting back and forth and her body started twitching, as if she were replaying something in her mind. My hands became red hot. I'd never felt anything like it. I quietly asked whether she were all right. She quietly replied, "Yes." I kept my mind completely clear and added absolutely no thoughts into the process. I simply pictured a calm beach-type setting. The treatment continued for another minute or so when tears started streaming from the corners of her eyes and into her ears. I quietly asked again whether she was all right. She replied with another quiet "Yes." After about two minutes of holding my hands in the same place, her face and body relaxed completely.

I took my hands away and asked her to take a few deep breaths before getting up. After the treatment, we talked for a few minutes about the experience. She described an overwhelming sense of relaxation and relief. She also informed me that her body felt great, with absolutely no pain. I asked her about the tears, and she said, "Those were tears of understanding." When I asked what she meant, she replied, "I've been going through some major things in my home life, with my adult children. The therapy you just provided has cleared the cobwebs from my brain. I can clearly think about my situation now, and I know exactly what to do." I asked her what she had envisioned throughout the experience. What she said blew my mind. She told me she had pictured a reddish sunset over a beach, and heard the waves gently lapping at the sand.

Such situations were not an every day occurrence in my office. But treatments like that certainly showed me the importance of human touch and intention.

### *Point of Responsibility*

*7. Do you both give and receive love and genuine touch on a daily basis? This is a large part of connecting to and using a power that's greater than any one of us as humans. Giving energy to and taking energy from others through a loving hug is a great way to recalibrate your own energy levels and to help others through an unspoken tough moment. Hug your friends and family tightly, and smile when you do it. You will both appreciate it.*

People started coming from many miles away to receive treatment at my clinic. I was seeing difficult cases, cases that hadn't been resolved by traditional health care methods or other chiropractors. I treated various types of headaches, carpal tunnel symptoms, fibromyalgia, chronic fatigue, scoliosis, sciatica, TMJ disorder, acid reflux, and tinnitus successfully.

### *Point of Responsibility*

*8. Seeking the proper type of health care in America is a confusing process, at best. Studies show that most Americans defer treatment until the symptoms of their condition become too much to deal with alone. I had one patient who suffered with neck pain since falling off her horse five years prior. Within one week of treatment, the symptoms were diminished by 90%. If you are experiencing a condition, or conditions, for which you simply don't know what type of health care practitioner to see, check out the "Responsibility in Personal Healthcare" link on www.responsibilitymovement.com for a detailed description of types of practitioners and their respective fields of expertise. Along with the empowering information provided on the site are links to other informational sites to help you make an educated decision on how to proceed into the realm of the American healthcare system.*

One woman who visited my office hadn't been able to swallow normally for about thirty-five years as a result of a wicked car crash. Monica suffered with a mild to moderate pain every time she swallowed. It didn't matter whether it was a liquid or a solid. She looked emaciated from being unable to eat with any pleasure. Her mood was dull; she was depressed and had a tinge of anger. Monica heard about my clinic from a friend who had been hounding her for months to come see me. Monica finally decided to give it a shot, although she informed me on her first visit that she didn't believe in chiropractic. I smiled and told her, "That's great, because chiropractic is a common sense approach to alleviate physical ailments. It's not something that warrants faith. It's not a belief system. Think about it this way: if you have a rock in your shoe, a physical alteration from the norm, you have two options: 1) you take some pain killers and maybe an anti-anxiety pill to help you deal with it, or 2) you take the rock out of your shoe, remove the physical alteration." She liked the story, but she was still skeptical.

I gently and specifically adjusted her Atlas that same day and sent her home with post adjustment instructions. Two days later, Monica was a completely different woman. Her smile was radiant, her skin glowed, and she said she had more energy than ever before. I evaluated her spine and made some minor adjustments. But the most truly amazing thing was that after only one specific Atlas adjustment, she was able to swallow fully and without pain. And the bone stayed in place; I didn't need to readjust it for almost a year. Through the next few months, Monica began to live the truest representation of herself, treating everyday as if it were her last.

Word started getting out into the community that I had a new approach to healthcare. When I started giving health lectures to various community clubs and organizations, I found I had a real passion for public speaking and for coaching others. I enjoyed explaining the techniques I used and discussing health and wellness with inquisitive people. A palpable charisma was around me, and a reciprocated desire for knowledge.

As those first few months quickly passed, I found myself incredibly busy. I started my day around 6:00 a.m., saw patients in the morning, gave talks or visited various networking groups at lunch, and saw patients in the afternoon. After that, I would grab a bite to eat and head home to create marketing and advertising copy for the upcoming week's ad campaign. I was married to my work. Building and managing my practice was the only thing that mattered to me. I was completely consumed and strangely happy that I had very little down time.

My pinpoint focus paid off almost immediately. I was getting new patients from all over the place. The health talks and ad campaign were quite successful. The largest influx, however, came from personal referrals. People were talking, and they talked a lot. The community was buzzing about my clinic. I was deeply humbled, and I appreciated all that was coming my way.

I became heavily involved in a number of charities and met new people everywhere I went. I met local government officials, small and large business owners, socialites and literally hundreds of soccer and little league moms. Soon I couldn't walk down the street without passing someone I knew. It felt good finally to belong to a community.

The new influx of patients was rewarding since I knew they were coming to my office due to my efforts. I no longer relied on the momentum created by the previous doctor. I did what was necessary to run my business successfully. Seeing it all come to fruition was incredibly gratifying, to say the least.

## *Point of Responsibility*

*9. List in your notebook those things for which you're most grateful. Be as specific and as colorful as possible. Focus on the intangible elements of your life such as: your abilities, your positive relationships, and your children.*

In one particularly interesting two-week period, I met five individuals who would come to shape my life significantly, each in his or her own way. One of those individuals was Atia. Atia heard about me from a good friend of hers in the community I'd helped a couple of months earlier. She was hoping I could help her with some of the issues she'd been suffering from for years.

When Atia entered my office, I was writing notes at my desk. My desk was out of plain view, but I could hear almost everything that happened in the office. Atia immediately struck up a conversation with two of the staff members, as if she had known them for years. She was engaging and friendly, so they all got along famously. The three of them talked for almost thirty minutes before I even saw her.

I peeked my head out to see what was taking so long; Atia was modeling for the girls her new little schoolgirl outfit, complete with knee-high socks, a short, plaid skirt, a half-length button-down, white, collared shirt and dark brown shoes. All of that was set onto a 5'2", middle-aged frame with an obvious workout obsession. Her attire wasn't something one saw in Atherton every day, at least on any adult.

I looked at my schedule for the remainder of the day; it was completely full. I needed to get things rolling if I wanted to fit Atia in. I walked up to the front desk where everyone was congregated. I introduced myself and asked Atia to follow me so we could get started. After she said goodbye to the girls, we went back to an exam room for our first conversation. We talked at great length about the issues she wanted addressed. She was eloquent throughout the process as I asked the necessary professional questions. I got the sense that she was sizing me up, although I wouldn't understand why until much later.

I followed our little talk with a spinal exam and X-rays. I remember thinking to myself that her short skirt probably wasn't the proper thing to wear to a doctor's office. But it was no big deal to me. I simply used a blanket to cover her lower body. I completed the spinal exam and asked her to come back later in the week so we could talk about the things I found.

When Atia returned a couple of days later, she brought treats, something she would continue doing for years to come. After a few minutes of surface talk between her and the girls at the front desk, I met with Atia in the exam room to discuss her case. She was interestingly lackadaisical about the whole thing. She declared, "I don't care what you do; just make the pain stop a little." She didn't care about why she had pain or what she could do to stop it from coming back in the future. She just said, "If I ever hurt, in any way, I'll just come and see you, and you'll fix me up, right?" That was how I came to know Atia.

Over the next few months, we became pretty good friends. We saw each other often, sometimes in the office, but usually around in the community. Atia decided to "take me under her wing," as she put it. She felt the need to help integrate me into the community further. She introduced me to many people, and would then give me the dirt on them, such as who was cheating on whom, legal battles, who were the drunks, who did drugs, etc. She seemed to know everything about everyone. I was finally getting to know the underworld of Atherton.

On the surface, it was glaringly obvious that Seattleites were decent about greeting outsiders with open arms. But I also noticed that very few of the people I met were interested in accumulating friends. They held me at arm's length, just long enough to put me into a category they could understand. Once I was perceived as basically non-threatening, the relationship remained at that superficial level indefinitely.

When I explained my theory on people in Seattle to Atia one afternoon, she just laughed. She told me the people of the Pacific Northwest were notoriously that way. They typically looked at all newcomers as outsiders, so it was a difficult place to make friends. I didn't want to believe that. I had always believed in a story a mentor had told me many years earlier, so I shared the story with Atia:

> Once a guy was thinking of moving to a small town where there lived a monk. He decided to go see this monk, to get a true view of the way of life in this small town. The monk received him, and they sat facing each other in the Great Temple. The monk asked the man how he could help. The man replied with his story, and that he wanted to know what things were like in that small town. The monk asked, "How are things where you're from?" The man replied, "The people are angry and inconsiderate. They yell and scream at each other for no good reason. The pace is hurried, and it's difficult to meet good people." The monk quickly offered, "That's exactly what people are like here." The man, dumbfounded, paused for a few seconds. But before he could formulate another question, the monk asked whether the man needed help with anything else. The man said, "No, but thank you," got up and left the town, never to be seen again by the monk.

> A few years later, another man had the same notion to move to this town where the monk lived. He, too, visited the monk and asked, "What are people like here, in your town?" The monk asked, "What are people like where you're from?" The man replied, "Well, people are wonderful. They are giving, loving, and look out for one another. Most people are happy." The monk quickly offered, "That's exactly what people are like here." The man thanked the monk for his time, and respectfully got up and left.

I explained to Atia, "This story tells us that our environment is controlled by us alone. We control the type of people who surround us. We control our actions, and thereby our reactions." She gave me a sarcastic little laugh, and said, "Whatever. It's still hard to meet good people here."

Later that same week, I met an old patient of the previous doctor. It was the first time we'd seen one another, although it had been three months since I had taken over. He admitted to me on that first day that he was afraid to see a new doctor, so he waited as long as he could before coming in. And that was why he looked like a human pretzel in the corner of the treatment room. Bobby was a very well dressed, obviously gay gentleman. He had a calm, caring nature about him. And right from the get go, he and I hit it off. In fact, on that first day, he and I sat and talked for about thirty minutes. I didn't usually get that kind of time to spend with people. But there we were, shooting the breeze as if we had known each other for years. At one point, he came right out and asked me whether I was gay. I told him I wasn't, and that I had a fiancée who had moved to Seattle with me. He replied, "We'll see what we can do about that." We laughed and began to talk about Atherton. He was full of gossip and clearly loved to share everything he knew about the area and the people who inhabited it. As a local proprietor, Bobby had been in the area for years and done quite well.

On our way up to the front desk after treatment, Bobby invited Natalie and me over for dinner later that week, and I accepted. We went over with a great bottle of wine and the three of us had a wonderful time gossiping and getting to know one another. Atherton was starting to be a lot of fun. I never knew what was going to happen next. Bobby became a long-term patient and an important friend of mine through thick and thin. We got along splendidly.

A day after I met Bobby, I was walking down the street in the Village and happened upon a cute little boutique. I enjoyed looking for women's clothing for Natalie, so I went in to check out the merchandise. While I was there, I picked out a little top and went to purchase it. Behind the counter was a beautiful blonde, Italian woman with huge blue eyes named Chloe. As she rang me up, she complained to one of her employees that her neck had been giving her trouble for over a week. As she rubbed it, I told her I was the new chiropractor down the road. She laughed and said she had actually been thinking of coming down to see me later that day. We continued to talk a bit. When she asked how I liked Atherton, I said I hadn't really had much chance to check things out, what with the new clinic and all. She gave me a piece of paper with her cell number on it and said, "I'm not trying to pick you up or anything, but it can be difficult to meet people here. If you ever need anything, just give me a buzz. I can show you around a bit if you like. And I'll see you later this afternoon. I have to have this neck worked on." Good people were coming out of the woodwork. Chloe and I became the best of friends and confided in each other the most secret of secrets. She introduced me to her family and friends, showed me the best places to eat and drink, and kept me abreast of the local gossip, of which she was always privy due to her high-profile clientele. She was wonderful.

A few days later at the clinic, I was introduced to a new patient named Sonya. Sonya had just moved to Seattle from California with her boyfriend, Gabe. They came north looking for a future together. The job market in California left quite a bit to be desired, so they were seeking a new start and didn't know anyone in the area.

After a couple of months, Sonya and I had become well acquainted during her treatment sessions. Gabe had extensive training in acting and was involved in small local productions, so Sonya asked Natalie and I to meet her and Gabe at one of his productions. Natalie and I agreed, and after the production, we all went out for a drink and had a great time. Gabe was a lot of fun and had more stories than Vince

Vaughn. I really liked him a lot. Over the next few months, we had tons of fun with those two.

That first summer in Atherton was special in many ways, and enlightening in others. New friendships were growing stronger by the week. I continued meeting more people. The clinic was running efficiently. Money wasn't a concern anymore as collections were rolling in with consistency. But on the personal side of things, I could feel my relationship with Natalie was changing. We were drifting apart.

## *Point of Responsibility*

*10. With what type of people do you surround yourself? Write in your notebook the nature of every relationship in your life. Again, be specific. Describe the emotions that come to the surface when you think about each relationship. Is each relationship balanced with give and take actions?*

Chapter Four:

# Trouble in Paradise

People were right; summer in Seattle was absolutely amazing. The weather was bright and sunny most days. In fact, the rain visited us only a few times between June and August.

Seattleites know they live in a real gem of a city, so much so that many actively discourage others from moving to the area. In fact, a number of Pacific Northwest residents told me directly to keep the natural splendor to myself. The first time someone said that to me I laughed, but when it wasn't reciprocated with as much as a chuckle, I quickly deduced that people from that particular locale didn't like outsiders much at all. They tolerated such folks, but didn't necessarily like them.

I thought the whole thing a bit trivial and interestingly twisted with entitlement. But what did I know? The place was gorgeous, and I appreciated living there, people and all.

As that first autumn approached and the leaves started their annual color change, I began to notice that sunlight was different in Seattle. The light rays projected at a lower angle than anywhere I had lived in the past. They created an interesting optical effect that made the greenery seem to shimmer and dance with life. Blades of grass became translucent and were illuminated. Flowers were more colorful and vibrant. The sunlight bounced and highlighted the contrast between the dark, volcanic Earth, the snow-covered mountains and the dewy, evergreen backdrop. It was a completely different world to me.

Chloe and I decided to grab some lunch at the local pub one random day. When I described my perception of Seattle, she just laughed a little and continued eating. As I took a bite, she said, "Seattle is pretty, but I don't ever remember thinking of any place the way you do. I grew up here, and things have always been kind of cool, but you're describing some sort of fairytale wonderland!" We laughed and then she said, "You're just different. You really appreciate the little things in life. But beware; the devil's in the details." That comment always stuck with me for some reason. Much later, I would come to appreciate it fully.

After lunch that day, I sat in treatment Room 1 by myself and waited for patients to start rolling in. I gazed out the giant windows to the busy intersection just twenty feet away. It was supposed to be a four-way stop, but most people just rolled through it. I recognized many of the people who didn't heed the big red blinking light nor the stop signs. They were the pillars of the community, the highly caffeinated soccer moms, business people on their cell phones, and patients. I wondered to myself, would these people scoff at the law if they knew I was watching? People seemed to take on a different persona when they were alone in their cars. Some people I knew as bright and bubbly banged the steering wheel and yelled at the driver in front of them when he or she took too long at the stop sign. Some people I knew as being morally upright, thoughtful and conscientious flipped the bird to other drivers. It was an interesting intersection, to say the least.

## *Point of Responsibility*

*11. When you're alone, do you act differently than you would when with others? Think for a few minutes about your actions, your voice and your manner of being when alone, and in your notebook, compare and contrast them with how you are in the presence of others. Learn and acknowledge the subtle differences, and figure out how you came to act that way.*

As I sat there with my feet up on the adjusting table and pondered random thoughts, I began to reflect on the maelstrom that was my summer. My life had become quite intense. Things were going very well on the business side of things. I bought a new truck and we started looking for a house. I was creating friendships with some great people. I did realize, however, that I was married to my practice and had stopped doing the things that made me happy as an individual. I no longer played hockey, worked out with weights consistently or read self-growth books. These were things I'd done my whole life, but I was starting to lose my way. I should have been feeling wonderful, but all I could feel at that point, when alone, was an eerie feeling of being unbalanced.

## *Point of Responsibility*

*12. Are you living your life passionately? If not, why have you chosen not to? Do you lose sight of your most favorite activities when in a relationship? Understand that no one can take passion from you except yourself. In your notebook, write a list of five things you're going to insert into your weekly schedule to recapture your passion for life and learning. Take a class to learn about something that interests you. Schedule time to read, take day trips, sign up to play a sport you like or one you'd like to try for the first time. The time allotment for each activity doesn't matter. Start with one activity. Then every two months or so, pick up something new. We'll talk about the steps to achieve this later in the book. The key to a long life is differentiation. We must learn new things and creatively challenge our brains to thrive in life. This is quite literally what keeps us young. Don't cheat yourself or make excuses. Make the decision and do it, whatever it takes.*

*13. Are you leading a balanced life? Are you physically, financially, emotionally and spiritually healthy? This step is designed as an awareness step only. Challenge yourself to come up with the reasons why you've chosen to be unbalanced in your life. Do you blame others? Is it just because that's the way you've always lived? Write your introspections in your notebook.*

I was snapped back to reality when the door opened quickly and in walked Natalie. I was surprised by her appearance because she didn't like being at the clinic much at all. She said she had come down to do her work for the week. Natalie was responsible for bookkeeping and paying the bills. She didn't exactly like the job, but she did it as an expression of good will since she wasn't working and hadn't enrolled in school up to that point.

As Natalie and I discussed the week's particulars, it was obvious that her mind wasn't all there. It wasn't until later that night that I understood why.

Later that day, Sonya called my office to invite Natalie and me to dinner with her and Gabe at their place that evening. When I got home to ask Natalie whether she wanted to go, the apartment was dark and the couch covered with bedroom pillows and blankets. The bathroom door was closed and light was coming from the crack beneath the door. Obviously, something was not right. I went upstairs and put on a pair of jeans and a T-shirt. When I came downstairs, Natalie was sitting on the couch. She looked so little sitting there by herself. I turned on the light and sat next to her, moving Archie and a few pillows to make room. Her eyes were puffy and red. Her hair was all messed up, and I noticed snot tissues scattered throughout the pillows and bedding. I asked what was wrong. She said she was just having a bad day. Not wanting to stir the pot, I left it at that for the moment.

Trying to pump some energy into the situation, I asked whether she wanted to go to dinner over at Sonya and Gabe's place. She was less than interested.

Over the previous couple of weeks, I had become increasingly frustrated with our situation. Natalie didn't want to do anything, go anywhere, or meet anyone. It was like pulling teeth to get her to come with me to Bobby's place the week before. And now her perpetual funk was forcing me to decline spending time with genuinely nice people who just wanted to be our friends.

All I wanted was for Natalie to be with me and have some fun. It was obvious we had some relationship issues, but getting out of our heads and experiencing new things together would have been great for us. We needed some downtime to chill and relax.

But Natalie was becoming increasingly closed off. In fact, when I was professionally obligated to attend an event, I would have to go solo. I took seriously every advantage I could to meld with people in the community. Oftentimes, people would ask whether I had a girlfriend or a wife, and I had to make up an excuse as to why Natalie couldn't make it. It was getting old, and I started to feel alone again as I had in Colorado. Up to that point, I had decided not share my feelings with her, as I didn't want to add to her cloudiness. But I was sure she knew I felt some anxiety about the way she was behaving.

## *Point of Responsibility*

*14. Do you give more thought to the needs of others than to your own needs (the raising of children being exempt)? Do you sacrifice more than you gain? Why do you think this is? Are you afraid your ideas aren't worthy? Do you believe you don't deserve a voice? No matter who you are or what your situation, YOUR voice and ideas are paramount to humanity's success. Each of us adds up to a whole, and without your input, you're depriving not just yourself, but all of us. Speak your mind; go get what you're worth.*

As I looked Natalie in the eye, I asked, "What's going on? I can't do this all alone. Can you help me out a little?" I knew I was always stressed with work, so I wasn't giving her the attention she deserved, but I had an inkling something else was amiss. It wasn't just me. "Please?" I asked. She wouldn't look at me, but bowed her head forward and started to cry. She spoke a few words about how she was generally unhappy and lost in life. She was anxious and was quickly becoming depressed because she didn't know what she wanted to do with the rest of her life. And further, the idea of committing to one vocation caused her genuine fear. Anytime Natalie thought of enrolling in the acupuncture program, she began to think of all the things she was not going to be able to do. Her thoughts and actions were irrational, but that didn't stop them. Indecision was the only decision Natalie made. She was rapidly losing weight, couldn't sleep and seemed to walk around in a haze. She stopped working out and wasn't eating well. Her eyes weren't clear like they once were, and her smile looked more like a frown. I could certainly understand her situation. I'd felt the same way before I got onto my life's path. But it was also evident something much deeper was happening within her psyche. What that was, I couldn't be sure, and I didn't think it my place to tell her what to do and how to do it. I would, however, nurture her and wait it out. Her state of being didn't affect the way I felt about our relationship. I just felt bad that she felt so forlorn.

After a few minutes on the couch together, I called Sonya and postponed dinner. She seemed a little upset because she and Gabe had gone all out on a big feast of foods from all over the world. I sincerely apologized and suggested maybe next week we could all get together. Natalie and I held each other that night until we fell asleep.

Over the next few months, Natalie continued to battle her issues, which took her down a dark road. Her anxiety and depression came and went, as she continued to withdraw from public life, limiting herself to going food shopping, to coffee shops and to the local bookstores.

I tried to make things as stress free as possible, but it just made our situation even more glaringly obvious. Over the next few months, Natalie closed up like a clam under attack. And I eventually mirrored her. I became absorbed in my work to escape from my personal life. I decided just to wait until Natalie came back to me.

### *Point of Responsibility*

*15. Have you ever lost a relationship due to putting too much time in other places? Do you make excuses or escape from your relationships under the guise of "having to pay the bills," or by some other ego-based declaration? Write in your notebook the ways you escape from emotionally taxing situations. Describe the cascade of events that take place, all the way from the initial emotion, through the escapism activity, and then into how you feel after that activity. Do you feel happier, or do you feel worse? Does the escapism lift you up, or bring you down?*

In the meantime, I took every opportunity to meet and hang out with the local people of Atherton and Seattle. I spent most of my time after work creating my reputation and attending business events. I was definitely torn by the desire to spend more time at home with Natalie. But when I did, it was awkward. I never quite knew what to say in her presence. It broke my heart, but I also owed it to myself to keep pushing for what I wanted in my life.

Atia, Chloe and Bobby began to suspect things were not going well on the home front. As small business owners, we could often be found entertaining and being entertained within the same circles. They saw me attending luncheons, dinners, wine-tasting events and various other functions without Natalie. After a couple of glasses of wine, they would inevitably begin asking questions, always trying for the inside dirt, but I never went there with them. My relationship with Natalie was ours alone. When engaged in one-on-one conversation with one of my newfound friends, it was clear each of them, in his or her own way, was genuinely concerned about my well-being. It was relatively simple for anyone to notice that my always-upbeat attitude was beginning to show some wear. Having friends on my team, people who cared about me, was comforting, even if I didn't tell them much. I usually just changed the subject and started talking about someone else's gossip—there was certainly enough of that to go around.

The stress at home was starting to bleed over into business. Getting up in the morning was becoming a burden. I was drinking way too much coffee and my diet started suffering. I began to lose a little weight due to all the stress in my life. I was obviously losing my edge.

My conversations with patients became a bit shorter. Although I was still extremely focused during treatment, the explanations of treatment became mottled and more confusing, at least to me. I felt tired most of the time, and the staff called me cranky on most days. It was true I was more easily agitated and more irritable. I felt I had a two hundred pound rock on my shoulders, and I couldn't shake it.

I became frustrated with patients for not adhering to care plans I'd put a lot of work into. And it was getting increasingly annoying to say the same things over and over to the same people. I began to focus more on the patients who were not doing their homework and exercises instead of the patients who were putting in the time and getting good results. My thoughts were consumed by the people who wanted to be fixed quickly, didn't want to take an active part in their own healthcare, and didn't want to pay anything for services rendered. By focusing on difficult people and negative experiences, I was reinforcing the negative in my life. I knew I was doing it, but I couldn't seem to stop. I was becoming increasingly closed in and introverted.

Until recently, I had cherished the opportunity to discuss and explain health and wellness with anyone and everyone. I had always enjoyed the chance to help patients switch their modes of thought from the traditional American sick care model to one of conservative health care with focus on self-responsibility.

I had also trained myself to be a master at dealing with confrontation and diffusing emotional situations. I realized people had emotional baggage, and I had very little to do with their happiness, or unhappiness, if anything at all. I'd always perceived such situations as a welcome challenge for me to show a patient objectively how the baggage of life hindered his or her progression to health. And, up until then, I had thrived on it.

But by that point, the cloud around me must have been quite palpable. I wasn't able to concentrate the way I normally could. I began to feel burdened by opportunities to help people grow and achieve. I started to feel a sense of despair. The tasks at hand seemed daunting, at best.

## *Point of Responsibility*

*16. Are you, or have you ever been burnt out? If so, what were the exact circumstances? Can you uncover a pattern of such behavior in your life? If you've every found yourself in a state of burnout, write in your notebook why you believe you allowed it to happen. In what ways might you put too much unnecessary pressure on yourself? Do you allow others to put too much pressure on you? Are you escaping from something? Do you, or did you, seek the adulation of others?*

One major conflict was time. I consciously structured each day with the utmost respect for the time of others. I prided myself on being efficient, methodical and meticulous. Sometimes, however, I would run a bit behind for legitimate purposes. On many occasions, I had three unscheduled patients walk in at once seeking treatment. And I wasn't about to turn someone away or deny treatment. Other occasions, some patients simply required more time than others. Inevitably, at those busy moments, a patient would show up late for his or her appointment and have to wait until I was finished with the patients who were on time. Of course, no one liked to wait, which created a dicey situation every now and again.

## *Point Of Responsibility*

*17. Do you actively manage your time on a daily basis? In your notebook, come up with two lists; one that describes the things you "want" to do, and the other the things that you "need" to do. Make this list all-inclusive with regard to everything you do on any regular basis. Include things like buying gas for your car, shopping for groceries, going to the gym, spending time with friends, date night, etc. Clearly define each of these categories. In the next column, define the frequency of each of those events. For example, if your list of things you need to do includes paying bills, write down how frequently you plan to do so. I pay bills twice each month. Then place those days into the daily calendar. Once you've completed that, organize each of those days to create your daily to-do list. It might seem like a lot of work at first, but once you complete the beginning part of this exercise, you'll begin to understand how you basically repeat the same things each week. And with a detailed plan of attack, you will waste no time in trying to remember what your next task might be. And because you have more time, you'll be able to insert things you've been trying to accomplish for years. Balancing your time between your needs and wants will also allow you to have time for unexpected things that have a way of popping up in life. Another great tip to save some time is the "touch it once" rule. Every time you get mail, touch each piece of mail one time. Don't set it on the counter for later. Stand above the recycle bin and decide what you're going to do with each piece of mail. If it's junk, throw it out. If it's a bill, throw away the ads that came with it and file it in the "bills to pay" folder for later in the month. If it's something you have interest in pursuing, such as education, research, or anything else, file it in your file drawer under something you'll remember, and then write on your calendar a note to remember to research that piece. For many other tips on time management and efficiency training, visit www.responsibilitymovement.com. And don't forget to sign up for the free newsletter. It's packed with useful tools that are guaranteed to make your life easier, and much more fun.*

After being with a patient for longer than usual, I would enter the next room with a sincere smile and thank the person who was waiting for his or her patience. This approach usually diffused any frustration from patients, but sometimes, particularly negative people liked to hang onto their misguided sense of being disrespected, even after I tried to clear the air. Since I never treated patients who hung onto this emotionally negative state, I would have to explain further that I wasn't being malicious by making them wait. I'd state that if they were in the same type of pain as the person next door, I would afford them the same courtesy of taking as much of my time as necessary to get the problem resolved.

This discussion helped many to relax, grow calmer and become more thankful that they weren't in as bad shape as that other person. I used my influence to bring to light for patients a clearer understanding of the exact moments when humans decided to be angry, hurt, happy or joyous. Some patients allowed for growth. We would talk about techniques to diffuse the negative by illuminating the positive.

Some patients, however, still liked to hang on to the negative emotion. The addiction to it was more powerful than their resolve. Even as they pretended by wearing a mask of happiness for the rest of the office visit, it was clear anger and resentment were still present. The emotions were irrational and selfish, and they were clouded further by guilt and shame. A few patients felt so much anger for having to wait, or guilt about feeling angry that they actually told me they weren't coming back to my office.

## Point of Responsibility

*18. Do you focus more on the negative in your life than you do the positive? Do you hang on to negative emotion, or do you move past them into reason? Write in your notebook how both negative emotions and reason have served you in your past. Do you think it plausible you might be addicted to the endorphins that circulate through your body when such negative emotions are present? How would it look if your life had no negative emotion in it? What thoughts, ideas and actions would fill the time? Write a list of ten things you would think about, create and do if you didn't focus on the negative in your life.*

Over that first summer, losing any patient was devastating. I felt hurt if my services were viewed as unsatisfactory, even though treatments were usually more than successful. I was incredibly emotional and took everything way too personally.

Constantly having to deal with things and people like that was draining. It was the worst part of my job and took the most energy. I started to feel zapped after confrontations. I was no longer navigating negative situations successfully. They left me with a pit in my stomach, or an inability to gain a full breath. The feelings I mimicked were those of being in shock, like I had just gone through a major trauma.

On one random evening, I received a phone call from my sister. Kris and I were close, even though we lived two thousand miles apart and talked only once a quarter. She was a loving mother of one, and, like me, tended to wear her heart on her sleeve. After a few minutes of catching up, our conversation switched gears; she began to talk about the deteriorating health of our mother, whom I hadn't talked to for years. My mother and Kris had maintained an on-and-off relationship through the years, but my mother and I had become permanently estranged when I decided two years prior that I didn't want manipulative, controlling people in my life any longer. As Kris and I talked, my heart beat harder within my chest. My breathing literally stopped. My jaw became clenched, and my face stoic. All were characteristics of the fight or flight response to my mother's former daily attack on my life. After a few minutes of listening to Kris talk about my mother, I became angry with her. We started yelling at each other about our parents' divorce and who was to blame for what. I had flashes of my mother's indifference to my life as the divorce got into full swing. As Kris blamed my dad for the downfall of the family, my mind was consumed with visions of our mother's new boyfriend who moved into the house literally weeks after our father left. After only a few more minutes, we both ended up slamming our phones shut simultaneously as we screamed at one another over the loudspeaker. When it was over, I paced back and forth in my kitchen trying to figure out why I was so angry. Before Kris and I had talked, I was in a wonderful mood. It was like any other day. But the mere mention of my mother brought back the constant fight or flight situation I had lived with every day of my adolescent life. At that point in my life, I was so incredibly scared. I was uncertain of everything around me. And I had no support from anyone. My extended family didn't seem to care much about our situation, and my friends didn't know how to help me.

As I sat on the couch, I made every attempt to keep all the emotions in; all except anger, that is. My face tightened and I put my left fist to my lips, as if to keep it all pushed in. I began to rock uncontrollably back and forth. I heard my voice, stuck deep in my throat, trying to escape in a low-pitched, wavering whimper. I put my palms over my ears, as if I could stifle the sound. But it was only magnified. I put my palms over my eyes, as if to hide from the pain, but it only enhanced the visions of being young and scared. Like bringing down the lights in a movie theater, my awkward and uncertain adolescence played vividly in the recesses of my mind. The movie detailed all the emotional situations that had taken place, those emotions that I seemed to mirror throughout my life. As I watched, I put my head in my hands and began to cry.

After about five minutes of listening to me, Archie jumped up next to me and cocked his head from left to right as he inspected the situation. I pulled him to me and cried even more deeply as he licked my tears away. When the tears finally subsided, I took him for a little walk. As we meandered through the rose garden down the street from our place, I had a personal revelation. I realized I was living my life by the emotions of others. And doing so was my modus operandi. It was an obvious trend in my life. From a very young age and in all relationships, both personal and business, I was like a chameleon. I bent and folded to wishes and emotions of others. I lacked my own voice and looked from without to fill the holes I had within. Although I was very strong, I was also riddled with uncertainty and inconsistency.

In my past, I simply mirrored the emotions of those around me, and that became the Me whom everyone knew. I was unknowable because I was a loose cannon. I couldn't be figured out because I only mirrored what I'd seen around me. And I was doing the very same thing in my adult life. My mood was based on Natalie's mood, the negative moods of patients, and of any other random person with whom I came into contact. Such a realization was empowering.

As our walk continued, my mind worked with clarity. Points of light continued to flow. With regard to work, I was so very happy to be achieving my newfound successes. From the outside, I was young, powerful, confident, and intelligent. And I was most definitely a good businessman. I appeared to have it all together. But a strange internal battle was being waged that I had never recognized before. On the inside, I was never happy with living in the moment. I always wanted more. I was anxious and I was afraid it would all be taken away, or I would be found out a sham or something, which logically couldn't be further from the truth. On a deep level, I felt I didn't deserve anything good, even though I had put in the time. All these negative emotions came and went throughout any given day, and they made no sense whatsoever. They were completely irrational. I suffered with this constant dichotomy between living my dream and then fighting against it every single day. I started to feel I was two different people, the real Me whom very few knew, and the Me whom I put out there for the public to see. I was tearing myself apart and was quickly getting bogged down.

Archie and I finished our long walk as we watched the sun go down over the Olympic Mountains. As I walked the long sidewalk up to the apartment, I vowed

I would change my life for the better. I didn't know how I was going to do it, but I knew I needed to change my thought patterns to become the person I wanted to be.

## *Point of Responsibility*

*19. Do you live your life by mirroring the emotions of others? Or are you solid enough in yourself to let the negative emotions of others slide right by you with no interaction? Do you take things personally? Do you look outside to fill the void within? Do you feel like two different people; one seeking a dream and the other fighting it? Honestly answer each one of these introspections separately in your notebook. As you do so, begin to tweeze apart how you react to the emotions of those around you; what you feel in your body, what's happening in your mind, what your actions look like. Write it all down and be specific. We'll talk much more about how to change such activity later in the book.*

To add to the stress, Natalie and I had recently started searching for a home to purchase. For my agent, I decided to use one of my patients, who seemed to be well connected in the community. Jeff was one of about three hundred possibilities from which to choose in Atherton alone. It seemed like everyone had "his own guy or girl" who was the absolute best. Jeff was about 6'5", and as lovable as a teddy bear. He was one of the nicest people I'd ever met, and that's all I could go on. I had no experience in that particular market.

The three of us spent many weekends house hunting. It was fun at first, but became a real chore. I was up against a wall as far as time was concerned. We had to be out of our apartment by the end of October. I only had a couple of months to close on something, and I was becoming increasingly cynical with the search.

The second issue was the down payment. Although things were good at the office, I didn't have much cash to lie on the table. So we were limited in the number of houses we could afford. On the positive side, because this would be my first house, I was only required to put down five percent.

The biggest detractor from purchasing was the outrageous home values. People were quite proud of their homes in the West, and Atherton was one of the worst. The rumor on the street was that home values in Atherton increased by an average of no less than 17% each year. It was unbelievable!

A few times I actually found a house I liked, but when I called up Jeff to arrange a showing, he would inevitably inform me the house was either pending or sold. It was incredibly discouraging. After six weeks, I just decided to lay low and hope for the best. I felt I was pushing too hard. It was like what people said about finding one's soul mate; you'll find him or her as soon as you stop looking. That's exactly what I planned to do. The home search was postponed indefinitely. I needed to take some pressure off. Between the stress of my recent career moves, searching for a home, my new realizations, and my relationship with Natalie, I knew I needed some help. I felt it was time I seek some counseling.

## Chapter Five:

# Outreach

I called up a therapist I'd met a few times and made an appointment. Because his office was miles from Atherton, I knew he wouldn't know anyone I spoke about. I needed some objective advice. Unfortunately for me, he was a very busy guy. I was going to have to wait a month before seeing him.

Not two hours later, the previous clinic doctor stopped in to pick up some odds and ends before his big move out of town. We were back in my office talking a bit when he said I looked really tired. He asked what the problem was, but I had difficulty putting everything into words. With my permission, he carefully and meticulously picked my brain. His questions were pinpointed, and his understanding of my situation was unbelievable. He followed by giving me some action steps and some sage advice, "Just relax; everything will be all right." I'd heard that one before.

I thanked him for his words, got up and walked him out to his car. On the way, I asked him where he picked up his ability to tweeze apart complex emotions so easily and turn them into coherent action steps. I was always looking for new and exciting tools to put in my toolbox, things I could use with patients and myself. He opened his car door and handed me the book Dianetics, one of Scientology's primary publications.

I had a brief interest in Scientology back in college, as I did with all religions and philosophies. I devoured books that offered any kind of insight on life's purpose, the relationship between our souls and personalities, and with each other. I explored it all. I, like many other people, was actively on the hunt for my place in the Universe.

So I took the book and started to read it immediately. I was definitely intrigued with the concept that our minds could be made more efficient using simple, objective techniques. I was less intrigued with Scientologists calling themselves a religion. I felt they were more about human growth and improvement than fostering belief in a Higher Power. But I didn't know enough about it to wager an intelligent opinion. After finding myself unable to read the unbelievably tedious book, I decided instead to visit the local Scientology branch to experience it for myself.

The "Church," as they called it, was a lively little place full of sincere smiles and a mix of all types of people. Natalie and I were invited in by the receptionist and given some initial paperwork to fill out. Within the paperwork was an in-depth personality test. I told the receptionist we just wanted to talk with someone for a few minutes to see what Scientology was all about. She just smiled and asked us to continue with the paperwork, and someone would be with us promptly to discuss everything in great detail. I was being put in my place! But I smiled back and said, "Okay."

As we continued filling out the arduous forms, I became more intrigued with the thought-inspiring questions. I noticed Natalie, squirming around next to me, was obviously not comfortable. Neither was I, but we plugged on to completion. Even if I didn't agree with the procedures, I felt it was good to be forced out of my comfort zone.

After I returned the forms to the receptionist, she invited us to follow her back to a little office where we were promptly greeted by the Church director. He seemed like your average American guy. We talked for a few minutes while he took us through a couple of exercises to become more aware of our own minds, and how to access them instantaneously.

I was definitely interested in the process of controlling my mind. I remembered back to my college days, and specifically to a conversation I had with an old roommate who had been in the Master's program for psychology. One evening, as we ate our ramen noodle dinners, he told me he had run across an experiment that a fellow researcher created. The experiment was to determine whether, through pain stimulus, one could become more efficient with staying on task. The first thing he did was organize his day by writing down absolutely everything he wanted to accomplish, including recreation, on his personal calendar. He was to keep the calendar next to him twenty-four hours per day. He then used an alarm clock that was set to go off at random times throughout each day. The last part of the experiment was to wear a rubber band around one of his wrists. The process was quite simple. When the timer went off, he evaluated whether he was "on task" at that exact moment. If he was, he got an extra segment of recreation the next day. If not, he had to snap the rubber band on his wrist, causing pain. The most interesting part of the study was that he went from something like 5% efficiency (i.e. being on task) to 95% efficiency within the trial of his experiment. Ever since, I had admired his ability to change his actions to achieve a desired outcome. He had figured out a way to create his own life, and in the process, expand his relationship to his environment. That was exactly what I had always wanted out of my life.

### *Point Of Responsibility*

*20. Find a rubber band and put it on your wrist. Make sure it doesn't cut off circulation. You want it to be loose fitting. In your notebook, create a list of your top ten behaviors that you realize are not self-serving. Then choose the one that would, by your own estimation, influence your life the best if it no longer existed. Focus on things like negative thoughts, cravings, gossip, judgment of others and/or yourself, compulsions anytime you're off-task, any time you say, "Yes, but," or when you think you can't do something. Which one negative behavior takes priority over all the others? Then, as you go through each day, every time you find yourself thinking those negative thoughts or behaving in that unserving way, give yourself a snap on the wrist. Do it hard enough to elicit the pain response. With time, the behavior will become significantly diminished. If need be, alternate the rubber band to the other wrist daily.*

As we talked with the director, my interest became piqued. Even though I didn't like the idea of being involved with any type of church, I understood that controlling our own minds was the only way to change our lives. We each decided to sign up for a separate eight-week course offered by the church. We chose courses based on our individual goals; Natalie started one on getting in touch with oneself, and I started the course on Personal Integrity.

We had a couple of hours that day, so we sat down and started going through our respective books. We were instructed not to talk to each other or anyone else in the room. I liked that they wanted only our input into the completion of the workbooks. No room existed for fooling around.

As I thumbed through the book and began to provide answers to some of the questions, I started to feel ashamed. I hunched over and protected it with my elbows so no one could see what I was writing. I was incredibly relieved when someone told me we had to leave our workbooks at the Church in between sessions. It would have been catastrophic to our relationship if Natalie perused the contents of my writings.

Over that first two-hour session, I was amazed at how much I wrote about the things that brought me shame, disrespect, anger and despair. It felt good to get everything out onto paper. And I began to feel relieved as I wrote within the pages of that book some of the things I had been responsible for in my past. I clung to the fact that I wasn't a bad person, and I never did bad things to people directly. But I did most certainly hang onto negative emotions associated with my rationalizations and justifications of things I had done. I thought about the times I had been irresponsible and manipulative with others' emotions and feelings. Little pangs of ego shot up to declare how those people had also wronged me, and my action was justified. A constant back and forth existed between my ego fighting this change for the better and my soul releasing all the pain associated with it. I had a widely varying deluge of emotions as I sat and wrote in the workbook. I was ecstatic finally to get this crap out of my mind, while simultaneously feeling I could not admit to those closest to me all my downfalls in life. I couldn't just tell everyone the things I had done and go on with life as usual. There would be serious consequences and life-altering events if I followed through with what they were instructing me to do. I couldn't bring myself to tell Natalie that I had cheated on her when I was in Florida for my internship, or about that one slip-up I had in Colorado with a young co-ed. At the time, I'd justified to myself that I wasn't getting what I needed from her. But the truth was that I wasn't strong enough to deal proactively with my needs and concerns within our relationship. I simply saw the grass as greener on the other side of the hill. As for the present situation, I admitted to myself that my previous activity was inappropriate, and I didn't want to do it again. That seemed a much more positive solution—a win-win, if you will. That way Natalie wouldn't have to go through any pain because of me, and I would treat this opportunity as a second chance.

## *Points of Responsibility*

*21. At some point in each of our lives, we feel shame, guilt, fear, and anxiety. In your notebook, describe four separate stories from your own personal experience where you've had to deal with each emotion. Be very specific in your story telling with regards to how you feel, or felt. Notice any patterns that emerge. Where do those emotions come from? How often do they occur? Are they mirrored? Are they learned?*

*22. How and why do you rationalize or justify poor or personally undesirable behavior? (For example, yelling at your partner. You could justify such behavior by saying he or she deserves it, but in reality, no one deserves to be yelled at, ever. It's a serious lack of respect, both for yourself and the other person. If there is yelling in a relationship, a power struggle exists that must be deflated before moving forward. Something in the relationship must change. We'll talk later in the book about how to slow emotional situations down and bring reason to the forefront). Describe in your notebook three separate occasions in your life where you have rationalized, either to yourself or to another person, personally undesirable behavior. Seek out any patterns. Do you blame others? Be honest and take responsibility.*

*23. Do you manipulate the emotions of others to get a desired result? Would it possibly be more productive if you simply asked for what you want from life and those around you? Verbalizing your desires significantly reduces your ability to harbor ill will, resistance and negative emotions toward others.*

After a few weeks of those sessions, Natalie and I both lost interest. Making it downtown was difficult during the week, and we soon decided it wasn't for us. I did, however, make a few resolutions. I vowed I would voice clearly what I wanted in my life, rather than trying to get what I wanted by manipulating others, and I promised myself I would never lie again, not even the little white lies I often used to get out of doing little things I just didn't want to do. These resolutions made me feel relieved and rediscovered, but only for a little while.

Through the month of August, Natalie and I had taken a few weekend trips to the Olympic and Cascade Mountains and Mount Rainier, to check things out. We had fun, but I couldn't shake the feeling that she was more like a sister than a love interest. I didn't want to believe it, but our relationship had changed significantly over the previous few months. I still adored her and felt the need to continue protecting her, but I didn't love her the way I once had.

I had tried many things to build a cohesive relationship with her, including positive affirmations, traditional counseling, moving across the country for a new start, and finally, Scientology. Nothing worked. I still felt anxious and uncertain about our relationship. I hoped going to my first therapy session would help.

By late August, the warm days of summer were numbered. During our first treatment session, the therapist and I took advantage of the sun and went outside on the porch to discuss some of the things I wanted to address. I told him about the Scientology experiment, how it made me feel, and some of the things wrapped around it. We were quickly consumed in conversation, and before I knew it, the hour turned into two. Things just seemed to flow. His methods were concise and cut deeply into my psyche. Even within that first session, I had major revelations.

We met weekly for the next month. Things were going well with regard to the treatment. I was actually enjoying the chance to explore myself with the help of a seasoned facilitator. The sessions were clean, clear and pure.

One of the primary issues my therapist and I discussed was the setting of proper boundaries. Upon introspection, it was clear I did have issues maintaining healthy boundaries with people. The most obvious manifestation was my relationship with

Atia. She wasn't just a patient anymore. We spent time together outside of the office having lunch or going for a run. Natalie didn't seem to mind—I think because Atia had a boyfriend—and she trusted me, but I definitely sensed Atia and I were getting closer to one another. We held each other's gazes and hugs just a little too long. And just because it was comfortable and I trusted her didn't make it right or acceptable. After wrestling with the facts, and with my therapist's advice, I decided to squash my personal relationship with Atia.

## Point Of Responsibility

*24. Do you maintain healthy boundaries within both your professional and your personal life? Personal integrity is paramount to achieving and maintaining self-esteem, and there is no mincing words when it comes to integrity. For example, necessary boundaries must exist between a professional and a client or co-worker; if you choose to take a professional relationship into the realm of the personal, professional dealings should be halted, and vice-versa. You will better respect others and be respected when you maintain healthy boundaries.*

I was fully willing to heed my therapist's advice. I planned to tell Atia on our weekly jog through the park that it was inappropriate for us to spend time together outside the clinic. I was committed to my own care much more than I was to having a relationship with her.

Two days later, as we were getting warmed up with wet-toed shoes on the dewy grass, I quietly told Atia that I wouldn't be lunching or running with her anymore. She instantly got angry. She screamed, "Is this because of your stupid therapy? Are you a new man now?"

"No," I quietly replied, trying to keep the energy of the situation to a minimum. "I just want to do the right thing. We can still see each other at the office, but I have to continue treatment to figure out a few things about myself. I just don't want any confusion right now. You can understand that, can't you?"

She stared at me for a second, and then just took off onto the trail ahead of us. I followed. We ran through the thicket quickly, with chests heaving and sweat dripping. I'd never been down that particular trail. And as we progressed, it closed in around us. It clearly hadn't been traveled much. After about thirty minutes she stopped, put her hands on her hips, turned to me as I came to a stop, and planted a huge kiss on me. She rubbed against me forcefully. I didn't have any time to think, and before I knew it, the run had become something much more than I'd expected. Atia pushed me against a tree and lifted up my shirt. She began to kiss my chest, stomach, and then went further south. As she continued, I thought ever-so-briefly about making her stop. But those thoughts were fleeting. I was caught up in the moment and allowed her to continue. When finished, she stood up and smiled at me right before she turned and started jogging back to the parking area. We quickly said our good-byes and walked toward our respective cars.

Afterward, I sat in my vehicle, dumbfounded, asking myself what the heck had just happened. Should I regret it? Of course I should! I never should have let it happen. The whole event made me ill. I truly wished I hadn't done it.

I had to head back to work within the hour, so I hurried home and jumped in the shower. The dirt and sweat were easy to wash away. The shame, however, remained for further contemplation.

Later that day, Atia came in for an appointment. She was grinning from ear to ear. When I entered the room, she immediately said she wanted to do that every week. I was torn between liking it and knowing it wasn't right. On more than one occasion, I caught myself replaying that morning's events. I justified the behavior by saying she was the pursuer. But I knew it wasn't proper to allow such behavior.

How could I let things get to that point? Although I hadn't been in town for long, the friendship I had with Atia had become complicated and quite entangled. Atia referred a ton of new patients to me. She was well connected, and if I didn't maintain our friendship, I would most certainly lose business. But I also had to take into account what to do if Natalie found out. And what about Atia's boyfriend? He certainly wouldn't be happy if he knew. I just stuffed it all down inside and told myself I'd deal with such things if and when the time came. Everything was all messed up, to say the least.

## *Point Of Responsibility*

*25. Every thought and action affects others, whether directly or indirectly. How do you think your actions and moods affect your friends and family members? Write down all of your typical daily emotions. Then write down all the people with whom you come into contact every day. Follow that by writing down your suppositions about how each person may feel when you run your life based on each of your emotions. How do they perceive your emotional actions?*

I told Atia that what we had done could never happen again; major consequences could result for us both if anyone found out. Rather than be concerned, she tried to convince me to meet her once a week. I told her there was no way that would ever happen and quickly left the room after the adjustment.

I had a few minutes before more patients were scheduled so I went back to my office. I was still feeling dirty and used. I couldn't let it happen again, no matter what. I had too much to lose. I still needed to see my therapist, but I didn't want to tell him about Atia. I had already made my decision to stop meeting her outside the office. It was already dealt with, and no one could help me any further with it. I stuffed it down deep inside, never to talk about it to anyone.

That night at therapy, I purposely started talking about anything but the events of the morning. We were in our fourth week of therapy and began to touch on the events surrounding my birth. After an hour or so, the therapist asked me whether I was willing to follow through with an abstract type of therapy. I said, "As long as there are no blindfolds and sheep involved. I already trust you." He chuckled and asked me to stand.

The therapy studio was the size of a large bedroom; it was painted a light blue and had plenty of natural light. It was adorned with various healing icons, candles and a few timeless books. In one corner of the room, laid directly on the hardwood floor, were two thin mattresses stacked one atop the other. He asked me to walk over and climb in between them. I did so. He asked whether I were okay; I told him yes. Then he slowly began to apply pressure around the edges and on the top of me. He was holding me inside. I asked him what the therapy was supposed to represent, but he ignored me. I tried to look at my sweaty palms, but it was complete darkness. My breathing quickly became labored, even though I had plenty of oxygen. I was inexplicably and irrationally fearful as I lay in a very strange position. I was on my back, completely submissive, and my legs were folded to the left of me. My spine was torqued, but it felt comfortable. My head was turned all the way to the right. As he applied increasing weight, he asked me why I wasn't moving. I told him I didn't know. Then he told me to get the heck out of there. He said I should fight for my life, instead of waiting for others to give me life. It hit me like a ton of bricks. The maneuver was mimicking the birthing process. As I began to move around slightly, I felt incredibly scared. Why couldn't I throw the guy off of me? I outweighed him by thirty pounds! I felt weak and poisoned with fear. I had lived with those feelings for most of my life, manifesting as a deep pit in my solar plexus and an endless anxiety.

Then I started to get really angry. "Get off of me!" I yelled. I summoned everything I had to push him off. He must have been superhumanly strong because I gave it my all and he still wouldn't let me out. I grunted and groaned and kicked and screamed. Then I broke free! I saw the light and went toward it with everything I had. The therapist tried to keep me inside, but I was too strong for him. I came out and lay on the floor, my clothes completely soaked in sweat. I lay on my side to get air, but I couldn't. I was absolutely drained as I had never been drained before. In my past, I'd been through some of the most intense workouts devised by man. I'd worked out to the point of exhaustion and vomiting on a number of occasions, but nothing was like that. I literally couldn't get my breath for fifteen minutes. I didn't have the energy to contemplate what was happening to me. I felt like I was going to vomit. I grabbed a can and dry heaved for a minute before lying back on the floor.

After a few minutes, the therapist explained that I had a lot of protection I didn't acknowledge. My puzzled look was invitation enough for him to continue with his explanation that I was surrounded by powerful entities who were looking out for me and who protected me as I evolved into the soul I had agreed to become before entering this lifetime. He also told me of a horrible entity I had grown up with who was attached to my mother and her family. He explained that the entity looked like the Grim Reaper, and that he just hung around, being pissed that I didn't let him into my life anymore. I laughed a little and he said, "It's not really that funny. How would you like to see that every night before you go to bed?" I told him I'd had many frightful encounters with that very entity when I was a kid. Many mysterious events had happened around the house and barn, including unexplained broken windows in the middle of the night, loud snoring from rooms where no one lived, small, black clouds that quickly whooshed up the living room stairs, and a baby who could be heard crying upstairs, even though my sister was the youngest person to inhabit the house. And it was the Grim Reaper entity that scared the crap out of me when I had to go out to water the horses every night in the haunted barn. I shared the story of how I'd run full speed out of that barn all the way to the house every night, hoping to stay just one step ahead of whatever was chasing me. I'll never know whether something was really there. But it sure felt like it at the time.

The therapist finished our session that night by asking me to pay attention to my dreams and report back on them during our next session. His process was certainly unconventional, but I was intrigued. I simply didn't know what to make of it. It was new, and opened up different avenues of thought. I decided to let the treatment run its course, without adding my intellect into the equation.

When my therapist and I talked later that week, I told him the few facts I knew about my birth—that I was born two and a half months premature so I had to stay at the hospital for over a month before being discharged. That was basically all I knew since my parents didn't talk about it in any greater detail.

Then my therapist asked me about my dreams since our last meeting. I explained, "The night after our last session, I dreamt I was first surrounded by a poisonous fluid within my mother's womb. I knew I had to get out if I wanted to live. She was killing me with her chemicals. As I attempted to leave, something grabbed me around the back of my head and right eye, and it pulled me with great force. The pain on the right side of my neck was like a searing white heat. After the commotion, I was laid in a tiny bed, my eyes were covered with bandages, and I couldn't see. I lay there for weeks. There was no touch, just voices. I lay on my back, with my head facing to the right, trying to peer out from underneath the bandages. My legs were torqued to the left, but it was comfortable. At that point, I woke up from my dream, drenched in sweat. I'd never been one to equate dreams with reality, but I was curious about the new parts of my dream experience."

When I woke from the dream, it was four a.m. I knew my dad would be awake by then since he lived on the East coast, so I called him. At first, rather than divulging any information, I asked him to tell me, blow by blow, what happened during my birth. Interestingly enough, he took a different tack than he ever had before while explaining it. He said that my mother was extremely worried during the pregnancy; she was constantly fearful and anxious for some unknown reason. When I decided to come out, the doctor used forceps on me for added leverage, except he placed them incorrectly and put them over my right eye and back of my head. He messed my face up so much that I had a black eye for a month. My dad explained, "That's why we don't have baby pictures of you." Without missing a beat, he added, "And then we had to leave you there for six weeks under the bilirubin lights in an incubator, until you were healthy enough to take home. You were so tiny, and so pitiful looking with those bandages on your eyes." I was blown away. My dream, not twenty minutes before, had explicitly detailed my real birth. I asked him why they didn't come and see me, hold me, or touch me. That's when he got angry and said, "They wouldn't let us touch you! They told us you had no idea what was happening in the first place. They just told us you were sleeping! Do you think we just wanted to leave you there all by yourself?" I didn't know what to say except, "I don't blame you. You were just following doctors' orders." He had to go get ready for work, so I told him I loved him and hung up the phone.

As I told the therapist about my dreams and my conversation with my father, I noticed I could breathe deeper and more clearly. The gnawing pit in my gut was significantly diminished. I felt calmer. We sat there and discussed a few more things before calling it a night.

The next day, I was taking a walk during my lunch hour when Atia pulled her car up next to me. She asked whether I wanted to come up to her place for lunch—nothing else, just lunch. I made her agree that it would just be lunch, and she did. As I hopped in, I consciously hoped she wouldn't try anything. But subconsciously, I wanted her to do just that. I simply didn't listen to my inner voice. On the way to her place, we picked up our witty banter like we never missed a beat. We had lunch and talked for a few minutes, and then she said it, "You know, if you want to stop by later tonight, I'll be around."

"You and I both know that's probably not a good idea, right?" I said.

"Just thought I'd throw it out there. The offer still stands," she replied.

She grabbed her keys and took me back to work with no further drama.

Later that night, I went to a wine tasting event with some local people I knew. The event ended early, but I was pretty wound up from the drinks. Since I was already on the city's north side, I decided to stop by Atia's place. My defenses were low. But more truthfully, I wanted sex with someone aggressive. And Atia fit the bill. She made us a couple of drinks and within minutes she was straddling me on the couch. I allowed her to do whatever she wanted. The whole time I was there, I knew what we were doing was wrong. But it felt good, with no strings attached.

Afterward, the reality of my situation brought glimpses of shame and self-loathing. What was I doing? I had to tell my therapist. I needed his help, regardless of how he might react or perceive me. Our sessions were confidential so he wouldn't tell anyone. I needed help to figure out why I allowed such things to happen!

I met my therapist at his office a couple of days after that second encounter with Atia. It wasn't easy, but I belted out everything about my relationship with Atia.

When I was finished, he looked at me and couldn't hide his emotion. His face turned pink and he started taking deeper breaths. I didn't know what else to do, so I just sat there waiting for him to say something. After what seemed like an eternity, he regained his composure and asked me whether my behavior was helping my life, or hurting it. I replied with the latter. My actions were certainly not proper. For the rest of the session, we discussed very specific actions I could take to disallow such activity. That was the evening I learned about consequential thinking. He taught me how to live from a different perspective than what I had been. I learned the difference between living from the front of the eyes, and from behind the eyes. It wasn't simply a metaphorical analogy, but a truly practical way of viewing the world. To live from the eyes is to direct your view on the world, to be aggressive and potentially overbearing. It is subhuman and is manifested in an uncultivated, or undercultivated, mind. And it's based more in motor activity. To live from behind your eyes is the cultivated ability to take in your environment and provide a well-thought-out plan of action, or inaction, as it were. It's based more on reason and the understanding of sensation. I learned how to take every situation in my life, as it came up, and drive it to the back of my skull for immediate contemplation. The idea was to separate the self from the external occurrences, to view experiences as if they were an out-of-body event. As the therapist and I continued with our discussion, I became fully committed to taking the extra few seconds for evaluation through the filters of responsibility, experience and knowledge. Thinking of the consequences of each of my potential actions was a powerfully enlightening way of becoming proactive, instead of reactive, in my life. We discussed situations in my past in this new light. He instructed me to breathe deeply, to relax my body and to think of each of those events consequentially. I was to choose my next action based only in personal responsibly. If it served me responsibly, I was to embrace it. If not, I was to think of another option. And if the situation was too intense for me to think consequentially, I was to cease immediately and leave the situation. The session was long and arduous, and there was still much work to do, but I felt more intelligent, and much more well-equipped with my new tools. I felt my own evolution was progressing positively.

After our discussion on consequential thinking, the therapist described what things were probably like for Atia. Her aggression was probably due to some event in her past, a situation over which she had no control. She was reenacting the event, except she was now the aggressor instead of the victim.

I found it interesting that my therapist viewed me as a victim in all of it. He said I shouldn't have done it, but I wasn't completely to blame. He reiterated that he didn't want me hanging around with Atia at all, not even as a patient. It was a recipe for disaster. I completely agreed.

## *Point of Responsibility*

*26. Do you create your own obstacles in life? It's your ego's attempt to make you important. Think of any obstacles you're up against at the present moment. Ask yourself whether a fight is necessary, or whether you can move past the hurdle without confrontation or resentment? Are you creating an issue where there need not be one?*

Chapter Six:

# New Beginnings, Again

The next day, I met a new patient who had some pain from lifting packing boxes; she and her husband were moving to San Francisco in a month, and she wanted to take care of her back with all the new stress and strain. During the treatment, she asked me whether I knew anyone who might be interested in buying their house with no agents. I couldn't believe it! I told her I might be interested, and I agreed to view it during lunch that day. I was both excited and nervous. The monthly payments were certainly manageable with the new income, but having the added commitment of a half million-dollar debt was daunting.

When Natalie and I saw the house, we both fell in love with it immediately. It was the perfect mix of elegance and potential. The place was very comfortable and had a beautifully finished basement with an additional bathroom. The thing I really liked was that both the kitchen and main bathroom needed to be overhauled, and they were huge. The place was a find, so we came to an agreement right there on the spot. We didn't need agents and the whole thing went as fluidly as could be. It was a win-win situation. We all shook hands on it.

On the way back to my office, I called my new hockey buddy Joe, who happened to run his own mortgage lending operation.

As Joe and I talked, I voiced my concern over being able to handle the additional debt. He literally laughed at me and said, "Buddy, you're in the top 5% of all wage earners in the richest country in the world. Finding a loan for you isn't the issue. It's deciding which loan to take. The house is as good as yours." After the inspection and the necessary due diligence, we closed on October 21.

The next afternoon, I moved our belongings from the apartment to the new house. We only had a few large pieces of furniture, a bed, a dresser, an entertainment center, and a TV. Most everything else I was able to box up. I literally dragged the larger pieces of furniture into their respective rooms. Natalie made it her job to unpack everything and arrange it. I gratefully agreed.

A few days later, I invited Bobby to lunch to share with him the great news. I felt on top of the world, and I wanted everyone good to be part of it. We dined and gossiped about the locals, and we talked about how our businesses were going. And then, as he raised his wine glass, he asked me what seemed to be an off the wall question, "Why do you try so hard to make it work with Natalie?" I was thrown aback.

I paused for a few seconds while I collected my thoughts and said, "Well, what do you mean? Isn't that what we're supposed to do when in a relationship?" I could feel my confused emotions rise up within me. My statement declared I was strong and had fortitude. I thought I should fight for her honor and our relationship. But I knew I wasn't in love with Natalie anymore. I felt guilty for even thinking of leaving her, and I couldn't bear the emotional ordeal of going through a breakup. The relationship was comfortable; that was all I needed for the time being. After all, people fell in and out of love all the time in relationships.

"You guys clearly don't belong together. I mean, you don't even spend time together," Bobby replied, keeping me in the hot seat.

"She's busy, I'm busy; you know how it is, Bobby," I said, just as he watched my eyes follow a young, beautiful woman across the room.

"Yeah, I know how it is," he laughed. "I think you should come over to my side!"

"But I find nothing sexy about dudes! It just isn't my thing, man!" We laughed and drank our wine as we ate some ox tail stew and the best fish tacos I'd ever had.

When I got home that evening, Natalie wasn't around. She had left a note for me on the counter that said, "Went to bookstore. See you around 7 p.m.!" As I walked through the dark house, I looked at all the boxes and wondered why she hadn't unpacked anything. We'd been there for three days, and I didn't even know where my socks were.

It was six-thirty, so I called her cell phone, and we talked for a few minutes. She was in the middle of reading something good, and wasn't coming home for a little while. I agreed that was fine and hung up.

I jumped in the truck and went down to the village. Chloe's storefront was still lit up so I stopped in to see whether she wanted to get a margarita up the street. She told me I was a welcome surprise, grabbed her jacket and we were off. We ended up having a great conversation that night over too much booze. We ate and laughed and she told me things people were saying about me. "Don't let this go to your head or anything, but you're known on the street around here as 'The Hot Doc.' The women love to gossip about you! There's even one woman who cut out your picture from your weekly flier and taped it to her pen so she could look at you all day long!"

We laughed out loud together and then I said, "Hey, whatever brings in business!"

Then she got a little serious, leaned in, and said, "There's another story I have for you that you might not like, but I thought you should know."

I could feel the heat rising up within me. "Oh yeah? What's that?" I asked.

"There's this old real estate developer who stopped into my shop the other day. His name is Scott, and he's a raging alcoholic, with alcohol oozing from his pores. He likes to come in and hit on me every now and again, usually under the guise of collecting money for some sort of charity. The other day, he asked whether I was interested in joining one of the local organizations he belongs to. I remember you said you gave some presentations there, so I asked him whether he knew you. He sneered, threw his head back, and asked me, "That chiropractor? He's a punk. What are you doing hanging out with the likes of him?" I told him you were a really nice guy, unlike him, and that he should go home to his wife. So he left, but not before he tried planting one on me."

I remembered meeting Scott at the presentations I'd given and thought he was a decent guy. It tore me up to think someone didn't like me. I never did anything to him. Why was he trashing my name? I had a mind to go visit him, but Chloe told me he probably wouldn't even remember talking to her that day because he was so drunk. It was difficult, but I just had to let it go.

Most stories I heard about myself were good, but there are always jealous people who despise someone for being young and successful. I simply tried to steer clear of anyone who gave me a strange vibe, and I learned to be more vigilant with whom I talked.

I was getting to understand how things worked in Atherton, but I was also becoming cynical. The real Atherton was beginning to show itself; it was full of well-to-do, emotionally teen-aged people. I was beginning to notice that people were quite stuck up. Snooty moms plagued the place with their venti coffees, five hundred dollar black walking suits and two-and-a-half kids. At every table inside the local coffee shop one could hear the latest gossip about so and so. Everyone talked trash about everyone else.

## *Point Of Responsibility*

*27. Are you addicted to gossip? If you truly want to gain happiness in your own life, you're going to have to stop gossiping. Throughout your day tomorrow, analyze the conversations you're a part of and that happen around you. Take notice of the words and contents of each conversation. If gossip is prevalent, know you must change how and with whom you converse to make an effectual change in your own mindset. From the next day forward, don't interject with things you've heard second hand or ask questions about the local gossip in any way, no matter how good you think it would feel to divulge or share in the information. That feeling is the inherent addiction. And that is what you're working to change. Stick to the facts. You'll be much more productive and will respect yourself more.*

*28. Are you consumed by what others think about you or your actions? This is a horribly disempowering trend in American culture. Instead of thinking how we'll be perceived from the outside, we must first determine whether our present thoughts and actions serve us. Write in your notebook some of your thoughts from the next twenty-four hours. Be sure to include both positive and negative self-conversation. On the following day, analyze those thoughts and determine whether they are working for or against you. The next step is to create our own thoughts, which lead us to powerful action and to our One True Life. We'll discuss this process more thoroughly later in the book. For now, focus on the analysis of your thoughts, and whether those thoughts are responsible to the self. Stop looking to the outside for what to do or how to be. Remember to be authentic. That's the only thing that reduces anxiety.*

*29. Are you driven by envy and/or jealousy? Do you always have to keep up with your friends and neighbors, or do you always have to have the best of everything? When you buy a new toy for yourself, if your thoughts are about how you think others will perceive it, you have some work to do. Before making any purchases, no matter what the size, ask yourself what your motive is. Motive is your inherent intention. If it's anything other than for your own enjoyment, don't make the purchase. There is an addiction to always having the Next Big Thing that is consuming Americans. We buy when we want to feel better. We buy when we can't afford it. We buy before our other items are worn out. We buy for status. Our culture is killing us from the inside out. It ends up being more about purchasing things than it does about the item purchased. The only way to stop the epidemic of our "throw it away" culture is to evaluate closer the motives that cause us to open our individual purses and wallets. For the next week, buy only items you need to sustain your life. Come back to your center. Don't buy the gum, the entertainment, the meal at 11p.m., the beef jerky at the checkout counter. Don't buy the magazines, booze or clothes. At the end of the week, you'll feel empowered. Continue the process. Make purchases only when you need something for survival. You'll begin to appreciate people and things so much more.*

The next morning, a new patient came to me with a severe migraine. She wore dark sunglasses and was as pale as a ghost. After being gently adjusted and given the chance to relax for half an hour, she stood up and started crying. I asked whether she was all right. She patted her tears with a tissue, looked at me and said, "Thank you so much. I've lived with these migraines for forty-five years, and no one had ever been able to get rid of them." Tears continued to fall down her cheeks. "I usually have to go for a week at a time with pain throughout my whole body. And now, after only a few minutes, I feel no headache whatsoever. Where have you been my whole life?" We chuckled together for a moment before she hugged me with the deepest gratitude. I truly loved moments like that. The breakthroughs made all the stress worthwhile. At the end of her treatment, I released her for the day and continued into the next room. Atia was sitting in the chair.

I closed the door and greeted her. It wasn't awkward. We just seemed to pick up where we left off. I asked, "Are you here for an adjustment, or just to heckle me?"

She laughed and asked me whether I knew that Laurie, my office manager, was soliciting patients to come to her Bible study groups.

I knew Laurie was an evangelical Christian and she and her husband were quite active in their Church. When I first came into the clinic, she and I had a short discussion about her religion. I supported her fully in her belief in her God, but told her it had to stay out of the workplace because it was intrusive and unprofessional for a clinic to propagate religious paraphernalia and ideas.

I told Atia that Laurie and I had already discussed the matter months ago, and she understood not to mention religion in the office. Atia replied, "Then why did she just invite me to one of her Church events?" Atia wasn't so much offended; she liked stirring the pot. "I just thought you'd want to know something like that," she said with a tilt of the head and a flick of the wrist. I told her thanks, adjusted and released her for the day.

Before I left for lunch, I asked to talk with Laurie. When she entered my office, she smiled from ear to ear, as usual. The girl was constantly smiling, the kind of smile people use to hide deeper, more aggressive motives. I asked her whether she had been inviting patients to religious events. She quickly replied, with the smile never leaving her face, "No, I just invite people over to my house for barbecues on weekends. Why do you ask?"

She wasn't going to make it easy for me. "Is one of the purposes of these barbecues to increase your church's membership?"

She looked around, trying to think up the logical reply. "Well…sometimes when they ask questions about my church, we talk about it."

I never knew Laurie to be a liar. In fact, she was the most honest person I'd ever met. But she didn't exactly offer up the whole truth either. I could see right through her like a piece of clean glass. I asked her, under no uncertain terms, to stop soliciting my patients, period. She smiled, agreed it would not happen again, and went about her day. She walked out of my office with a sense of passive defiance, and with a smile. She and I both knew she had leverage within the clinic. She was great at her job; I doubted any other office manager could be so incredibly efficient, but I also knew she would find some way to continue the dissemination of her beliefs, making the issue rear its ugly head again.

After lunch that same day, one of the most interesting people I'd ever met came into the clinic for her monthly office visit. Betsy was a middle-aged, flamboyant woman of the town. She wore suits that were throwbacks to the twenties and thirties and drove around in early model American muscle cars, for which we shared a mutual affection. She loved the sheer power of them; the way they threw her back in her seat when she hammered on the gas. Betsy walked like Betty Davis, talked as dramatically as a movie star, and had the confidence of a bull. She told the greatest stories and controlled the conversation, talking nonstop from the moment she entered the office until she walked out the door.

When I finished treating her that day, she asked me to come outside. She had a surprise to show me. We walked around the building to where stood one of the most beautiful vehicles I'd ever seen. The car was a powerful, yellow hot rod with more chrome than a Harley. The interior was wrapped in flawless flat black leather. She offered to let me take it for a spin, but I had patients coming soon. She cocked her head to the side and said, "Maybe next time, Doc," as she got in and started the car. She rolled the car into the street and squawked the tires as she waved goodbye out the driver's side window. What a beautiful piece of artwork.

The leaves changed color and shed quickly that first November. And autumn receded into winter in the bat of an eye. The first month at the new house was quite uneventful. I wasn't around much, and Natalie was always busy with her own thing.

On one evening when we found ourselves home together, we decided to have a nice dinner down in the Village. As we walked through the village that night, we ran into five or six people I knew to whom I introduced Natalie. As we walked the quaint street together and ran into more people, I said to Natalie, "This place tries awful hard to look like a Norman Rockwell painting, but it's probably ten times more dysfunctional than your average town."

She laughed and said, "Maybe people with money believe they can do whatever they want, thinking they're more privileged, so they try to cover up their less than noble activity with fake fronts like this village."

I was definitely impressed with her estimation. It was certainly true that Atherton looked good on the surface. But it also had its share of shady individuals. And it was true they covered up their social misgivings with pretty things that cost a lot. But Atherton wasn't unlike any other community. I was just beginning to understand what people everywhere were like. We all had our idiosyncrasies. That's part of being human.

Since being in Atherton, I'd done my best to keep my ears open and my mouth shut. I listened much more than I talked. Quite a few people in town loved to hear the sound of their own voices, and those voices were easy to hear after a couple of glasses of wine. While at dinner functions, wine tastings and cocktail parties, I learned that unbelievable numbers of parents smoked pot daily; some even supplied their kids' habits. I learned about the weekday mothers who went out on weekends together to use cocaine and ecstasy while slugging down martinis. I learned about the closet alcoholics with DUI's. And, of course, the swinging parties where people shared sex partners until everyone was satisfied. Atherton had an underworld not visible through the plate glass windows adorned with expensive furs and fine Italian shoes.

Natalie and I ducked into a trendy little French restaurant and had a wonderful meal that night. It was a nice, quiet dinner with excellent service. We talked of many things, but we never really seemed to pierce the surface. I thought maybe life was supposed to be that way, but I wasn't comfortable with it.

After our meal, Natalie and I slowly walked back to our car and got in. Neither of us said a word. Somewhere between the appetizer and dessert, I lost her. She was back within her own head. On the way home, the air was heavy with angst. I could barely breathe, so I asked her whether everything was okay. She just said she was tired. It had apparently been a long day for her, so she wanted to go home and go to bed. I honestly wasn't all that interested in being around her. Her moodiness made me so tired. So I asked whether she minded if I went back to the office to get caught up on some work. She agreed; she obviously couldn't care less what I did.

As we said goodbye, I didn't like that our relationship was so humdrum, so I threw out an idea I'd been mulling over to try to shake things up. I asked her to look online to see what it would cost for a two week Christmas vacation in Hawaii. She looked at me completely befuddled and said, "Are you serious?"

I told her, "Absolutely! I think we deserve it. Don't you?"

She agreed it would be a ton of fun and said she'd start looking right away.

On my way down to the office, I realized I had never been on a vacation as an adult. I'd taken plenty of weekend trips, but never a two-week vacation. I was getting excited.

I quickly completed my paperwork while down at the office that night and decided to go across the street to the local pub for a beer. I hung out with an eclectic mix of longshoremen and bratty "ghetto" wanna-be's. We all had a good time playing pool and giving each other shit. I quickly became one of the crew and won the favor of the owner, Kyle. That guy was a trip. Nobody seemed to know how old he was, but he had bright gray wisps of hair that stuck out of either side of his mesh-backed Mariners cap. He was one of those guys who, when he talked to you, always sounded like he was yelling. He was about six feet tall and had a big beer gut that forced his untucked Polo shirt to hang about six inches out from the rest of his body. I think I heard about a thousand stories and jokes that night. He never stopped.

At closing time, I said adios to the guys and went back to my office across the street to get my keys. I couldn't find the little guys anywhere. I became seriously annoyed with having to open and close all the office doors. Doors were all over the place, and they unnecessarily chopped the office up. They were more annoying than functional, so I took all the dysfunctional doors off their hinges and put them behind the building in the dumpster. I was amazed at how much of a positive difference it made. The place had been a little stagnant, and now there was more flow. It actually looked great.

When I was finished with the doors, I looked at the wall that split the building in two. It completely separated one half of the building from the other. And in order to get to the other side of the clinic, one had to exit one side of the building, walk outside, and then enter the other half through another door. It was the weirdest thing ever. Since I'd been there, I'd wanted to demolish the thing and connect both halves. And that's exactly what I did that night. I opened up the wall with a hammer and a saw I had in my truck. That was the weekend I started the office remodel. I was going to make that place even more efficient.

I had done remodeling at many points in my past, so it was no big thing to me. In fact, I liked using my hands to create a warmer, more comfortable and flowing space. That first weekend I carefully removed all unnecessary walls and doorways and resituated the location of the front desk and retail area. I estimated that the remodel would be completed in about six weeks. It was to consist of new carpet, warmer colored paints in every room, new tile in the reception area and a completely new front office. The idea was to have a much more open floor plan where it was easier to access all treatment rooms and offices from one large open room.

The first week was quite a change for everyone. The patients loved the remodeling ideas I had and asked tons of questions. They loved being in the middle of it all, being involved. Some even wanted to hire me to do some work at their houses. I would treat a few people, do some paperwork and then go build a doorframe. Then I'd treat a few more people, do some paperwork and put up some drywall. It was really a lot of fun.

Later that week, Natalie and I went to Bobby's for Thanksgiving. We had a wonderful time and stayed late into the night talking and sharing stories. The next day we lay in bed and booked our travel plans for the Christmas holiday. We were really excited to see Hawaii, and it was only three weeks away!

Time was flying by and the remodel was going smoothly. By the end of the second week, the drywall was completed and the mud was sanded. I primed the walls for paint and installed tile in the reception area.

On Friday, I got a phone call from Atia. She asked whether Natalie and I were coming to her annual holiday party scheduled for the following night. She'd been pestering me about it for the previous two weeks, but I didn't want to commit in either direction. I genuinely wanted to go, but I was trying to heed the advice of my therapist. Atia still came into the office for treatment every now and again, and I already felt so guilty for treating her behind my therapist's back that I hadn't been to a session with him in weeks.

The whole thing was just too much for me. I despised cloudy situations, and this one was muddier than heck. I told Atia that Natalie and I had previously committed to another party and thanked her for the invitation. She was silent for a moment before she switched gears completely.

She said, "Did you know I took Natalie to lunch the other day?"

I was genuinely shocked. "You did what?"

"I took her to lunch. We had some great conversation."

"Why the heck would you do that?" I asked.

"Keep your pants on; I didn't tell her anything. I just thought she and I should get to know each other, that's all."

"Leave Natalie out of everything, just like I keep your boyfriend out of it," I warned.

"Okay, Doc. I don't need any more friends anyway. I don't even like her. She's boring. Enjoy your other party tomorrow," she said, before hanging up on me. I didn't like that Atia had dirt on me, but at least I had the same dirt on her.

The next evening, Natalie and I went to a party hosted by a woman I'd known for a couple of months. Katy and I gathered in the same circles and could oftentimes be found at the same networking or wine tasting events. She was a partier, and I heard from a mutual friend that she had a thing for me. I wasn't planning to act on it, but the attention was nice. More importantly, I figured her party would be a lot of fun so we went. I knew Katy's crowd was more inclined to downing vodka than wine, so I brought a fifth of Vox with us.

Katy greeted us at the door. She was wearing a short, red leather skirt with black boots and a tight angora sweater. She adorned her head with a cute little Santa hat. We all hugged. I sat the bottle down next to all the others. At that early hour, already about twelve fifths were sitting on the sideboard. It was going to be a long night.

The party was a little slow at first, but as soon as the booze started taking effect, it was a lot more fun. It got louder and people started spitting a lot more when they talked. A group of about eight people took turns going into the bathroom with each other. Everyone talked a million miles an hour, sniffed a lot and had eyes that constantly darted around the room. A second group was just sitting on the couch in their expensive suits and dresses with glazed eyes. A bunch of winos at the dining room table were each trying to prove himself more educated about booze than the next.

I downed my sixth drink within two hours and decided to pump it up a little bit. I made my way around the room, introduced myself to people I didn't know, told jokes and laughed too much at the boring, incoherent stories coming out of the drunks' mouths. By that point, Natalie looked like she wanted to pass out. Katy had been feeding her drinks all night. I asked Natalie whether she wanted to leave, but she said with a silly little grin that she wanted to people watch for a while. She went into the next room and sat on a chair that faced the crowd.

Katy immediately came up to me and aggressively asked, "What's her problem? Doesn't the little girl know how to have a good time?"

I laughed at her over-the-top theatrics, "Leave the girl alone. She's just not a seasoned alcoholic like you."

She replied, trying to keep herself upright, "I've been watching you throw down quite a few yourself, so don't chastise me. I just don't think she has what it takes to be with someone like you. She's obviously not enough."

She stumbled into me, grabbed my arm and whispered in my ear, "Join me outside in a few minutes, in the garden."

What? There was no way that was going to happen! I couldn't believe what she was asking. I openly laughed at her complete lack of self-respect. But that didn't stop me from envisioning what could happen.

She looked around, and then said with a come-hither smile, "Nobody will ever know except us." I knew I shouldn't even think about what she was offering, but I couldn't stop.

## *Point Of Responsibility*

*30. Do you find yourself fantasizing, glorifying or even obsessing about events that would probably do more harm than good to yourself and others? Such thoughts oftentimes lead to internal emotional disturbances. We might begin to feel guilty for having such thoughts, and act out the emotional confusion on those around us. If the thoughts continue, they can easily spiral into isolated external incidents, and ultimately into compulsions. In your notebook, describe one thought that seems to play over and over in your head, either one from your real past, or one from your imagined future. Write the story out in specific detail. When finished, write a list of ten things you could think about that would be more proactive and positive to focus on? Any time you find yourself in a negative daydream, practice taking yourself out of the fictitious moment and into one of your proactively created moments. Practicing this process can help you to function properly. Do this over and over, as many times as you must throughout each day.*

*31. Are there situations in your life where you act, or have acted, without integrity? We have all done so. But acting with integrity is at the heart of self-respect. Without it, we feel bad, guilty and low. List five specific situations where you've acted without integrity. When finished with your list, ask yourself why you acted as you did. Were you creating a situation of self-sabotage? Deep down, did you want to be found out so your true self would be known to the world? Were the actions a muffled scream for help? Are such actions habits for you? Have they become your "way of being"? What are the consequences of your lack of integrity to those around you? Write a list of your three closest relationships. Describe in your notebook how your lack of integrity could potentially affect those three individuals. Then describe how those actions could potentially affect you personally, as well as affect your reputation as an upstanding individual.*

I reaffirmed to Katy, "No matter how tempting that may be, it's not going to happen. But thanks for the offer."

"Your loss, Doc," she said.

I looked over to Natalie. She was out cold. I told Katy to get herself a new drink while I checked on Natalie. I gently nudged her and asked her to get up. It was time to go home. We said our goodbyes and went home for the night. We passed out as soon as our heads hit the pillows.

Over the next two weeks, I finished remodeling the office. The place looked astonishingly beautiful. We had made a wonderful transition and the place felt great. It was everything I had hoped it to be. I felt a comforting sense of accomplishment.

It was finally time for vacation! We flew into Honolulu and stayed at one of the boutique hotels on Waikiki. The time seemed to fly by as we filled every day with sightseeing adventures and every night with fine dinners, dancing and shows. Things were great. I was finally able to unwind, to relax and to appreciate everything around me.

Unfortunately, the connection between Natalie and I refused to reignite. I enjoyed the time we spent together, but it felt like she and I were not just on different pages, but part of completely different books.

Chapter Seven:

# Everything Anew

It was a new year, and I had big plans. I decided I needed additional training in marketing and advertising. I had been doing very well and was in the top 5% of all chiropractic clinics nationwide with regard to income. It was time for me to expand my operations by opening other clinics. I needed help from outside of the industry to take my dreams to the next level.

I'd recently heard about an international executive program from a colleague. The innovator prided himself on having created a successful program to help individuals achieve their goals in all areas of life. After some research, I determined it was no sham. His program was legitimate, and he was helping people achieve their dreams using sound principles I hadn't yet mastered. Of course, the program cost some dough, but I firmly believed that fortifying one's education was the only way to achieve increasingly progressive success. My first seminar was scheduled for April, and I anticipated it like a child would Christmas.

Back on the home front, the New Year brought good moods from patients and vendors and things were light and quick. Life was much less stressful. My primary receptionist informed me on the first week back that she was going to get married and her new husband didn't want her to work anymore. Under previous circumstances, that news would have sent me into a fit of anxiety and worry. I would have been tearing my hair out trying to figure out how all the work was going to get done. But, surprisingly even to me, the news came and went relatively easily. Maybe I was changing. I congratulated her with genuine joy and promptly initiated a search for someone new.

Two weeks later, Natalie and I had dinner with Sonya and Gabe. I told them I was hunting for someone who could do a little marketing, advertising and some administrative work. Sonya said, "You know, Mark, I'm not really happy with my job right now. It's too boring and my skills aren't being utilized at all." As she described in great detail why I should hire her, I thought of how comforting it would be to have someone I could truly trust in a position of power in my clinic.

Although it felt like Sonya would work well in the clinic, I still had to call her references and do the background work. After all, I didn't know her on a professional level. After making the necessary phone calls, I decided Sonya was indeed, a good fit for the office. I let her know again that the job was administrative in nature, but it would evolve into self-initiated, internal and external marketing and advertising. I needed a right hand person I could trust long-term. I told her the base pay, and that bonuses would be available based on her performance. I was a firm believer that employees must produce in order to make what they were worth. I had no problem paying out big bonuses; it meant I was making more money. She agreed it was a great opportunity and started two weeks later.

From the very beginning, Sonya was a natural. Her skill set was clearly above simple administration. She quickly became competent in running the entire front office; by the time the previous receptionist left, Sonya was doing the job much more efficiently. After only two weeks, Sonya started cross training with Laurie to learn the inner workings of the business. She quickly picked up the abilities to do both paper and electronic billing, insurance coverage negotiations and callbacks, inventory, accounts payable and receivable. The pace around the office was swift. It ran like a well-oiled machine or a beautiful dance. I was so grateful everything was working out.

Within weeks, it was clear Sonya was overqualified simply to run the front office, so we started the hunt for a full time front office person. Sonya could then work on things like a new logo, taglines, getting me booked for more speaking engagements and creating better advertising copy. I didn't like the idea of having three full-time employees, but I stayed focused on the future. In order to increase volume, I had to create a solid infrastructure of personnel to handle that new volume.

After a couple of weeks, we hired a little firecracker blonde to run the front of the house. Cynthia was young and had a powerful disposition. Sonya and I both liked her and the way she dominated her responsibilities. Unfortunately, after only one week, she decided to work for another company that could pay her more. I was sad to see her go, but I couldn't blame her for going for the money. I simply couldn't budget more money for employee wages. I wasn't too disappointed because a long-term patient of mine, Kendra, had come in close second when I had interviewed Cynthia, so I offered her the position. Kendra screamed into the phone with excitement and told me she could start in a week.

My team quickly came together. Kendra picked up her job with ease and everyone got along exceptionally well. We worked together with very little friction, resulting in a direct upswing in business. Good energy flowed throughout everything associated with the clinic.

The same Friday I hired Kendra, I was ready to go home, throw back a nice glass of wine, and relax for the weekend. But first, I had to drive Natalie to the airport because she had planned a weeklong trip to visit her aunt in Colorado for a quick spring vacation. I took her out for dinner on the way to the airport and told her to have a good time and to relax. I would hold down the fort. She pecked me on the lips and was off. It was just the pug and I for the next two weeks. I felt like I too had a vacation.

The weekend was quite eventful. I went out with Bobby on Saturday to a trendy new restaurant with overpriced tapas and scantily clad patrons. After dinner, we hung out for a little while and ran into some people I knew from hockey. Shortly thereafter, Bobby was feeling a bit tired and decided to go home. I, on the other hand, made it a night on the town. The guys and I went to a few different clubs for dancing and too much booze. Later that night, the guys went home and I ended up sleeping with an investment banker who was just in town for the weekend. I stayed the night at her hotel with her and a few of her local college friends. And early the next morning, she and one of her more amorous friends awakened me for some more fun. It wasn't exactly my typical night out in Seattle, but it was a welcome change of pace just to let loose with no inhibitions.

On my drive home that morning, I began to feel guilty for cheating on Natalie. As the previous night progressed, I remembered feeling happier than I had in a long time. I wanted it to last forever. The conversation was good. Being with friends outside of my typical microcosm was invigorating. And having adoration from beautiful women made me feel good. I felt I deserved to have fun; that nothing should hold me back from living my life to the fullest. But during my alcohol-distorted consequential thinking practice, I didn't recognize there was also a sense of acting out, a sense of passive aggressiveness on my part. The child inside wanted to prove to Natalie, and to itself, that I had the power to do whatever I wanted with limited repercussions. But Natalie wasn't even going to know what had happened. The whole game was in my mind. The bottom line was that I wasn't strong enough to tell Natalie my position. I was afraid of what might happen. My ego didn't want her completely gone, as she offered some comfort when I needed it. Of course, having someone in my life solely for comfort was incredibly selfish on my part. But I paid no attention to that. Any time I thought about how my activities might make Natalie feel, my ego would remind me that I wasn't getting what I wanted and needed from her anyway. So I simply tried to sabotage my relationship from the inside out. Deep down, however, I knew my actions were not right. I was a coward. And it did nothing but bring on a wave of depression.

At work on Monday, I got a phone call from someone I thought I'd never hear from again. It was Cynthia. She said she was sorry it hadn't worked out at the office, and she hoped I didn't have any hard feelings. I told her I understood her position, and I just wanted her to do well. Then she said, "I have a question for you."

"What's that?"

"I know it's short notice, but this firm I'm working for has invited all of its employees to some celebratory event downtown tomorrow night. Would you like to go with me?"

I didn't think twice. "That sounds great! I don't have any other plans, and it will be good to see you outside the office for a change. We can loosen up a little bit!"

"Awesome! I can't wait!" she replied. After giving me directions and discussing the attire for the evening, we bid each other adieu and hung up the phone.

The next two days flew by, and before I knew it, I was on my way to pick her up. When she opened the door, she invited me in. She poured us each a glass of wine and showed me around the place. She said she had to put on the finishing touches of her makeup, so I sat down on the living room couch. As she stood in front of the bathroom mirror, we gently talked about nothing. After a couple of minutes, she came out and sat down in the chair next to me. She was so beautiful. We sat there for a few minutes with the gas fireplace roaring in front of us. Then she said, "You know, I have to be honest. I'm a little tired. I'm not so excited to go to this thing. But I'm glad you came over."

"Do you want me to leave?" I asked, feeling a little unsure.

"No, that's not what I meant. I was just thinking maybe we could just sit here and talk."

"That sounds perfect to me," I said. "It gets tiring talking to people all day long. It's nice just to relax with someone once in a while."

She quickly refilled our glasses, then perched herself next to me on the edge of the couch. "You know," she said, "it wouldn't have worked out with me working for you."

"Why's that?"

"Well, I'm a little embarrassed to say…."

I knew then Cynthia was going to make a serious pass at me, one I would reciprocate. I didn't think twice when she leaned in to kiss me. I was quite attracted to her when she worked at the office. I remembered back to some of the insidious thoughts I had to stifle when she was around. As the evening continued, one thing led to another. When I was on my way home, I figured it probably was a good thing she wasn't working in my office anymore. I couldn't trust myself to be in her presence while thinking of the possibilities every day. As for my consequential thinking practice, it seemed to become disengaged anytime an alcoholic beverage was around. I had to come up with a way to think of the consequences before the inebriation. I truthfully had to figure out the thought that precipitated the final events that were making themselves a pattern in my life.

A couple of days later, Sonya and I were working late at the office. Things had been pretty intense around there lately with all the new business and cross training that was going on. The place was like a whirlwind. Around eight at night, we finally started gathering our things together to take off. We stepped outside, I locked the door, and as I turned around, she asked me whether I wanted to go blow off some steam somewhere.

"What do you have in mind?" I asked.

"Let's go get some Mexican food and too many margaritas!" she said.

"That sounds perfect! I'll drive."

It was nice just to hang out with her away from the office for a change. It had been weeks since the four of us had done anything together. And even when we did, it seemed like she and I couldn't really talk candidly. I liked Sonya. She was a genuinely good person—empathetic and strong.

As we ate, the conversation was easy. We drank and laughed and drank some more. At about ten-thirty, I thought we should probably call it a night.

Then she asked out of nowhere, "Hey, sorry I have to ask, but do you think I could stay at your place tonight? Our apartment is so far away, and I shouldn't be driving."

## *Point Of Responsibility*

*32. Have you ever engaged in compulsive behavior? Use the list below to create your own all-inclusive list of the various types of compulsions you've lived with over the years. (Examples: overeating, undereating, filling every waking moment with activity and/or talk, lacking integrity, lying, passive aggressiveness, overworking, wishing, day dreaming, procrastination, control, manipulation, guilting others, sex, spending money irresponsibly, self-deprecation, drugs, alcohol, fighting, ego proliferation, sugar consumption, searching for the "next big thing," worrying....) These are the types of behaviors that are tied into our emotions. This is an awareness step. Write as many of your compulsions as you can recall.*

I quickly replayed the last few days in my mind. I had been with three different women in three days—the overnight businesswoman, her friend the next morning, and Cynthia. And now Sonya might be the fourth in as many days. I knew Sonya wasn't inebriated; she'd only had one margarita over dinner. For once, my better judgment came into play. I knew it would be a potential disaster if she and I had any form of sex. I offered to call Gabe to pick her up, but she declined. We paid the bill and I drove Sonya back to her car before heading home for the night.

The next day, I was out in the backyard working when I heard a vehicle pull up. I looked around the house into the driveway; it was Atia. She walked up the sidewalk with a plateful of cookies in her hand. "Hey, what's up?" I asked.

"Just thought I'd bring you some cookies. You look like you're working too hard. Can't you hire somebody for that?" She handed the cookies to me as I put down my shovel.

"It's good work, working with the earth, getting dirty," I said. "It heals your soul. Maybe you should try it."

She quickly quipped with a dramatic scowl on her face, "Yeah, right. Like I'm going to work in the garden. And my soul's just fine, thank you." We walked inside the house. I washed my hands and unwrapped the cellophane, pulled out a cookie and took a bite. But before I could chew and swallow, Atia did exactly what she did on that trail weeks before. It was a surprise, but even after a few seconds, I couldn't bring myself to make her stop. Even though the rational part of me screamed to end it, the more cunning compulsive part of me won out. When Atia left, I felt disgusted and anxious. Something about the way she went about things didn't jibe with me, but something else did. The whole thing was obviously irrational.

The next day, I picked Natalie up from the airport. She asked me how things had been. "Uneventful," I said. "How 'bout you?"

"It was nice to see my aunt, but I'm glad to be home."

We shared a nice, quiet evening together before things became unraveled.

It was a beautiful spring Monday. Natalie and I went out for a nice dinner and started talking deeply after a couple of glasses of wine. We talked about our relationship and discussed her unhappiness in her own life from her not knowing what she wanted to do with it. And we talked about how my addiction to work and our mutual resentment of one another had driven a wedge between us. We acknowledged that we had grown apart. It was all very calm and sincere. She asked me plainly whether I thought she should move out, maybe just to shake things up a bit. I gently agreed that it might be good for both of us. Two weeks later, we found her an apartment close to her school's campus.

## *Point Of Responsibility*

*33. Do you stay in negative relationships longer than you know you should? Or do you leave relationships as soon as the going gets tough? Do you do both at different times? Evaluate in your notebook your last five relationships, and take notice of any such patterns.*

Over the next two weeks, Natalie and I talked in great detail about the expectations for the experiment. We wanted to remain exclusive with one another; we shared the hope that with some temporary space between us, we would eventually come back together. I told her I would pay for the apartment, and she agreed to get a job to pay for all her other expenses.

After setting up the apartment and helping her unpack, I left. On the drive home, I started to grieve over our five-year relationship that had taken us so many places. We both knew it was over, although we weren't fully willing to admit it yet.

At work, things were very busy, but going well. I was on autopilot for a few weeks. But Sonya was a bit sidetracked. I noticed her starting to withdraw, and at the same time, I caught her staring at me on quite a few occasions. I figured she was probably just embarrassed for making a minor pass at me the night we went to the restaurant. I just hoped it would pass with time.

I didn't want to make a big deal out of it. I ignored her stares as much as I could. But then she started asking me to lunch almost every day and asking about Natalie and me; she knew things weren't going well between us. I felt like she expected me to talk with her about it. The only thing I wanted was for her to continue being a good, hard-working employee. I was amazed at how quickly a margarita could change a relationship.

### *Point Of Responsibility*

*34. Does it seem, in your life, that things happen TO you, instead of you creating your existence? In my past, I would set up a situation to get a desired result, making it appear that someone did something TO me. The whole thing would be planned just under the conscious radar. This allowed the other person to think he or she was controlling the shots, when, in fact, they were only playing off my body language. If you envision things happening TO you in life, take a closer look. For one reason or another, you're probably allowing others to control your environment. You're giving away your power and being passive about your own life.*

I decided to spend most of my social time with both Bobby and Chloe. We shared great conversation, lunches, dinners and went to parties together. Atia stopped by every so often to offer her insincere condolences with regard to the probable failing of my relationship. Natalie and I shared time at the bookstore and continued exploring the Pacific Northwest together. For a little while, we appreciated each other's company like we had in the distant past.

In early April, I attended my first executive seminar in L.A., and I had a great time. It was a whole new world to me. I met hundreds of people like myself with great ideas and opportunities, all looking to achieve the next level of success.

I learned many things that week, including how to write more stimulating marketing and advertising copy and how to focus on particular niche groups. I learned how to accumulate and interpret statistical evaluations of my marketing efforts. I also learned how to systemize my business and how to reproduce the system over and over to maximize my efforts. The week was fruitful, to say the least.

When I came back to my patients, I was busier than ever. On that first day, Atia stopped by and told me that she took Sonya to dinner and got her really drunk, so much so that Sonya had to spend the night at Atia's place.

"Sounds like you guys are becoming good friends," I said.

"I guess so. Just know that you and I are on the same team, and she's on the outside. I'm just making it comfortable for her to share her deepest darkest secrets with me, so I can keep you up to date with what's going on in her head. You gotta keep your enemies close."

"She's not my enemy Atia; she's an employee."

"Well your employee's in love with you."

I immediately felt ill as she smiled, stood up and walked out of the treatment room.

At that moment, I made a conscious decision to stop all negative activity with both Sonya and Atia. It was time to take my life back.

Chapter Eight:

# Seminars and Emails

With the help of Sonya, I began to implement some of the ideas and procedures I picked up at the executive training seminar. We systematically organized all clinic policies and procedures and created manuals that easily and efficiently explained the inner workings of the business. We left nothing to chance. We created a hierarchy, budgets, clear and concise job descriptions, and patient flow charts. I bought the necessary equipment to bring billing in-house, and also made the billing and note taking system paperless. Systems became much clearer for everyone to use over time, and I erased all uncertainty anywhere I found it. We role-played, had weekly focus meetings, and came together as a group. It was a lot of work to get it done, but the whole process was worth it tenfold when I stepped back to see what we had created.

I also decided to move forward with my own personal seminar series. I created four different presentations that focused on various topics such as self-responsibility in personal health care, wellness, human physiology and weight loss. I presented the talks to corporate groups, charitable organizations and clubs of various sizes; anywhere from fifteen to two hundred people were in attendance. It was an excellent way to get face time in front of as many people as possible. And I flourished as a speaker and educator.

The next executive seminar came up quickly. Coincidentally, it was all about training the people that do the training in organizations. I learned successful and practical management techniques, how to give more powerful presentations, and how to structure them for maximum effect upon the audience. I was grateful to learn the techniques employed by the classic orators of the past, as well as the great speakers of our own time.

When I came back from that seminar, I increased my number of talks per week to an average of four. I was really pumping them out. And it didn't seem like work because I had uncovered a new passion. I enjoyed immensely the opportunity to connect with people in a way I never had before. Along with an easy, practical approach to life and real health, I offered them something healthcare practitioners seldom allow into the equation: I offered them hope and the belief that they didn't have to live with illness the rest of their lives.

The practice was running on all cylinders. The first quarter was coming to a close and things were quickly becoming excitingly efficient. Patients appreciated the newfound values I had recently injected into their healthcare experience. I sent out newsletters, presented free health seminars, gave out coupons that deeply discounted products and services, and supported as many charities as I possibly could.

Sonya was working hard, but she still seemed to be sullen more often than not. She always looked tired. I knew she wanted me to ask her how she was, but I stayed away from Pandora's Box. I simply hoped she could shake it off at some point. Things were going so well, and in a large part because of her.

The attempt to distance myself from both Sonya and Atia was working well. I still treated Atia once in a while, but I didn't allow her the time to get going with the latest gossip. I simply wasn't interested in the rumor mill anymore. I knew she and Sonya lunched together on most days, and I didn't mind that they spent time together. It was fine they had a friend in each other. It seemed to take a lot of pressure off me. I felt cleaner, happier and quieter.

Meanwhile, Natalie and I continued seeing each other a few times a week. We had fun going on hikes, exploring Seattle and seeing movies. But the fire was clearly out. It would be just a matter of time before we decided to call it quits, but for the time being, it was nice to have an old friend with whom to read a book and explore.

Near the end of May, I went to yet another seminar that focused on business and marketing. Instead of closing the clinic for the entire week, I brought in an out-of-state doctor to cover for me. It was a win-win, as they say. He made a little dough, and the clinic didn't miss a beat.

Before I left, I asked Sonya to make Dr. Smithson feel at home. I asked her to show him around my house, where he would be staying, and to show him the sights and sounds of Seattle. I gave her some extra cash to spend however they saw fit.

The week went well on both fronts. The practice ran seamlessly, and I picked up priceless knowledge from many masters.

On the evening before the seminar ended, I noticed I had a missed call from Atia. I took a deep breath and reluctantly gave her a call back as I walked around the parking lot. She answered the phone and proceeded to drop it. As she fumbled around for what seemed an eternity, I heard Sonya and a man's voice in the background. The noise made it obvious they were in a restaurant together. When Atia finally put the phone to her ear, I could tell they had been drinking for a while.

"What are you guys up to?" I asked, already knowing the answer.

"Oh, Sonya, Dr. Smithson and I are at a restaurant downtown. We're pretty messed up. I don't know how long we've been here, but I think it's been longer than twenty minutes." They all laughed.

"Nice," I said.

I figured Sonya asked Atia to come to avoid any awkward silences. Atia was usually great at filling those with something useless. She loved to sit and rip on unsuspecting individuals as she sank deeper into inebriation. To me, both were quite humorous.

"What did you call for? I'm kind of in a hurry," I asked.

I heard her grunting as she got out of her chair. She told the other two she was going to use the little girls' room, and then said, "Well, I was wondering whether you wanted me to give Dr. Smithson the 'Doctor Treatment.'"

"What the heck are you talking about?" I knew full well what she meant. I just wanted to hear her say it. I had no idea why I liked listening to her trying to shock me. I just did, even though it was so inconsequential.

"You know, the 'Doctor Treatment', Doc," she hinted.

She wasn't going to give out any more, and my impatience spiked. "Do whatever you want," I said. "You guys are both adults; I think you can both figure it out. Don't you? And why are you asking me for permission anyway?"

"Well, he's a nice guy, and the babysitter has my kid for a few more hours. So I think we'll just go back to your place when we leave here. Any objections?"

"I gotta go. You're ridiculous," I said, even more annoyed. I hung up the phone and went back inside. I hadn't seen much of Atia over the past few months, and that phone call reinforced why I didn't want to be part of her life. But I still wondered why it was so tough to convince myself of it.

That same night, I had random sex with a stunningly beautiful woman who was at the seminar visiting from Southern California. She was a successful real estate developer with a natural confidence and a quiet, intelligent demeanor. She and I hit it off right from the get go. We partnered up for most of the day at the seminar and decided to continue the union into the night. We shared wonderful conversation, food and wine before going back to her room for the evening. During conversation, we talked about many things, including my current relationship; she said one thing that brought light to some of the cloudiness I'd been experiencing. "I'm worried about you're keeping your integrity intact. All a man truly has is his integrity you know," she prophetically declared.

## *Point Of Responsibility*

*35. Have you ever tried to stop an unwanted behavior within yourself and failed? Why do you think that is? List in your notebook three situations in which you did so. How did you feel after resuming the negative behavior? Be very specific in detailing your emotions here.*

Her words struck me hard. I knew them as true, just not at the surface. But she was absolutely right. Every time I had sex with someone else, with it came more guilt, shame and anxiety. I was going to have to end my relationship with Natalie soon. Closing the door on it for good was the right thing to do.

When I came back from the seminar, Atia was one of my first patients the following Monday. She apparently had a lot to tell me about the week. As I treated her, she shared with me how she seduced Dr. Smithson at my house. I just looked at her until she said with her scowl, "Don't worry; I washed the sheets."

"I'm happy for you," I said. I quickly finished her treatment and opened the door, forcefully implying that I couldn't care less.

She walked out, obviously annoyed that I didn't indulge her in storytelling time. The only thing I was focused on was implementing the newest ideas I'd learned at the seminar. I wished I didn't have anymore to do with Atia, but for some reason, I still didn't cut the ties completely.

About this time, I began hanging out with Chloe more. Sometimes we talked shop, other times we just goofed off or went for a walk. Our relationship was easy. It was comfortable. It didn't revolve around gossip, but was infused with light and truth. We shared good stories with one another, but more importantly, we calmed each other. Many times that summer, we laid out the yoga mats in the park to watch the clouds roll by. I cherished those moments and didn't want to them to end. But they had to; they always had to.

About a month after I'd returned from the last seminar, I felt implementation of the new ideas was going way too slow. Laurie and Kendra were doing well at their jobs, but Sonya was in a major tailspin.

Since the night at the restaurant, conversation between Sonya and I had deteriorated to the point where I would purposefully refrain from asking personal questions of any type. I knew Sonya had a bit of an obsession with me, but I didn't want to acknowledge it. I was dead set on it not affecting the clinic in any way. But after a short time, it was obvious she wasn't going to let it lay. Sonya had become much more emotional and withdrawn at work. Her staring was getting worse, and many times, I saw her dart in or out of the bathroom with red, puffy eyes. I had hoped her feelings would peter out, but that clearly wasn't happening. I began avoiding her at any cost.

To add insult to injury, Sonya made it common practice to miss deadlines and was often late to work. I found myself micromanaging her daily activities to make sure her tasks were completed, which added to my stress and hers.

We still attended marketing events together, but I made a point to remain as separate as possible. We would drive separately, mingle as separate individuals representing one company, and we would never debrief until the next day at work. I didn't want to poke the elephant in the corner, but now the animal was standing up and coming right for me! I just pretended not to notice, hoping everything would work itself out.

## *Point Of Responsibility*

*36. Do you avoid uncomfortable situations, or pretend that such situations don't exist? Do you hope that they just pass with inactivity? Wonderful opportunities for growth exist within every perceptibly negative situation. Think of some of the negative things in your life that you might want to work on. Make a declaration to yourself to change the situation into something less cloudy. Anxiety lies in the uncertainty of life and relations. Aim to make things clearer and more understood. Take responsibility for your actions and words. Say what you mean and mean what you say. Choose your words carefully, as every word is a declaration of the things you want to surround you and your family. Make the best of those uncomfortable situations. In your notebook, write down a list of no fewer than five negative situations you presently have in your life. Follow that with describing in detail the possible lessons you could take from each one.*

The next time Atia arrived back at the clinic, she had a huge tray of cupcakes. I openly thanked her with a smile, and we went back to the treatment room. As I adjusted her, she mentioned she and Sonya had had dinner the night before; they had been sharing quite a bit of time together since she and Gabe had broken up. I had heard there were rumblings in their relationship, but that was the first I'd heard that they were no longer together. Could it be possible Atia's estimations about how Sonya felt about me were wrong? Maybe she was just emotional over the ending of her relationship, and it had nothing to do with me.

And then Atia dropped the bomb. "I spent last weekend finding an apartment for your employee. We found a place two blocks from your house! Isn't that great?"

"Are you serious?" I asked, my eyes protruding out of my head.

"And then, after we went shopping for some odds and ends, we had some dinner. But it was really pitiful. All she could talk about was you. Before long, she was crying in her pizza. I acted like a good friend and gave her a shoulder to cry on, for six hours! She said she was completely in love with you, and that you don't even give her the time of day anymore."

"Why on Earth did you find her a place right down the hill from me?" I couldn't understand why she would do such a thing. I felt the heat rise up within me.

"It's all that was available with the peanuts you pay her," she said with a smile. Atia was having fun with all of this! She was creating chaos and loved it!

I blurted out, "I pay her well! Especially when you take into account that she cries all the time and hardly works anymore!"

Atia continued talking about something, but all I could think about was how the situation had reached its boiling point. It was time to deal with everything. Sonya had called me several times that week outside of work to discuss things, but I let the calls go straight to voicemail. I needed the weekend to collect my thoughts; then I planned to call her on Sunday.

That Friday, Betsy pulled into the parking lot with her latest hot rod purchase. It was quite a beauty. After her treatment, I had a couple of free hours, so I checked out the car with her and she offered me the keys.

We jumped in and took a stroll with the top down. It was like riding on air. She navigated us to a small house that was up for sale and asked me to pull into the driveway. It was another of her latest purchases. We walked in and she showed me around. I lost track of her as I checked out the views of the city. When I went downstairs into the master bedroom, there she lay across the staged bed, completely naked. My eyes must have been as big as saucers!

The inevitable occurred that day. And afterward, she dropped me off at the office in plenty of time for me to run home for a quick shower before returning to work. Unfortunately, I had to pass Sonya's new apartment every time I went home. And each time I did, I was reminded that I would have to deal with her. Sunday would be the day. The uncertainty had to end.

After a nice, relaxing weekend, I finally found the courage to give Sonya a call on Sunday night. As I walked through my gardens, I dialed her digits. I didn't want the conversation to ramble on ad infinitum, so I told her I had about ten minutes for her to discuss her issues. She said ten minutes was not enough, and she would stop by instead. She hung up on me. I heard her car start up a couple of blocks away. She raced up the hill, slammed on the brakes in front of my house and threw her door open. Then, with her phone still in hand, she started cursing at me about God knew what.

I puffed up my chest and said in a low voice, "You're way out of line! You need to get back in your car and leave. The weekend is my time! We'll talk about this on Monday!" I didn't like that she put me on the spot, and my ego got the best of me.

## Point Of Responsibility

*37. Have you ever acted harshly toward another, even when you knew you brought the situation upon yourself? In your notebook, describe three specific situations where you have done so and take notice of any patterns.*

Sonya angrily stomped her foot and ran back to her car crying. Then she peeled out and tore off in the direction of Atia's house. I couldn't believe what had just happened. I didn't want to believe she'd finally gone off the deep end.

Sonya had obviously been through a lot in recent times. But regardless of that, she should have been professional enough to keep her personal life separate. And I should have been more professional by not sending signals of availability to her. Neither of us was being honest.

I'd spent a lot of money, time and effort training Sonya, and the last thing I wanted was for her to quit or make me fire her. I thought I'd give her one more shot. I had a lot invested.

So I shot her an email later that night. I told her how bad I felt that communications had broken down between us, and that I truly wanted resolution to the issues that muddied the waters. I didn't want emotions to cloud our conversation, so I asked her to contact me by email. I asked her to detail all the things that gave her grief, and how I could help. I tried to keep it as professional as possible, while still showing genuine compassion. At the end, I apologized for allowing her to believe there was any hope for a possible relationship between us.

I didn't hear anything back, and Sonya wasn't at work the next day. I gave her some time and space, as I knew she was still helping Gabe with his move out of town. I received her reply that Monday night.

She apologized for her behavior, but she also admitted that the most important thing to her was our personal relationship, which indicated to me that things were probably going to end badly. But I figured I owed it to both of us to try. Even though she was backing me into a corner, I agreed to meet with her later that night at her apartment down the hill to see whether we could resolve things.

When I got there, she opened the door and invited me in with a smile. Candles were lit all over the place and not a single light was on. She was certainly setting the mood.

I sat down and thanked her for meeting with me. I wanted her to be at ease. But I also wanted to control the conversation. So I candidly told her how I felt about everything and asked her to speak her mind. Things were calm as we discussed our general dynamic and how we thought things were going at the office. I let her know I wanted her to be part of my team at work, but it wouldn't work unless we could let go of the past. She agreed we just needed a fresh start, with no hard feelings. The meeting went exactly like I had hoped. The drama was dashed, and I felt our team was back in action.

That night, I got a call from Natalie. She informed me she was leaving immediately to attend a four-week religious retreat in Georgia. I wasn't necessarily surprised; I knew her mother was a devout Evangelical Christian who desperately wanted Natalie to "find the light of God" again. Due to recent events in Natalie's life, her mother saw the chance to fight for her daughter's soul, so she paid for the entire trip.

The religious issue with Natalie and her mother was deeper than I could understand, even after five years of trying. I had always believed people should follow their own paths to enlightenment, as long as they harmed no one in the process, but Natalie had literally been brought up in a cult by the name of The Children of God. They had raised many well-known people throughout the world, and when she was five, her father moved her family to Europe to become fully involved in their way of life. Unfortunately, the cult was fraught with bad, bad people doing bad, bad things to kids and each other. Although their supposed focus was on the rigid idealism of Christianity, it had, at some point, evolved into something much more humanistic. It was based on control, manipulation and the satiation of inappropriate sexual urges and activities. Prostitution was used to lure men with money to the group. They called it "flirty fishing." And Natalie's mom had been one of the fisherwomen. The donations provided by these international sex-seeking men allowed the cult to continue into prosperity, and for the egomaniacal leader to justify his own behavior. Natalie's father was apparently a really smart fellow, but he fell prey to the manipulation of the cult leader. He thought it all right to bring his family into the communal living structure of the cult, to allow the constant degradation of his wife, and to allow the incessant sexual advances by the group elders toward his young daughter.

After living within the cult for almost a decade, Natalie's mom finally decided it was too much. She moved back to The States, but she still stayed involved in organized religion.

Natalie remained in the cult with her father until she was seventeen. She raised money for The Children of God by playing in a band and by singing on street corners all over Europe. When she'd finally had enough, Natalie left under the cover of darkness. She flew to the U.S. and began to integrate herself into traditional American society. She remained estranged from her father for many years.

When I met her, Natalie didn't believe in organized religion, and as we got to know one another, I understood why. Instead, she studied various types of spirituality and made a practice of daily meditation. Our mutual belief in unbound spiritualism had been a major point of resonation in our relationship. But, for some reason, Natalie now found it necessary to explore extremist Christianity again. I didn't ask why; I just told her I hoped she ultimately found what she was looking for.

## *Point Of Responsibility*

*38. Spirituality is the thread that all religions share. A religion is functional as long as 1) it is inclusive, not exclusive; meaning it teaches principles that bring people together, and doesn't seek to segregate based on faith, 2) it helps to achieve personal spiritual growth by providing a framework of dynamic principles aimed at evolving the souls of its believers, and 3) it is all-accepting and teaches no harm. Within the framework of spirituality, do you live your ideals without judgment of others? Do you accept people for who they are? Or do you place people who don't think your way into a different, usually subordinate category within your mind? Did you inherit such negative behavior? Do you take the lives and issues of others and apply new, more functional ideas and actions into your own life? Do you remain rigid and determined at the thought of something different from your beliefs? Do such conversations take you out of your comfort zone, or create anxiety within you, or make your heart beat faster? Do you feel attacked when discussing these beliefs with others? That is your ego trying to make a case for your "rightness." God is in the calm, while the mind is the ruler of tumult. Take the time to write your thoughts about spirituality and religion and where those thoughts originated.*

Even at that point, Natalie and I weren't completely broken up. I wanted to believe there was still some hope. We told each other our relationship would be exclusive until her return six weeks later. I wanted her to feel I supported her. I knew she was fragile, and I didn't want to add to her stress. I also didn't have the strength to tell her it was over.

She spent the first two weeks at her parents' house just hanging out. We talked on the phone a few times, but the conversations were tough and forced. After that, she went to the retreat. Midway through the retreat, we talked again. It was like talking to an alien. The Natalie I had lived with for five years had seemingly been brainwashed within two weeks. She talked of conspiracies to obliterate religion, about how a cosmic battle was being waged in the heavens for humans' souls, and that we must all repent before the inevitable rapture. I couldn't believe what I was hearing. We were completely disconnected. It was really strange, but it was also a relief. Despite her fragility, I knew she was capable of making her own decisions. I didn't talk to her again until I picked her up from the airport.

While Natalie was gone, and only a mere week since our little heart-to-heart, Sonya decided she wasn't finished fighting for our "relationship," so she sent me a lengthy email. Part of me wanted to know immediately what she had to say. In my experience though, emails of that length were never good. I decided not to succumb to the urge, but to ignore it until I could read through it without emotion when I felt myself under control.

Over the next couple of weeks, Sonya asked me numerous times whether I'd had a chance to read her email. I would reply, "Does it involve work only?" She would answer with a quiet, "No." I could tell she was upset by my response, but I was not going to let her backslide on me. I needed her to be strong, to live up to her side of the bargain. We were going to remain business only.

Within that same two-week period, I had also met someone new. While at a birthday party for my friend Bethany, I took notice of a woman who really stood out from others. What instantly struck me about Esther were her exotic looks and her seemingly intuitive, yet funny, demeanor. I asked Bethany to introduce us, and then Esther and I shared a few words before she and her friends left. Later that night, when I asked Bethany for Esther's phone number, she cocked her head to the right and said, "Trust me; I've known Esther for a while, and you don't want anything to do with her. She's more than a handful."

"Just give me the number. I can handle myself; don't worry."

"As you wish, sir, but mark my words!"

I called Esther a few days later from the office. We went out to lunch a few times and had a couple of successful dates over the next week and a half. It was low stress and exciting to learn about someone new. She lived in a funky neighborhood that was fun to explore, and we shared stories of our past. She had lived most of her life in New York and L.A. pursuing an acting career. When she was finished with that, she moved to Seattle six months earlier to start up a dating service.

I didn't want to screw up the new thing with Esther, so we put sex on the backburner until I could completely resolve things with Natalie. I knew it was time to move on.

I picked up Natalie from the airport that week. When I saw her, I gave her a hug and she reciprocated with one of those junior high school dance maneuvers, hands on the shoulders and butt out. It was the creepiest hug I'd ever received.

During the ride to her apartment, the conversation was like walking through quicksand. After a few sentences, silence followed for twenty minutes. She had a Stepford Wife smile on her face as she sat on her hands.

Finally, I had to break the silence. "I honestly don't know how to relate to you right now. After that last phone call, I was kind of creeped out."

She tilted her head back slightly and began gently to sway from left to right, back and forth, like she was appreciating sweet songs within her head. Then she started laughing and crying simultaneously. I just sat there waiting for her head to spin in a three-sixty. I was more freaked out than ever. After about twenty seconds she emphatically said, "These are tears of joy! My eyes have been opened! I can now see! I am so happy with my life!"

At that point, I definitely didn't know what to say. I just kept driving as she started speaking gibberish. I asked her what she was saying. She replied that it was an ancient language she allowed to flow from within. The woman was sitting in my car speaking in Tongues. I pounded on the gas pedal and couldn't get to her place fast enough.

A couple of days later, as I was getting ready for work, she popped in at the house. She wanted to talk about our relationship because time was of the essence. I was already late. As I donned my tie, I told her we could talk later that evening over dinner. We both knew what it was going to be about.

Then she asked, "Who's Esther?"

I was blown away. My mind couldn't draw a parallel between Natalie and Esther. "How do you know Esther?" I was at a loss, which seldom happened. I was the king of carefully chosen words and keeping my indiscretions to myself, or so I thought.

"Sonya called me a few days ago, while I was still in Georgia, to let me know what's been going on since I left. She said you were dating lots of women and you were having sex with this Esther girl. Is that true?"

"Listen, she's a girl I've been seeing for a week or so. And we haven't had sex. I wanted to wait for you and I to get closure to our relationship."

"Oh, that's nice. How considerate," she said sarcastically.

"I really have to go to work. Let's have dinner tonight; we'll discuss it all then, okay?"

"Fine," she agreed.

I walked out absolutely furious with Sonya. How could she do that? Having an infatuation with me was one thing, but calling Natalie to tell her things she knew nothing about was unbelievable! That day at work was as slow as molasses. I was tired and completely ignored Sonya, and everyone else, for that matter.

When I walked into the house that night, things were different. Little things were missing. The pug was still there, but pictures were gone, various knickknacks were no longer there, small pieces of furniture had vanished. Natalie had left, for good. There wasn't going to be any dinner together that evening. There wasn't going to be any closure.

But as I walked around the house, I felt a weight being lifted from my shoulders. I even felt a little guilt for feeling happy when I should probably feel sad. And then came an overriding sense of calm, quiet and stillness. I felt like my head was completely submerged under water. All stimuli were gone. I took a deep breath, stood up straight, and felt relief. I was finally released of all the burdens imposed by our relationship. I no longer had to pretend we were meant to be together. I no longer had to house resentment for her lack of support. I was no longer responsible for paying her way. I was liberated.

I thought it a great time to review the emails Sonya had sent to me a couple of weeks earlier. I wasn't necessarily angry at her for sabotaging things with Natalie. I couldn't place blame on her for my failed relationship. But I began to understand Sonya's capacity for vengeance. She wanted to be heard, and she was going to be heard, whether I liked it or not. I calmly perused the email line by line. What I read was the worst possible outcome of my hiring a friend to be my marketing specialist.

Sonya told me how she had intended to declare her feelings for me when I went over to her place for our discussion weeks earlier. But in my presence, she shut down and just agreed with me on all fronts. So now she shared with me all the reasons why she thought we would be great together, including a Relationship Horoscope detailing the commingling of our two signs.

My heart sank. This was the deathblow to any hope we might be able to work together in any professional capacity. She discussed how she had actively pursued a relationship with me, even though she knew I wasn't interested. And I realized she never really had any interest in helping to run my business; it was all a front to get me into a relationship with her; she even made this clear by including lengthy, unedited passages from her personal journal about her feelings for me.

As I read through the entries, I felt physically ill. She detailed how her personal feelings for me had paralyzed her and made her ineffective at work. Her words implied a sense of entitlement to me, even though we both had significant others. She sounded like she was living her life solely to be with me. I was surprised and saddened by her devotion and longing for me. I didn't understand where it came from. She went on for pages and pages about how lonely she felt. It was almost too much to bear. She was obviously hurting deeply, and I didn't think it my place to give her advice. I wanted to be her boss, nothing more. I was on my own emotional roller coaster with failed love and inappropriate relationships.

Her emails made it clear she understood my confusion and that I was in no position to be in a relationship with anyone, let alone her. But that didn't stop her pursuit. By her actions, she was obviously vindictive, even though she saw no problem with what she did.

As the entries labored on, I felt pity for Sonya. I admitted to myself that I had toyed with her emotions, albeit without purpose. She was so lost that she became consumed with believing a relationship with me would fix all of her issues. She seemed to be living inside her head instead of in the real world. Her behavior was unhealthy, but I also understood my part in her dysfunctional perceptions. By not dealing directly with the issues between us and keeping her employed at the clinic, I had given her hope we might one day be together.

By the end of her email and her trying to hurt me by talking to Natalie, it was obvious something sinister and insidious was unfolding within Sonya. I couldn't allow such activity in my life any longer. Her dysfunction didn't have to be my dysfunction.

I was annoyed with how much time, money and effort went into cultivating Sonya as the ideal employee, just to have her become the ideal basket case. But as I sat alone and came to grips with the situation, I began to blame myself. I couldn't believe I had hired her. I was largely responsible, both directly and indirectly, for the whole mess.

It was time to make a clean cut: Atia = gone; Natalie = gone; Sonya = gone. I would cut the dead wood out of my life yet again, but this graft would be much deeper.

I immediately called Sonya to tell her that her employment at my clinic was over. Of course, she put up quite a fight, but I'd made my decision. I was moving forward without her.

The week after all that happened, Laurie informed me she was pregnant, so she was only going to keep working at the clinic for a few months. I congratulated her and truly wished her all the success in life. She was going to be a great mom. It wasn't much of a shock because I knew she and her husband had been trying to get pregnant. Laurie said she would be happy to train Kendra fully. In the past, I would have been pulling my hair out, but all I felt was relief. Laurie was a great employee, but she was getting paid way more than the position commanded, and I wasn't sure how to deal with her continued solicitation of patients to her religious events. The pregnancy seemed to solve many problems simultaneously.

I would soon have only Kendra to run the office. When I talked to her, Kendra declared she was on my team 100%. I told her Laurie would train her on everything she needed to learn, and we'd hire someone for the front desk operations. Things would be fun and new again, so we were both excited.

## Points Of Responsibility

*39. Recall your list of friends from Chapter Three. Think about each of them individually. How does each relationship serve you? Is it a mechanical relationship, or is there love and excitement? Does it help you to evolve into a positive force? Does it enable your negative behavior? Does it give you a false, external purpose for being? Does it satiate your ego in any way? Is one person perceived as more important than the other? Does it keep either party subordinated? If, after conscious thought, you perceive a relationship as negative, or even questionable, how would your life look without that relationship? Can the relationship be modified to be more useful to both parties? Many people are walking through life with blinders on. Could an inspirational and truthful conversation between the two of you bring a new light to your relationship? Think of a few scenarios where you could gently tell the other person you'd like your relationship to be more functional, less trivial, and more meaningful. Tell him or her you need more presence, not necessarily more talk, but more presence. A good technique to use is to ask for his or her help in this process. Most people love the opportunity to help others. But if your plea isn't heard, you need to determine whether it is the kind of relationship you want in your life. Don't simply throw things away; make an honest and responsible attempt to recycle and recreate your relationships. Everything you do, directly and indirectly, affects the lives of others. So be responsible with your thoughts and emotions. Slow down. It's imperative that you make good choices.*

*40. Do you place blame on others for occurrences in your life? The most liberating of actions is to take your power back by taking responsibility for every little thing in your life. View every single action and occurrence in your life as your own construction, because it is. Ultimately, you are the architect of your own life. You choose to attract the positive and the negative people and occurrences. When you open that door to eradicating blame and you take responsibility for everything in your life, you inherently create and allow purpose, consciousness and authenticity to shine through, and calm confidence and self-esteem are born.*

Chapter Nine:

# Getting Back on the Horse

After relegating Natalie, Atia and Sonya to my past, I thought it necessary to take it a bit slow on the dating scene. I just liked to go out, meet nice people, drink a few beers and maybe have some good conversation. I wasn't so interested in sex. I would just talk the girls to death, and then go home. I didn't ask for phone numbers or pretend I was interested, no matter how nice or how gorgeous the girl.

Esther and I started seeing each other a couple of times a week, which was nice. But her noncommittal and elusive nature was mildly frustrating. When I used to juggle four or five dates a week like her, I probably seemed the same way. Now I saw what it was like from the other side. But I didn't really mind. I found her mysterious nature and elusive banter both interesting and endearing. When we were together, we just enjoyed each other's company without it getting heavy or stressful.

One afternoon, Esther invited me to a party in Fremont following a dating event she had planned. I had nothing else going on, and was curious to see one of her events, so I agreed. I wondered what type of clients she represented. Were they high-powered execs who were just too busy every day to slow down and talk to anybody? Were they hideous monsters with no social graces? I had no idea what I was in for, but I was interested to find out.

I walked into the bar at about 7 p.m. I couldn't help but notice everyone was adorned with one of those sticky name cards, creatively scribbled up with his or her name and some personally motivational epithet. The girl at the front door offered me one. I graciously declined. I hated those things. I preferred to begin a conversation by offering my name as a greeting. I thought it rude and presumptuous for anyone to walk up and stare at a card on my breast without acknowledging me first. Oh, how I despised those things.

Nevertheless, I walked toward the bar to get a drink. On my stroll over, I greeted a few people who looked at me strangely, presumably because I was a person and not a sticky nameplate. Everyone looked so confused. All these silly little nametags were attached to obviously uncomfortable patrons stumbling around pretending not to look at each other. Everyone sipped from their little red straws as they looked down to avoid as much eye contact as possible. I'd never seen so much closed off body language. Out of about fifty people, only six were actually talking to each other.

As I waited for my drink, I saw Esther in the corner, one of the six, talking to a beautiful, tall Asian girl. They were looking straight at me, but they didn't come over or even wave. When I smiled and gave a small wave, they just sat there. At the last possible moment, Esther finally gave an almost unnoticeable wave and a nice fake smile. I thought it quite comical how she played the hard-to-get role in such an obvious manner.

I asked the bartender how the night was going. "Weird," she said.

I laughed out loud. "This is a strange little event, isn't it? Sorry you have to go through it. I guess there's something to be said for meeting people in a more natural environment."

She leaned in and passed me my drink, "These people are just trying too hard. I can't believe people have to pay for this stuff."

"It is true though, some people need a little push back into the human fold," I offered.

"Well, I indirectly heard the leader chick's spiel. Don't get me wrong, she's got a lot of energy, and she tries to be nice, but the things she was teaching her people were just dumb. She had no idea what she was talking about. And on top of that, they pay double for this!"

"What do you mean?" I asked.

"First, they pay her to come to this thing. Then they pay the bar for their drinks and cover charge. But it looks to me like they're all doing the same thing they would if they didn't have to pay for her services."

"Let's hope they all find what they're looking for." I raised my drink to toast them all and took a sip. I tapped the bar and thanked the bartender.

I then walked toward Esther. When I was within ten feet of her and her friend, they turned their backs toward me in an obvious manner. I knew they saw me coming, and I realized Esther was trying to teach this new girl one of her "techniques" to make the guy want the girl more. So I plowed my way in between them to show the girl that Esther knew what she was talking about.

"Hello, ladies. Very nice to see you this evening." Esther pretended she was surprised to see me, even though we had just waved to one another a couple of minutes before. The other girl just looked at Esther.

"Oh, hi there!" Esther said. "I was wondering whether you were coming tonight." All of her conversation was so rehearsed. She introduced me to her friend, Amber, and we shared some tedious conversation. The whole time, it was clear Esther wanted Amber to practice her conversation skills while pretending to be uninterested. It was the dumbest conversation of my life, but I pushed through it for Amber's sake. I felt she needed some confidence, so I played along and talked her up as much as I could.

When I couldn't take anymore, I politely excused myself and meandered around. I introduced myself to people and started conversations with obviously less than comfortable individuals. I felt it my mission to get these people started on their paths to functional conversation.

In the next couple of hours, I only talked with Esther a few times. I caught her staring at me on a few occasions, which made me feel a little strange, but I didn't say anything about it. By the end, I anticipated Esther and I would leave soon to go to dinner, but as I grabbed my coat, Esther came up to tell me she was leaving. A guy in a tight black T-shirt came up with her coat and held it for her as she wriggled into it. She leaned over, gave me a hug, said goodbye in my ear, pulled away, sent over another fake smile, and walked out the door with him.

I just stood there dumbfounded. I certainly didn't expect her to leave without me, and especially with some other guy. It was one of the rudest things anyone had ever done to me. I thought things between us were slowly developing. But that was obviously not the case from her viewpoint. I was genuinely hurt, but I realized we weren't exclusive. I had absolutely no say in what she did with other people. I decided, due to recent events in my life, that there was no place for people like her in my space.

All of a sudden, going home wasn't the first thing on my agenda. I decided to ramp things back up, so I went to the bar and ordered another drink. As I waited, a woman to the right of me turned around and said, "Hello." Poetically enough, it was Amber. I sat down and we started talking again. As we drank together, she apologized about the conversation earlier. She said she was trying to take instruction from Esther, but was less than enthused when the talk seemed strained, unconventional and shallow. It wasn't who she really was.

"Seems to me like your conversation skills are fine, when you're being authentic," I said.

"It does feel more comfortable just to be me," she agreed.

"I'm no professional dating coach or anything," I offered, "but in my opinion, we'll all meet our soul mates much quicker if we actually allow our truest selves to shine through. We tend to get stuck in how we 'should' be, or how we think others want us to be. But that's where we go wrong. All conversations and thoughts become flawed because we're not representing ourselves. We seem fake, because we are fake."

"Wow, I guess you're right," she said, still thinking about what I said.

"Listen, it's not that difficult to meet people; you just can't have expectations. Have fun and appreciate people for who they are. Doesn't that seem to take all the stress out of meeting people? It does for me!"

She agreed. We hung out for a couple of more hours talking and drinking. When it was time to leave, I walked Amber to her car. We continued to talk a little more, and as she stood there with her car door open, we both gently leaned in and kissed each other. I pulled her close to me and felt her slender body against mine. It immediately started to rain and she asked whether I wanted to jump into her car until it blew over, so we did. It was completely dark out, and the whole event reminded me of an innocent high school make-out session. It was exciting and invigorating. We were just two people exploring each other, exploring ourselves, and having a genuinely good time.

After a little while, I slowly pulled away and said that maybe we should stop. Neither of us felt like going further that night. I told her it would be nice to see her again, maybe after the upcoming weekend, and I took down her phone number.

As I walked back to my car, I still hadn't gotten Esther completely out of my mind. Why would she do something like that? I just decided to forget about it as much as I could and move on with the healing. It felt good to meet Amber that night. It restored my confidence.

That following Tuesday, Esther gave me a surprise phone call. I had no plan to call her, so it was good to see I still had an opportunity to razz her about leaving the event with that other guy. She invited me to dinner at some high profile sushi joint after a speed-dating event scheduled for Thursday. Part of me wanted to tell her to go mess with someone else, but the other part of me that wanted to razz her won out. I agreed to meet up with her.

When I got there, most of her clients had filtered out of the place. Only a few couples were sitting here and there. I greeted Esther with a smile, and we sat at one of the tables near the sushi bar. There was little conversation. She would usually be talking my ear off. Obviously, something was on her mind. But I didn't indulge her with my curiosity. I figured if she needed to talk about something, she could cowboy up and spit it out. I just pretended to be happy-go-lucky and oblivious.

We ordered some food and she asked about my weekend. I decided to be vague and elusive, to give her a taste of her own medicine. I had a reminiscing look in my eye and a smile on my face as I told her as little as possible. I was really enjoying the opportunity until she interrupted me. "Weren't you angry that I just up and left with Peter after the event last week?"

I knew Esther had been playing games with me, but her curiosity about my feelings had become the chink in her armor. She had no idea what she was doing, and she had no idea I knew what she was doing. I could barely contain my laughter and sense of gloating. She was something else.

Rather than answer the question right away, I slowly chewed my food and made her wait it out. As her impatience grew, I finally said, "Why should I be angry that you left with some other guy? We're not exclusive." I took another delicious bite of her ego, as well as a piece of unagi.

"You don't care that I left with somebody else?" She appeared shocked.

Chew, chew, gloat, "Nope," I said.

"That's weird. Most boys would be really pissed."

"First of all, I'm not most boys, Esther. I'm a man. And I'm sure you're not used to dating men. Second of all, you've dated mostly boys in the past because it maintains your ego and controlling sense of self. And even though you're seven years older than me, I'm not easily controlled or manipulated."

Looking anywhere but my eyes, she said, "Whatever" and took a drink.

After a few minutes, she told me how leaving with another guy was one of her techniques to make the guy she was really interested in jealous. I just about spewed sake from my nostrils.

"Are you kidding me? It makes you look more like a lady of the night, if you know what I mean," I quipped.

"It was just to make you jealous. I don't even date Peter."

In my experience, when someone tried to control or show dominance in a relationship, he or she actually had one of two situations going on. Either 1) he or she has low self-esteem and/or self-worth and the ego inflates to make up for that lack with attention-getting, flamboyant behavior. Or 2) he or she is trying to keep others at arm's length so as not to feel hurt and pain. Esther was obviously the latter. She was cunning, and had mastered the art of manipulating people and situations to get a desired result. She came across as a bit aloof, but I could see her shark's fin just below the surface. Rather than think of her as evil or bad, I realized she had probably been hurt significantly at various points throughout her life. I tolerated it. I was testing myself more than she was testing me.

## *Point Of Responsibility*

*41. Do you hide behind a façade, a fake representation of self? Regardless of your initial answer to the first question, write in your notebook specifically what you have to hide from others. Write down the things that bring you shame, guilt and fear. Are they rational, or are they irrational beliefs? On a less-than-conscious level, do you consider yourself "less than" because you've done things you're not proud of? Know that every human has such a history. Those are the events that create opportunities for growth. Accept that the events happened, take the necessary lessons, and move past them. Don't allow yourself or others to use them against you for any other reason than growth. Think deeply about the real reasons why you put up walls to keep people away from your heart and your mind. We all do so in some way. Understand that our walls are representations of a dysfunctional ego that wants to keep you in your comfort zone; it sees that you inherently have a choice to act differently so it puts up walls and floods you with vague emotion. First notice what's happening when you think about closing yourself off to others for any reason. Then get rid of the negative thoughts that allow for such activities to continue ruining your life and that keep you separate. Allowing vague and senseless fear to control you and your relationships dooms you to repeat the negative feedback loops that keep your mind cloudy. Keep your past in the past. Live in the present.*

*42. Are you a chameleon? Do you act differently with different groups or individuals? Humans shouldn't strive to fit in with others. By being authentic and showing our true selves, we're inherently respecting those people with whom we interact. We're showing them they are worthy of knowing the real person inside of us. Being true to yourself makes you trustworthy. Being true to yourself perpetuates self-confidence and positive mental health and self-awareness. Be who you are, and know that it is more than good enough.*

Then it was time for me to up the ante. I needed her to know that I knew what she was doing. Firmly but gently, I said, "Esther, I don't like your games. I do like you. I think we have a good time together. But unless you stop actively playing this hard-to-get routine, including all your silly dating rules, I'm going to have to move on."

She had nothing to say in reply. It was clearly the first time she'd ever been called out on her crap. She sat there with a calm look of openness. She understood I wasn't like the many others she had dated. I was calm, confident and secure. I wasn't going to be manipulated with the hope of eventually getting into her pants.

"You've got it all figured out, don't you?" she said.

"Not so much. But I do like you, and I don't want ridiculous games to get in the way of a possibly good thing. We all have enough to deal with in life without having to play games with each other."

She didn't reply, which was fine by me. We finished dinner and I went over to her place to hang out. We made out passionately that night, but didn't take it to the next level. A deeper bond, however, had developed since our earlier conversation. It felt comfortable and solid. I told her we should think about dating exclusively. I didn't want to waste my time with a "serial dater." I wanted to see whether we could turn it into something great.

"Well," she replied, "I've slowed down on the dating front since meeting you. In fact, I've only been dating you and a dentist for the past two weeks. And based on our conversation tonight, I think I like you better. You don't put up with crap. It's hot. So yeah, let's see where it goes."

I gave her a kiss and we talked for another hour before I had to return home. As I fell asleep, I thought about how I had just gotten myself into another relationship so quickly. Was it going to be good for me? Was it what I needed? After a couple of minutes, I put the issue to bed. I decided just to have fun with it, chill out and relax.

At work, one of my patients, Heather, asked me whether she could do some of my business accounting to work off the balance of her bill. I thought about it for a couple of days and finally decided it would definitely take some pressure off me if she did so. She started coming in weekly to pay bills and reconcile the accounts. After only a month, I realized what a big help she was. I no longer dreaded doing the books, which was a major load off.

Around that same time, one of my best friends from college decided to move out to Seattle. Mike decided he'd had enough of snowy Michigan winters so he wanted a change of scenery. He moved into my place and got a job at the local pub down the street. It was great having Mike around. I needed some guy friends back in my life. It seemed everywhere I turned was another woman. The added testosterone was a welcome change.

Esther and I started to see more and more of each other. It was like no other relationship I'd ever been in. She was very strong and independent, but she was also self-effacing and codependent. I found both sides of her equally endearing, and I was completely engaged in our relationship. I wanted it to work and was happy to do my part.

Those first two months were interesting, to say the least. Most of the time, we laughed long and hard. We were sexually compatible, and seldom had a night gone by without us being together. We were very affectionate and enjoyed doing things with and for one another.

But some obvious differences existed in how we looked at and lived life. In the public eye, Esther put forth her confident side. She was daring, vocal, and had no boundaries. On the private side of things, she was quite scattered and lived from moment to moment. In my opinion, she ran the inner workings of her business and her personal life in reaction to her emotions. When she was happy, everything and everyone was happy around her. When she was angry or sad, a cloud consumed her and everything around. When confused, the waters around her muddied. I never knew which Esther would show up to dinner or answer the phone.

There was absolutely never a rational discussion with Esther. She had to have her feelings heard and understood completely before moving past anything. Inevitably, I would have to fold to her behavior if I wanted to get past the situation. But I was all right with it most of the time. I had all these new issues to deal with that made me think I was growing, becoming more tolerant, less reactionary and less emotional myself. I welcomed the opportunities.

But as time went on, it was increasingly obvious I wasn't getting what I needed from the relationship. When I stood my ground on mutual disagreements, a power struggle would inevitably ensue. Unfortunately, the power struggles erupted more often as time went by. Even on beautiful days and completely out of the blue, when Esther didn't like something, she had to make it known at any cost. I felt I was always walking on eggshells. Her battle for constant attention was draining and confused the heck out of me.

One evening when we came home from dinner, I had two desserts, one in each hand. At the entrance to her apartment building, Esther stood aside and waited for me to open the door for her. I'd always been a gentleman; it's how I was raised. But I also think that relationships are teamwork, and not opening a door for your girlfriend because your hands are full is completely acceptable. She told me to put down the desserts to open the door for her; she was serious. I told her just to open the door, and after a heavy sigh, she jerked the door open and walked in. "Thanks for holding it for me," I said, barely wedging my foot in before it closed. On the elevator ride up, I got to hear how I wasn't a real man because I didn't open the door for my girl. She was always making a big deal about me opening doors for her, carrying bags for her, buying her flowers, and waiting for her to take the first bite. I couldn't even eat a potato chip while watching football without having to offer her one first. Those weren't fights for proper etiquette and chivalry; they were fights for control and power.

A couple of months into our relationship, I came to understand such games were just a part of her being. They weren't daily, but maybe two or three times a week. So I put up with it. The rest of our relationship was good. We had conversations during which I didn't have to think much, and we were spontaneous. It was just those little, isolated events I had to endure whenever she found it necessary.

### *Point Of Responsibility*

*43. Do you control situations and relationships to try to influence a desired response? How would it make you feel if you didn't have to think about how to control people and situations? Might you have more energy? Do you think you would have more time for functional thought, instead of dysfunctional ego-based living? Could a lack of control open your life to more unforeseen happiness and unexpected joy? This way of being is more open-ended, and inherently creates a life full of adaptability, acceptance and flexibility. Let go of the pointless manipulation, stale thought and dogma. Practice thinking and expressing yourself in open-ended conversation. Allow for the unexpected to occur. It will spur on creativity from within you. Work diligently to avoid "yes/no" conversations.*

As the months passed, I realized how I was being manipulated and shaken around. I was falling prey to her "push-pull" technique. She would push until I was on the verge of saying something that would blow the whole thing up. Then she would pull me close and be affectionate. I felt like I was holding on to one end of a rope while she was dangling me from the other end over a high precipice. I had very little control within our relationship and was completely out of my comfort zone.

On the other hand, I was learning a great deal about myself. I was being forced to think in a different way, and that part intrigued me.

When we went out on the town, her friends always surrounded Esther. They were a completely transparent lot. Upon meeting them for the first time, I noticed the only thing her friends had in common with Esther was they were all closing in on forty years old, were unmarried and had no children. As time went by, I noticed that for them, going out on the town wasn't so much about having fun with friends; it was a consistently frantic attempt to meet the man who would hopefully father their children. The whole proposition was all so disgustingly mechanical. So many of Esther's friends longed for a meaningful relationship, but they sought such a relationship among the inebriated and lost. Instead of creating value within themselves, which is incredibly attractive to everyone, most of them were looking for someone to fill the void within.

Another of the issues that consistently came up between Esther and me was her need to let me know about all the guys she had dated in the past. Not one time when we went out on the weekend did we avoid running into one of her beaus. I would actually make fun of her for flirting with all the guys in my presence. I knew she did it on purpose; it was part of her silly push-pull thing, and she obviously liked the attention. I tried not to let it faze me, but I also felt it was disrespectful of me. I didn't push it too much simply because I didn't want to rock the boat.

### Point Of Responsibility

*44. Do you allow others to disrespect you with their words and/or actions? It's NOT all right for people to do so. And it's NOT all right for you to allow such behavior. It's a horrible thing for others to talk down to you, to poke fun at you, or to belittle you. It's an atrocious thing for you to allow such behavior. From this point forward, respect yourself enough to tell others that disrespectful behavior toward you will not be tolerated. Chances are good they won't take you seriously. So when you let them know, be calm and collected. Breathe deeply and stop whatever you're doing. Look them in the eye and confidently let them know you're serious. Don't be confrontational; you're simply letting them know you're moving past being disrespected. If they attempt to be confrontational or emotional, know they are afraid of losing their control over you. You must pass through the entanglements of this emotion into freedom if you desire true emotional health. A diffusing statement from you might be, "Your disrespectful comments are hurtful to me." This will hopefully create a sense of introspection within the other person. If he or she continues to display excessive emotion, it may be best to leave the situation.*

*If you're the type of person who speaks sarcastically to others, evaluate why you feel the need to disrespect the people around you. If you're making fun of others at their expense, know it's just your ego trying to make you feel more important or knowledgeable than you think you are. Gain some self-respect and stop talking down to people. Know that you're inherently powerful. You don't need to stoop to such undermining, passive-aggressive behavior.*

Esther started one particular advertising campaign that included a picture of four guys ogling over her on the side of thirty metro buses that canvassed Seattle every day. She was very proud that she had dated all of the guys in the ad, even though they all looked the same: short blond gelled-up spiky hair, 5'10", big cheesy smile, deer-in-the-headlights gaze, designer jeans, light blue crew neck long sleeved shirts that were too tight, ridiculously-colored, square-toed shoes. How original. Each was basically the same guy, only with a different name. Every time I saw one of those buses, I laughed out loud, whether I was alone or with someone else. And when Esther was present, my laughter always started a fight.

As our relationship continued, I realized Esther knew almost nothing about running a business. Although she had good ideas, she had no clue how to be successful. At one point, she decided to buy a Volkswagen Beetle and have it painted up with bright colors and the phone number of the company. When she first told me this idea, I laughed, but when she didn't laugh with me, I tried to sound serious as I said, "I hope that goes well for you."

"Don't you think it will be great?" she asked. "People will see it all over the place!"

"You definitely don't want my opinion," I replied.

"Oh come on. Don't you think it will bring tons of people through the door?"

"No. I think it's a see through gimmick. No one in their right mind will entrust you with helping them change their lives in an intimate way. You won't be taken seriously. It will be funny, but your services shouldn't be a joke to you. What are you going to do, jump out of it with a costume on and entertain them until they sign on the dotted line? This clown car is a ridiculous idea, Esther. And further, you don't have a lot of money to be spending on things like this. The best marketing and advertising is accessing word-of-mouth referrals. The grass-roots approach is what will grow your business, not shots in the dark."

"Whatever. I think it will be great," she insisted.

The campaign was a complete bust. She lost a bunch of dough and ended up getting only one client.

Esther and I shared many of our nights in the Belltown neighborhood, the more trendy part of Seattle where one would go to be seen, drink expensive drinks and eat overpriced food. Like Vegas, it was fun, for what it was worth. People don't exactly go to Vegas for spiritual fodder and fellowship; it's understood there's a lot of silicone and plastic, but you have fun with it; that's how I considered Belltown, fun, but not real life.

Esther was the epitome of Belltown. In that environment, she transformed herself into what she thought others wanted.

One evening there, I was drinking martinis and having a great time with a couple of Canadian hockey players I had just met. Esther entertained a couple of guys and a girl. I recognized one of the guys from the side of the bus. I laughed to myself and turned back to the fellas. As I did, I was pleasantly surprised to see the rest of their party, four stunning beauties, had met up with them. We all sat there and got drunk, doing shot after shot, laughing loudly and telling stories all night. When one of the girls asked me whether I was alone, I pointed to Esther, who was sending some pretty ugly scowls to our end of the bar. The girl turned back to me and whispered, "She doesn't look too happy."

"Let me put it to you this way," I said. "As soon as we got here, she ran off to talk to some friends at the other end of the bar, one of whom she recently dated. You ever see that picture for that Seattle dating company with four guys and a girl?"

"Do you mean that cheesy picture of that girl in the red dress with the boys looking up at her?"

"Yes, that's the one. Well, two of the people are right down there. So I've now been sitting here for two hours having great conversation with your friends. And I'm not about to stop. So let's have some fun!"

I bought another round of shots and we quickly finished them off.

It didn't take long after that. About five minutes later, Esther stormed down to our end of the bar and grabbed my arm.

"What are you doing?" she asked.

"I'm having a hell of a time with some old hockey buddies, and you?"

"You're humiliating me in front of my friends!"

"Do you mean the dude you dated and his entourage?"

"Whatever; can we go outside and talk for a minute?"

"It's a little cold; I think you can say anything you need right here, don't you?"

"I'm not going to talk about this with you in the middle of a bar," she replied.

"Sure, why not; I'll go outside." I then told the guys and gals I was with, "If I'm not back in ten minutes, send the cavalry." They all laughed as Esther and I walked outside.

"Why are you acting all stupid with those hookers?" she asked.

"Hookers? They probably wouldn't like it if you called them that."

"I don't care! Why are you being a jerk?"

"Esther, when we got here, you made a beeline for an ex and left me standing at the door with your coat, and I don't really want to have a conversation with that Cretan. I have a hard time believing he could talk about anything other than the color of the highlights in his hair or where he goes shopping every day. So I kept myself busy. I took a seat at the bar and started talking with some intelligent people. Every once in a while, I would glance over to see your hand on Cretan's shoulder, or laughing at Cretan's story, or leaning on Cretan's thigh. I know how you are, so I didn't think anything of it. Two hours later, you take notice of me talking with some women, and now you're interested? I don't get it."

"You know what?" she replied. "I think maybe you just don't belong here. Belltown is full of my type of people, not yours."

I was honestly shocked. After I took a drink I said, "That's interesting, because it seems a little funny that every time I come to Belltown I meet some great people, and at the same time, I get a chance to be amused at the delinquents and clowns you call friends and exes."

She immediately said loudly, "You just don't belong here!"

"Esther, you're right. I don't belong here. I don't belong here with you, your double standards or your lack of respect for our relationship. Find your own way home, not that it will be difficult. We're surrounded by about a hundred different guys you've dated."

As I walked to my car, she attempted to chase me down in her stilettos and silly little skirt. It wasn't difficult to gain distance between us and before I knew it, she had given up hope on reaching me and went into another bar. I knew she'd meet up with one of her old boyfriends and she'd be fine.

## *Point of Responsibility*

*45. Do you create chaos in your life? No? Think again. All chaos is self-created. Know that this is the ego needing to be heard. It has an incessant need to show its importance. When things are chaotic in your life, stop everything, take a breath and laugh off the unnecessary influence of your ego. Be yourself.*

I drove home calmly, but still disappointed. We were three months into a relationship and it was constantly up and down, push and pull, happy and sad. I was tired. Work was stagnant. I wasn't spending as much time as I wanted with my other friends like Mike. And I hadn't been playing much hockey since meeting Esther. Being in a relationship with her was like an endless black hole of inconsequential events.

When I got home, Mike was just getting home from work. We opened up a bottle of wine and quickly downed the whole thing over stories from the past. We opened up a few more that night and talked into the early hours of the morning. It was good to have him around, a true and real friend.

That night, Esther called me no fewer than twenty times. That was her modus operandi. Ever since I'd known her, her cell phone was attached to her ear. When I was pissed at her, I never picked up the phone. And that time was no different.

The next day, I finally picked up one of her calls when I was on break. She sobbed into the phone about how sorry she was and that it would never happen again. I decided to let it slide. I felt too weak to break up with her.

That night we decided we needed some alone time, a little vacation in the sun. So we jumped online and found a great cruise in the Caribbean. We were both very excited to get away and just start over fresh.

Up to that point, our relationship had been both incredibly fun, and incredibly stressful. It was consistent in its inconsistency. It wore on my nerves, but for some reason, I felt like I couldn't just quit. It wasn't like my stagnant relationship with Natalie. It was high-octane, constant blue-flame intensity. I didn't understand it fully at the time, but I felt it necessary to do everything in my power to hold onto our relationship. I wanted to continue working on it, even though I was knowingly being manipulated and controlled by her. In my past, I would have escaped from the turmoil in some way. I would drink more; cheat on my partner; turn off my emotions; or simply leave the relationship completely, with no explanation. This time, I needed to prove to myself that I had what it took to push through the bad times. I didn't want to just throw it all away at the drop of a hat, or act irresponsibly by sabotaging the relationship. I knew that Esther loved me, and I thought that love would conquer all. I didn't take into account, however, how her version of love was manipulative and controlling. I knew I deserved to be in a good relationship, but I couldn't come to grips how her behavior was never okay. I simply allowed it, hoping it would change when she realized I wasn't going to run out on her. Her actions hurt me, but again, I hoped she would see the light at some point and ultimately become comfortable in our relationship.

Even my workdays were affected by my relationship with Esther. My energy levels were all over the place. Any time things weren't going well, which was often, Kendra would just stare at me, cock her head to the side, place her hand on her hip and say, "When are you going to get rid of that witch? She's not good for you, and you know it." Soon she was giving me this advice once a week.

I knew I could do better than to live that lifestyle, but I couldn't just quit it. In the grand scheme of things, I felt I had a handle on everything. It was just the day-to-day that suffered. I knew Esther had been deeply hurt in the past, and our incongruencies brought her residual baggage to the surface. I knew she wanted a long-term relationship, but she also pushed it away at the same time. It couldn't be any more obvious from the outside. She didn't want anyone to mess her up again; it was tough for her to let anyone get close. She was completely selfish, but her selfishness stemmed from how she was raised—or wasn't raised. She'd had no possessions, so she'd had to fight for everything material. She was just living out her past. Unfortunately for me, I mistook pity for love, and attention for affection. But I wasn't willing to bail out, not without giving it my all. I just held onto the hope that Esther's acting out would diminish over time.

Our cruise was coming up in a week, so before making any decisions, I wanted to wait and see how things were going to play out.

It was a tough flight down with layovers and a shuttle ride to port. It wasn't fun and took way too long, but we finally arrived late in the afternoon. As expected, I was responsible for carrying the luggage the entire way, as well as organizing, planning and paying for everything. When we finally boarded the ship, I just wanted to fall into bed and take a little catnap, but Esther wanted to explore. I did too, but just not yet. I needed a few minutes. I told her to go by herself and bring back some coffee when she came back. That's when Esther went off the deep end. "We came on this trip to be together! You need to get up! We can sleep later!"

"Esther, give me a break," I said, beaten like a rented mule.

"No, get up!" She pulled the covers off me.

I jumped up and grabbed the covers back, scowled at her and told her to go. I jumped back in bed with the rumpled covers only to have her pull them off me again. She was determined and pissed as a hornet. "I just want to go look at the ship with you! What's so wrong with that?"

As we stared at each other, I said, "Esther, I don't know what your malfunction is, but you're not the only one in this relationship. I need things too. And right now I need a few minutes to myself! Now leave!!!"

She screamed and came at me with both fists flailing at my chest. I grabbed her arms and threw her on the bed. "Knock it off! Are you crazy?" She kept coming at me until I just left the room with her screaming all the way. I couldn't believe what had just happened. After less than an hour on the cruise ship, we were in a fight. It was unbelievable and incredibly discouraging.

## Point of Responsibility

*46. Do you allow physical, verbal or emotional violence in your life? Do you strike others? Do you allow others to strike you? Write down the patterns that repeat in your life that allow for such behavior. There is a major disconnection within the communication process that allows for such events to occur. When things are good between you and your partner, that is the time to discuss when that disconnection may occur. Don't get involved into the reasons "why" you fight, but focus on finding the specific point at which both parties allow a confrontation to escalate. You're discussing emotions, so it's highly likely the arguments won't be rational, but whether one party is rational or irrational is of no importance. The important thing is that both people must be acknowledged while in the heat of the moment. When things get hot, simply stop and agree to disagree for the time being. Agree on a place and time to work through the issues if need be. Know there is an addiction to the chemicals within the body during such events. And those cloud judgment when put into action. Know that most arguments are the manifestations of a power struggle. The ego confrontation can be quite a confusing web. So it's always better to know that both of your lives will be all right. Everything will be all right. Just breathe and relax. Everything will be all right. For the individual, the true issue at hand is why one needs to struggle with others for power. If you desire true love and peace, such activity is not congruent and must be eliminated at all cost. If after discussion and taking disarming action steps, the behavior continues, it must be acknowledged that it is time to move on. It is time to take the lesson and act upon it. You are good enough and worthy enough to live a happy life. Immediately following a split with your partner, avoid looking for another to fill the void that momentarily remains. Become solid within yourself. Grieve the loss. Reaffirm and visualize the life you're building, allowing negative thoughts, hatred, rage, guilt and shame to leave your body and mind. Be grateful you're alive and keep moving forward. Keep moving forward.*

As I took a walk to cool off, I came up with two reasons as to why she flipped out. 1.) She felt abandoned, or 2.) She really was crazy. I couldn't put off the inevitable any longer. I started on my way back to the room. We were going to be on that ship together for seven days in tight quarters. There was no escaping that.

I unlocked the door from the outside and entered the room. She was sitting on the edge of the bed with her knees to her chest. When she looked up at me, it was obvious she'd been crying. She started immediately, "I'm so sorry. I don't know what got into me. I just wanted to have a good time with you. Security came by after you left and wanted to know what the screaming was all about. I just told them it wouldn't happen again. They told me if it did, one of us would be kicked off the ship. I'm so sorry. I shouldn't have screamed and hit you."

"You know what, Esther, we can talk about it later. The only thing we should focus on is what's happening right now. Let's just have fun on this trip. I spent a lot of money on it, and I know you want to enjoy the sun and sand as much as I do. Let's just have a good time. When we get back home, if we're still alive, we can discuss our relationship and what we want to do from there. Does that sound all right?" I always had to talk to her like a little girl instead of as an adult. I thought it weird at times, but I just needed her to chill out, by any means necessary.

Strangely enough, the rest of the cruise was uncharacteristically fun for both of us. We had a great time and saw some incredible things. When we came back home, things were good for about six weeks before the wheels started coming off again.

It was self-evident there were things in my life I wanted and wasn't getting. I wanted growth for the clinic and for myself. I wanted peace in my life. I wanted a healthy relationship with a thoughtful and loving woman.

Another executive training seminar quickly approached. And it was none too soon. It was the end of February, and I was ready for a little break from everything. Unfortunately, while I was there, Esther called me no fewer than fifteen times a day. During the day, she left messages with no meaning and groveled on about nothing in particular. She told me she missed me and loved me and couldn't wait for me to get back.

At night, however, things were completely different. When I would call her to talk about the day and say goodnight, she would be out having drinks with this person or that person. She was always talking to someone else at the same time as me. She was just cold and rude, and I didn't like it. When I finally told her after the third night how I felt, she started to fight with me. She said I was too sensitive and being selfish. She asked whether I just expected her to be by herself while I was gone. From that point, the conversations didn't go well. Neither one of us was happy.

By the end of that week, an overwhelming sense of doom and gloom slowly came over me. I sat in my lonely hotel room at night thinking about my life and relationship with Esther. I realized we had little in common. I liked to read, hike and play. Her life revolved around her business and partying, while I had hopes and dreams for my future. She lived day to day with no thought about anything but herself while I loved with reckless abandon. She was controlling and manipulative. What the heck was I doing with her?

On the plane ride home, something snapped within me. In fact, I lost it. As I sat there waiting for the plane to take off, I stewed in my confusion and unhappiness. I wondered what I was going to do. I felt like my throat was going to explode at any moment with a hyper-audible scream. As the plane started to gain speed, I bowed my head forward to counter the force pushing me back into the seat. I had a crushing pain in my stomach and tears started flowing down my face. The plane traveled forcefully down the runway. The small bumps we hit were magnified and seemed to shake something from within me. I leaned further forward and metaphorically felt I was traveling at a million miles an hour, completely out of control. I wanted to scream, but I couldn't. All I could do was sit in my seat and wait, wait for the inevitable confrontation.

Chapter Ten:

# Revelation

"Esther, I'm sorry, but I can't do this anymore. This constant push-pull thing that exists between us is unbearable. It changes who I am and the things I do in my life."

"You're not breaking up with me! I've been through all of this too!" She slid over to my end of the couch and grabbed both of my hands.

"Esther, please. We both know this relationship is tearing us apart. It's not good for either of us. We're always emotional. Excelling at anything else is impossible with such low energy. I don't remember the last time I went on a hike, or even read a book, which are two things I love passionately."

"I've never stopped you from doing any of that. Don't blame me. You're a big boy. And you're not breaking up with me. Don't be a quitter, Mark. You owe it to me to work hard for this relationship."

"I have worked hard, Esther. And I have nothing left to give. I've lost ten pounds from all stress this relationship brings me."

"You're just a quitter. Fine. Leave then. I don't date quitters." She got up and ran back to her room. I had already stealthily collected all my belongings from her apartment in a small bag on a dining room chair. After only a few seconds, she reemerged into the giant loft space overlooking the Seattle waterfront. "I was going to get your clothes, but it looks like you've already put them somewhere! I never knew you were such a quitter! You're a jerk, Mark, and you should be ashamed of yourself!" It was Esther true to form. She was a victim from day one. Everyone was always doing things to her, never with her.

"Maybe we could both take some responsibility for the relationship ending," I firmly stated.

"No way!" she screamed. "You're the quitter! You did this, not me! I want to be in a relationship with you!"

"No Esther, what you want is someone to control and manipulate. I told you when we first met I wasn't going to put up with your games. Unfortunately, I lied to myself for the past nine months that your crap was endearing."

"What's that mean?" She genuinely had no idea what endearing meant.

"You'll figure it out, Esther. You just won't have me to throw around while you're doing it. Don't worry; as you always let me know, many other men would love to date you. As for me, I'm out." I got up and went for my bag.

"No! Don't leave!" She ran over and embraced me, put her head on my chest and made me drag her across the room as I walked toward my bag.

"Esther, get off of me. It's over. Your games have finally messed this relationship up beyond repair and I'm done!" I kept trying to maneuver for my bag.

"No!" she screamed. "I'm sorry I called you a quitter! You're not a quitter! I don't want you to go! Don't make me be alone!" She squeezed tighter. At moments like that, she always said what she thought I wanted to hear or screamed things that were sure to ensnare me emotionally. But the only thing I thought about was my exit strategy.

I saw my chance when she unwrapped her arms to regrip. I immediately made a beeline for the door. She got up to give chase. "Stop it, Esther! We can talk about it later! But right now I need to leave." I opened the door and quickly shut it behind me. I ran down the hall and down the stairs. I heard her open her apartment door and give chase. I knew that using the stairs would buy me enough time to escape the situation, as she always waited for the elevator, no matter what.

I had parked my car about three blocks from her apartment, in a completely different spot than usual; I wanted to make it difficult for her to find me on foot. As I pulled out, Esther came running around the building at top speed. Over our nine-month relationship, I'd never seen her break walking speed. Luckily, the car was pointed in the right direction for a quick escape. I jammed it into gear and sped off, Esther in the rearview mirror screaming obscenities to the world.

Over the next month, the real Esther continued to reveal herself. She tried everything under the sun to get me to talk with her. She called me no fewer than fifteen times a day and matched that with twenty texts. She left messages at the office using another name, but she used her office phone number, which I knew by heart. I never responded; there was no way I was going to allow her to manipulate me with her siren songs.

I often thought I caught glimpses of her driving slowly past my house in her clown car. She had no reason to be in Atherton, so I hoped it was a horrible coincidence, or a nightmarish flashback.

After about three weeks, Esther realized I wasn't coming back. Then the calls started getting mean and angry. In her voicemails, she called me a quitter and a loser, and told me yet again that I wasn't a real man. She even let me know that my BMW was a stupid car. I couldn't believe I'd actually taken her seriously for so long. I was relieved not to be with her anymore.

I immediately began to strengthen myself from the inside with quiet time, meditation and gently working out. I'd forgotten how vital the "me" time was, and I cherished it more fully than ever. For the first time in many months, my mind was becoming clear and quiet. I couldn't believe what I had put myself through. All I could do was speculate why I stayed with her for so long.

On one of my first post-Esther weekends, I went out to do my favorite hike in the Olympic Forest. As typically happened when I roamed the prehistoric land, I became keenly aware of self. I breathed heavy from the difficult hiking. Slowly, a wave of introspection crept into my head. I felt calm, positive and quiet.

As I walked up the treacherous mountain path, the patterns of my past relationships began to reveal themselves. Over and over, I entered into relationships with women who were unavailable, couldn't communicate functionally, didn't show emotion well, and were passively aggressive. They were just like my mother. And the parallels were strikingly obvious. My earlier speculation was transformed into solid knowledge.

Over the next several weeks, I thought deeply about my relationship with my mother and how it had affected my life in the present. She had basically abandoned my sister and me after divorcing my father. She invited a guy to live with us who clearly didn't like kids. I thought about how many times I had been chastised by her for doing nothing more than carefully exploring my own life. She continuously pushed my sister and me away. She was always angry about something ridiculous, yelled at whoever was within earshot, and then waited for us to come back and apologize. It got tiring, so my sister and I would put space between our mother and us for our own protection.

As time went on, it became evident my mom felt we were abandoning her, even though most people would call it growing up. She was angry most of the time and became increasingly paranoid about everything. She seemed to think everyone was out to get her.

Things worsened after my sister and I both left for college. She was less than concerned about our lives in any way. In fact, over ten years of college, and even though my school was only two hours away, the only times she ever visited me were my two graduations. Her antics finally came to a head on the day I graduated from doctor school.

I invited everyone to Atlanta for a great celebration. I booked hotels, made party reservations and planned to have a wonderful time with family and friends over a long weekend. I invited everyone well in advance and everyone RSVP'd. It was going to be a ton of fun. I was with Natalie at the time and we were excited to have everyone around.

Before we knew it, the weekend was upon us. My best friends and family from around the country started showing up. Friday night and into Saturday was great, except that my best friend Erik, my sister, Kris, and Mom were nowhere to be found. They were all supposed to ride down together after work on Thursday, but they didn't show or call, and when I tried to reach them, they didn't answer their cell phones. Horrible thoughts flashed through my mind. I knew the mountain drive could be treacherous with weather. Had they been in an accident? Who would I call to investigate the possibility? Should I just continue entertaining?

Finally Saturday evening, I got a call from Erik, who said my mom had decided to work into Saturday, so they expected to arrive late that night. I was a little pissed, but that was my mom, business first, at any cost. I told Erik where to find us that night and hung up the phone.

At about one in the morning, my sister and Erik finally showed up at the bar. We all hugged and I asked, "Where's Mom?"

My sister replied, "She decided to stay at your apartment instead of coming out. She was acting kind of weird for some reason. So Erik and I came out to have some fun!" The rest of the night was a blast. We all ate, drank and danced the night away.

The next morning, Natalie and I woke up to make breakfast for everyone who stayed at our place. Everyone slowly started getting up, and they shared stories about the nights before. I was getting ready for an early graduation rehearsal when I finally heard the bathroom door in my mom's room close loudly.

"Everything okay in there?" I asked through the door.

Almost immediately, she whipped the door open and came out to where everyone else was. I smiled and wrapped my arms around her, "Nice of you to make it!"

Her arms hung limp at her sides. She didn't hug me back. I pulled away and put my hands on her shoulders as I looked into her eyes. "What's your problem?" I asked. "Wake up on the wrong side of the bed?"

"I've never been so disrespected in my life," she replied.

Everyone was a little puzzled. The conversation hushed. I said, "Sorry, but no one has disrespected you in any way. We're all just getting ready for the ceremony. Do you want some pancakes?"

She looked at Natalie, and then at everyone else. Her jaw was clenched and she remained rigid. "I have never been disrespected like the way I was last night."

"What are you talking about?"

"You know what I'm talking about, Mark."

"Let me tell you what I know. I know that I graciously and happily planned a fun weekend for all my friends and family, including you. I know everyone here is having a great time helping me celebrate the completion of ten long years of school. I also know you decided to work instead of being here with me, forcing Erik and Kris to wait for you. And further, you have completely disrespected everyone here, including me, by forcing me to deal with your crap on my day. So here's what's going to happen: If you don't change your tune immediately, I expect you to pack up your things and get out of my apartment. We're busy having a good time." I looked her in the eye as she stewed over her next move.

No way would her ego allow itself to back down. "Fine, I'll go! I've never been so disrespected," she repeated as she stomped back into the bedroom and started throwing her crap back into her suitcase.

"Nobody even knows what you're talking about," I said to her from the hallway. I just shook my head and wanted the situation to end as quickly as possible. I said, "If you need help getting your stuff together, I'll be glad to help you expedite the process."

"I got it!" she screamed.

I opened up the door and waited a few seconds before she dragged her unwheeled suitcase through the doorway.

"Have a great graduation, Mark," she scowled.

"Don't think I won't. It was fun before you got here, and I expect it to continue after you're gone." I shut the door and turned around to everyone staring at me, no doubt wondering what the next step should be.

"Okay, everyone," I lifted my head high and smiled, "let's forget about all that nonsense and just have a good day. Sound good?"

"Did that really just happen?" asked Natalie as she flipped another pancake.

My dad answered, "It's a pretty common occurrence around Mark's mother." He had an interesting way of detaching himself from people. He never referred to "him" or "her" in terms of his relationship with them, but in relationship to the person with whom he was talking. When he talked about my mother, he said "Mark's mother," instead of using the words "my ex-wife," or actually using her name. When he talked about my sister, he'd say, "your sister," instead of using her name. It was a little technique his ego used to lack any serious ownership of a situation. Every time he did it was like nails on a chalkboard. But I didn't say anything. I wouldn't let it bother me.

"I need a beer," Erik declared as he reached into the fridge for a cold one and broke the awkwardness.

We all chuckled pitifully at what had just transpired. I had to arrange a flight for Erik and my sister, since their ride had just left. They weren't exactly happy about being left in Atlanta, and I was incredibly embarrassed by my mother's selfish actions. But we made do. And interestingly enough, the place was light and fun from then on. We all had a great time.

I had no contact with my mother from that point forward. I decided for the first time I didn't want that kind of person in my life, regardless of whether he or she was family.

As I came running back down the mountain on that rainy day in the Olympics, I drew the parallels between my personal relationships and the relationship with my mother. I acknowledged that I allowed myself to enter into relationships that didn't serve me. I simply repeated negative patterns. I finally understood how allowing that type of person in my life affected me on a daily basis.

After acknowledging everything, I felt free, I felt clean. No longer would I allow anyone to disrespect me, including myself. I was back to creating my life instead of allowing others to control my emotions. I was once again strong and centered.

## *Point of Responsibility*

*47. The family dynamic can be one of the most challenging parts of life, which inherently makes it a wonderful vehicle for the greatest of growth opportunities. Ask for your family members' support in creating a more conscious and purposeful family unit. Write in your notebook how you envision your immediate family relationships, and then your extended family relationships. Share it with everyone. Let your family members know you seek something meaningful and mutually beneficial from your relationships with them. If after much hard work, you determine that the lives of specific family members are too much of a drain on you and your positive relationships, step aside and ultimately accept those people for who they are. In many cases, rigid members of your family will not allow for the changing of an individual. You may be always perceived as a little child who has a lot to learn, even though you're an adult with a family of your own. Truthfully, we're all children with a lot to learn; no one is above that. Let people have their perceptions. Those perceptions mean nothing with regard to who you are. When you accept such a rigid individual and stop judging, it diffuses tension, and there's a greater possibility that something might positively develop in the future. Whatever you do, don't throw barbs at anyone, ever. When we chastise and blame others, it does nothing except create another level of competition. Avoid the habits and addictions to the negative emotions associated with confrontation. Don't allow the entanglements, emotions and guilt-based loyalty to control your life. Rise above them and get to a place of acceptance. It's the only thing that truly matters. Embrace the ego of your perceived enemy and work with him or her to create instead of continuing the process of degradation. You may end up with a great friend in the end, for you probably have more in common than you think. That's why he or she gets under your skin. Also, taking the high road means you don't say you're taking the high road. Don't put your nose up in the air and be self-righteous. Just sit back and listen. In the most extreme situations, it might be necessary to cut ties completely with a friend or family member who is malicious, especially toward your children. Family is sacred, but sometimes family can be destructive. It is your responsibility to your children to know when such things are occurring and to take appropriate action. More often than not, if we learn how to appreciate and reinforce the positive qualities of each family member, the bonds become stronger. When we show interest in others, the walls come tumbling down. Question people's opinions and just let them talk. Actively listen and have no expectations in the process. Don't offer your own opinions unless asked to do so, which will come shortly after they put their walls down. The whole point is to get the lines of communication open. Once open, keep them that way by staying away from "yes/no" questions. Be open-ended and flexible.*

Chapter Eleven:

# Back to Normal

The day after I came back from the woods, the office bustled with patients. Kendra ran around like a chicken with her head cut off. The girl we hired for the front desk didn't work out, so Kendra was forced to do it all herself. I helped where I could as we looked for someone new, but it took time to find good help.

Finally, she couldn't take it anymore, so Kendra gave me her two-week notice. She was, understandably, completely burnt out and unhappy. The feeling of dread was racing up from behind me. I had to find an office manager AND a front desk person within the next two weeks! There was nothing like putting the pressure on.

The very next day, Heather informed me she was going to take a full-time position she had recently been offered, so she wasn't going to be able to do my books anymore. When it rained, it poured. I told her that she had done enough work to pay off her bill, so she could consider it paid in full.

I spent every extra second I had looking for someone to fill Kendra's shoes. I was certainly concerned, but I also knew everything would work out. It always did one way or another. After everything I had dealt with over the past three years, I was confident things would ultimately be okay.

After about a week and a half, I found a new graduate from a local training program. Claudia seemed to be a good fit. She was very confident and had a commanding presence. She was exactly what I needed. The first couple of weeks were hectic, of course, but after that, Claudia really seemed to take over.

On the home front, I started my kitchen remodel. I felt I needed to start making some changes around the house. I had plenty of nice furniture, but the place wasn't set up for entertaining. So one night around eleven p.m., Mike and I drank a bottle of wine and decided to start demolishing the walls that encircled the kitchen. We had a blast physically pounding the drywall off the studs. Within two hours, we were finished, and we piled the rubble into the truck under the moonlight. By the time we scooped the last of the refuse into the truck, it was time for bed.

Over the next few months, I researched, designed and contracted the reconstruction of my kitchen, complete with slab granite, pendant and recessed lighting, wood floors, custom cherry cabinets, a cathedral ceiling and overpriced appliances I'd probably never even fully utilize. I realized I had a knack for remodeling, right down to the last detail. And most importantly, it was a lot of fun!

Things seemed to be going in the right direction with the business and my personal life. I was feeling stronger and decided I could start dating again. So I jumped on a popular dating website for busy professionals and quickly started making contacts and having fun little conversations. I went on a few dates just to get out of the house and meet some new people. I felt I was finally doing it the right way. I was in control.

After a few weeks, online dating became second nature for me. I learned not to have any expectations but simply to enjoy each person for whom she was. If I didn't get a good feeling about her motives, I'd usually just be honest and tell her after the first ten or fifteen minutes that I just wasn't feeling it. I felt no sense in forcing the issue. Most times, however, a stimulating conversation ensued. Being completely detached from outcome brought a comforting element to the process.

One of my dates was with a cute little dancer named Jennifer at a coffee joint. I had an idea what she looked like from her uploaded photograph on the web site. As I took a sip of coffee, I glanced to my left and noticed a little blonde girl sheepishly approaching me. We made eye contact; I lowered my drink, smiled, and said, "You must be Jennifer."

"Heeeey, you're Mark?" She offered her hand, so I did the same.

"You guessed it! Can I get you a latte or something?" I liked to keep the energy up in awkward situations like that. "Yaaa, that sounds good," she replied.

She had a way of drawling out her "heys" and "yaaas," and she fidgeted with her hair and clothing constantly. It was kind of cute. She was obviously nervous. As we sat there sipping our drinks at the table in front of the fire, she kept tucking her hair behind her left ear and avoiding eye contact.

I was surprised by her appearance of low self-esteem. She wasn't really confident the way I expected a professional dancer to be. But she was soft and sincere, which was a welcome change for me.

We ended up having some wonderful conversation that afternoon. And since the first date was a success, we decided to date a couple of more times. We had a lot of fun together. Jennifer lived in a completely different world than me. Her life revolved around the arts, food, conversation and entertainment.

Jennifer was always close to the action. She attended huge benefit dinners and gala events; she was deeply rooted within the Seattle scene. It was easy for me to get caught up in meeting the people who made Seattle function. After only three dates, I was talking with multimillionaires, socialites and pro athletes.

After one such evening, on our third date, Jennifer and I sat in the back of a little martini bar gossiping and people watching. As we talked, she smiled, cocked her head to the side, and gently asked, "Have you been dating anyone else since we've been seeing each other?"

I hadn't even thought about the fact that she was the only one I was still seeing. "Nope. You're the only one, which is a little strange."

"What do you mean…strange?" she asked.

I laughed at the way she said it before I replied, "I just mean I hadn't really thought about it before you asked. Before we met I was dating a few girls. But I haven't even thought about them. You're keeping me too busy! But how about you? Have you been dating anyone else?"

"Not since our first date."

"Hmmm, interesting," I said.

Then she asked, "Sooo, maybe we can just keep that going?"

"I love the idea." I raised my wine glass, "To a budding relationship!"

We clanged our glasses and continued our evening out. Things were going great!

A mere two nights later, the fledgling relationship was put to the test when we went out for a nice dinner. Afterward, I invited her back to my place for a glass of wine. Things were going along smoothly, and I showed her around the place. The upstairs was still torn up due to the remodel, so we retired to the media room in the basement. I put on some music and opened a bottle of wine. Things were quiet, light and happy. But it was the calm before the storm.

As we raised our glasses to finding one another, I heard a knock at the front door.

"Whoever it is, they'll go away," I said. "We're in the middle of something here." We smiled at each other and kissed a little.

Knock, knock, knock. It was getting more aggressive. I didn't want to leave the couch, but the person was pretty darned determined. I set down my glass and gave Jennifer a kiss on the forehead. "I'll be right back. Don't you go anywhere."

I walked upstairs and into the living room. The house was dark and most of the shades were pulled. I quietly walked in my socks over to the window that had a view of the porch and carefully tweezed apart two of the shades. What stood in front of my door horrified me. It was Esther, and she was forcefully pounding on the door. I let the shades come back together and wondered what I should do.

"Mark, I know you're in there! I saw you come home! Who is she?" she screamed through the door as she continued to pound even harder. Why the heck was she at my house? I hadn't talked with or seen her in about six weeks. I thought all the chaos had ended. "Mark, open the door!"

Then she started pounding on the plate glass window where I was standing. My heart started to pound. She continued to scream at the house. I could only imagine what the neighbors were thinking. I didn't want to fuel her fire, so I didn't say anything. I just quickly walked back downstairs to reassure Jennifer. Why was this happening to me? The night was going so well. And now I had to deal with Esther, of all people. As I entered the room, I noticed Jennifer was standing now. She was obviously scared. Esther had noticed the light through the basement window and was now pounding on that glass.

"I'm so sorry, Jennifer. The woman's crazy. Let's just keep quiet; after a few minutes, she'll hopefully go away." I embraced her as we weathered the storm together. Why couldn't Esther let go? Why couldn't she just leave me alone?

She stopped for a moment. There was silence. I took a deep breath, pulled away from Jennifer, and said, "God, I hope that's it."

No sooner did I say that when Esther started screaming through the window, "I can hear you!" Her face was literally right next to the basement window. "Let me in! I know there's someone in there with you, Mark!" She then continued pounding on the glass. I had no idea what was holding the glass together. It should have broken from any of her latest strikes.

"Esther! Stop pounding on the glass! It's going to break! Just leave me alone!" I yelled through the window.

"I just want to talk with you! Who's in there with you?"

"It's none of your business, Esther! We're broken up! You need to get over it!"

Then I heard her stomping away from the window. I wanted to think that she would just leave, but in my heart, I knew that wasn't a possibility.

I looked at Jennifer, who was absolutely mortified, and said, "This is so ridiculous. I'm sorry you have to be here right now. It's like an episode of Jerry Springer in here."

"Should I leave?" Jennifer asked.

"I think this is the best place for us right now. We'll just hole up until she's gone."

Pound! Pound! Pound! Now she was at the side door, at the top of the basement stairs. The woman was relentless! She pounded on the glass door harder than ever; I knew it was going to give way. As I ran up the stairs to tell her to stop, it happened. The glass exploded into the kitchen and onto the first few steps. I got to the top of the stairs and was face to face with pure evil. She had an obvious look of surprise on her face, like she couldn't believe she had actually just broken a glass door with her bare hands. "I just want to talk! I'm so sorry! Don't step in the glass. Oh my God, I'm so sorry!" she screamed.

"Are you insane, woman?" I screamed. She was trying to open the door to get inside. I pushed her out the doorway and onto the patio. "What are you doing? Get out of here! What are you going to do next, Esther; shoot me? Do you have a gun, Esther?"

"No, I don't have a gun, Mark! I just want to talk."

"This is the kind of stuff you see in the movies! Except this isn't a movie, Esther! What you're doing is real, and you need to stop! Get off my property or I'm calling the cops!"

She paced back and forth and pulled on her hair with both hands. "I just wanted to talk to you! I'm so sorry for breaking the window. I'll pay for it. Just hug me!"

She attempted to enter the house again, but I pushed her out. This time though, I followed her. I pulled out my cell phone and dialed 911. "Do you see what I'm doing, Esther? I'm dialing the cops now. Unless you start walking down the sidewalk to your car, I'm going to push the green button. And then you'll go to jail. Is that what you want, Esther? Do you want to go to jail tonight?"

"No, I don't want to go to jail. Fine, I'll leave," she said. She reluctantly started walking down the driveway, looking over her shoulder.

I couldn't believe what had just happened. My life was a circus. As I walked back into the house, I sidestepped to miss the glass. Then I heard someone walking up the sidewalk. In disbelief, I jumped outside to see Esther standing there in front of me. I said nothing. She just looked at me for a second, and then said, "I just want to talk. Can we talk?"

I didn't say anything. I simply pulled my phone out of my pocket and pretended to push the send button. Then I held it up to show her the number was being dialed. She turned and ran away for the last time. I put the phone in my pocket and went back inside. Hopefully Esther and I were finished for good.

Jennifer was at the bottom of the stairs. "Is everything okay?" she asked, her voice trembling.

"Yeah, just a little mess to clean up. I'm so sorry about all of this. I really don't know what to say. It's completely unacceptable. I wouldn't blame you if you wanted nothing to do with me. But you have to believe me when I say that my relationship with her is so far in the past for me."

"Weeelll, it really didn't have much to do with you. I thought she was going to kill us and cut us up or something," she said half seriously, half jokingly.

I walked down the stairs and pulled her onto the couch. The music was still playing so we just hung out for a few minutes before I got up and cleaned up the glass that lay on the floor. The rest of our evening was much less eventful. We reconnected, continued talking and fell asleep together.

My work life was beginning to have troubles also. On the business side of things, collections were dropping significantly. I was doing just as much business as I always had, but Claudia wasn't collecting payments on much of it. The accounts receivable skyrocketed, so I started to get a little nervous. I typically ruled the roost with a soft hand, as I wasn't a big fan of micromanaging, but I knew two more months of not getting paid could be a disaster. So I talked daily with her about the state of affairs. She constantly reassured me everything was okay, and I shouldn't worry. She told me she had quite a few things to clean up because of the previous office manager's mistakes. I knew that to be at least partially true, so I took her word for it. After all, I had noticed how she was extremely busy every day. When I'd walk by her desk, she was either on the phone or working on the computer. All that work had to be for some purpose. I had confidence that she could right the ship.

Each night, I went home to more progress on the kitchen remodel. It was coming along beautifully. The subcontractors had just recently finished buttoning up the walls and installing the lighting. The floors were complete and the cabinets were delivered and ready for installation.

On evenings and weekends, I worked on the landscaping. It felt good to dig my hands into the earth. I started to feel rejuvenated, reconnected to self. I would work until the sun went down and then head over to Jennifer's for the evening.

Our relationship was progressing nicely. We went out together on most nights and had a lot of fun. Living the dancer lifestyle was quite a bit different from what I was used to. It seemed to me that dancers were used to partying almost every night. They gossiped about everyone, swapped relationships and partners, and spent all their money on food and entertainment. Although they were completely self-absorbed, very few of the dancers had plans for their futures. They just lived in the now. It was like being with a bunch of twenty and thirty year old teenagers. Fun was had by all, but there was really no substance to any of it. And Jennifer was truly no different than the others, but I didn't mind. My personal life needed to be carefree. It was light and experimental. No one put demands or expectations on me, and it was nice not thinking about the big picture for a change.

Over time, I realized Jennifer wasn't exactly the sharpest knife in the drawer, but she was honest and sincere. She and I never talked about God, philosophy, goals, destiny, or anything else heavy, for that matter. It was just day-to-day surface nothingness that we discussed. We lived in the present, which was comfortable. It was good for the time being, but I also knew ours probably wasn't the relationship of my lifetime. It was just a well-deserved break.

Unfortunately, Jennifer, although incredibly sweet and older than most of her cohorts, was still a part of the dancer's drama. She had recently divorced her husband, who was another dancer, because he cheated on her with another female dancer. That type of activity wasn't all that shocking, as the dancers' community was known to be quite incestuous. It was my belief that they all dated each other at some point, and it was even common for both sexes to swap gender every now and then. Jennifer was incredibly hurt by what she'd been through, and she still wasn't over it completely.

Just how hurt she'd been became a glaring reality during a phone call one Friday afternoon. When I asked whether she wanted to have dinner that night at a local hangout, she said, "Mmmm, I don't think so."

"Okay, what does that mean?" I asked.

"I don't know; I just don't feel like it." Her reply was completely uncharacteristic.

"That's fine. Do you still want to go to the party tomorrow night?"

"No, not really. I just don't think we're having as much fun as we should."

I thought back to the few times she had expressed fear I would dump her out of the blue, that I would probably become bored with her and find someone new. Now those thoughts and words were her own prophetic musings. I was obviously being dumped, and I never saw it coming. But my ego had to fight it. "I don't understand. We do something fun almost every night. I get along great with all your friends and family. And I take you all over the place. What other kind of fun are you talking about?"

"Weeeelll…I don't know. I just don't think we're having as much fun as we should." I was silent and confused.

She continued, “Maybe you could come and pick up your things tonight after work. I’ll be away so we won’t have to see each other.” I hated what was happening, but I hated even more that it was premeditated, and I hadn’t seen it coming.

“Well, I don’t really understand what’s happened,” I said. “Did you meet someone new? It’s fine if you did, but just be honest with me. The ‘not having fun’ statement doesn’t really hold water. It doesn’t make any sense.”

“No, I didn’t meet anybody else. I just don’t want to get hurt.”

“So you’re getting out before you get hurt?”

“I’ve been hurt by guys a lot, and I can’t go through it again.”

“Are you becoming a nun or something? You’re going to have to trust someone at some point, aren’t you?”

“I just don’t think we’re having as much fun as we should.”

I was blindsided and angry that I didn’t see it coming, but I couldn’t do anything about it. I told her I’d pick up my stuff and leave my key behind that night, which I did.

The rest of that weekend was like living under water. I was screwed up, big time. I spent the whole time reliving the relationship. I had known it wouldn’t last forever, but I’d thought I was in control. The strange thing was I didn’t even really like her that much. We didn’t have anything in common, I didn’t like her friends, and her lifestyle was absolutely ridiculous. I didn’t even enjoy our sex that much. So what was my problem? Why was I so hurt? I couldn’t shake that I was dumped by someone like her, someone over whom I thought I had the upper hand. But the joke was on me.

Eventually, I understood I was Jennifer’s rebound. She was finally in control and her subconscious reveled in the pain of another man. And it was I who got the shaft for all the men in her past. But besides Jennifer’s part in everything, I had to come to grips with my own input. I was the one who had put myself in a position that wasn’t truthful. I was the one who viewed myself as having an upper hand in our relationship. How distorted I was. That was certainly no way to be in a relationship.

I was simply biding my time until I had the strength to move on. It was the same I'd always done, except the pain was getting worse.

## *Point of Responsibility*

*48. How do you cope with moderately life-altering events like break-ups or losing your job? Do you act out by binging on food, alcohol and/or drugs? Do you grieve the relationship, or do you stuff the pain of loss down deep within you? The only constant in life is constant change. It's how we grow, and it's what life is all about. Properly grieving a loss is necessary. Take the time to do so, but let the pain go in a positive way. Cry, gently work out, and talk with someone uplifting. Stay away from people who enable your pity party. Take the good lessons from the perceptibly negative event and move forward with confidence that you're closer to being in a wonderful situation, whether in work or personally. Treat yourself well, and know you're on the right track, because you are. And remember, you're not alone. Everyone deals with such issues.*

The next couple of weeks were brutal for me. It took all the energy I could muster just to get to work every day. The days were long and foggy. I couldn't eat. I couldn't sleep. And I was running on fumes.

In my mind, I knew the breakup with Jennifer was best for both of us. But in my heart, I felt such deep pain that I almost couldn't function. It didn't make sense to me that the emotions bubbling up were incongruent with the minute nature of the relationship I was mourning.

Many people realized things weren't going well for me. Patients knew something was up, but I couldn't share my personal life with the very people I was helping to heal. I just shrugged off their inquisitions, assuring them I was fine. Bobby and Chloe even tried to get me out of my funk with conversation, entertainment and drinking. But I was completely inconsolable. Nothing pulled me out of it.

I'd obviously been through breakups before, but the pain was different than anything I'd ever lived. I knew it wasn't directly due to the breakup. The breakup had simply triggered some deep emotions from my past and inserted them into my present-day life for processing.

After a couple of weeks, I noticed I had a huge opportunity to shed much of the baggage I'd accumulated over the years. It was raw, painful and visible, like it never had been before. All the negative structures I used to function were suddenly staring back at me, bolding waiting for me to make my move. Would I look away, pretending they didn't exist? Would I talk gently with them, to try to figure them out, like I did with other people? Would I try to love them, as I had tried to love other unavailable objects of affection in my life? Would I angrily chop them into pieces and try to manipulate and control the situation, like I was prone to doing? What was next? What was I going to do now? It was a moment of truth.

## *Point Of Responsibility*

*49. How does your ego influence your life? Do you attempt to control as many variables as possible? Do you seek compliments from others? Do you always need to be heard, and/or to be right? Are you completely dedicated, at any cost, to your work? Why do you think that might be? Are you trying to fill a void? Are you looking for something from the outside to fill something on the inside? Does your situation cause an imbalance in the rest of your life? The key is to live with a balanced ego. For the ego does have a functional purpose; otherwise we wouldn't have it. Learn to feel when the ego flares. And when it does, listen with your heart to its screams for power, for struggle, and its battles for more. Simply sit quietly and evaluate it. Physically put your hands to your heart before you make any important decisions in life. Just doing this alone separates the "real you" from the ego's "you" that you've identified with for so long. Acknowledging your emotions is the first and most important step in separating your true self from this overbearing entity that resides only in your head. Realize that you are NOT your ego, and that proliferation of your ego is detrimental to the evolution of your soul. Again, the ego has a function, but that function must be managed and balanced by YOU through reason. We'll talk much more about this later.*

*For now, write in your notebook five events where your ego has sought control. Think of situations where you've been angry, frustrated, and challenged by others. Think of power struggles and times you've fought just to be right. Write them down; become aware of your own patterns.*

Ultimately, I decided to take the opportunity to break down the barriers in my life that falsely shrouded who I was. Those behaviors kept me from manifesting my true authentic self. Most of the things I'd achieved up to that point I'd done by brute force, logic, intelligence and willpower. I acted in my best interest, or what my ego saw as my best interest, in every situation. I wasn't responsible with the lives of others. I was very good at reading people and manipulating situations to get what I wanted. I empathized with people, but only to learn how they "felt" about their relationships to their environments. I would change conversation patterns when with different types of people. With some I was loving, with others I was harsh. I picked up systems from everyone and everything around me, kept the ones that were solid and served me, discarded the ones that were dysfunctional or slow. My primary goals were to cultivate the abilities that would make me the most efficient and adaptive person I possibly could be. The world was like my own little experiment.

I thought all people were like me, and maybe they were. But within my conscious acts to better myself, I had also created a lot of noise. I hid from myself, and from others, the parts of me that brought shame, anger, guilt and anxiety. My ego shielded from my conscious mind the emotions that eked out during trying situations. I pretended they did not exist, and they were unimportant. After looking back at all the opportunities to heal myself from within, I finally realized I had cheated myself out of most of them. I didn't use my emotions as they were meant to be used, as a tool for self-discovery and re-creation.

Until now, I had understood emotions from a negative standpoint. They just got in the way. They were cumbersome and clouded situations. They were uncontrollable, and I wanted nothing to do with them. When confronted with emotions, both within myself and others, I would simply react. No attempt was made to understand anything about why they existed. I didn't care what caused them to surface; I thought them inappropriate in most situations.

And then, out of the blue, it dawned on me: In almost every part of my life, I was reacting to emotions. I never honored my own; I was always living for and through the emotions of others. I laid others' emotions into my own dysfunctional blueprint. No wonder my life was so chaotic! I wasn't living for myself. I simply mirrored whatever others were doing! I was the ultimate chameleon. I, in the ultimate search for acceptance, had given my power to everyone else with whom I came into contact. And I did it all day, every day.

After that major personal revelation, I determined I was honestly ready to rid myself of the recurring negative blueprint that had become my way of understanding, manipulating and controlling my environment. I was actually ready to move forward. I didn't want to awaken every morning and walk backward into my future. I was going to face it by digging deep within myself and by clearing the cobwebs once and for all.

## *Point of Responsibility*

*50. Do you give your power away? Do you allow the ideas, words and actions of others to dictate more of your life than your own? If you do, to whom do you give your power and why? Take it back by actively choosing to make your own decisions. If in a partnership, bring new things to the table. Be assertive and challenge accepted truths and actions. Do things for the right reasons, and not because that's how they've always been done. Certainly don't disregard your partner's wishes, but have within your relationship a better balance of power if you notice it has been disrupted. Try new things, grow in any way possible, and begin to reclaim your responsibility to yourself. It is up to YOU to live a full life and to manifest your gifts for the whole world to experience.*

Chapter Twelve:

# The Dichotomy Manifested

I felt like I was reborn. I had a new lease on life, as it were. It was my time to capture and live the truest essence of me. But first, I had to dive deeply within my psyche to uncover the culprits of my repeating, self-allowed, pain and anguish. I had no more patience for such things to exist within me. They must be purged. I knew it would take time, but I was okay with it. "What else do I have to do?" I often thought. "This is the type of work everyone should be doing all the time. Work like this is much more important than gossiping or entertainment, or anything else, for that matter." I felt good about being on this leg of the journey.

## *Point Of Responsibility*

*51. Do you often escape into things like gossip and entertainment? Do you spend hours on the Internet, in front of the television or playing video games? Such habits can easily lead to compulsions and ultimately become addictions, eating up major chunks of your life. Write in your notebook the number of hours each week you spend on entertainment. Include things like movies, unfocused Internet browsing, video games, and television. Be honest with yourself. Then determine the amount of time you spend on self-creation, things like active meditation, creating your day in your mind, envisioning positive outcomes in relationships, goal assertions, etc. And then determine the amount of time you spend on your responsibilities, work, exercise and education. How much money do you spend on entertainment each month in comparison to everything else? A responsible approach would be to spend a full ten percent of your net income on things entertainment related. Entertainment is absolutely necessary and should be enjoyed by everyone. But unless balance exists with the other parts of your life, something is not getting the attention it deserves. One important concept of living a balanced life is to reward yourself with entertainment after the achievement of responsibilities. Claiming entitlement to entertainment before being responsible ends up leading to escapism and a lack of self-worth.*

But I had to do it my way. I had never been a fan of psychotherapy. I'd used it in the past to help get through tough times, but it seldom worked. I was the only one who could get myself through such times. No one else could make the decision to change but me. In my opinion, psychotherapy allowed for too many scapegoat opportunities. And I wasn't about to blame anyone other than myself for my predicaments. That would be the easy way out. In fact, it was the American way. I could easily blame all of my problems on any number of things from my past and present, but that's ultimately placing blame on something other than what was actually creating everything in my life: me. I attracted everything that was in my life. That was the bottom line. I had to take responsibility and that was all there was to it.

I first began my introspection within the pages of various books that discussed philosophy, spirituality, quantum physics and functional thought. I'd studied such writings in my past, but not with the same understanding from which I was now working. I devoured the writings with an inspired and deeper knowing. I was able to pull together many systems, ideas and concepts into my own doctrine, to recreate and live my life.

### *Point Of Responsibility*

*52. Read from a book for thirty minutes every day. Although newspapers and magazines might occasionally have a thought-inspiring article, they should be considered entertainment. Most books, on the other hand, expand the mind. Choose books that inspire you or that teach you something. A great time to do this is in the morning, but anytime will work. You won't be disappointed. And you'll probably even notice other avenues of thought open up within you. Open a book to open your mind.*

I wanted to live within that peaceful realm twenty-four hours a day. I was slowly unlocking the door to my mind. As I searched externally for things that could aid in my evolution, I realized I must simultaneously attack the demons from within. It was time to get to work.

The first step was to acknowledge the lowest common denominator within each negative structure in life. I found that the easiest and most relevant way to evaluate my emotions, which were the window to the ego, and eventually, to the soul's evolution. Under what circumstances did I feel joy in my life? When was I frustrated? Who made me feel anxious? Why was I on the verge of being angry all the time? I asked and answered dozens of questions like those honestly and with integrity. I wrote my answers down and continued the process by diving further into my psyche.

I spent every available minute fine-tuning my systems of understanding. As I did, I understood more fully the dysfunctional therapeutic systems in popular American culture originally designed to help people overcome emotional and mental issues. Patients rarely did the activities therapists prescribed, and therapists seldom held their patients accountable. The only people who seemed to get better were the ones determined to improve, regardless of the therapy employed. Most patients just continued to live in sickness, which began to define them. Patients decided to accept their illness as an identity of victimization. Being a victim is the ego's way of telling the world that one's lot in life isn't his or her fault, but someone else's.

Interestingly enough, as I dug into my beliefs to learn why I behaved as I did, I realized it wasn't really that difficult. The horned devils were right below the surface the whole time. I started to process the issues at hand. I immediately wrestled with my feelings of abandonment, my need for constant external acceptance, feelings of impending doom and being taken advantage of, as well as the emotions and subsequent patterns associated with being molested as a young boy. Little did I know it, but the next six weeks of my life would be monumentally life changing.

It was the beginning of August, and vacation season was in full swing. I took advantage of the slow days at work to continue working on myself. Claudia seemed to be figuring things out, and I gave her the space to do so.

I was often lost in focused thought. One day, I realized it had only been a few weeks since the breakup with Jennifer. I felt like that relationship was a lifetime ago. I hadn't thought about her much since last seeing her; I was more focused on getting to the bottom of my issues. I wondered how she was doing, but I was genuinely happy to be out of that relationship.

Things had been intense for some time. I felt the need to blow off some steam and just have some fun for a change. It was time to meet some people who didn't live in Atherton. I decided to use the same popular dating site as before, and I started making small talk with some of the more interesting individuals. It was a nice break from the tedious nature of my recent days. Every second seemed to be filled with something. Not only was I focusing heavily on my thoughts, I was still working as hard as ever at the office and contracting the remodel at home. Over the next couple of weeks, I met some great women. There were no love connections, but good conversation and friendship. It was nice to be out there again, and not constantly living in my head. I began to have an appreciation for how life really worked. Sometimes things were good. Sometimes things were bad. But life is ultimately about our reactions to those events, and how to tweak our actions so the negative events don't become repetitious.

### *Point Of Responsibility*

*53. We all learn things at our own pace. Sometimes we can get frustrated with others for not understanding, or for not having the wherewithal to take their lives to the next level. Others may have that same frustration toward us. Each life is relevant only unto itself. No logic or honor comes from comparing people. In your life, do you attempt to force people into being how you want them to be, instead of accepting them for who they are? If so, this represents your lack of acceptance for what is. Let people be who they are. We're all on our own paths.*

*When you offer guidance, do it with love and acceptance, and only do it once. No one likes unsolicited advice. It's much more functional to show someone you care instead of ramming something down his or her throat. When people know you care, and see you living with responsibility, they will come to you for advice. That advice then becomes solicited, and will be well received.*

On one of those lazy summer days, an old patient named Summer came back to the clinic. We had become good friends, previously, although I suspected she wanted something more. I had first treated her daughter, Emily, and then her, and when she was going through a divorce, she had talked to me about the situation and the anxiety it was causing her daughter. I expressed my concern for her, but I had declined an invitation from her a few months prior to go to lunch, thinking it best to keep our relationship on a professional level. Now she was back from a long visit in Arizona with her parents as she went through the divorce. As soon as we saw each other, we started talking and laughing, and picked up right where we had left off. She again asked me to lunch, and this time, I accepted. I liked talking with her, and I wasn't going to deny myself good conversation just because she was a patient once in a while.

A couple of days later, I picked her up from her office, which was downtown, and we meandered into a small café. As we talked, she told me about the details of being in the middle of divorcing her husband. I listened and told her I thought it was for the best, then told her about my current soul searching, including that I was doing some writing to clean out the cobwebs, and I was finally starting to pull myself out of the fog.

We decided to meet for lunch again later that week. As we stood at the portal to her office, she smiled at me, leaned over, and kissed my cheek; she held the kiss for just a little bit too long. When she released and opened the door, I said goodbye and she was off. Until that point, I hadn't really thought of Summer in a sexual way. I left downtown with a confused mind, but I tried not to think anything more of it. I just wanted to get back to work; it was like my sanctuary.

On our next meeting, Summer and I took a little walk down the sidewalk. As we walked past the storefronts of glass, cement and the latest in fashion, the conversation trailed off into nothing. The silence was comfortable, and then she took my hand in hers. I didn't want to offend her by pulling away, and her warm hand felt good intertwined with mine. Summer giggled a little, and we continued down the street quietly. On the way back to her office, she asked whether I would be interested in going with her to an office function the next week.

I had made an evening date with a woman I'd met online on the same day as Summer's event, so I told her I had something going on early that evening, but maybe I could meet her afterward. I could tell she was hurt and wanted to ask whether I was going on a date with someone else, but she didn't. As we sat in the car in front of her building, she said, "I like your style." Then she leaned over and kissed me on the lips. I kissed her gently, and then quickly pulled away. She looked a little confused, smiled coyly, and opened the door to the lobby.

"Call me when you're done with whatever you have going on that night," she said. "It would be fun to meet up." I reassured her I would. She smiled, turned and walked into the high rise.

As I drove back to my office, I felt confused about whether I was attracted to her. The kiss had been like kissing my mother, except that I was turned on a bit. The feelings were muddy, but that only intrigued me to contemplate the sensations further. There was obviously more to it.

## *Point Of Responsibility*

*54. Do you have emotions that seem to come out of nowhere? Write in your notebook three situations in your life when you've said something harsh, flied off the handle, or reacted irrationally. Calmly think back to each event, and try to figure out where those emotions came from. Did you inherit them from a family member, friend or love interest? How long had that type of emotion existed within you when the situation occurred? Take your time and don't get frustrated. It may take a little while to uncover such things. Remember, such emotions might have been buried for some time.*

The rest of that day, I felt I was in the fog again. It was like being in shock. I was able to function, but something within me was fighting.

When I got home, a package from my sister was waiting on the front step. I went inside and unwrapped a beautiful leather-bound diary. We'd recently rekindled our relationship, and she knew I'd been doing a lot of writing. I was deeply appreciative of her reaching out to me. We hadn't spent much time together since our parents divorced in 1988. We certainly loved each other, but since she lived in the Midwest, the distance made it difficult to have a successful relationship. I immediately wrote her a thank you note and dropped it in the mailbox with an extra little note to my nephew, whom I adored.

As I prepared my dinner, I noticed the diary on the counter top and recalled something an old man told me once, "Don't ever write anything down that you don't want the whole world to know about." I had never been interested in diary writing, but I appreciated the gift. It was very thoughtful, and I loved that about my sister.

Later that night, I was tired, but incredibly restless. I tried reading, but nothing sunk in. I kept reading the same lines over and over. I couldn't focus enough to do any of the exercises I'd created to explore my mind, so I gave up and went to the pub for a beer.

Atherton was an extremely small community. Everywhere I went, I was engaged by someone: present patients, past patients, someone who had seen my face in an advertisement, or people who felt it necessary to tell me chiropractic was quackery. I never knew whom I was going to run into; such situations were inescapable, and created a self-imposed anxiety as I walked the village streets. Unfortunately, it was getting much worse due to my recent dredging up of the past. The anxiety and my past were obviously connected in some way. I parked in a dark spot near the back door of the pub. As I sat in my car, it dawned on me that the reason for my anxiety was quite simple. On the inside, I felt "less than." Although I lived a highly successful extroverted lifestyle, the "me" with whom I identified constantly searched for external reassurance. I would set people up within conversations and actions to give me the desired response, which was reassurance and positive feedback. The reassurance felt good to my ego, but didn't satiate the deeper realms within. Words were the easiest form of reassurance for me. They were free, and people liked giving kind, reassuring words. It made them feel they were a deeper part of my life. We both received something from the transaction.

The second most common form of reassurance for me was the act of sex. It was relatively easy for me to seduce others, or allow myself to be seduced by others. I actively cultivated the art of putting myself in the position of availability, from meeting new people in line at the coffee shop, to the produce section at the market, and the most recent manifestation within my clinic. The self-imposed anxiety with which I'd been living was most obviously my deepest self that screamed all the way into my conscious, "Stop! This isn't me! This activity is killing me, and harming others!"

## Point Of Responsibility

*55. If you want to be respected, be someone worthy of respect.*

I had always been a genuinely likable fellow. People were drawn to my charisma and love of life. I was also drawn to having happy, healthy conversations with folks everywhere I went. I'd really learned to love talking with people of all types. But, as the anxiety resurfaced at various points throughout my life, with it came the manipulation of healthy conversation from a need for insatiable external reassurance.

I was at a loss with what to do next, so I shook it off and went into the pub through the back door. I was quickly greeted with, "Hey, jerk, what's new?" from my generally angry buddy Dave. Scott was next to him, bobbing his head forward and then quickly back, just before his nose touched the bar. They'd obviously been drinking for a while. Dave and Scott were a couple of pub regulars and fellow Harley riders. I knew them through Dave's wife, who was a patient each year during softball season. We shared some conversation, razzed each other and drank too much booze.

I was on my fourth drink when I got a phone call from a number I didn't recognize. I excused myself from the bar and stepped outside to take it.

"Heeey, is this Doctor Mark?" The woman was obviously a little inebriated.

"Maybe. Maybe not. Who's calling?"

"It's Heather! What are you up to?"

"Just drinking too much. How about you?"

She laughed, "Yeah, me too! I just broke up with my boyfriend, and my girlfriends don't want to stay out! Do you need a partner?"

"You bet! I'm at the pub. Come on down!"

"I'll be there in about a half hour," she said.

"See you then."

I went back inside to play some silly video game and have another drink. Dave and Scott took off and my buddy Mike showed up for a few minutes. We did a couple of shots of Jaegermeister. That stuff was brutal.

Heather showed up on time. She commanded quite a few stares as she made her way over to me. I stood up and gave her a big hug. I got us a round of drinks and introduced her to Mike. We all did another shot. As we stood there, Heather said, "Wow! You better be careful; I do some crazy things when I drink too much!"

"Well, I don't know about you, but I have to work tomorrow. Maybe we should get out of here and go back to my place before it gets too late."

She looked at me for a second, trying to evaluate whether I was serious. She grabbed her full glass, raised it up and said, "I'm ready when you are," before slamming the contents.

"Let me clear up the tab, and we'll be on our way."

I paid the tab and Heather followed me back to my place. We walked in the door and made our way downstairs. I grabbed us a couple of glasses of water on the way.

Within seconds of sitting on the couch, we were engaged in a kiss. But I couldn't get into it. I was having the same strange feeling I'd had with Summer earlier that day, except I was definitely attracted to Heather, and she was offering herself up with no strings attached. I didn't know what my problem was. I'd done the same exact thing many times before, with many different partners. But for some reason, the present event was purely mechanical. I'd never been so detached from a carnal experience in my life.

We lay on the couch for a few minutes before commencing the inevitable parting of ways. As we put our clothes back on, she said, "I guess it's a good thing I don't work for you anymore. That'd be a little awkward!"

"Yeah, I guess you're right. But it was fun!" I said, trying to keep the energy up.

I walked her out and gave her a quick kiss goodbye. Then I took a shower and went to bed wondering what was stirring within me.

The next day flew by relatively quickly, but I still felt some remnants of the day before's emotions. Things just weren't right between my ears. After work as I meditated for a couple of hours, some interesting things happened. I had fleeting visions of literally being crucified for things I hadn't done. That was shortly followed by what I can only explain as a super fast tunnel ride. As it slowed down, my consciousness came back to my body. I slowly stretched out my neck and back, still seated. I tilted my head back and felt heat rising up from within my throat. My diaphragm tightened and the lump that had been in my throat for as long as I could remember started to move upward. My head tilted forward to accommodate its motion from below. My breathing became shallower. My eyes opened widely. I got the distinct sensation of the moment just before fear arises. It was a state of bewilderment, with no expectations. I just had to sit and wait for the next piece of the puzzle to drop. I tried to shake off the stress by stretching out my shoulders, arms and neck. But my diaphragm tensed up again, causing a physical retching motion. My head tilted forward and the hot lump moved up to where my tongue attached at the back of my throat. I tried to clear my throat, but I wasn't in control of the process. I just had to sit and wait. Before I noticed what I was doing, I started humming deeply. It resonated within all parts of my body and seemed to relax the process that was occurring. Then, on one exhale, my diaphragm pushed that hot lump past the constrictions of the throat and into the back of my mouth. I gagged and tried to swallow, but the lump was determined. I felt I was going to choke, when the humming became deeper yet, and seemed to work in unison with the diaphragm to push the little ball of shame, guilt, anger, frustration, and all those things left unsaid out of me where they belonged. The humming quickly turned into my voice, at its lowest frequency. My throat expanded, like before a yawn, and my mouth stretched to reveal a sound I had never heard before. It was a deep, painful, and quiet howl. It shook me from within. I visualized it as releasing the black tentacles that had been wrapping themselves around my insides for many, many years.

Tears began to stream down both cheeks. I had never been through anything like this before. Although I was scared, I wasn't going to stop. I sat there howling in my basement, alone, naked and warm, for as long as it took. Time was irrelevant. With each breath, the howl became deeper and longer. It continued to gain momentum and my full lung capacity was quickly reached. I took a deep breath in until it stretched my back and torso in all directions, followed by a deep howl out until my whole body tensed at the end of the exhalation. The tears continued. The lump was now in the back of my mouth, and I had that feeling one has just before vomiting. The glands in my mouth watered, my head tilted down, my chest out. I started to clear my throat, gently at first, and then forcefully. The lump was no longer purely metaphorical. It was all real, and it was coming up. I had the sensations of salty and bitter within my mouth just before I jumped up and went to the bathroom to vomit that crap out of me. I ran to the toilet and lifted the lid. I gagged and spit into the bowl. My chest heaved, my heart pounded, and I cleared my mouth and throat. What came up was absolutely disgusting. There was no vomit, but a yellowish-brownish-greenish mucous. Where the hell did it come from? And what exactly was it? The scientist in me wanted to reach in and pull it out, but the spiritual me wanted nothing to do with it. I flushed the toilet and got up. I took a deep breath and took stock of my body and mind. It was then I realized what it was like to take a full, deep breath. I had never had the sensation that I needed more air until that moment when

I actually had the capacity for it. I looked at myself in the mirror and seemed to be standing up straighter. My eyes and throat felt cooler. They no longer felt hot and full. My body was relaxed and felt ten pounds lighter. I came out of the meditation completely drenched in a foul-smelling sweat.

Immediately afterward, in the forefront of my mind, I began to understand my emotions were wrapped around my older half-brother molesting me so many years before.

My relationship with Steve changed forever one day when I was about eight, and he was seventeen. Mom and Dad left to go grocery shopping and they took my sister with them, so it was just my brother and I at home. He told me to come upstairs with him, into his room. His room was typically off limits to me, so it was a treat that I got to hang out with him that day. He pulled out some porno magazines and proceeded to take off his pants. Then he took off my pants. When I asked him what he was doing, he just said it would feel good. Then he started licking me down there, and he wanted me to do the same thing to him. At that point in my life, that type of activity was like taking out the garbage, or feeding the dog. There was no emotional attachment whatsoever. So we did that until he suddenly pulled away. It was obviously strange to me, but I didn't know what was going on. I was a little kid who got to hang out in my brother's room for a little while. I don't remember exactly how many times it happened; my mind blocked it out. I do know that it was at least a half a dozen times.

Before my brother turned eighteen, he was kicked out of the house by my father for doing drugs and getting kicked out of school for the second time that year. I always wondered if they knew what he'd done to me, and if he'd done the same thing to my sister.

## Point Of Responsibility

*56. Are there negative events in your life that you hang onto? Have you wronged others? Have others wronged you? Have you been verbally, physically, emotionally or sexually abused by family members in any way? How about friends of the family? Have you been made to feel insignificant, always to blame, dumb, or anything else that unfairly projects negativity unto you? Detail all such situations and people in your notebook and clearly mark the page for later discussion. Be honest; get them out of your head.*

I had never really reconciled within myself the sexual abuse I experienced from my brother. I'd always known it had happened, but I had never felt the need to analyze it. I didn't feel ashamed or dirty, and I knew I wasn't to blame since I'd had very little control over it. Nor did I see the need to blame my brother. That would just cause more issues. I had always thought it best just to ignore it.

But now my recent understanding of its impact on me inspired me to rehash its ugliness. I realized that subconsciously, I had no problem pretending boundaries did not exist for me. From an early age, and due to the molestation, I'd learned that boundaries were something talked about, but not necessarily enforced. And many times in my adult life, I had recreated that exact idea. I would sleep with married women, or with women in relationships, and I always found ways to justify my wandering penis.

Acknowledging that the situation had happened now made me think I could move past it, and I felt I could begin to demonstrate more acceptable behavior on my part. I was tearing down the old framework. Most of the time, it felt good.

On occasion, however, I used alcohol to stifle the demons tormenting me. Most nights I could be found at one of Atherton's surrounding watering holes. I knew I wasn't an alcoholic; I was just choosing not to deal with all the recent upheaval twenty-four hours a day. I needed a little break during the evenings, and moderate alcohol consumption, coupled with being around people, seemed to do the trick. (In hindsight, meditation, working out, and filling my time with more creative endeavors would have been more soothing and productive, but I wasn't quite there yet.)

One evening, after coming home from the pub, my phone erupted with constant text messages. I had hated texts ever since Esther. Every time I heard the message signal, I got a gnawing sensation in the pit of my stomach. But I checked it anyway. It was Atia. She was notorious for sending me senseless texts at all hours. I usually just discarded them without reading. But this one was a bit more interesting, "My place, twenty min?"

Obviously, the boyfriend was on another business trip, and she was feeling frisky. And so was I. I jumped in the truck and drove to her place. On the way, I began to think of the consequences of what I was about to do. I wondered what would happen if her boyfriend pulled into the driveway while I was there at one in the morning. What would I do if he caught us in the act? If it were before or afterward, would I just hang out with a stupid look on my face? Would I jump out the bathroom window like in the movies? More importantly, why was I even making this trek? I knew I shouldn't, but that didn't stop me. The urge to have sexual contact overpowered any thoughts of impropriety. I quickly suppressed all thoughts that inspired me to turn around and go home and began to focus on what I was walking into. I was clearly the object of one of her fantasies, yet I was letting her take advantage of me. When I reached her place, I walked up the steep stairway and opened the gate from the outside. She was sitting at the bottom of the porch stairs smoking a joint.

Quietly, I asked, "Is anyone home?"

"The baby's asleep. It's just you and I, Doc. So come on over here."

I did as she instructed and let her do her thing. The moon shined down, illuminating the foliage, rooftops and swing set. Unfortunately, it didn't illuminate my better judgment. The moonlight created a silhouette of her face and body, making her features invisible. She could have been anyone. The event was quickly over and the cool summer air made my sweaty skin tighten. Within minutes, Atia went back inside and I was on my way home. I wondered to myself, even though I had zero respect for her and knew she was completely vindictive, why I allowed her to manipulate me. When I got home, I grabbed another beer from the fridge and drowned any possible insight until I fell asleep.

Since the next day was Saturday, I woke up early and immediately started working on the landscaping. I had finished the sixty-foot long retaining wall earlier in the week and started building the 1200 square foot, multi-tiered deck. Mike gave me until lunchtime when he had to get ready for work. As he walked back inside,

Summer pulled up in her car. She jumped out and pulled a picnic basket from the back seat. I watched her walk her spindly legs up the sidewalk and to the side of the house. She didn't take notice of me, so I yelled down to her and waved.

Once she walked back to where I was, I asked, "Whatcha got there?"

"I knew you'd be working on this landscape of yours, and I also knew you wouldn't stop for lunch, so I made a couple of sandwiches for you."

"That's awesome! Are they edible?"

"What's that supposed to mean?"

"Didn't you tell me you're not exactly a whiz around the kitchen?"

She laughed through her crooked little smile. "Yeah, I guess you're right."

I jumped down from the top of the wall and took my gloves off. She sat down on the patio and assembled a nice little lunch. I washed my hands under the spigot outside, and we sat eating and talking. Mike came out, quickly met Summer and left for work. When I told Summer I needed some furniture for the house, she offered to go shopping with me; wanting a second opinion, I agreed. We decided to go the next day. Once we finished lunch, she was on her way. She gave me a little peck on the cheek, and I thanked her for the sandwich.

That night, I met Mike at the pub for a beer. When he asked what the deal was with Summer, I told him we just went to lunch a couple of times a week. He asked whether we were having sex.

"No. I don't really find her attractive, but she's cool to talk with."

"Does she always show up unannounced?"

"Nope; first time. It was all right though; she brought me a sandwich."

"That chick's got an agenda."

"Maybe; maybe not. We're just having a good time."

Our conversations were always like that, quick one-liners. I appreciated the "no thought" approach to our discussions.

The next day at work, my old friend and patient Betsy came back in for treatment and a pillow, but she forgot to take the pillow with her. She later called me about it, and I agreed to drop it off at her house around eight o'clock.

When I knocked on Betsy's door later that evening, she invited me inside. She was wearing a tight, red leather skirt and a flowing, ruffled blouse that caught air. She told me to have a seat in the living room; then she asked whether I wanted a Heineken as she went into the kitchen. I gladly accepted the drink.

From the other room she said, "Thanks for bringing the pillow. I really appreciate that. I've just been working so hard all day. I don't think I could've come back down to get it. I need more hours in my day!"

Almost immediately, Betsy was in front of me again. She leaned over me to set my beer on the table next to my chair, meanwhile putting her chest in my face. She kept talking about something. Before I knew it, my blazer was off and she was rubbing my neck. "You work so hard every day. You must need a massage. Why don't you take off your T-shirt so I can get to those muscles?"

"Sounds good to me," I said.

She proceeded to undress me under the guise of "massage." I just let her continue. The attention felt good, and she had good hands. She worked her way down my body until one thing led to another. I had only fleeting thoughts that it shouldn't be happening; I found it interesting that I wasn't turned on by her, but by the attention. After it was over, I didn't think much more about it. I just went home.

The next day, I was working on building my deck when Summer dropped by again. She woke Mike up by her incessant pounding on the front door. When he opened it, he grumpily told her I was in the backyard, where she soon greeted me with another sandwich. Coming over unannounced wasn't a big deal the first time. But this time, it rubbed me the wrong way. It implied a bit of entitlement, and I didn't like it. I asked her to call next time, as I was always in and out. And I didn't want her to go to all that trouble just to come over to an empty house. She agreed. I gulped down my sandwich, thanked her, and quickly got back to work.

Mike came out after she left. "That chick's annoying."

"Yeah, she's getting to be." He went back inside, and I continued working.

On the eve of Summer's office party, I had a quick happy hour date with a woman who had to wear slip-ons because she couldn't tie her own laces. The date ended after the first glass of wine. I called Summer and we met at her office building shortly thereafter. The party was over, so we decided to get a drink somewhere else. As I waited for her in the high rise's lobby, I heard high-heeled footsteps clunking on the marble behind me. I turned around to see Summer in a little black dress, covered up with a salmon-colored shawl.

"Don't you look nice," I said.

"So do you," she replied. "But that's typical, isn't it?" We hugged. "Well, here we are. What do you want to do?" We had made no plans past that very moment.

"I don't know. How about you show me your office?"

"Sure, no problem! It's up a few floors, though. But I'm sure we'll see a nice view of the city below."

"Let's do it." We jumped into the elevator and went up to her floor. We got off and she showed me around. Surprisingly, another person was still working. Summer introduced us before we continued on to her cubicle. She offered me her chair and knelt beside me. She turned on the computer and showed me some of the things she'd been working on.

After a few minutes, Summer went to the washroom, and I rolled my chair over to the windows. She was right; the view was spectacular. The city lights shone brightly off the sides of buildings. Being up that high muted the noise from below. It was peaceful, and I was caught in a daydream.

"Nice, isn't it?" She handed me a bottle of water.

"I could certainly get used to this."

I stood up and rolled the chair back to the desk. I sat down; she sat on the desk.

Summer's co-worker walked over to let us know she was leaving. We both said good night. A few long seconds passed before I broke the silence with a small laugh.

"What?" Summer asked.

I smiled and said, "You could cut the tension in here with a knife!"

She laughed and sat on my lap. Before long, our relationship had been taken to the next level. We kissed for a little while before calling it a night.

I went home and took a quick shower before jumping into bed with the pug. I needed some sleep. I had one more day of work before the weekend projects were to continue in earnest.

The whole next day, I felt I was in that "shock fog" that had become so familiar recently. I knew I shouldn't have let things snowball like they had between Summer and me. I just didn't feel right about it.

At work early the next morning, I had a surprise visit from Erika, a patient I'd met a few times when I first took over the clinic. Erika was a runner, and twice a year she would come in for a wellness treatment. She had a natural beauty about her, not only visible on the outside, but that shined brightly through from the inside. She was about 5'8', had a feminine but muscular build, and long, flowing brown hair. Her skin was perfectly tan and her eyes were a deep green. She was truly striking.

Since the morning was slow, we sat and talked for quite some time after the adjustment. While we typically shared good conversation, this time it was deeper.

Out of nowhere, she said, "You look a little sad. You know, when I'm not feeling right, I go for a long walk. Maybe that's what you should do."

"That's a great idea; maybe I'll go at lunch today. I don't have anything else planned."

As we kept talking, me leaning against the counter top while she sat on the treatment bench about three feet away, I noticed she was giving off some interesting body language. She would hold a gaze longer than acceptable in normal conversation. She kept fidgeting with her hair and shyly tilted her head as she looked up to me. She even reached out to touch my hand when she talked. I knew she was married, but all she ever said about her husband was that he was always away, and then she would change the conversation to something different.

When I had to go see my next patient, she got up and asked, "Can I give you a hug? You look like you need one."

I didn't see any problem with it, so I said, "Yes" and we embraced. She squeezed me tightly and buried her head into my left shoulder. She slowly ran both of her hands up and down my back. Again, the attention felt good. We held the embrace for about fifteen seconds before I pulled away. I put my hand on the doorknob, and she grabbed her running coat from the chair. She then asked, "Do you want some company on your walk at lunch today?"

I wasn't sure what to say. I wanted to, but I knew it could open up a can of worms. Things were so cloudy for me at that point, but I conceded. She agreed to pick me up at my place and I gave her the address.

After my last patient before lunch, I ran home to change my clothes, and she came to pick me up. I jumped in her SUV and we were on our way. We got to the park and started walking at a brisk pace. Neither of us said much, but I felt an obvious gravitation toward her. We turned off at a seldom-used trail. After five minutes, we came to a bench that overlooked the lighthouse and further north to the Straits of Juan de Fuca. We stood next to one another admiring the view, breathing deeper and longer than normal. She turned to look at my face as I peered at the sea. I didn't turn to her. I just stood there looking forward, fully aware that she awaited my next move. I took a deep breath and said, "This place is a little piece of heaven. It's so beautiful here."

"You should take a walk here every day if it makes you feel like that. Do you want to go back? Or do you want to have a seat on the bench?"

I didn't want to leave. It was a peaceful area closed off from the rest of the park. "Let's have a seat and just relax." I wiped the dew off the bench with my sleeve and we sat down.

She sat to my left and twisted her spine to give a few cracks. "Who needs a chiropractor?" she said. As we laughed, she placed her hand on my thigh and leaned her head on my shoulder. "This is nice," she said.

We sat in silence for a few minutes taking in the environment. White clouds billowed over the Olympic Mountains and above Puget Sound. The sun was almost finished burning off the morning marine layer and revealed itself in angelic streaks through the mixture of alders and evergreen trees. I put my arm around her and began to play with her hair. She sighed deeply and began to rub my thigh. She looked up at me for a moment before gently kissing the left side of my neck. I closed my eyes and enjoyed her lips and tongue on my skin. I pulled away, looked at her and kissed her salty lips. She brought her left hand up to my chest and slowly moved it back downward as we kissed. That was how we initiated our sexual relationship.

Afterward, she rested her head on my shoulder and rubbed my chest as we sat on the bench. It all seemed so natural. No little voice in my head tried to second-guess the situation. It was clearly just two individuals looking to connect with one another. It was the most relaxing carnal experience I'd had in a long time. After a few minutes, we slowly walked back to the car while talking and laughing.

The next weekend, I finished putting the top boards on the deck. It looked awesome, even better than I had imagined. Things were starting to come together around the house.

As I cleaned up the site, Atia walked into the backyard. "Hey, Doc. Whatcha doin'?"

"Just cleaning up. What are you up to?"

She walked up the stairs onto the deck. "Wow, this looks great! Is there anything you can't do?"

"I'm sure there's plenty. But it's nice to have a place to barbecue now. And you can even see a little of the bay from here."

She leaned over to look at the peek-a-boo view as she hung onto me for support. "I don't know, Doc; you probably won't be able to put that in the listing when you go to sell." We laughed at my optimism. As we stood there, she started rubbing up against me and pushed me onto the cooler of Vitamin Water I had next to me. She then proceeded to do what she had so many times before. The woman was shameless.

Afterward, I asked her what our little agreement was really all about. She just lay there for a few seconds before saying it was just something she liked, and I shouldn't question it.

I knew I had very little to do with her ecstasy, but I didn't mind so much. I just reaped the benefits and called it good. We talked for a few minutes before she left. I continued working on planting shrubs and trees in the front yard.

On Sunday morning, I got a text message from Erika. She wanted to come over and check out the kitchen remodel; she was thinking about remodeling her own kitchen and needed some ideas. I called her back and told her to come over.

Erika knocked at the door as Mike was leaving for work. He let her in, and shut the door behind him.

I showed her around before we ended up in the media room. We sat and talked for a few minutes before she leaned over to kiss me. We didn't have sex that day, but other things did happen.

As the late morning turned to afternoon, we sat together, laughed, and told stories. The comfort between us was natural and stress-free as if we'd known each other for years. It was too bad she was married. My curiosity led me to ask, "Is your husband around much?"

"My husband?"

"Yeah, you know, the guy you're married to?"

She laughed, “I think I’ve seen him around.”

“No, seriously. Do you guys have some kind of open relationship or something? Would he be okay with this?”

“Our relationship isn’t necessarily open, but more of a ‘don’t ask, don’t tell’ kind of thing. We’re good to each other, but we don’t spend a lot of time together. We have other objects of interest every now and then, and we don’t hold back that natural urge.”

Around one o’clock, Erika had to get to an appointment, so I went back to my landscaping.

No sooner did I step outside than Atia pulled up across the street. I went down to the driveway and greeted her as she walked toward me carrying Tupperware.

“Hey, Doc. Want some cupcakes?”

“You know it’s the second quickest way to my heart!”

She opened up the container and I took one.

“Is Mike home?” she asked.

“He’s at work. Why do you ask?”

“Because I think we should go inside. I only have a few minutes, and yesterday wasn’t enough. I need more!”

Before answering, I needed time to figure out how to make it happen since I feared I still smelled of Erika. “Okay, but I need to take a quick shower first. I haven’t taken one yet today.”

“Whatever, just hurry up,” she said.

We both went inside and I told her to meet me in my bedroom in ten minutes. I don’t remember thinking about absolutely anything as I took a shower. Having random sex was what I’d always done.

I came out wrapped only in a towel. She was already in my bed and pulled back the comforter to invite me in. Without thought, I jumped in next to her.

She took the lead and my body immediately submitted. We were having sex, but I was in that strange "shock fog" that had become so familiar. It was like an out-of-body experience. I realized I had passively become a puppet for her fantasies. I became angry that she was manipulating me. She had been the portal that led to my recent increased sexual activity. She was the first to seduce me since I moved to Seattle, and like my brother, she was aggressive.

Afterward, I didn't say anything. Atia put her arm over my chest and told me how much of a turn-on it had been. I, on the other hand, felt ill. The whole event made me sick. I knew I shouldn't have even been with Atia. The carnal portion of our relationship wasn't love or even a manifestation of two individuals' mutual affection. It had become an outlet for aggression, both hers and mine. It was a manifestation of misplaced control, and possibly even anger. We lay there for a few minutes before she got up to go back to her real life. I took another shower to wash off the dirtiness.

Not twenty minutes after Atia left, Summer stopped by again, unannounced. Not surprisingly, she had another sandwich for me. I let her in, but I was really agitated by what had just happened with Atia, and because Summer kept showing up. As we stood in the foyer, I told her much more forcefully that she couldn't just stop by anymore without calling first. I told her I was dating others, and it would be uncomfortable for everyone if she showed up while I was entertaining another woman. I had quite an edge, as recent events percolated within me. My anger, frustration and anxiety resurfaced in a focused, deeper, clearer voice and a puffed up stature.

I could see her mood change as I scolded her. She looked at the floor, but when I was finished, she looked up and said, "You know what? You're not the only one I'm interested in. I'm also seeing a guy named Charlie from my office. At least he treats me with respect and appreciates me!"

## *Point Of Responsibility*

*57. Are you a reactionary person? Do you live your life running from one emotion to the next? Unfortunately, when we do so, we're not using our emotions most efficiently. Emotions are meant to provide a window to the ego. They tell us how the ego perceives our current environment, and what it wants to do about it. Under what circumstances do you feel joy in your life? When are you frustrated? Around whom are you anxious? Are you easily angered? When emotions flare, step back and evaluate them. Take a few deep breaths and stand up straight. Gently twist your body from left to right. Stretch out. Breathe. Reevaluate the emotion. Does it really matter in the grand scheme of things? Would the situation matter a year from now? Does it have relevance to the evolution of your soul? Chances are good that the emotion does not help your cause. When you become the observer of your own life in this way, your perceptions quickly change from the "right now," into "truth." Live in the state of being present, instead of in the state of emotion.*

*58. Do you, or have you ever in your past, projected your emotions onto others? Do you take out your misery, anger or frustration on those around you? If the answer is no, the world is a lovelier place with you in it. But if you have been known to do so, you have a responsibility to yourself and your environment to change your negative behavior into positive. When you're showing others the selfish story of your ego, it is less than becoming. Those in control and who have self-confidence are more able to put irrationality aside and respect those around them. As the saying goes, we attract more with honey than we do vinegar. Think for a moment how it might feel to those around you when you're visibly stewing about something. Does it give you a sense of power over your environment when others have to walk around on eggshells to avoid angering you further? Investigate all the subtle nuances of this topic, for it has wide-reaching implications and may reveal patterns throughout your life. It's a tough one, but be diligent and honest with yourself. You will not regret the process. When you find yourself in an emotional state, use the techniques you've already learned to recalibrate. Let the emotion recede. Practice this every single time emotions flare, and then quickly move into constructive thought patterns. Control your environment. Don't let it control you.*

Things were going south quickly. So I physically stepped back, took a deep breath and said, "Okay, look, we're both pretty stressed out here. I don't mean anything bad, but I just don't think it's a good idea for you to show up without letting me know you're coming. Can you at least understand that?"

"Yes, and I promise I won't do it anymore," she agreed.

"Thank you," I said. "That's all I want, just a little heads up. It's no big deal, right?"

"Yeah, you're right," she said. We stood there facing each other for a few seconds before she passed me the cellophane-wrapped sandwich. "You might as well have the sandwich."

"There's no poison in it, right?" I joked.

"Not this time," she laughed.

We went outside and sat on the front steps to share some meaningless banter. As I took a bite of the sandwich, I noticed Atia's little sports car rolling down the street toward my house. I hoped to God she wasn't going to stop. I was supremely relieved when she just gave a quick honk and a wave. Summer didn't think anything of it. When I was done, I got up, gave her a hug and went back to planting trees.

Working in the garden and on remodels always allowed plenty of time for introspective thought. As I worked that day, I began to think about the previous two weeks. I'd had a lot of sex, by any standard. I hadn't aggressively gone after women; I just let things happen. Most of them had been patients at one point or another, but I rationalized it by telling myself it was okay since we weren't having sex within the office. We were all consenting adults. I could not be held one hundred percent accountable for what was happening, and I was sure no one would say anything. Since we all had major things to lose, I felt I had some form of leverage on each woman involved. And if something ever did come up, or a complaint was ever filed,

I could just say the women had pursued me. I made sure I never pursued anyone. The women always took the first step. I felt I had protected myself the best I could.

The following week got off to a busy start. Atia stopped by work for a quick hello and brought up the "drive-by."

"So who's the chick you were with the other day?"

"Just a friend," I said.

"That's okay; you don't have to tell. I have my ways, so I already know who she is. Atherton's a small community, you know. All I'm going to say is that she's bad news, and none of the other Atherton moms like her. She's just weird, and I think you can do better." She quickly turned and walked out. "Bye Doc!"

A few minutes later, Summer called to invite me over for lunch. I was bored and hungry, so I obliged.

When I reached Summer's house, I walked up the stairs to the side door. Some groovy jazz tunes rolled through the partially opened screen door. When I knocked, Summer's voice invited me in. She was putting the finishing touches on some kind of salad. She put down the wooden spatula and gave me a hug. "I'm so glad you could come over. I figured you were getting sick of meeting me at your place, so I thought I would change the venue. Do you want a quick tour?"

I turned and looked out the picture windows that framed the Olympic Mountains. "Yeah, but I think this is probably the best view, isn't it?"

"I guess so. But let me show you the rest of the house."

"All right," I agreed.

As she showed me around, I quickly realized the only asset she had was the view. The house was dark, old, and the layout was horrible. The furniture that filled the joint was weird and eclectic, none of it comfortable. I had previously thought the woman had an eye for beauty, but I was obviously wrong.

We came back down to the kitchen and had a bite to eat. Afterward, we sat on the pink velvet couch. She almost immediately planted a kiss on me. After only a few seconds, I got that same weird feeling like I was kissing my mother. It really grossed me out. The internal sensations were so incredibly mottled. As we kissed, I wondered why I kept hanging out with her. Being with her was really starting to repulse me, but not enough for me to deny her propositions. We fooled around a little. Afterward, I went to the gym for a quick workout and a shower before heading back to work.

I'd been living quite a pace in the recent weeks. Not only was I continuing to dredge up the past, but I was having a lot of sex. And I hadn't tied the two together. I worked nonstop on various parts of the remodel, as well as running the clinic on a full time basis. I had a ton of energy and was never quite satiated with anything. I felt I had to fill every moment with something. The noise in my head was getting louder, and I was attempting to cover it up with more unserving activity each passing day.

Two nights later, I decided to check out the new Italian joint in the village. It was supposed to be all the rage, with truly authentic cuisine. When I got there, I was quickly seated at a small table along the wall. It was great for people watching. The place was comfortable, quiet and charming.

As I perused the menu, a server came up to inform me that a man across the restaurant had sent over a fine bottle of Bordeaux for me. I looked over to see who had done such a nice thing. It was a fellow I'd seen a few times who had a carpal tunnel problem that we quickly reconditioned. He was a well-known commercial developer in the area, and an all-around nice guy. The guy was worth tens of millions and he and I got along quite well. I sent him a wave and a smile and allowed the server to uncork the wine. He poured a taster and I took a sip. It was unbelievable. After the pour, I raised my glass to the fine gentleman, nodded, took another sip and enjoyed.

No sooner did I set my glass down than a patient, named Erin, came waddling over in her high heels. I hadn't seen Erin for months, but she was always a welcome surprise. She was a little firecracker and never at a loss during story time. One of the things I found enjoyable about her was her stylistically flamboyant nature, among other things. She was always dressed to the nines in the latest fashion. She had beautifully styled hair and nails, and impeccable skin.

Erin was also a bundle of energy. She never stopped. The woman was always doing something. During her last few visits to my office, she invited me to meet her and her friends for happy hour. But every time she asked, I was already dating someone new, so I declined.

I stood up, gave her a hug and invited her to sit. She immediately started talking, even before she sat down. She told me she was returning to Atherton from a happy hour event downtown.

I asked whether she was meeting someone for dinner. "No, I just don't want to go home yet. It's been a long day and I want a good glass of wine."

"Well, look at what I have." I picked up the bottle and poured a glass for her. I hadn't even finished pouring before she started telling me about her crappy day at work. She fully detailed her massive consumption at happy hour and laughed about how amazing it was that she had actually made the drive to Atherton without being pulled over.

We went through a whole bottle of wine with bread and a fried zucchini appetizer. I just sat listening to her as I ate my food. After half an hour, I became bored with her incessant droning on. She didn't interest me at all. I wondered why I'd ever put her on a pedestal. I tried to focus as the white-collared, early thirties woman talked crap about her fiancé, who was out of town, as well as her friends, job, city and everything else.

As Erin continued on, I threw around some pretty interesting questions in my head. Why did I continue to bring people like her into my life? Why was I becoming increasingly anxious as I sifted through my emotions? Why was I living in that cloudy, murky and uncertain place every hour of my existence over the past couple of weeks? What was going on within me? Why couldn't I just be okay?

I took a drink of wine and the switch flipped again. I started to think about how attractive she was, even as she talked her gibberish. After a few more drinks, I found her voice and conversation increasingly annoyed me. I despised how she blamed everyone else for her unhappiness.

But Erin was so pretty. I could smell her cocoa butter caressed, light brown skin. Her big brown eyes and long eyelashes seemed to drag me in like a Venus flytrap. Her long, wavy brown hair bounced and flowed as she became more animated with more wine.

I began to tear myself apart with the ridiculous dichotomy manifesting within me. On one hand, I was turned on by Erin's incredible allure, yet she genuinely repulsed me. It was all so confusing.

That was when the front door opened and in walked one of my favorite patients of all time, with her handsome husband. Nila was a local, well-to-do artist. She was sharp as a tack, self-confident and had a mouth like a trucker. She had a certain, magnetic charisma that was highly attractive. When she would come into the office, it wasn't uncommon to hear us cackle on behind closed doors. We simply had a great time chewing the fat with one another. It was relaxing and jovial; exactly what life was meant to be.

Nila and I waved to one another as she took her seat. Meanwhile, Erin was just saying the same thing over and over. But even Erin needed a break every now and again. She excused herself to visit the restroom.

After Erin disappeared, Nila came up, grabbed my face between both hands, smiled and said, "I love you so much. What a shining light you are!"

"What are you talking about?" I asked.

"I just like how you handle yourself. It's refreshing, especially in such a stuffy neighborhood like this. Everyone wishes they were you, you know."

"Why wouldn't they? I have a great life! You know you're the coolest patient I have, right?"

"I think I'm just one of many, deary. Just one of many with a crush on the good doctor."

"Get out of here. Your husband awaits your return. And I'm awaiting Miss Talkative." We laughed and hugged, and I waved to her husband as she made her way back to their table.

As I sat there alone for a few moments, I felt guilty that Nila thought I was such a wonderful person. She obviously didn't know about my recent activities. That one cascade of thoughts sparked a moment of clarity. I had convinced myself that the last couple of weeks had just been me having a good time, blowing off steam. I wasn't worried about what others thought. I was just living my life. On the other hand, I knew what I was doing was less than honorable. But it was difficult to care too much. I was getting what I needed, and so was everyone else.

Erin made her return in mid-thought. When she sat down, her butt almost missed the chair. We softly laughed together and finished our second bottle of wine. It only took a few more minutes before we decided to take off. I paid the tab and donned my tweed blazer.

Once we were outside, Erin asked whether I could drive her home. I wasn't at all stunned by the request, as she had been slurring her words for about an hour. I agreed, and as we started driving, I asked where she lived. She answered by asking whether she could see the work I'd done on the house. I wasn't allowed to answer, and was forced to listen to her go on about how she was a whiz in the kitchen and how she wanted to see whether I set it up properly. When she was finally finished, I quipped, "This better not be some crazy attempt to take advantage of me." I laughed after I said it, but noticed she didn't. As I stared forward, negotiating the road, she held her gaze on my face.

We pulled up to my house and went in. I filled up a couple of glasses of water and I gave her the general tour, finishing in the media room.

"You did a great job on the kitchen. I'm impressed. Most guys have no idea how to design one. It's obvious you have taste."

I raised my glass of water, "To taste!" We clanged glasses and took a drink. We sat on the carpet in front of the new gas fireplace. After less than five seconds of silence, she jumped on top of me and we started down the road on which I'd been so recently active. After a few minutes, I was confronted with my ever-familiar dichotomous thoughts again. I tasted the cocoa butter on her skin. Then I thought about how her fiancé would feel if he knew where his girlfriend was. What would he do if he found out? And then I thought about how I was about to have sex with yet another patient. Even though it had been some time since Erin had been to my office, that activity was inappropriate. Then she kissed my neck and came back to my lips. It wasn't a good idea. But soon enough, there were no more thoughts of anything except the obvious.

Afterward, she kissed me, put her dress back on and asked me to take her back to her truck. She was quiet for the first time ever in my presence. I took her back and we parted ways for the evening.

Later in the week, I received a text message from Erin. She asked whether I would like to meet her for cocktails downtown after work. It was Friday, and I could always use a drink on Fridays, so I quickly shot her back a text letting her know I'd be there at around seven o'clock. After work, I met her and a couple of her friends. We all shared some conversation and drank a few martinis. Then she received a phone call from a friend who was having a boyfriend breakup crisis. Erin decided she better go comfort her friend. I had no desire to hang out with Erin's other friends, so I left when she did. I burned a few hours at the pub before heading to a party at the home of my friends, Sara and Dave.

I arrived at their place around nine p.m. The place was already jumping; people had obviously been drinking for some time. One funny thing about the people in Atherton was that they never missed a chance to booze it up. High society was fun and had its perks.

I walked in to a small uproar. I was immediately handed a margarita, which I quickly downed and had refilled. Sara took me by the arm and introduced me to everyone. I met no fewer than twenty-five real estate agents, who were always trying to meet new people for whom to buy or sell. There were bankers, accountants, developers and the like present. The place was full of the big players within Atherton. I recognized most of them from various events, and I had drunk with most of them at one point or another.

The music bumped into the warm summer night as we all continued with the inebriation. At around one in the morning, people started stumbling home, and by three, only a handful were left. I sat on the couch with a cool woman named Sophia who was telling me about her business. We were both a little too drunk to drive home, so we stayed the night, each of us on a separate couch. But as the night turned into morning, Sophia had made her way to my couch, and there was yet another random hookup. It reminded me of college, but that was as far as the thought went. It was basically just more of the same, simply going through the motions.

The next day I worked around the house and then put in some hours at the office. That night, I got a text message from Summer. She was wondering whether I wanted some company. I knew exactly what that meant. I was tired and my defenses were low, so I gave her a phone call and asked her whether she wanted to meet me at a little hole-in-the-wall bar for a drink. She told me she was only a couple of blocks from my house, which wasn't really surprising, given her past behavior. I told her it had been a long day, so I just wanted to freshen up a bit. She agreed to meet me at the bar.

When I got there, Summer and I had a couple of drinks before heading outside. I walked her to her car as we shared some meaningless conversation.

I knew where it was all headed. It seemed like I couldn't get away from my compulsions. They followed me everywhere I went. I wasn't actively seeking out their reinforcement, but at the end of the day, they always got what they wanted.

Summer turned to face me, grasped my upper arms, and pulled me toward her for a kiss. She leaned her back up against the passenger door and said, "I want you to take control and do what you want with me."

It was the first time we'd actually gone all the way. Through the whole thing I heard a thousand screams from above and within telling me to stop, but I was in the fog again and didn't listen. Afterward, she tried to hug and kiss me, but I was mentally and emotionally vacant. I wasn't there anymore. I told her I didn't feel very well and needed to go home. We parted ways and I went home. All I wanted to do was cry.

## Point Of Responsibility

*59. Are there compulsions of any type in your life that create anxiety? (Compulsions are feelings of being compelled to some irrational action, which is always unnecessary and often repetitive. Some examples are overeating, overworking, over emoting, drinking too much, being in your head all the time, underachieving, boredom, procrastinating, living in constant entertainment, and the like.) If so, do you wish you could stop these behaviors, but by rationalizing them, you allow yourself to continue the behaviors? Do you spend most of your time wondering "why" such behaviors recur? The primary key to eradicating such unwanted behavior is to acknowledge it exists. Second, you must choose whether you want to continue letting life control you, or if you want to step up and claim your power to create your own life. Third, when you figure out why the compulsions have manifested, deal with the issue(s) once and for all. Be honest with yourself. With some inspired meditation, determine where your issues stem from. Don't let them control you any longer, and don't cover them up by pretending everything's all right, because it's obviously not. If it were, you wouldn't have compulsive behavior. This part of the process can be difficult if you choose it to be. But it can also be tremendously growth-rich. Responsibly say what you need to say and do what you need to do to let the uncovered emotions free. Talk with friends and family members about the issues that pertain to them. Apologize to the people you need to. Forgive those who've wronged you. Forgive yourself for the things you've done. This is your chance to live in the present and to atone, so allow the currents to run deep to clear out the negative. Some people might say they don't retain the power to choose because they are physiologically addicted to their compulsions. But the truth is most of us DO have the power to choose. We've just been led to believe, by mainstream life and by our ego, that we are victims; that once we have a mild to moderate dysfunction within us, we haven't the ability to change it. This couldn't be further from the truth. We are the ONLY ones who can change it. WE have the power, not therapists, not drugs, and not the compulsions themselves. The most difficult part is flying in the face of your fear toward that which you inherently know as good. I challenge you to abandon the negative feedback loops that you may be addicted to by filling your head with visions and thoughts that reinforce your wonderful life. To review: 1) Acknowledge that you live with a compulsion. Don't justify it. Just notice it. 2) Choose to let go of the compulsion; otherwise, you're choosing to keep it. 3) Deal with the compulsion responsibly so it no longer carries any weight in your life. Take all the time you need, as this is an incredibly important step in the process. It will help you to stop living in the past, and bring you into the present. Only as a last result, seek talk therapy to get you over any remaining hurdles. 4) When the negative feedback loops try to reintroduce themselves, or you start thinking of compulsions and addictions from the past, STOP! Get out of your head immediately. Disengage them, and realize they're just projections of your ego telling you how much better you felt with the activity, when in reality, it is ruining your life. If possible, engage in a conversation with someone. Don't talk about the compulsion or thought. Let it die. If there's no one around, or conversation is inappropriate, get up and go outside. Take a walk. Stretch out. As you do so, reaffirm your positive life with visions and verbal affirmations that reinforce it. When you get back inside, get back on track with the action steps that reinforce the same. When you choose to reclaim your own power, there is no doubt that your environment will, and must, change to allow for new growth. Know that relationships might be transformed or lost, and more gratifying and productive people will begin to show up in your life. Keep moving forward. Don't look back, except to appreciate how far you've come. Remember, the compulsions are only manifestations of deeper anxieties. They are NOT the primary issue. And the primary issue to which you may attribute your negative behavior is still only a crutch that enables you with an excuse to continue behaving poorly.*

The next two weeks were a blur of sex, drinking and more sex. I had opened up a portal that I wasn't able to close. I rotated between Erika, Summer, Atia and anyone else I could fit into my heavy schedule. All I wanted to do was act compulsively. I felt subhuman, like a crocodile must feel. Nothing else was important.

Those two weeks were like an out-of-body experience for me. I felt I wasn't a part of my own life, like I was watching everything from above. I was completely caught up in the muck and was thoroughly confused. When I wasn't at work, I walked around in that ever familiar "shock fog" as I tried to fulfill my daily responsibilities. The only thing I could concentrate on was who I was going to meet and when. I had consciously made the decision just to let things happen. It was all I knew. Whatever the consequences of the activity, I would just power through it, like I did everything else in my life.

As each encounter ended, I told myself I wouldn't do it again. But the next day would bring new waves of fear and anxiety. I reached out to satiate the demons temporarily, at any cost. The behavior kept getting riskier. It was like each experience upped the ante to the next one. I'd drive to Atia's place close to the times her boyfriend was likely to get off work and show up unannounced. And the next day, I would visit Erika at her house, the whole time worrying whether her husband would suddenly walk through the door, home early from a business trip.

I even exploited my friendship with Chloe. She was sincerely concerned with me, and tried everything in her power to get me out of the funk I was living. But she didn't know the truth, or the extent of my depravity. On one particular evening, we ate and drank, and ultimately turned our relationship into a sexual one. I felt guilty that I had slept with her under the guise of friendship, when it was really just more acting out on my part. I took advantage of her. It made me feel sick to my stomach. As we lay there on the bed, I felt it necessary to apologize to her for these things. After I did so, she just told me to chill out. She didn't think I had taken advantage of her at all. She told me she gotten something out of it too. And then she said something that surprised me. "You know I have feelings for you, right?"

"Well, yeah," I said.

"Okay. I know who you really are, and that person is beautiful. And whenever you're ready, I'd love for us to pursue a good relationship with one another. I want to give you a beautiful baby. I think you'd be a great father."

"You know I'm not ready for that," I replied.

"I know, sweetheart; I know you're not. But I'm here whenever you're done with whatever it is you think you need to do."

I left the next morning and seemed to be more confused than ever.

I started to escape heavily into the landscape remodel. I worked harder than I'd ever worked before. It was like running a marathon every evening after work, and then running another one late into each night to fill my voracious appetite for escapism. I felt like I was going crazy.

As far as the business was concerned, I finally came to the conclusion that Claudia was lying and possibly even stealing cash. I realized that my pie-in-the-sky attitude toward her evolution as a good employee was unwarranted. The fact was that everything was messed up, and it was getting worse. Patients were increasingly unhappy with her service. It was time to find someone new, and I had to do it quietly.

Physically, I was losing weight and felt beaten down. I couldn't recall being more stressed and tired in my whole life.

I thought seriously about selling the practice, but quickly came to the conclusion that selling wouldn't solve any of the issues at hand. The issues were mine, no matter where I worked and what I did. I had to continue my own evolution to get past all of it. I was still a very good doctor and the clinic was growing. I just needed to figure out my personal crap, and I had to do it quickly.

Between work and all the dalliances, I was surprisingly able to finish both the landscape and the kitchen. In fact, they were both completed within the same week. As Mike and I uncorked our first bottle of wine in the new kitchen, I had a metaphorical understanding of what the kitchen and landscape represented for me. They were representations of the endless pursuit of bettering myself. I had hope that since the remodel was complete, maybe I too, could become new and improved on the inside. As Mike and I sipped wine and sat in the living room, I noticed that the diary from my sister was sitting out on a side table. I wrote a few things in it to clear my mind and to process the metaphors rolling around within it. After doing so, the next couple of nights were the best sleep I ever had.

Three nights later, I was in my bed sleeping when I heard a knock at my bedroom door. It was Summer. I looked at the clock. It was 2 a.m. I jumped up and asked what she was doing.

"I put Emily to bed and wasn't very tired. So I was just stopping by to see whether you needed anything." Her breath reeked of alcohol.

But it wasn't out of the question for me. I was still half asleep and didn't think it would cause any harm. So I let her in. Right in the middle of it all, as Summer was on top of me, I started to hear what sounded like a girl urinating. And then I felt warmth beginning to surround my pelvis. That was when my life changed forever.

As Summer relieved herself on me, I finally realized I was in the middle of living the complete manifestation of the worst-case scenario for my life. I had completely bottomed out emotionally. I was more out of control than I had ever been. I hadn't consciously realized that my recent actions had been elicited by dredging up the past. It was the most obvious and direct manifestation of old structures, habits and events revisited, and I couldn't even see it. My ego didn't want to let those things go; it wanted me to stay within my comfort zone, and it fought hard to cloud my judgment. I was making poorer decisions and living for escapism more than ever before. I had no respect for anything—not the women I was with, not how my actions would impact the lives of their family members, and least of all, I had no respect for myself.

I had thoroughly executed my plan to break down my old dysfunctional blueprint, but I hadn't filled that space with anything functional. Since I had created no new operating software, meaning good habits, the remnants of old habits forced their way into my daily life, and with a vengeance. I hadn't fully purged them because I was too "in my head" to understand what I was doing was not good. I had rationalized and justified everything, and never took full responsibility for my actions.

### *Point Of Responsibility*

*60. Our lives are ultimately determined by decisions we make throughout each day. Every decision you make leads to your future. Active decision-making is much more powerful than passive decision-making. When confronted with a decision, no matter what the magnitude, first make sure the directions you decide to take fall in line with your personal philosophy. If the decision is an emotional one, stop where you are, breathe deeply, close your eyes and envision being illuminated with a wonderful light from above; the light of truth. Let it illuminate the truth within you and allow it to wash remnants of ego away. When ready, ask yourself again which direction you feel is best. The truth will be illuminated; all you have to do is trust it. Learn to follow that intuition always. Follow your heart, or your sixth sense. We all know the difference between right and wrong. Don't forget that the ego will always steer you back to the way you've always done things, back into your comfort zone. It doesn't care what's right or wrong. Its sole purpose is to make a name for itself. When the ego flares, think of the consequences of your actions. If they don't fall in line with your core ideals and philosophy, you mustn't follow that path, no matter how much your ego pushes. When you make decisions this way, you will honestly be able to stand by them. You'll have confidence because you're living consciously. Make sound, educated decisions. And stick to them with integrity.*

# Part Two:

# Taking Responsibility

Chapter Thirteen:

# Throwing Out the Trash

It was about six-thirty on a Sunday morning. Rays of sun made their way across my bedroom. I felt strangely wonderful. Nothing ached and I was fully rested. I pulled the covers off myself and swung my feet to the floor.

For the past half hour, my phone had been blowing up with that ever-familiar text message signal. I was amazed at how I was still so viscerally attached to the connection between that noise and Esther's face. I wondered whether it would ever go away.

I jumped up and gently twisted my spine to the left, to the right, and then stretched out my neck. I took a few deep breaths and walked across the room to pick up the phone. It was probably my dad or sister just saying hello. I scrolled to check the most recent messages. As the number became illuminated, I felt an immediate weakness in my knees and had the sense like I might vomit. It was Esther.

I wondered what she wanted. It had been almost five months since the great window-breaking incident. Before I stopped to think about it, I texted her back, "How can I help you?"

She replied within seconds, "Church this morning?" When we were still together, we attended a church on the north side of town a couple of times. She was scouting for new clients, and I knew a couple of patients who frequented the place. It was an enjoyable experience; good stories, good people, spirituality without much religion or dogma. It was refreshing.

I shook off the cobwebs and sent her back a message telling her to pick me up at eight.

As I showered, I tried to figure out Esther's motives. She never did anything without careful planning. My mind screamed, "She wants to get back together, stupid!" But I allowed her to surprise me. I didn't create any expectations around it. I felt powerful. I had to prove to myself that if I were ever thrown back into the lion's den, I could safely make it out alive. I smiled at the opportunity as I washed my hair.

Before long, she was out in front, waiting in her clown car. I grabbed a light coat and ran down to meet her. I opened the car door and peeked inside.

"Hi," I said.

"Hi," she replied through a fake smile.

"Are you going to shoot me or anything?"

She laughed a little, embarrassed by her previous behavior. "No."

"Are you going to drive really fast to some kind of human chop shop and drop me off for someone else to shoot me?"

"What's a chop shop? Do you mean like Chinese food or something?"

"Forget it. I'm just being silly." I smiled and jumped in. I knew she wasn't sharp enough to put a plan like that together if she had three years to coordinate it.

We attended the ceremony and decided to get some lunch afterward. The inevitable conversation was about to begin. I knew she couldn't hold out forever.

"Mark, I'm really sorry for the way things went down. I should have listened to you more. I was really a jerk, but I do love you. Can we try again? Please? Can we just try again?" She continued on to describe the things that floated around in her head.

I was amazed, not with her efforts to get me back, but that she was actually trying to tell me how she felt. And she wasn't yelling, screaming or scheming. But there was no way I would ever let myself enter into a relationship with her again. All I now felt for her was pity.

I calmly told her I loved her when we were together, but I didn't want to be with her that way any longer. I told her I had tried everything within my power to make it work between us, but it simply wasn't meant to be.

She told me how much she had changed since we'd broken up, but I didn't believe it. I knew who she really was. I leaned over and gave her a true, honest and sincere hug, something I'd never been able to do before without disdain or contempt. It felt good. By giving her that hug, I released many of the demons from within myself. I honored their existence and understood much of my recent pain was due to turning a blind eye to them. Squeezing that confused, angry and frustrated being allowed me to see how I had projected myself onto others on many occasions.

Esther wept on my shoulder for a few seconds before her ego showed up. She recoiled tightly and wiped her eyes. "That's fine. It was worth a shot, right?" She sent over another fake smile.

We spent much of the day together walking around downtown. Around four in the afternoon, I was getting a little tired and wanted to go home. On the way there, we stopped to pick up a pizza. We got to my place, and I threw it in the oven. We sat on the couch as we waited for it to bake, her head buried into my shoulder.

Then she said, "See? This feels good, doesn't it? It could be like this all the time. You just have to give it a chance. Don't be a quitter. Let's give it another chance." She awaited my response.

Still, the only emotion that came up was pity. The saying, "I still love you, I'm just not in love with you" ran through my mind, but I'd never use it. I didn't use clichés. "Esther, we can do what we're doing right now, but I won't be in a relationship with you again. I'm sorry."

"Do you want to fool around?" She was upping the ante, but I was up to the task.

"No, I don't want to fool around." I laughed a little bit. "You'll do anything to get your way, won't you?"

"I just want us to be together. Let's give it another shot! Please?"

For about ten minutes, she pushed hard, but I didn't allow it. For one of the first times in my life, I was acting from the inside. And I wasn't going to be persuaded. I held strong. I was both empathetic and confident. She subsequently went through all the emotions within our conversation. But I was as strong as a rock. I didn't get overemotional. I didn't overreact. I didn't raise my voice. I didn't allow her to sting me with her verbal barbs. And ultimately, she just stopped. She gave up, at least for the time being. I reached over and pulled her toward me again. "I'm sorry, Esther. I think you see how this is going to go, right?"

"Fine. But I still think it would be better the second time."

"You can think that if you want to, but it's not going to happen."

She excused herself to go out to check her phone in the car.

When she came back inside, we ate the pizza and watched a movie. She ended up spending the night. We slept in the same bed. She tried a few times to get things going, but I thwarted each of her advances. Taking my own power back was gratifying. At no point in my life could I remember ever having done that.

In the morning, I walked her to her car and noticed I hadn't rolled up my car windows the night before. They must've been open the whole previous day. That was definitely not like me. But I had been a little off in recent times, so I just let it go. On the way past my car, I also noticed the diary sitting on the back seat, on the other side of the open window. That was a little strange because I didn't remember taking it out of the house. But it was obvious I must have.

I gave Esther a hug as we stood next to her car. "Are you sure we can't be together?" she asked.

"Come on; give me a break here," I said with a smile on my face. "We can hang out as friends, but that's as far as it's going, period."

"Well, okay. I guess I'll see you later then."

Esther and I hung out a few more times that week; it was actually a lot of fun. But I knew she was just on her best behavior. The real Esther would eventually show up to wreak some kind of havoc. It was just a matter of time, and I knew that time was quickly approaching. On each of our successive friendly meetings, I could feel the anxiety within her increasing. I didn't want any part of what she would release. I needed to get out of that environment, so I finally told her it wasn't a good idea to hang out anymore. We were finished, and I wished her the best.

As expected, Esther's voicemails and text messages over the next week grew increasingly angry. She peppered me with the same old inferences that I wasn't a real man and that I was a quitter. I stopped fielding her phone calls and text messages. I just deleted them. I remained powerful and calm, and I continued to make good decisions.

It was early September, and I hadn't dated anyone other than Esther for a little over a week. I didn't even have sex with anyone. I did, however, continue to receive phone calls and text messages from women. I didn't answer any of them. I laid low. The storm was over, and I had to figure out a way to let them all know I was done living my life the way I had. I was finished with noisy, useless, unserving behavior. I had to treat each situation a little differently, so as to not anger any of the women. The last thing I needed was an angry patient I'd had sex with, so I calculated how each of the situations could go. It was time to manipulate for the greater good. I was no longer going to put myself in a submissive position. I would live on my terms, and those terms didn't involve being in questionable relationships.

I told Atia over the phone that I wasn't going to allow the sexual relationship with her anymore. Since she was a patient, such activity was completely inappropriate. I told her I was cleaning up my act, and I was going to live my life with integrity. I even asked her help to make sure things like we'd been through didn't happen again. I didn't actually expect her to do so, but I wanted to give her the idea that I was asking her for help. She took pity on me and agreed she wouldn't force herself on me anymore.

When I called Betsy, she more than understood my situation. "I just want to see you happy, Doc. Don't worry about me. I'd never do anything to hurt you. Our little fling is between you and me, and no one else." I thanked her and went to the next person on the list.

Things seemed to be going relatively smoothly until I talked with Erika. I didn't think it proper to end our deal over the phone. I genuinely cared for her and wanted to tell her to her face. So I invited her over to my house for a glass of wine. I was sure she thought the evening was going to end up like it had on most other occasions, so I waited until we were a couple of glasses deep into conversation before I told her I didn't think it appropriate we have sexual relations from that point forward. She put her hand on my arm and said, "Oh, I could take or leave that part of our relationship. I just want to be close to you."

She had thrown me a curve ball. Not knowing what to say next, I asked, "What do you mean?"

"It's just nice to be close to you. You're a good person, and this world doesn't have many good people in it. So I just cherish the time we get to spend together."

I really liked her. I wondered whether we could have a platonic relationship. But with my new resolve, I couldn't put myself in that position. I didn't want to risk it. If I slipped, the results could be catastrophic. Even though I was still attracted to Erika and she presented an opportunity for a more subdued relationship, it was still improper. "I really like you, Erika. You're just so cool. And we get along really well. But I can't be in any type of relationship with you. It has to end."

Her eyes quickly filled with tears. I hated it, but I was doing the right thing. "We can still hang out, can't we?" she asked.

"I'd really like to, but it's not right. I'm cleaning up my life, and it's bad for both of us. I'm done with self-destructive behavior."

She smiled through the mess of tears and hair, "Okay, but I don't like it. I think we're great together. If you ever change your mind, you know where to find me." She gave me a huge hug and said, "I'm so sorry you haven't been doing well. I'm here for you, however, you need me to be." I again told her I was sorry, and after a few minutes, she was gone.

A couple of days later, I was working in my yard while I contemplated how to approach things with Summer. Our situation was the most delicate. I didn't know where she was within her own head, and I hadn't talked to her since she urinated on me. As I pulled some weeds and contemplated my options, Summer's SUV pulled up across the street. She got out and walked up the driveway. I greeted her with a "Hello" as she slowly came up the stairs to the front yard.

She said, "Hi," but nothing else. I could tell she wanted to talk about something, but refrained. I was happy she came over so I could end things on a decent note. But as I struggled for something to say, I felt the heat rise up from my gut. I was feeling a little angry that she showed up unannounced yet again.

I blurted out, "Did we have a date today?" She just looked at me as if I had caught her off guard.

"No," she softly replied.

"What are you doing here?" I asked.

She stumbled for some words to fill the space. "Uhh, I just wanted to talk to you about my friend and some other things."

"I'm sorry, but I can't get over the promise you made to call before coming over. Are you checking up on me?" I was being irrational. I hated the way I had let everyone control me, so I felt the need to stand my ground. "Do you want to catch me with someone else?" I knew it was harsh, but she hadn't received the clear picture that we weren't in a relationship. She had no rights to me.

She stopped coming up the stairs. "I just wanted to talk about us."

"What do you mean by 'us'?" I asked.

"Our relationship, Mark."

"Summer, we don't have a relationship. We've had some good times together and some decent conversation. But your lack of respect for my wishes and your stalker-like behavior is just too much for me right now. In case you haven't noticed, I have a lot on my plate. And I thought keeping you up to date with all of it would win me some points in the 'let's keep it relaxed' category. But I guess I'm wrong. You and your drama tire me out. And the fact that we had sex is completely wrong, even if you are separated from your husband. I shouldn't have allowed it to happen, any of it. Now, can you please stop showing up at all hours unannounced?" I hadn't any idea where all my rage was coming from. I just threw it out there like a rain of bullets.

Behind her eyes was a raging fire. She screamed that she was done with me, turned and walked quickly back to her car. Before she got in, she turned to me and said, "You're a coward!" Then she stomped her foot, got in her car and took off down the street.

The situation could have gone better, but I was glad it was over. I had significantly reduced the drama in my life and no longer had to wonder whether Summer lurked around every corner.

Unfortunately, the festivities weren't quite finished. Later that day, I received an email from her that erased any curiosity as to how she was looking at everything. She proceeded to tell me the real reason for her visit earlier that day. She told me she was completely in love with me, but she had gotten angry after I started reprimanding her. She was angry I had shut her down, called her a stalker, and said she was dramatic.

But there was still more. She then tried to psychoanalyze me using her high school-level understanding of psychotherapy that left all of her suppositions logically flawed. As I read the words, I couldn't believe I'd actually let her into my life.

She continued by letting me know how much of a prize she was, that it was my fault I hadn't allowed our "relationship" to bear fruit, and that she could have been my one true love.

I had never thought of Summer as my meal ticket, but I did understand my role in our "relationship." I had indirectly taken advantage of her being a little lost in life. I had never been forceful with her in any way, but I had gone along for the ride, letting her take the lead. I allowed her to create a fake relationship and to live her fantasies through me. I hadn't seen the harm in it before. But in hindsight, allowing her to create such a fantasy was horribly irresponsible on my part.

That night, I received some great news for a change. The Porsche I had purchased from the East Coast as a gift to myself two weeks earlier was being delivered to me at five the next morning. I was like a little kid on Christmas Eve! I didn't recall ever feeling such anticipation and happiness.

Early the next day, as the sun eked through the marine layer, Natasha sat before me. I'd never named a vehicle before. But from the first moment I saw her, I felt that this car was a representation of my idealistic nature. It embodied the characteristics of not only myself, but of the woman I was seeking as my life partner. The name Natasha was strong, worldly and confident. And it held a vision of beauty, sophistication and practicality. In our first face-to-face meeting, we shared a mutual respect and love that transcended emotion.

The morning was completely quiet as I became familiar with the vehicle I'd wanted since I was eight years old. At that moment, I finally felt a sense of accomplishment. After all the things I'd been through in my life; all the education, all the meaningless jobs, all the situations I'd made it through, and all the great things I'd created, at that very moment I had a sense of accomplishment. The attachment to the vehicle was not materially oriented. It was more metaphorical in nature. It was a manifestation of unbelievable hard work and dedication over many years. It was the first cosmic "Thank you" that actually stirred up deep emotions within me. All the others, like the house, the remodel, the businesses, they were "supposed" to happen. Those things were a part of how it was simply meant to be. The Porsche, on the other hand, was just for my pleasure.

The car glistened in the dew. Her curves created an iridescence across her body as the sun met the metal-flake brown of her skin. She was low to the ground and took a stance of readiness. The car was a piece of artwork.

When I opened the door, it had that vintage car smell. The leather seats and dashboard gleamed. Absolutely no dirt or wear was visible anywhere on her. I jumped in, closed the door and grabbed the steering wheel. I took a deep breath. "Thank you," I said aloud. I melted into the seat and poked around to figure out some of the gauges and controls. After a few minutes, I reached my left hand down and twisted the key to the right. The engine roared to life. It was deep, tough, and sexy. After it warmed for a few minutes and the RPM came to below eight hundred, I tapped the gas as a call to attention. The engine screamed. She was ready to go.

I shifted into first gear and pulled away from the curb. I noticed right away what it was like to drive a car with no power steering. It was tight and highly responsive. As I drove slowly down the road, I could feel every dip and bump. It was the stiffest car I'd ever driven.

I got out to the main road and put the pedal down further for takeoff. It immediately shot me back into my seat. I shifted to second and third, where I had to stay until I hit the interstate. As Natasha and I became acquainted, I noticed I had a silly smile plastered across my face. It wasn't because I was driving a Porsche. It was because I was driving that Porsche. The car and I got along famously. It was like nothing I'd driven before. The BMW was classy. The Mustang was powerful. The little sports cars were fun. But this car was in a league of her own. I eventually pulled onto the interstate and jumped on the gas. I held myself steady in the seat as the engine screamed us quickly up to 80 mph. I laughed out loud with enjoyment. This car was better than any roller coaster, any drug, and certainly any woman. I was in love for real.

I drove around for a couple of hours, but I had to cut it short to make it to work on time. I had a limited schedule that day. After my last patient, I gathered a few things into a duffel bag, jumped back into Natasha and drove toward the Cascades. I'd decided to take a mini road trip to get my bearings and to reconnect with myself. I also had some more relationship issues I intended to sort out during this time.

On my way up to the mountains, I noticed autumn was changing ever more quickly at the higher elevations. Big yellow leaves fell from the maple trees and the evergreens swayed in the gusty, cool mountain air. Natasha and I tested one another in the turns and on the straight-aways. It was the most fun I'd had in years, without a doubt. I pulled into one of the first small towns and stopped for coffee. I checked out the local antique shops and talked with a few business owners. The sun played hide and seek, and the weather was cool and windy. I sat on a park bench and watched the river below as it tumultuously churned over some rocks and then immediately became calm as it continued its journey.

I had some family issues to address. I finished my coffee and took a deep breath before calling my dad. I knew I needed to say some things to him, but I couldn't imagine how it was going to play out. It wasn't like one of those seminar talks I'd practiced over and over. It was going to be a real life conversation where I wouldn't know the outcome beforehand. My heart beat faster.

I made the call and my dad picked up. We discussed the weather before I broached my purpose. "Dad, I'd like to share some things with you that are quite alarming. Some of the things you already know about; others you don't. I sincerely want you to listen to me, so I don't expect or want you to say anything. I'm not accusing you of anything. Okay?"

"Okay, go ahead." His tone told me he was trying to be present.

"First of all, Dad, I love you. And I really love the relationship we've created in recent years. In fact, I cherish it. There's no sense in holding back now, so here it comes. When we all lived back at the farmhouse, Steve molested me. I don't know how many times it happened, but it was more than a few. It's affected my life significantly up until the past week, until I was finally able to get a grasp on it."

"I'm sorry that happened to you. I had no idea." He was already fading.

"I figured you didn't, and I don't blame you. In fact, I don't even really blame Steve. Someone probably did the same thing to him, and he was just recreating it. On to topic number two." He took a deep breath. He knew what was coming next. It was the event that drove a wedge between us for many years. "When I was back in college, you asked my to put my tuition, room, board and food on a credit card that I had. So

I did. As the months went on, the total on that bill neared twenty thousand dollars. You didn't want me to work. And you told me you would pay for it. Unfortunately, that didn't happen. It took me six years to pay that thing off. I missed an awful lot of college down time because I had to work more than forty hours each week to pay for that card. It pissed me off for a long time. If I would have only known that I was going to get stuck with that bill, I could have planned much more efficiently. I could have applied for student loans. That would've been an easy thing to do. I'm no longer pissed about any of that. It was my schooling, and I'm responsible for it. What I wish I never had to go through was the realization that I couldn't count on or trust my own father. Coupled with the fact that I had a mother who could care less where I was or what I was doing created an environment of loneliness. I always felt alone. I harbored these feelings for a long time, but not anymore. I just need you to know I have been negatively impacted by your actions."

"I'm not very proud of the things I did," he said unemotionally.

"I don't expect you to say anything, Dad. It's over for me. I've dealt with it. Anything you feel the need to say, you should just make right within yourself. I have no investment in it anymore."

"Okay," he said.

I quickly changed the subject to talk about how Natasha handled and that I was on my way to a lodge in the mountains for the weekend. We talked for a few more minutes before I hung up the phone. Our relationship was going to be just fine.

One phone call was finished, but there were still two to go. I dialed up my mom—this would be the big one. One ring, two rings, three rings, four rings, "Hi, you've reached…" She didn't pick up. I left a message for her to call me back because it was urgent—after all, we hadn't talked in five years.

Then I dialed my brother's phone number. It was disconnected. I knew he had been living in Flint, Michigan in a meth house. He'd graduated from a daily weed habit to cocaine, to crack and finally to crystal meth. By my sister's account, he'd lost his house, lost his girlfriend of twenty years, all of his toys, and was basically just waiting for the day he would die. So I wasn't surprised not to reach him.

At least I had started getting rid of owning problems that were unnecessary. I already felt a little lighter from my brief conversation with my father.

I looked at the water pounding against the rocks again. Then I jumped back in the car. The drive to the lodge took a few hours as I stopped to take some autumn photos. It was my favorite time of year, and I couldn't capture enough of it.

When I did finally get to the lodge, I checked in and immediately went to my room. The room had a stunning view of the waterfall. A fire was already roaring in the fireplace. I dropped all my things and opened up the large patio doors to let in the cool air and rushing noise of the river. I sat in the chaise lounge next to the fire, covered myself with a large blanket, and coiled up in a fetal position. I lay that way while my brain processed the day's activities until I cleaned my system with tears. I fell asleep there until three in the morning.

Upon awakening, I was really hungry. I grabbed a Snickers bar from the forbidden mini bar. I wolfed it down as I closed the patio doors and threw a couple of more logs on the fire. I washed it down with a soda. I laughed a little to myself as I thought, "Wow, I'm the epitome of health."

I unpacked my notebook and began to write to people I had wronged. I wrote how in high school I had betrayed a long-time buddy by talking smack about him to his girlfriend. They were already having problems and their breakup was inevitable, but the conversation I had with her finished the job. I tore myself up over that one for years. I wondered why I would do something like that. It was simply because I was unhappy in my own life. And talking badly about another person helped my ego. It was time to let the self-loathing from that event be eradicated. I wrote down a very specific apology to my friend Matt on one side of the paper. On the other, I wrote down, "I forgive myself for…" and continued on with the full explanation. When finished, I tore up the paper and threw it into the fire, watching it burn completely.

I apologized to the many, many women I'd used over the years to try to fill the black hole that was my lack of self-worth and self-responsibility. Though never intentionally malicious, I knew many had been indirectly affected by my acts.

I had a lot of sex in college with many different partners. I was, in fact, envied by a lot of my friends, which enabled the behavior under the guise of "just having fun." I thought it was just part of the college experience. I didn't pay attention to the people who were disgusted by what I did. I just figured they were jealous. I'd clearly deluded myself for quite some time. I forgave myself for not being able to see through the cloudiness of those times, and I allowed that I did the best I could with what I had. I didn't let myself off the hook; it was obviously wrong. I just forgave the past.

I continued by forgiving myself for the many things I'd done to girlfriends in college; things like lying, cheating, getting angry, manipulating and attempting to control situations. I wrote about very specific events to each woman, forgave her when it applied, and subsequently forgave myself. I ripped up each one with all the forgiving intention I could muster. I felt things deeply as I watched each letter burn. I forgave myself for staying in destructive relationships. I forgave myself for thinking bad thoughts about people. I forgave myself for not being more honest with myself about the destructive nature of my most recent actions, like having sex with married women. I wrote about the encounters, describing each in great detail. I apologized to each woman, each husband and boyfriend, and each family I had directly or indirectly affected. I followed that by forgiving each woman for her part, and subsequently myself.

I forgave myself for the disrespect and poor decision-making I willingly brought into my life. I forgave myself for feelings of inadequacy. I forgave myself for losing my way in the world, and for not representing my true and authentic self. I forgave myself for how I had defiled the essence of me. I forgave my brother for what he had done to me. I forgave my father for his part in everything. I forgave myself for the guilt I had around despising my father and hating my brother. I forgave my mother for her anger, envy, abandonment and conditional love that peppered our relationship. The last one took the longest to burn. As it did, tears fell uncontrollably from my eyes. I sobbed heavy and hard. My body writhed with pain as I finally decided to let all associations with my mother go. I was, in effect, at my mother's funeral.

The whole process took about six hours. When I was finished, it was nine in the morning. I jumped up, took a quick shower and went down to the tiny restaurant for some pancakes and bacon. It was like the very first time I'd ever eaten. The strawberries were robust, the pancakes light and fluffy, the syrup perfectly blended with butter, and the bacon thick and juicy. I adored and cherished every single bite until the plates were empty. It was the best breakfast I'd ever eaten.

I grabbed my coat and headed outside to take a gander at the falls through the thick mist. They were quite impressive. The calm water on the river above gave way to a towering shaft of white that ended hundreds of feet below as it thundered into yet another calm river. I climbed down as far as I could go and stayed there for quite a while. I let the billowing mist from below land on my face and hair. After a few minutes, I was covered in ice. The cold air had frozen the water on the hair of my face and head. It pulled the skin on my face tighter. But I wasn't cold. I was calm. I was calm like I had never been.

I made it back to my room before lunch. I started another fire and picked up my notebook. I was a little chilly, so I decided to keep the doors closed. It was time to write a couple of farewell letters. I had already scratched on a piece of paper the relationships that served me and that I wanted to keep in my life. Interestingly, the only people in Seattle were Mike, Chloe and Bobby. The "good" list also had my father, best friends across the nation, and family on it.

The only two people who had to be actively dealt with were my brother and my mother. I had already, in effect, released both of those relationships earlier that morning. But I felt the need to say goodbye with absolutely no expectations. I knew neither of them would come running with arms wide open screaming, "Please don't let me go! I need you in my life!" They possessed two of the most monstrous egos I'd ever run across. I knew because the apple didn't fall far from the tree. I sent the letters to let each of them know where I stood. I never expected anything out of it. And that was why it felt good to send them.

I wrote a short note to my brother detailing exactly how I felt about what he had done so many years before. I described how the event had resulted in a lack of clear boundaries in my present life. I informed him that I never wanted to see or hear from him again. I wrote it clearly and confidently. I felt strong and relieved that it didn't create any sort of pangs within my gut. There was very little emotion, if any at all, wrapped within it. I called my sister for his latest address and dropped it in the outgoing mail immediately.

I was actually excited to write the final letter to my mother. I had done it before. About three years after she stormed out of my apartment before my graduation, I sent her a letter trying to stimulate some type of conversation. I had told her that if she couldn't treat me better, and actually take some ownership with regard to what had happened, then I didn't want her in my life. I never heard another thing from her. So my next letter was the final one. I took a deep breath and started writing.

I wrote for a couple of hours that afternoon. I discussed in vivid detail the utterly atrocious things she had done as a mother, the things for which I had forgiven her. I told her it was wrong to bring a stranger into our house immediately after she kicked our father out, especially when she knew the guy didn't like kids. I told her it was mean and vindictive of her to call me a user and a thief the time I came home from college and took a blanket back to school because I was cold at night. I told her it wasn't right to change the locks on all the doors of the house we'd grown up in without giving us a key. I told her it was wrong to abandon my sister and I under the guise of "working all the time." She treated us like trash after she divorced my father. No wonder my sister and I had low self-esteem. I told her I thought it was weird she had told me she was envious of the great life I'd created. She should have wanted that for me!

The letter seemed to go on forever. But as it did, I felt increasingly liberated. Why would I want that kind of person in my life? For many years, I had tried to cultivate a relationship with that woman. But there was no bend in her. At any given moment, she could go off. And for no reason at all. I hated the feeling I got when I was near her. It was true she was my mother, and somehow I was still able to love her. But that didn't mean I had to put up with her mental and emotional abuse for the rest of my life. I had finally made the decision to let her go. It had been five years since I last saw her, and my life was better for it. Some people weren't meant to be mothers.

I again started to think of the uncanny emotional parallels between my mother and Esther. The women were basically one and the same. And it was rewarding to see how differently I'd handled myself the second time around with Esther. I was making positive progress. And I was happily over both of them.

I finished the letter, folded it and put it in the envelope. I marched right down to the front desk to buy another stamp, and proudly dropped it in the outgoing mail. The letter must have weighed twenty pounds, because I immediately felt that much lighter.

I ran back upstairs and changed into my hiking gear. I went out for a brisk hike to clear my head and to get some fresh air. The hike was a wonderful meditation, and the day sped by. By the time I looked at my cell phone, it was four o'clock. I quickly made my way back to the lodge before the sun went down and went to the bar for some dinner. The evening was short, as I was both physically and mentally drained from the day's activities. I was asleep by nine.

The next day I woke up at the crack of dawn and felt completely revitalized. As I rolled out of the oversized bed, I realized how quiet my head was. There was no incessant buzz around all the things I had to do, or where I was in my life. It was quiet.

I opened up the shades to reveal sunny skies. For the first time in ten years, I felt like myself. I was genuinely happy. Coffee percolated as I took a quick shower. I got out and dried off before pouring myself a cup. I walked over to the patio door and opened it. The falls were mesmerizing. My mind was clear, and I was well rested. I took a deep breath and walked over to the bed. I was in the mood to meditate. I jumped up on the bed and practiced the breathing techniques that allowed me to transcend the present. It was easier than I could ever remember. Almost immediately, I was off into the land of reconciliation.

## *Points Of Responsibility*

*61. Do you blame others for situations and occurrences in your life? Stop. YOU are the sole architect of your life, and that's the bottom line. It's up to you to create the life you want. Stop making excuses as to why you aren't happy, you don't have abundance, you're not surrounded by good people, or you aren't where you want to be in life. It's not anyone else's fault but your own if this is the case. When you blame, you're utilizing your power to recreate more blame, denial and unhappiness. You relinquish responsibility. So maybe it's time to change your paradigm. When those negative reels of tape from past experiences play in your mind, say aloud, "STOP!" And then fill that space with visions and statements that reinforce your life as you see it. Literally use the five senses to live the abundance that surrounds you. Notice all the good-natured, well-intentioned people around you helping you to succeed in life. Feel yourself doing the things that bring you passion. See yourself in your happy and satisfying relationship. Let's not forget, BLAME KILLS SELF-EVOLUTION.*

*62. How often do you get into emotional battles with others? Seek to become more objective and less reactive. When emotions bubble up, repeat the steps you've already learned to let the fire die down. Acknowledge what is happening. Choose to observe the situation from the back of your head instead of through your eyes. Take deep breaths, stand up straight and gently twist your spine one way and then the other. Respect yourself and the others involved. If the situation remains heated, take a walk. But before you leave, tell the other person that you're committed to creating an agreement and to figuring out a way to make things work. To leave the situation with no commitment to agree to a resolution is controlling and unacceptable. Calmly letting go of addictive emotions by the use of relaxation and reason reinforces your responsible and blame-free behavior.*

*63. When you were young, did you experience events that have negatively influenced you? We all have negative situations from our past. Write down each event on a separate piece of paper. Next write down how that event might have allowed for certain emotions or habits in your life. Write down how you believe it has affected you. Be explicit in your discussion. Get it all out on paper. Use every word in your vocabulary to describe the impact of those events on your psyche, your relationships and your perception of the world. Come back to it after a day or so and add more. Never delete anything, as each word has come to the surface for a reason. Keep the letters for later action.*

*64. Write, for yourself, a letter to each person you've wronged in your life. Again, use separate pieces of paper. While you're doing so, deeply feel all the shame, guilt, lack of self-confidence and negativity associated with your activity. If you're truly in a state of healing and non-ego, it will be easy for you to apologize meaningfully to each individual. Apologize for each specific event. Take responsibility for yourself. Avoid the tendency to blame or to explain. The point is to take responsibility for your thoughts, actions and words, without rationalizations and justifications. If you've offended groups or organizations, apologize to them as well. Put out into the Universe your willingness to step back and analyze, and to take full responsibility. It will breed more of the same, both within you and within others. Keep the pages for later action.*

*65. Write down all the ways you've caused chaos and negativity in your own life. Make this list all-inclusive, and keep the focus on yourself. Write about how self-destructive thoughts and actions have affected your life. Write about the various ways you've let your ego control you. Write about the times you've run from peace and/or happiness and the times you've been depressed and anxious. Write about the ways you've disrespected yourself, any feelings of inadequacy, and specific events where you've exhibited poor decision-making. Again, feel deeply every word you put on paper. Focus on how such emotions and actions have played a role in YOUR dysfunction. (For example, "I've been fearful. It's affected my life by my lack of ability to show my partner who I truly am.") Keep the pages for later action.*

*66. Collect all the pages from the last three steps. It is time to set yourself free from all the self-imposed burdens you've been writing about. It's time to leave them in the past where they belong. Pick up the first page. Read it slowly. Feel and literally live in the emotions that resurface when you read the things you wrote. Feel them deeply, and let them bubble to the surface. Bring every last haunting emotion into your consciousness. When the emotions have peaked, hold onto the paper and begin slowly to tear the page. As you tear the paper into tiny bits, infuse it with all of your emotions. Feel the anxiety and emotions transition away from your material body and into the paper. Visualize the tentacles of those emotions unwrapping themselves from your muscles, organs and nervous system. Let the emotions melt from you completely. When the process is complete, the emotions now reside within the fibers of the paper, not within you. When the action of tearing the paper becomes more mechanical, or when it's completely torn up, begin the process of apologizing and forgiving all involved. Apologize to those you've wronged and for the inappropriate things you've done. Forgive yourself for actions taken upon others and yourself. Forgive others for the things they've done to you. Take as much time as necessary. Accept that every experience in life is an opportunity for growth. Learn the lessons involved. After this, you cannot harbor ill feelings of any type. They have no power over you whatsoever. They were your past. And know that you are NOT your past, but whatever you choose in the present. When you are finished with each subsequent page, put the remains in a sealable container, like a box or a jar. When the whole process is complete, immediately seal the container and take it to a refuse container outside of your home. Throw it away and let it go forever. When you have discarded the contents of your past, relax and breathe deeply. Have no expectations as to how you "should" feel. Simply allow yourself the moment to be present. Don't force or allow any thought. Just be with yourself and smile. Hold the visions of your wonderful life.*

*67. Relationships, both personal and work-related, are the single-most important vehicle by which we can truly gauge our internal environment. When we have a good internal environment, we have strong, helpful and respectful people who surround us. When we have a negative internal environment, we tend to allow stagnant and destructive relationships to surround us, or we have few or no relationships at all. Relationships are important in that they are a direct representation of how we see the external world and interact with it. They should be actively and responsibly managed. Diligently work on the good ones and let the bad ones leave. You know the difference between the two, and it's time for some action. Locate your list of friends from chapter eight. Decisively determine whether you want to continue the relationships that don't serve you in a positive way. When you're ready to stop making excuses for their existence, it's time to write each person a letter. Think of all the good things that came out of your past relations with each person separately. Write them down and thank the person for the opportunity to be a part of his or her life. Feel the gratitude before you state it is your decision to cease further contact with him or her. Don't blame or get into details about specific situations. Simply say the relationship is not the type you want in your life and let it be done. Don't hold power over the other party or try to be manipulative. Sincerely thank the person for all the good times and look forward to your present. Send the letter. If the person comes back for discussion, don't avoid the confrontation. When in front of that person, look him or her in the eye, and with only love in your heart, state that you're not interested in being in a relationship with him or her any longer. Tell the person he or she will be all right. Have compassion and empathy, but not sympathy. Anger may arise from the other, but it is your responsibility not to be manipulated or controlled. Give a hug if it's appropriate. Otherwise, just walk away. Emotional situations are an inevitable part of life. And avoiding such opportunities for growth will keep you in a state of anxiety and stifle your life. When you think in such positive terms, it's easier to understand you're helping both parties to evolve. You're not enabling. You're disallowing negative past events into your present and future. And this you should hold on to at all cost.*

Chapter Fourteen:

# Building Blocks

As I sat on that oversized bed in the lodge, my life changed forever. I saw clearly how my ego affected everything in my life, including the sexual compulsion. My ego had brought about a few positive attributes, such as money, prestige and education. But unfortunately, there were more negative sides to it than I had ever wanted to admit. The thing was like a kid in a candy store. It had its greedy little paws all over everything. I saw how I constantly needed external admiration, how it reinforced a sense of scarcity that always needed more, and how it caused me to suffer with a constant sense of fear and anxiety. I'd always been a caring, loving and giving person. But what always took center stage for me were things that focused on achievement and increasing the ego. My ego was insatiable. It was constant and conniving. It entered into every part of my life and became elusive. It tried to be "me." It tried to be "victim." It tried to fight everything it could to gain importance and significance. It caused me never to trust and drove a wedge between me and everyone and everything else. It even reared its ugly little head within my meditation. It tried to tell me that my conclusions weren't true, that I was just making things up. It tried to tell me that there was no alternative to living with my ego. It was comfortable, and if I kept digging, things would be even messier. It asked me whether I really wanted to go through more upheaval.

## *Points Of Responsibility*

*68. What do you fear? Where do those fears come from? Did you inherit them from family members or friends? Do you live with fear just because that's what you've always done? Diligently dissect your fears and their suspected origins. Write about them in your notebook. Are you afraid of success, of failure, of never having enough, of never finding love, of not living your destiny, etc.? Know that fear is irrational and the only thing that can kill the spirit. Fear strangles life. After evaluating the situations in your life where you allow fear to creep in, figure out and write down how you're going to move your thoughts in those instances from fear to acceptance. Know that everyone has fear, and that successful people move past that fear into action. Use the principles you've already learned to move from fear into action. You have the power to reason your way through difficulty. Practice it.*

*69. Does your ego make excuses to allow compulsions and addictions to continue in your life? Is it time to take your power back yet? Are you ready to drop habits that don't serve you and those around you? By not choosing, you're still making a choice, and it's usually the choice to fail. Until you choose to take responsibility for your life, you are choosing not to. Don't enable your ego. When you notice your ego flaring up, step back, breathe, release yourself from the urge to fight those around you, and from the urge to fight the ego itself. Accept it. Smile at it. Then fill your next thought with an action that will put you back on track to creating a positive life. Read and feel your written visions. Do a walking meditation. Get physical and feel your body as you stimulate the release of endorphins, which reinforces your positive behavior. You are, in effect, becoming addicted to the positive action and conscious thought.*

*70. Understand that your ego is tricky. It will try anything and everything to get its way and to try to make itself "right." More importantly, understand that you are not your ego. You live above and observe your ego. It is a piece of you, but it does not define you unless you allow it to do so. To live your life by ego and emotion is to live a substandard life. We all have glimpses of glory, but releasing the ties that bind us to ego will allow those glimpses to diffuse throughout and become the norm. As you transition from an egoistic and humanistic framework into a more responsible, conscious and purpose-driven one, you will reduce confusion and resistance in your life. Since you're making decisions actively, and not passively, you no longer find yourself running from battle to battle, putting out emotional fire after emotional fire. With time and practice, you will have more energy because living a purpose-driven life is all about creation. It's about the uncovering of truth. And truth always invigorates us.*

I softly laughed to myself. The simple acknowledgement of ego caused a previously unimaginable shift in my state of being. It opened my eyes wider than ever before. Just acknowledging and accepting such things as fact caused it to crumble. Peace and warmth began to melt the ego almost immediately. All the things I'd brought into my life, all the prestige, all the money, all the accolades of achievement, none of it was important. The most important thing in my life was the achievement of that particular moment. It was truly priceless. All worldly things paled in comparison to the new focused intention I'd just uncovered within myself. The simple realization and understanding that I was now going to act in my life, not react with ego, was all empowering. I was so happy that I jumped off the bed, went to the window and screamed, "I want to live!" I danced around the room a little bit before running down to breakfast. Things were different within me. This wasn't simply a minor shift, but a seriously life-changing event. It wasn't like the many times before, when I'd promised myself I'd change, only to fall back into meaningless and destructive patterns. There would be no empty promises. I had decided to have only great people and relationships in my life. There was no room for anything other than good habits. I had finally made the choice to stop backing my way into my future.

After breakfast, I continued where I left off. I opened my notebook and thought deeper about the past six weeks; I hadn't done anything to accentuate and create more of the positive in my life. Most things were focused on the negative, or not focused at all. I revisited the old quotes, "Whatever you think about expands," and "Like attracts like." I knew these statements to be true in my own life. I usually got what I wanted through hard work and conscious focus on the desired effect. I always got what I actively and passionately thought about. And it was time to apply it again for the achievement of long-term joy. I was no longer going to focus on my past. I had been good at throwing out the trash, but I kept filling that same space with the same activities, the same types of relationships, and the same uninspired thought. It was time to fill my present and future with activities that served both humanity and myself. I was transforming my life from within and beginning to live my own purpose.

## Point Of Responsibility

*71. We attract people and situations into our lives that resonate at the same frequency as us. By being responsible, by being present in every moment of your life, by creating abundance and positivity, you will begin to resonate at like frequencies. Those activities become easier. You draw like-minded individuals into your life. When you think of joy, joy shows up. When you think about abundance, abundance shows up. Again, the Universe doesn't discriminate or create polarity (i.e. positive/negative, good/bad, black/white,) humans do so. And since what you think about literally becomes matter in your life, it would behoove all of us if you created things and situations in a positive manner instead of the opposite.*

My whole life had consisted of incessantly planning for my future. Enjoying vacations was difficult because I was focused elsewhere. Enjoying time off with friends brought me guilt for not spending my time more wisely on marketing or making money. The drive for more was constant and unrelenting. I wanted to live and enjoy my present.

When I wasn't thinking about my future, I was focused on the past. I'd replay negative conversations I'd had with patients or others. I'd focus on what I could have said, or should have said, to make myself feel better. I'd focus on bad relationships I'd gone through, decisions I would have made differently and pitfalls that consumed time, money, or both. I didn't want to lose anything more to such negative patterns of thought. I was finally beginning to focus on the present.

## Point of Responsibility

*72. Do you look to your past and back your way into the future? Do you incessantly plan for the future? Both are effects of the ego. Indirectly, it is stealing your present, and ultimately your life. Live in the present in every waking moment. When you catch yourself daydreaming, stop! Stay focused on the task at hand. It's necessary to plan for the future, and to learn from the past. But let go of the wanting, the wishing and the emotions associated with both. They have absolutely no relevance to your present. When you're finished planning and taking lessons, come back to the present and live here. It's the only place that truly matters. Know that your ego will battle constantly to take you to the extremes. And when it does, smile at it and come back to the now.*

Interestingly enough, it was in such times of upheaval and uncertainty that I was more prone to recreate the exact behavior I was trying to eradicate. But knowing that my ego was pushing hard to keep such structures in place made it easy to continue on in the right direction. The primary focus for me wasn't to continue diving deeply into self to figure out the intricate details of how I got to the horrible place I used to live, but how to get out of it. Anyone could spend a lifetime trying to figure out and tweeze apart the inner workings of his or her brain and how it might affect his or her life. But that was where the comfort zone made its residence, in the mind. And that's where the ego wants us to continue living. The difficulty lay in the decision to jump out of the comfort zone of one's own head and into the abyss that represents his or her connection to the universe. Such a proposition brought up an intriguing question. How does one get out of his or her head? I decided that anytime I found it necessary to dive deeper into my own mind, or replay negative occurrences, I would say aloud to myself, "Stop!" and continue on with some type of positive action step, like going over what I was grateful for in my life. It completely stopped the addiction to being in my own head all the time.

## *Point Of Responsibility*

*73. Revisit and focus on the things in your life for which you are gracious and joyous.*

The next step after acknowledging issues and actively managing the ego was to take complete responsibility for everything in my life. In my past, I had many situations and people I could blame, but to do that was self-victimizing, and yet another part of the ego, which took those things that happened to me in life and said, "Poor little Mark, how could you possibly do any more with such a crappy past?" The bad things that happened to me or around me became my way of being, so to speak. They defined me. It was much like many of the patients I'd treated over the years. So many of them became defined by their illnesses. They lived the illness every day, all day. Their egos liked to have something by which to define them, and an illness was a sturdy cause. Unfortunately, the patient seldom broke free of the illness because it would mean the ego had nothing else to work on, and it liked to be in the forefront.

## *Point Of Responsibility*

*74. Responsibility is the most fundamental underlying code and the binding agreement between all creatures on earth, including humans. Everything we do in life must be responsible, especially when no one is looking.*

*Responsibility is defined as "the social force that binds us to the courses of action demanded by that force; a form of trustworthiness; the state of being accountable or answerable, as for a trust, debt, or obligation." In effect, responsibility is the representation of our own reliability and dependability as it relates to our family, our community, our government, the earth and us. John D. Rockefeller Jr. said, "Every right implies a responsibility; every opportunity, an obligation; every possession, a duty." Notice that responsibility supersedes morality. Morals can be different between cultures, religions and regions. Again, responsibility is the fundamental thread that binds ALL of us. It has nothing to do with belief or tradition, but with underlying propagation of relevant truth with regard to healthy evolution of the earth.*

I no longer blamed my environment, my parents, or bad things that happened to me for anything in my life. Where I was in my life had absolutely nothing to do with anyone else. I was the sole architect of it all. I drew everything into my life, and I was the only one who could change it, period. Taking responsibility forced me to take complete control of everything around me. I couldn't blame another for anything. Taking that responsibility was the most empowering thing I'd ever done. It altered my mindset from one of weakness, affliction and blame to one of trust. Taking responsibility indirectly illuminated the part of me that could trust. I couldn't believe the things that were happening as I sat at the desk and wrote in my notebook. I was becoming more solid from the inside. A fundamental and powerful change had occurred within me over the past two days. I never remembered feeling so concrete in my whole life.

I continued to write, "We all have to make decisions every day about how we live. That's why every day is a new opportunity to change our actions. If we aren't living the way we like, we can change it. But first comes a decision. We must first make the conscious decision to make life different than our past. Most people make the decision, but then keep the same people, relationships and environment around them. They're doomed to failure. First we acknowledge that a problem exists. Second, we dive into our own mind to figure out the relationships between our past and present and how the ego plays into it. Third, we exit or release the negative components of our environment at any cost. There's no other way to do it. We don't get a 'do-over' in life. The sooner we start to live with responsibility, truth and purpose, the better."

On that particular Sunday, what came out of my mind onto paper simply amazed me. The whole day was a blur, as time became irrelevant. By early afternoon, I had come up with a complete, balanced process by which to transform my life from one of suffering and blame, into one of self-responsibility and joy. It ended up being the culmination of many different things I'd studied over the past fifteen years that had only made sense as individual units before. I drew from my extensive readings on Quantum Theory, philosophy, psychology, and from my own experience. I pulled together systems that shared common themes and involved the fundamentals of life for all of us. The program was rooted in responsibility, balance and common sense. And it cut out all extreme behavior that was geared toward satiation of the ego. It focused on presently and intently recreating relationships; first with self and then with others. It was the simplest and most effective approach to recreating one's life I'd ever known. The tenets couldn't be denied, and anyone could follow through with it. I employed easy steps to balance the physical, mental, emotional, spiritual and social parts of life. I couldn't believe what I had created out of such turmoil.

## *Point of Responsibility*

*75. My ideas, writings, activities and systems eventually evolved into a program called "The Responsibility Movement™." The program was designed to help you recapture your life with an easy, common sense approach. At the core of the program are The Seven Pillars of Balance. The Seven Pillars are: Wellness of the Mind, Love and Relationships, Success and Leadership, Finance, Physical Wellness, Codes of Living and Spirituality. We'll be discussing the basics later in the book. You can also find more information at www.responsibilitymovement.com.*

The things I continued to write on the blank pages of my notebook favored the entrance of deep substance. The words were mine, but the concepts had roots deeply planted in Universal truth. With time and calm, I created a practical process of events to help evolve the person, and inherently to evolve the soul. I wrote briefly about spirituality, and how we, as humans, tended to idealize what life "should" be. We hold a vision of a great afterlife, and of great God(s) above. But that vision usually got lost in the day-to-day acts of our lives. "We" become more important than our reason for being, which is the soul's evolution. We've become part-time spiritual and full-time human. I was finished living the "human experience." I was ready to move into a fully spiritual consciousness and to help others do the same.

I discussed my ideas about the need for humans to "polarize" everything in life. How we label things as right or wrong, good or bad, black or white, positive or negative, desired and feared. I knew such labels had no relevance to the human experience until we created them, or more specifically, the ego created them.

## Point Of Responsibility

*76. Do you polarize life by labeling situations and people in terms of right or wrong, good or bad, happy or sad, useful or useless, black or white, desired or feared, moral or amoral? Know that such labels have almost no relevance to evolving the soul. Such labels are ego-based; they're created to make a person or a group more right than another. When a situation occurs in your life, stand in a place where no polarity exists. Don't apply the egoistic forms of labeling. Be quiet and act from a place of truth. Do the best you can. Don't criticize or complain. Many are addicted to the emotion of a situation and don't get past it. They revel in the pain, the blame, in the fight to be right and in the confusion that consumes it. Then they relive the emotion every day, sometimes all day. This type of activity is what keeps us down. It degrades our life and steals from us our present. Don't be a part of it anymore. Act swiftly to utilize the action steps already learned in earlier chapters. Get past that moment and move on.*

I pondered how wonderful life would be when everyone lives using the "lowest common denominator" of truth and self-responsibility. We'll all have enough to eat, a place to live, and there will be enough abundance for everyone to thrive in every way he or she creates. Humans aren't to that point yet, but as a whole, our consciousness is expanding. My first goal was to work toward eventually mastering my new way of thinking and being, and to facilitate others to do the same.

The things I wrote were monumentally life-changing to me. The thoughts were idealistic, but they had practical appeal. Everyone who saw the obvious benefit could easily use the steps. He or she could simply insert clearly intended habits to begin to bridge that gap between idealism and the manifestation of those ideals in life.

Creating the new framework, or context, was the most difficult part for me, but I now had it within my grasp. It was time to move forward, to fill that context with good content, or habits. I had a lot of bad-habit time slots open and available in my schedule. What new, positive occurrences did I want in my life? What things and opportunities were the perfect representations of myself in my present incarnation? I pensively spent the next few hours writing, contemplating and uncovering the things I would use to fill my life.

## *Point Of Responsibility*

*77. Create a list in a notebook of your goals, your visions and your dreams. This is the first step in actively creating your life on a daily basis. Once you have the basic goals written down, you're going to form them into something incredibly powerful. But the first step is to figure out and write down your basic visions. Put some serious thought into this step and take your time. As you go through the initial part of the process, fine-tune your goals and dreams. Make them clear and concise in your head as you create them. Envision anything and everything you will be manifesting within this lifetime. Leave nothing out because the Universe is your catalogue. If you can think about it, you can achieve it. Organize your goals into four distinct categories: immediate future, one-year achievement, five-year achievement, and lifetime achievement. Use the seven basic categories from the Seven Pillars of Responsibility as your primary guide to goal creation. You will, of course, want to achieve specific things within each of the Seven Pillars.*

*When you've finished creating your list of goals, it's time to rewrite the contents in a new and refreshing way. Take out all statements in which you are "wishing" or "wanting." There can be none of that, or you will get exactly what you put into the Universe, wishing and wanting. And you don't want to continue wishing and wanting, right? You're creating manifestation! Second, the structure of your visions and affirmations must make use of a newly discovered process within the brain called neuroplasticity. This process allows us literally to change our minds.*

*The connections, or neuronet, that we currently have within our brains are merely due to the reinforcement of our own thoughts and actions. Unfortunately, most of us don't take an active part in creating our reality. We simply do things as we've always done them. We're addicted to the things that surround us, like entertainment, sugar, alcohol, food, indifference, creating obstacles and compulsions. And those addictions are the things we reinforce every single day by continuing such activity and incessantly replaying those thoughts and actions in our minds. But because of our brain's ability to change its neuronet, we have the distinct opportunity to create exactly the type of life we choose. Another of the greatest recent discoveries is that our brain also has the ability to generate new cells within the hippocampus, which is responsible for memory storage. The cells reach maturation at about six weeks. It's an astoundingly empowering concept to understand that you can actively add memories to your brain. In fact, you already do it every day. But how and why might this be functionally important? When you add new and positive memories to your history, those are the little reels of tape you recall because those are the thoughts and visions that have been most recently created and utilized over and over. Those visions have the most active connections. They make up your new neuronet and become your memory. So when we coalesce the concepts of neuroplasticity and generation of new memory cells, and that the brain doesn't know the difference between internal and external reality, we come to the basic conclusion that our thoughts truly do become reality. Rewrite your goals or visions utilizing a new format. "For as long as I can remember, I've always had peace and joy in my life. It's always been that way. Peace and joy have always been a part of me and the people who surround me." Start by writing three of your most important visions into the saying. Get creative. Say the words calmly aloud to yourself. Believe what you're saying. Hear the words as they resonate within you. Feel what your life looks like with the visions that you've created. This IS your life. It's nothing new. You're just reinforcing the things you've always known to be part of you. Don't stop repeating and working the visions until you begin to feel the endorphins released into your body. You'll feel uplifted, happier and on top of the world. Adding a walking meditation to the spoken visions increases its power exponentially. Do so as many times as you can every day, but at least three times, and at least ten minutes each time. The walking meditation is the most powerful way to start your day. Before you do anything else, go outside and start your day with this activity. It sets the tone, and you'll be acting from within yourself and your ideals as the day progresses.*

*78. Thought is all-powerful. The things you think about expand. Point of fact, thoughts become things. When you consciously focus on something, you will ALWAYS get that desired effect, and whether you label it positive or negative is irrelevant. This is why it's important for you to watch your thoughts as well as your actions. If you desire something, keep envisioning it in present time. Don't stop at any cost. Continue to develop and crystallize your greatest life. It will manifest.*

Over the next three weeks, my life changed dramatically. By employing the ideas and habits I put into my new system, I was the epitome of balance. Surprisingly, living my life with as little ego as possible wasn't all that difficult. In fact, it was easier to break the chains of egoistic living than I had ever imagined. It was the right way of being, and it always took less energy to do the right thing. To be clear, I hadn't completely eradicated the ego to a dysfunctional thing of the past, but I began to understand its true purpose: to lift oneself out of the depths of despair and a feeling of "less than," to a place where all humans aspire to be—a place of balance. It simply needed to be kept in check. Dealing with others' egos was a piece of cake because I wasn't emotionally invested anymore. I thought and spoke from the higher self.

The ease of meditation continued as the wormhole of clarity opened itself a bit more with each passing day. The little negative filmstrips became less intense and the meditations became a time of solace, of re-creation and not just "dealing."

All the steps within my new program helped my transition to healthy living. But the one that ignited the whole thing was responsibility. It was an epiphany to realize that responsibility was the most fundamental underlying code and the binding agreement between all of us. Our lives are a direct manifestation of the respect, or lack of respect, for that connection. Every single thing we do in life must be responsible, especially when no one's looking. Interestingly enough, the decision to be self-responsible was the one that melted away all anxiety and fear in my life. Justifications and rationalizations had no place within me anymore.

My daily habits were completely different, which allowed me to focus on those things in life that made me grateful and joyous. The six weeks before the trip to the lodge were a living hell, but I had pushed through it, and I was now functionally living in a great space.

The practice boomed with new life. That first week back to work, I was able to find someone to help out at the office. She was new to town and had significant knowledge about practice management. I asked Claudia to train Julie for the front desk and to cross-train her for the back office position, in case Claudia was ever sick. I held faith in Claudia and hoped that she would pick up some good habits from Julie. I was certainly feeling more comfortable since I was getting someone with significant experience back into the office.

Conversations with patients were smooth, and I had very little conflict for the first time in my professional career. The incessant phone calls from various women stopped for the most part, and things felt great.

## *Points Of Responsibility*

*79. Know that everything is all right.*

*80. You are responsible. You don't blame your environment, family or bad things for where you are in life. You are not a victim, but an innovator, the sole creator of your life. Focus on the life that you truly have, not the manifestations of past negative thoughts and behaviors.*

Chapter Fifteen:

# The Empire Thrives

The last week in September, after three weeks of living my new life, I decided I was ready to meet some new people. I figured some conversation with people who didn't live in Atherton would do me some good. I hadn't dated anyone exclusively since Jennifer, which was about ten weeks ago. But I'd also been through a lot in those ten weeks and was a much different person than before.

Both Atia and Erika had been trying to get a hold of me the whole time, but I never once returned a phone call or a text. Atia stopped by the office a few times, but I always made myself busy. I simply didn't want to have anything to do with any of the women from the past, and saying, "No" empowered me.

I was busy with work on most days, so the best way for me to meet people was online. I wasn't interested in doing the bar thing, or being set up on blind dates. Around the third day, I got a message from a girl who had just moved back to Seattle from Southern California. Sasha's note read, "Hey, check out my profile. If you like it, maybe you could send me an email." That was it, short and sweet. So I did exactly that. On paper, she was the coolest ever. Sasha was both extremely beautiful and intelligent. But she had two things that worked against her. The first was her profile picture. It was one of those where she was hugging someone, but that someone was obviously cut out. The second was the picture of her poor boxer dressed up like a pumpkin for Halloween. I laughed a little at how pitiful the poor thing looked and shot her back a funny and sarcastic email. "Unfortunately, it looks like we can't meet. I respect dogs, and you apparently don't. And who's the guy in the missing half of the photo?" I was hoping she would understand my humor and send back something witty.

Unfortunately, I didn't get a reply; she must have taken my dry sense of humor seriously. So I sent her a second email the next morning, hoping I hadn't messed things up before they even got started. "I would love to have lunch this weekend or something if you'd still like to. I look forward to meeting you." She emailed me back within a few hours to tell me her weekend was booked, but a late lunch on Sunday would be good. I wondered whether she was one of those "serial daters," like Esther. She probably had dates lined up for the whole weekend. But I wasn't going to let my past dictate my future, so I told her Sunday would be fine.

As I drove over the lake to meet Sasha on that sunny Sunday afternoon, I began to think about how calm and peaceful my mind was. It was like all the yuck had been completely swiped from my brain. I was seeing more of my good friends. I was playing hockey again. I meditated daily using a new technique that worked extremely well for creating each day. Conversations with everyone in my life were easier and freer. I offered great advice to patients without a fear of rejection. I was living in my present, and had recaptured the ability to live without polarity, and with truth and presence. For the first time in my life, I was living with a smile that came from the inside.

As I crossed the bridge, I noticed Natasha was going a bit fast, which made me think I should know where my wallet was, in case I was pulled over. I searched the passenger seat, the glove box, and all my pockets. I had left the thing in my BMW. And I was on a bridge, so I couldn't just turn around. If I went back for it, I would surely be a half hour late, which was unacceptable. I couldn't just show up without a wallet. Sasha would think I was either a bum or just testing her or something. I needed some help deciding what to do, so I called her up and asked, "Hey! Are you at the café yet?"

"I just got here. Are you on your way?"

"Yes, but I have a story to tell."

"Oh, really? And what's that?" I could tell she was already deciding I must be a con artist, liar, or juggler.

"It's no big deal," I said, "but I've forgotten my wallet and I'm on the bridge. I need to turn around to go get it, which means I won't get there for about forty-five minutes. I'm so sorry for wasting your time. If you like, we could reschedule."

But her reply made me realize she was one of the coolest women I'd ever met. "Don't worry about it. I have enough to pay for lunch. This isn't some kind of test, is it?"

"No, definitely not," I laughed. "I don't do it often, but I left my wallet at home. Are you sure? I have no problem going to get it."

"Seriously, it's no big deal, but you better hurry because I got us a couple of great seats to watch the sun go down over the lake!"

As I hung up the phone, I could already tell our date was going to be fun.

Once I arrived, the conversation flowed easily. We watched the sun go down as we shared a few appetizers and a bottle of wine. Sasha was the perfect combination of intelligence, good humor, depth and fun. And it helped that she was stunningly beautiful and her eyes were deeper than the ocean.

As the day sped by, I found it interesting I didn't feel anxious or nervous at all. I just genuinely wanted to get to know her. After all the dates and bad relationships I'd been in over the last two years, none of them involved the sense of peace and comfort I now felt, both emanating from deep within myself and being reciprocated by the person across the table. Even though I was attracted to Sasha, I remained in the present as we talked rather than letting my mind escape to the places it used to. No visions arose of how the night might play out. My intention was healthy and pure, and it shined through. I couldn't be more excited to turn the corner in relating with people. Living with focused intention and without expectations or limiting polarity fired me up.

## *Point Of Responsibility*

*81. Your intentions dictate your thoughts and become the manifestations that make up your life. So create positive intentions; otherwise, your positive thoughts and meditations will constantly be met with confrontation where they interface the physical world. Your relationship to your physical world must coincide with your thoughts and ideals. And that interface is by your intention. Your intention is the filter through which your thoughts are manifested to create your ideal internal environment. But when those thoughts and visions are translated into the physical world through intentions that are less than responsible, the manifestations will be cloudy and distorted. If your intentions are pure and clean, you will more easily and sooner manifest your ideal life. Remove resistance by creating congruent thoughts and interactions.*

On the way home from our date, I was back on the bridge. I started thinking about the next weekend. I had made plans to go to the Olympic Mountains to do some hiking. "I wonder whether Sasha would be interested in going with me," I thought. So I called her up.

The first thing she said after picking up the phone was, "Did you miraculously find your wallet?"

"Very funny," I said. "No. I just wanted to say thank you for the wonderful day. I really had a great time talking with you, and I'm heading to the Olympics next weekend to do some hiking. It's always more fun with two, so I was wondering whether you'd like to join me."

I heard nothing on the other end. Absolutely nothing. I pulled my phone away from my ear to see whether we'd been disconnected. The time was still rolling. So I said, "It's not like I'm a serial killer or anything. I'm just going for a little hike."

I felt I had really messed things up until she said, "Can I bring my boxer with me?"

"Of course! She'll have a great time! The only catch is that we'll probably have to spend the night, but we can get two rooms. So it's no big deal."

"Okay, that sounds like fun!" she said.

"Great, I'll give you a ring with the details later in the week."

"All right, have a good Monday," she said.

"You do the same; talk with you soon." We both hung up our phones. I worried for a moment about sounding too desperate and being too forward with Sasha. But I realized it was my ego bringing forth such notions. "Thanks for sharing," I told it, "but I have it under control."

I had made great strides that day, and was excited just to release it all into the Universe. I had no expectations wrapped around any of it. I felt like I was floating gently down a stream, with the rapids behind me, and the calm, wide river in front.

## *Point Of Responsibility*

*82. Expectations obliterate original thought. In our social lives, we are inundated with how things "should" be. Imagine what the world would look like if there were no expectations about how situations will go, or how someone will react to something. We wouldn't expect partners to be a certain way, but we'd learn to appreciate them for their true essences. We wouldn't find it necessary to use posturing in business, because every person would be acting from a place of responsibility. Expectations are created from past action; they're a comparison of how you perceived an event; expectations are all perception. The models you created from your past are projected onto your future, allowing nothing but the past to move forward. Dropping your expectations is a complete change in your mindset. It is extremely powerful to understand that each situation and person is different from your past. You will get a renewed sense of life. Having no expectations is, of course, intimately involved with trust. And trust must be achieved through positive dealings and with experience. Throughout the process of getting to know someone, or while reinventing your personal relationships, eliminate the projection of your own expectations upon such interactions. Simply appreciate the processes and people for what and who they are. Don't expect anything from anyone. Go into every conversation as if it's the first time you've talked to him or her. Always be on your best behavior. This process will inherently stimulate growth within you, as you will be forced to let go of the connections within your brain associated with expectation—expectations that haven't allowed you to progress beyond your past. Don't confuse expectations with codes of conduct. Expectations are emotional and irrational; they are not based in reality. Codes of conduct, however, are your preconceived, objective ideals and how you've chosen to relate actively with your environment.*

That weekend we went to the Olympics and had a great time. Before the hike, I took Sasha to a little joint that made the best pancakes in the world. When we had our fill, we drove up to a trailhead about fifteen miles from town. We put on our raingear and hiked into the green forest. About three hours in, we made it to my favorite place on Earth. In the middle of nowhere, a number of small springs bubbled up cold mountain water into a small pool that gently began to trickle down between black rocks covered with vibrant green moss. About a hundred feet below the springs was a confluence of various starting points where the creek began to flow with some speed. The springs created a small meadow within the delta that was covered with thyme, yellow asters and a myriad of other colorful mountain vegetation. The old-growth trees protected the oasis from the harsh weather above. The place was prehistoric in nature. Huge ferns encroached into the fresh creek and fed on stumps of trees that met their demise. It was the plushest landscape I'd ever seen, and I deeply enjoyed the place each time I reentered it. When there, I always had a sense of belonging to the Universe, yet I felt like a tiny speck in the grandness of it all. The place never ceased to leave me feeling humble and rejuvenated.

The drive home was comfortable and quiet. As we reluctantly drove back to civilization, we shared wonderful conversation and ate the leftover snacks we had packed for lunch. We laughed and showed our more delicate sides. We talked of our pasts, futures, and how each of us might fit into such a place. I dropped Sasha off at her apartment a few hours later and went home to get some sleep.

The next day was Sunday. After I called Sasha to thank her for the time we spent together, I went down to the pub to watch some football with a few friends.

I liked my new life. It was so much quieter and peaceful.

The next few weeks, I continued to date Sasha, but I felt it necessary not to be immediately drawn into another relationship, so I went on a few other dates as well. They were nothing special. I mostly just thought about Sasha. And then we had the talk that changed everything.

About a month into it, around Halloween, we sat and had a nice dinner and she asked me whether I was still seeing other people. "Mostly women," I answered coyly. I took a drink of wine.

"No, really," she said.

I'd been thinking about having this conversation for a few days. I knew it was coming and just spoke from the heart. "I've had a few other dates, but nothing spectacular. The women are usually just trying to find something they'll never find in another human being. I'm not so interested in trying to fit into someone else's life, or in filling their gaps of unhappiness. I want someone with whom to grow, and truly appreciate the journey of life. And all I've found are fearful, angry, frustrated, hurt people who refuse to let the past go. Most people like to talk about themselves constantly; how much they've achieved, how much they have, whom they know. I'm just so bored with all of that. I like people like you, Sasha; people who aren't afraid to own up to mistakes and who try not to repeat them. I like you because you realize your life is a blank slate, and you're the painter. You inspire me to continue to strive for love, understanding and responsibility. You've never labeled me. You've never judged me. You've just appreciated me for who I am. I love being with you, but I don't put any expectations on what this is becoming. I simply like it for what it is. The time we spend together doesn't fill any addiction for me. I genuinely like being with you." The words comfortably flowed out of me; I knew them as truth.

After a few seconds, she said in response, "I feel the same way. Let's just date each other then." The words were so matter-of-fact.

I thought for a second before I answered. I was a little afraid of entering into another relationship so quickly, but it had been almost four months since my last relationship and years since I had dated someone with substance. I had been through a lot recently, but I felt better and cleaner than ever. I was solid. Sasha and I had talked quite a bit in recent conversations about our pasts and what we'd learned from them. Sasha felt comfortable with my past, and I with hers. But even though I liked Sasha a lot, I couldn't allow one of her current activities in my own life. So I said, "I would love to give it a shot, but only on one condition."

She nervously chuckled and took a sip of wine. "What's that?"

"I will gladly date you exclusively if you stop smoking completely. I don't date smokers. I never have and I never will."

Nervously, she said, "Okay. Why's that?"

"I believe it's a major weakness," I asserted. "It's like saying to the world you don't have what it takes to deal with your problems and addictions, and you need chemical dependence and external acceptance to make it in the world. You don't strike me as the type of person who fits that bill. You're really adorable, clear and you have a brilliant mind. I think you're probably just doing it because it's what you've always done. But you don't need to do it anymore. It's not necessary. I truly want to date you, but I don't date smokers." Speaking with that kind of resolve was empowering. And even though I was risking a potential relationship with a wonderful woman, my assertion was honest and pure.

## *Point Of Responsibility*

*83. Do you stand up for your well-thought-out, rational beliefs, or do you fold under the pressures of others, or of society? If you know you don't want to date someone who parties all the time, don't date someone who parties all the time. If you don't want to work in an office setting, don't work in an office setting. Understand clearly the things you want in your life, and the things you don't. We get into trouble and create anxiety when we aren't living in line with our rational beliefs. Don't judge anyone for his or her behavior, but make active decisions about whether you want to live intimately with such things.*

She shook her head gently up and down for a few seconds before replying, "Okay. I hate it anyway. I don't even know why I do it. But how do I quit? I kinda crave it, you know?"

"You probably don't want to quit cold turkey. How about you give it a month to quit gradually? And when you finally do, we'll celebrate madly! And if you don't, I'll be forced to throw myself out into the general dating pool yet again. Please don't make me do that!" We laughed and clanged our wine glasses. It was hopefully the beginning of something wonderful.

Getting to know each other in a healthy, responsible way was unbelievably refreshing. We had no expectations. We just lived in the present. We spoke our minds and respected each other in all situations. We laughed and learned about one another daily. I was continually amazed at how there was actually someone else in the world who understood me, and who was on the same path.

On one overcast, Seattle day, I checked my voicemail as I drove home for lunch. The third message was from Summer. My body tightened and the heat in my gut rose up into my throat. It was the first time in weeks I had felt such an emotion. My breathing became shallower and the palms of my hands started to sweat. The mere sound of her voice stopped me dead in my tracks. I was so repulsed by the thought of having been with her. As I listened to her words, I caught a glimpse of my face in the rearview mirror. All the anxiety, disgust and fear had come back and showed themselves as muscular tension, furrowed brow and clenched jaw.

Summer's message was about three minutes long. She informed me that she took responsibility for her part in everything. Her voice was condescending and sure as she told me how sorry she was that she had pushed herself on me. I felt betrayed and taken advantage of by that statement, as if I were just a little pawn in her dysfunctional chaos. I was so glad to be over that disgusting part of my life. Then she said something that sent barbs throughout my body. She told me I still needed to take responsibility for my part. I could hear in her voice the absolution of guilt, with her passing the buck onto me. At first, I was just a little annoyed. But the more I thought about her words, the angrier I got. I listened to the message about five times. I couldn't believe the gall she had. My ego caused quite a ruckus as it defended my "rightness."

I took a twenty-minute walk before making it back to my car. I jumped back in without having lunch and went back to the office. On my way there, I got over the initial emotion and felt relieved that I no longer had to deal with such things. I wasn't about to bring them into my present, so I deleted the message. No way would I ever call her back to have her further absolve her sins.

I decided not to bring up the phone call to Sasha. It was over and I felt it unnecessary to discuss such revolting things with her. I just put it into the recycle bin of my brain and continued on.

Not three weeks after the phone call from Summer, I got another voicemail from some drunken guy babbling something into the phone. I didn't recognize the voice. It sounded like a little kid who was holding his nose to make his voice sound different. I laughed at first, until I heard what he was actually saying, "Hey, uhhh, just wanted to let you know that I know about, uhhh, you and my, uhhh, fiancée. This is Derek Jones, and I know about you." It was Erin's fiance. In a crazy voice, he continued on with various threats against both my person and my practice. I'd seen him before in the community, and I wasn't afraid of him physically, but I was mortified by the amount of potential destruction a person in his position could create in my life.

I'd heard it through the grapevine that he and Erin had broken up, and I couldn't say it came as much of a surprise. Erin was in the process of moving forward with her life, but he was on a path of destruction. I knew I wasn't the only man Erin had cheated on Derek with. I, however, was the one who got his attention. I could only guess he had found out Erin had cheated on him, and she had thrown my name in his face to flaunt him with the men she had been with. She was the gift that kept on giving.

My life had been going incredibly well, but this new glitch could potentially stir things up significantly. I had no idea how far Mr. Jones would go. I wondered whether I had to be concerned about him attacking me with a gun, or coming to my office as I treated patients. I didn't know what to expect, so I tried to go on without thinking about it. I didn't tell Sasha about the phone call. Again, I felt it was all in the past, and I definitely didn't want to lose her over it. I just hoped the guy would get over his anger and move on. I rationalized that I actually had very little to do with the demise of Erin and Derek's relationship. It was clearly over before she and I had our ridiculous little tryst. He was a smart fellow, so I was sure he would bring it to a rational close.

Shortly thereafter, I received yet another voicemail from Summer. At first, I didn't want to listen to it, but my curiosity got the better of me. She told me she was sorry for everything and wanted to get together for lunch. I couldn't believe it. The woman was sick. I quickly deleted the message and kept her where she belonged, deep in the past.

## *Point Of Responsibility*

*84. Have you been known to avoid or ignore challenging situations? Do you procrastinate? Do you live with blinders on, choosing not to deal with financial issues, business matters or matters of the heart? Dealing with the less desirable side of life is how we grow and learn about ourselves. We should jump at the opportunity to remove the veils of fear and shock, and to allow clarity and active thought to change our lives. Deal with your issues head-on when they come up. Don't allow them to fester and become more than they have to be. To do so will limit the consequences associated. If you don't do it now, you'll continue to live in fear and you won't become the truest representation of yourself.*

It was almost the holidays, and Sasha and I were doing very well. We quickly fell in love and shared most nights together. Around that time, I started looking for a second home. I wanted a little vacation place we could enjoy year around, so we spent weekends away searching for the perfect place. We looked everywhere within a five-hour drive, as far north as the Canadian Rockies, and as far south as the Oregon coast. In early December, we decided on a place in the mountains of northern Washington. It was everything we were looking for. The weather was warm in the summer, and there was world-class skiing in the winter. The drive was easy, as it took only a couple of hours from both Seattle and Vancouver, and the cabin itself was to die for. It was a new build with a ton of space. We loved it and were excited to have a place to go on weekends.

As we waited for the financing to go through, we spent the holiday season with her family and followed that up with a Caribbean cruise to celebrate all the new things in our lives.

When we returned home, we closed on the beautiful cabin and filled it with eclectic furniture. Even shopping for the place was fun. Unfortunately, Sasha was laid off from work at the same time. A silver lining, however, was when she asked whether I'd be interested in hiring her to work the front desk. She knew things with Claudia were tenuous, and Julie needed some help. I thought about it for a couple of days before we had a serious discussion about it. I was a little concerned about dating someone with whom I worked, but after talking about it at great length, we decided to give it a shot. She would start the next time Claudia mishandled her duties. Unfortunately for Claudia, that was only a few days. She simply self-destructed by not showing up to work for three days in a row. She used every excuse in the book, so it wasn't difficult to let her go.

I was so glad I decided to bring Sasha into the office. Patients immediately fell in love with her. Everything was working out so well.

In March, Sasha and I planned another trip to the Olympic Mountains. We hadn't been there since our second date, and I thought it would be a great place to ask her to marry me. Over the previous few weeks, it became clear Sasha was the woman with whom I wanted to spend the rest of my life. It was a no-brainer. I searched everywhere and found a beautiful ring for her. It was classy, sophisticated and genuinely beautiful, just like her. I knew it was hers the moment I saw it. I wrapped it in a T-shirt and stuffed it in my weekend bag.

When we got to Port Angeles, the weather was blustery and wet. Trees, branches and debris littered the roadway, but we made it to the hotel unscathed. We went out for dinner, but called it a night relatively quickly. We were both quite fatigued from the previous workweek.

The next morning, we got dressed for our hike and went to the pancake cafe for breakfast. I'd stuffed the ring into my breast pocket, and kept checking every couple of minutes to make sure I didn't drop it somewhere. I was petrified of losing the thing.

We went to the same trail we had visited six months previously. We hiked up the side of the mountain for hours as I videotaped the whole thing under the guise of trying out my new camera. The hike was cold, wet and ethereal. But I'd never remembered feeling warmer. I was delighted to be where I was, and I felt like I was walking in the clouds the whole time. The trek was like a pleasurable out-of-body experience. It was calm, light-hearted and pleasantly invigorating.

When we finally reached the clearing where the springs were, it was around lunchtime. Right on cue, the big snowflakes started falling to the ground from way above. The brook below meandered between rocks and under small shelves of ice on either side. About fourteen inches of snow were still on the ground. The place was silent. I walked down to the side of the brook and took video of the whole thing, including Sasha from a distance. She went down into the delta to check out the ornate rock formations.

After a few minutes, I pulled the ring out of my pocket and began to walk toward her. My heart started beating faster. I was increasingly paranoid about dropping the ring into the snow or the brook. I could just see it falling and never being recovered. I told myself not even to pretend it could be lost. I walked up behind her, video still rolling, when she turned around to greet me with a kiss. I pulled my lips away and started telling her why I really loved being with her, and how I wanted to spend the rest of my life with her. Then I finally offered the ring to her. Only a small part of me wondered what she would say. We already shared a deep knowing that we would be together forever. It was a relief to have that part of the equation solved. Nevertheless, I knew I was lucky to be with her, and I couldn't have been happier when she said,

"Yes." We rolled in the snow, kissing and hugging for a little while before making the trek back to the truck.

Anticipating her answer, I booked our next night at the lodge above the falls, the same place where I'd recaptured my life. I wanted to share that place with her. So we jumped in the truck and made our way to the lodge. We were there in just a few hours. One thing I loved about northern Washington was being able to see so many things over such a short time period. It was the land of the day trip.

We arrived at the lodge and immediately got a bite to eat. Afterward, we went up to the room and stoked a fire for a little while before heading to our evening spa treatments. The pools were dreamy and the massages heavenly. I wanted for absolutely nothing in my life. I was so grateful for all of it. I was excited to be on that journey with my life partner.

We lazed around into the next day before they kicked us out. It was time to head home. On the way there, I asked Sasha whether she wanted to check out some open houses. It was Sunday and there were always a few good houses to check out in Atherton. She agreed it would be a fun thing to do.

The first house we checked out was unbelievable. It was on the west side of a hill facing the Olympic Mountains and Puget Sound. Its neighborhood was extremely quiet, and even majestic. As we strolled through the grand rooms, I fell in love with the mission style, huge picture windows and the wood floors. Sasha fell in love with the kitchen and that each bedroom had its own private bathroom attached. Most importantly, even with all its charm, the place still had greater potential. It was awesome! I knew I couldn't afford the huge price tag, especially with two other mortgages. But it was good to dream. I could see myself living in a place like it within three years, if everything worked out well. We checked out a few other homes, but nothing compared to the first one. It was the house of our dreams.

The next day, I was talking to my good friend Joe who owned the mortgage company. We talked about the house and future dreams of owning such a place. At the end of the phone call, Joe told me he was going to check whether he could get me financed for the big house. I kind of laughed it off, but was curious to see how far my professional title and recent earnings could take me, so I told him to go for it.

I went back to look at the place a couple of days later with an agent who was a friend at the time. We went through the house with a fine-toothed comb and did all the cross comparisons on the property and others like it. The place was priced to sell, and I quickly got caught up in the thought of actually owning that particular house. To pull it off would be a wonderful engagement gift to Sasha.

After my conversation with my agent buddy, I called Joe and asked him how the numbers looked. He said we could get it financed with a good rate; lenders had little issue giving out money to professionals.

I next called my accountant for his view from a tax standpoint. He was the only one who really knew whether I could afford it. He told me I was making enough to pay for the house, and it would be a great tax write-off. He didn't have to sell me on it. I hung up before he could change his mind.

Later that night, we made an official offer on the house, and within fifteen days, we closed. I couldn't believe I had just bought the house of my dreams. I had everything I had ever wanted, and I was only thirty-three years old. I was so grateful for everything, most of all for Sasha. Our relationship helped me alter my long-term goals into short-term goals. Having children and a wife had always been at some point in the distance, but I could finally see those times coming nearer, and I welcomed them.

We moved over to the big house right away and put the smaller house up for sale. The real estate industry was leveling off a little. It had been red-hot for the previous six years, but my agent assured me we'd still make money on the smaller place, especially with all the work I'd done on it. It looked great and everyone loved it.

Julie and Sasha were doing very well at the office. The accounts receivable steadily declined and we became more efficient as the weeks and months passed. I had finally achieved a sense of balance within my life. All things were firing on all cylinders, and I was on top of the world. My relationships were healthy. My business life was quite solid with an expanding future. My personal life was incredibly different from just nine months before. I wanted for nothing for the first time in my life. I appreciated every single day, and everyone and everything in it.

As we created new routines within our new home, Sasha and I became closer than ever. While watching the sunsets over the Olympics that first week, we talked about planning our wedding. Effortlessly, we agreed on a quaint, intimate ceremony that would include only our family and closest friends. Neither of us was interested in having a big production. We wanted it to be passionate with a sense of practicality. We wanted everyone to appreciate the moment, not the stuff surrounding it. Stress and ritual would have no room, only love and affection. We quickly decided our new house would be the best place to share our nuptials. We were so excited to have our loved ones around us as we committed our lives to one another.

But almost immediately after creating the plan for our future together, I received notice that things had the potential to change, and change drastically for the worse.

# Part Three:

# The Awakening

Chapter Sixteen:

# The Wake-Up Call

It was a random Tuesday morning, and I was on my way to the office to take care of some pressing business. I didn't have patients for about five hours, and I relished the idea of being at the clinic alone to recollect my thoughts in a quiet atmosphere. I parked and walked toward the door. Kyle was across the street cleaning up the parking lot after a rowdy night at the bar. He shouted over a big, bellowing hello as he waved.

"Hey, Kyle! Don't you ever sleep?" I asked.

He just laughed and said, "I got my four hours! Why don't you come over for a beer tonight? I'm buying."

"I'll be around after work!" I unlocked the door and walked inside. A thick, white envelope was on the floor as I pushed the door open. I thought it must be a payment someone had dropped off after hours. I picked it up and tucked it under my arm as I turned up the thermostat and flipped on a few lights.

When I got over to the front desk, I put down my bag and read the front of the envelope: Dr. Mark Svetcos—Personal. I opened it up and unfolded the numerous pages. What I read made my knees buckle. As I began to understand what I grasped within my hands, my heart pounded faster and my hands shook uncontrollably. I read through the brief letter about a hundred times within two minutes. But it said the same thing each time. And it was no joke.

The letter stated very clearly that it was the writer's intention to pursue legal action against me for sexual misconduct with a patient, and the patient was his fiancée. He had already lined up the necessary media contacts to blow the story wide open, and retained an attorney to sue me civilly. He blamed me for being the sole cause of the downfall of his potential marriage, and he wanted retribution in all its forms.

I knew he was serious. But the interesting thing was that he said the next move was mine. The letter stated he hadn't taken it public yet; he was going to blackmail me. The last part of the letter described how to get a hold of him to learn of his requirements. It was signed…Derek Jones.

Attached to the letter were the numerous sexual misconduct laws he printed off from the Washington State Department of Health website, as well as recent newspaper articles about doctors who had lost their licenses for various egregious behaviors. He knew what he was talking about, and that such accusations would ruin my practice.

I paced back and forth in my office for a couple of minutes, wondering exactly what I should do. My chest was tight and I couldn't catch my breath. The heat inside my throat was unbearable. I felt like my head was going to pop off! I swallowed the cottony spit in my mouth, but it wouldn't go down my constricted, dry throat. I sat down at my desk, only to get up and continue pacing. I clearly wasn't going to get any work done, so I grabbed my keys and walked out the door. I turned to lock it and my hands shook so violently that the keys fell onto the wet cement pad. I picked them up and used two hands this time to steady the key. I turned and walked briskly to my car as Kyle said something to me from across the street. I waved without looking and jumped in the Porsche. I started her up and sat there for a couple of minutes.

My body was rigid and my spine erect. I felt I had a thousand-pound weight on my shoulders that forced my body to lean forward. I fought it, which caused my head and shoulders to touch the seat briefly until the weight took over again. It was a battle to keep my head up. As I physically rocked back and forth, I noticed my eyes didn't feel like they were my own. I could see out of them, but the sensations weren't what I would describe as typical vision. They were blurry, black and white. I couldn't feel my body. I would glance down at my hands and see them making a fist, but I couldn't feel the tightness of the muscles as they strained. My breathing was shallow, and I felt like if I didn't move, I would wake up from my dream and Sasha would be next to me saying, "Wow, that must've been a nightmare! You were jerking and groaning like I've never seen!"

But the dream continued. It was really happening. I jammed the shifter into first and took off like a rocket toward the park. Tears started falling as I contemplated what I should do. Should I keep it to myself and hope for the best? Should I tell Sasha now? That would be the right thing since I'd never kept anything from her in the past. And besides, there was no way I could hide something like that. She worked at my office! And I didn't want to hide it anyway. It wasn't how I lived my life anymore. It was all really happening. My worst nightmare was my conscious reality!

I drove ferociously past the multi-million dollar homes of Atherton and toward the park. I had only one mission at that point, getting to the The Cliffs. I screeched down the road and into the park. I almost killed myself and whoever was in the other car while negotiating the S-curves. I abandoned Natasha and briskly walked to the Cliffs as I ripped off my tie.

As I got to the edge of the sandy, limestone cliff, a deluge of tears accompanied tremendous sorrow for the things I had done. I stepped up onto the old growth log that one should never pass. I looked down at the cold, rocky surf below and outstretched my arms.

Chapter Seventeen:

# Strength

As I stood above the black rocks that sharply jutted up hundreds of feet below me, I took a deep breath and filled my lungs with the cool, salty, Puget Sound air. Tears had ceased and were dried to my cheeks. I put my arms down to my sides and continued to breathe deeply with the intention of clearing all the black emotion from every cell in my body. I stepped back, off the log, and closed my eyes. My head gently rolled forward as I elongated my spine with a full, deep breath. I stretched out my shoulders and back and continued to let the stress melt into each exhalation.

## *Point Of Responsibility*

*85. Have you ever been blindsided by something that has unexpectedly changed your life? Understand that you're not in control of all situations. There are many forces at work. The nature of life is a balance between complete organization and chaos, even though both are merely perception. The fact is that sometimes things just happen. This, however, should not become your mantra. Although there are parts of life over which we have little control, the much greater part of our lives we can control. Any time you're surprised by an event, or blindsided, be as productive, introspective and responsible as you possibly can. Simply accept the event as having happened, process the emotions and move forward. Don't allow yourself to get caught up in victimization and in reliving the events ad infinitum. Such events are major opportunities to help us, and those around us, to evolve. Learn the lessons. Learn the lessons. Learn the lessons.*

*In your notebook, list the five most life-changing events that have happened in your adult life. Carefully and responsibly step away from the emotions of loss, guilt, shame, fear, bewilderment, disbelief, anger and blame. Describe factually how you reacted to each situation. Then go back into each story, and with your newly uncovered ability to self-analyze calmly and unemotionally, write in extreme detail how you would handle yourself if that same situation happened to you today. Envision yourself standing up straight, not saying anything rash, taking long, deep breaths, listening, and letting emotion recede before taking a responsible, blame-free action. You've already lived through the situation the first time, so you know that you'll make it through yet again. In effect, what you're doing is resetting a new baseline with regard to how you deal with highly emotional situations. You're literally resetting and recreating new memory cells. And since you've now relived those tumultuous situations with success, you have a history of doing so. You've always been able to do it. It's always been that way, for as long as you can remember. This is a serious step forward in your progression to living a conscious life in the present. So be present. Relive and replace each situation as many times as necessary with your positive outcome. Do not consider this step complete until you're literally smiling by the end of each and every challenging situation. Be honest, and be responsible!*

It was right there, at that specific moment, that I decided to confront everything negative that was coming my way with the same calm and focused intention I had been living for the previous eight months of my life. I wasn't going to stop living with truth and purpose. I wasn't going to deny anything or blame anyone else. That was the point where the rubber met the road, so to speak. Living consciously was relatively easy while things were going well. But what a person did in times of adversity was what showed his or her character. It was my chance to prove to myself that I was strong on the inside; that I wasn't just a bunch of talk. I was going to face into the wind and confront head-on everything negative I had created in my life. And that was where it was all going to end.

After about a half-hour of meditative breathing, I walked slowly back to the car, taking notice of everything for which I was grateful. I still had a wonderful life. I didn't know what Sasha's reaction was going to be. I definitely wanted to be with her for the rest of my life, but if she saw things differently, I could do little about it. I just knew it would all work out for the best. That was the nature of life.

I drove back to work and completed the tasks at hand before seeing patients that day. I cherished the time I spent with each of them as I felt a stronger, deeper bond to the therapy and counsel I provided. I had a confidence that was unshakable.

During that day, I realized I had already changed for the better in three primary ways. First, I could now take my emotions and do something proactive with them. When I first read the letter, I had an extreme emotional response to the words on the paper, but within the hour, I had used those emotions to dissect what was going on inside me. In the past, I would not have fully inspected such things, or I might even have dismissed them completely.

Secondly, I was now able to let the emotions go after utilizing them. I didn't stew in their presence. I didn't think about them for hours on end and allow them to poison everything around me. It was nearly impossibly to deter my mind recalling the letter, but after repeatedly letting the visions go, I acted from a deeper place, not from an egoistic or emotional one. I acted from the "me" who observed. I simply kept telling myself there was nothing I could do at that point.

The third change was that I didn't allow others' emotions to affect me negatively. That had been a biggie in my past. I was prone to doing what many humans do every day. I would literally feel the anger, frustration and pain others felt, and mirror that back to them. I would basically resonate at the same frequency as the other person. The easiest example involved my mother. Whenever she decided to fly off the handle, I would mirror that activity. My heart would pound, my face become stoic, and my voice deeper. Even if I didn't say anything, or wasn't involved in her reason for anger, I would still have that fight or flight response. I wasn't my true authentic self. Basically, I was living the lives of others. I'd chosen not to be a party to such activity. I had always been a good sympathizer, but I'd finally become a good empathizer. I didn't have the need to be so close to the pain, anger, or frustration to feel I was a part of a situation, or to feel I was helping someone. I could do the job much better while first being strong within myself. I finally felt I was living my own life.

The present strife presented an opportunity to practice my new way of being. Everything I'd worked so hard for was on the line. I never once thought of running, escaping or hiding. I didn't place blame on others, but took the responsibility for myself. I couldn't change my past; it was complete. But I could most definitely change how I was to live while moving forward, while dealing with others' inevitable judgments of my past.

After work, Sasha and I jumped in the car and went home. We changed and decided to go out for dinner. I had no idea how to bring up the letter. So on the way to the restaurant, I took a deep breath and just started talking.

"I got a letter in the mail today that may change things for us significantly."

"What do you mean? From who?" she asked.

"It was from Derek Jones. He's Erin's ex-fiancé. I told you about my one-time affair with her, remember?"

"Yeah, I remember. Well, what did it say?"

"It said, well, here, just read it." I handed her the letter.

The silence was deafening. I had no idea how she would respond. Those were the longest few moments of my life. She read the letter, flipped it over to look for any writing on the backside, and then put it down.

"Doesn't he have anything better to do with his life? He should just be relieved he found out she was a cheater before he married her. So what's next? Can he really sue you?"

"I have no idea. She's not even the one, as my patient, making the complaint. And I don't know the rules that apply. I don't know much of anything at this point."

"So what do we do now? Live in fear?" she asked.

"We just live our lives like we have been. Nobody can make us feel any way we don't want to. We have a great life, with or without all the stuff. So let's just continue living with purpose, and we'll deal with everything as it comes. The most important thing to me is that I don't lose you. I think we're great together, and I hope we have a long life of happiness ahead of us, regardless of how all this turns out."

"I'm not leaving you," she said as she leaned over and kissed my cheek. "I love you more than anything in the world. I know who you really are, and I love you even with your faults. But the thing is, you don't even live that way anymore. So it's kind of irrelevant, isn't it?"

"Let's just hope that if this gets out, everyone else sees it that way. It was consensual sex, and it was one time. But people like this kind of gossip. Seeing the downfall of someone successful makes them feel better about their own lives. All we can hope is that Mr. Jones is making empty threats and none of it will matter. Let's just try to relax and live our own lives." Sasha agreed and we did the best we could with the rest of the night.

The next day, I read the letter again. The guy was obviously hurt by his fiancée's betrayal. I wondered whether he knew about the other guy she'd been with, and how far he might go to get back at someone. I lost hours worrying and replaying the situation in my mind. Again, I realized I was just a pawn and had no control over what was going to happen. I decided not to contact him. I wasn't interested in getting involved in a heated emotional battle, and I definitely wasn't going to pay him off. Whatever the consequences of my decision, I would endure.

I placed the letter in a file folder and filed it under "The Past."

### *Point Of Responsibility*

*86. Do you hold grudges? Doing so is the primary way we relive and recreate negative emotions. It's also how we attempt to control others. To hold a grudge is to give your power away. In your ego's struggle to control and devise, the power of both parties is consumed by the fight to be right, to be more important, or to be better. They are, in point of fact, simply fighting to be heard. Such behavior decimates and stifles growth and creation. Ego proliferation and positive creation cannot coexist. You're either doing one, or you're doing the other. When you choose to do battle for "rightness," you're actively choosing NOT to use reason. If there is a perceived "winner," that winner has only won until the next inevitable battle ensues. The ego needs more and more in the endless pursuit of "rightness." Balance your ego. Lose the grudge, and figure out how to create a mutually beneficial coexistence. The easiest way to diffuse such situations with perceived enemies is simply to ask their opinions about something. And then genuinely listen. Don't seek a lengthy conversation. Don't be fake. Don't laugh too much. Just be real, and completely non-confrontational.*

Chapter Eighteen:

# The Sidewalk

Most of my anxiety concerning Mr. Jones' threats faded over the next few months since we didn't hear anything new. Sasha and I decided to get married on the last day in June, so we focused our attention between that and the office. Julie was finally getting us paid on all the accidents that Claudia had created, and Sasha was excellent at running the front office. The practice was growing steadily again. Seldom were we not busy, and the place was as efficient as could be. A definite shift in consciousness had occurred over the past ten months. Normal daily conflicts easily melted away and my patients were happier than ever. The connections between everyone involved with the office were deeper and more meaningful than at any point in its existence. It had turned the corner into being a community health care center rather than just another medical clinic.

As the days turned into weeks, and then into months, the good fortune around the clinic and us continued. I decided to reward myself for my recent abundance with something I'd always wanted. For years, I'd admired Harley Davidson Motorcycles. And I was finally ready to pull the trigger on an especially classy one I found in Seattle. She had a mango-white paint job, had a brand new chromed-out engine and many refined customizations. The thing was a sight to behold and sounded just as elegant. I immediately fell in love with her and got a great deal to boot.

## *Point Of Responsibility*

*87. The end of the cycle with regard to goal creation is reward. Each time you create a goal, think of a modest reward for its achievement. Envision yourself enjoying that reward, and work diligently to reach your goal. Cut out pictures of it, write it down, and use all five senses to create it in your mind. Each time a goal is surpassed, be sure to reassess your life for balance. If imbalance exists, correct it. Then write your new goals and begin to envision both your goal and your reward being achieved. This is the Cycle of Enlightened Achievement, which you can further discover at www.responsibilitymovement.com.*

I quickly got my motorcycle riding endorsement and started riding around town most nights to get a feel for her. I always knew I'd love riding, but I didn't know until then how truly enlightening it was. My favorite rides were on small, two-lane country roads at about forty-five miles per hour, with Sasha holding on behind me. The smell of the grasses and trees, coupled with the myriad other sensations, made riding a spiritual event. With every ride, I felt closer to nature, closer to the Earth, closer to myself.

Sasha and I continued to plan the wedding together, and before we knew it, the date was upon us. I was excited to be marrying my best friend and life partner. The last couple of days before the wedding, all of our closest friends flew in from various regions of the country. We all talked, ate and drank while reliving the good stories of the past and integrating them with our future.

The night before our wedding, Sasha and I stayed downtown while the family and Bobby decorated our house for the nuptials. We had a wonderful dinner and spent the rest of the evening loving each other while watching the sun go down over the bay and mountains.

We woke up early the next morning and had breakfast in bed before Sasha left to get ready. I stayed behind and slowly got around. I had a couple of hours to go before my eleven-thirty arrival back at the house. So I put on some clothes and went to get some coffee. I took a leisurely walk downtown for a few minutes. I liked watching people briskly going about their days. I wondered what they were all doing. How many of them were getting married today? How many of them were still in love? Were they happy? I was most definitely in love, and I couldn't be happier. As I walked the streets, I remembered wondering when I was younger, if I would ever really want to get married. Would I ever want to be with just one person for the rest of my life? Could I be with just one person for the rest of my life? Was it within my power? I laughed a little to myself as I cherished the feelings that Sasha and I shared. I was so much in love with her, and it was healthy. There were absolutely no thoughts of "hoping for the best." I genuinely wanted to do everything in my power to make it a solid, functional and loving relationship. I was so excited that we had allowed each other the opportunity to share our lives.

I had about forty-five minutes before I was expected at the house, so I walked back upstairs to get ready to roll. I put on some music and took a long shower. When I got out, I looked at myself in the mirror, deep into my eyes. I was happy. Yes, many things in my life had not always been the most productive, but all that seemed lifetimes ago. I was humbly proud of the things I'd overcome. I'd learned from my mistakes, and I was now reaping the benefits of leading a life of purpose and intention.

I slowly shaved, put on some deodorant and lotion. When finished in the bathroom, I went into the bedroom to see the sun shimmering off the bay. It was a wonderful day. I sat on the bed and meditated for a few minutes. It was the quietest my mind had ever been. When I was ready, I got up, put on my suit and scooted out the door.

On the drive there, the sun shined through the open moon roof and onto my face. Cool, jazzy music played on the radio. I was in heaven. I paid no attention to the people cutting me off in traffic, to the construction barrels strewn all over, or to the overzealous bicyclists who owned the road. I was happy, deeply happy.

I pulled up to the house with a few minutes to spare. My dad greeted me with a big hug and we walked inside. The place was exquisitely beautiful. Bobby had done a superb job with the decorating and flowers. The sun's rays brightly filled the house and illuminated the thousands of roses and irises that adorned every corner and table. Everyone was quietly milling about with an interesting focused intensity. As I engaged a small group of our mutual friends, Sasha's mom came through the doorway and hugged me tightly before quickly going on about her business. Sasha's momma was adorable.

Within minutes, Sasha was walking down the foyer stairs looking absolutely stunning in her sleek, classically beautiful wedding gown. As her father led her toward me, I caught a glimpse of myself in the foyer mirror and noticed the perma-grin across my face. I couldn't stop it. I was so in love with her, and with everything our union represented.

Sasha's father handed her off, and we continued outside onto the front porch for the ceremony. All of our loved ones gathered on the green grass below the porch and looked on lovingly. Sasha and I faced the judge as we took in the beautiful view of the fine summer day and of each other. The gardens were beautifully manicured and gave way to The Puget Sound and the jagged Olympics Mountains in the distance. A warm, gentle breeze caressed our faces as the ceremony was conducted. And as quickly as it started, it quietly came to a close. We kissed each other and Sasha threw the bouquet into the mass of women below.

After a little while, the guests made their way to the reception, which Sasha booked at a high-end restaurant in West Seattle. The place literally sat on pilings over the water, and it faced downtown Seattle. I couldn't have dreamed up a better place.

Sasha and I shared conversation with everyone and handed out the wedding cupcakes when dinner was finished. We posed for pictures and shared a couple of hours of festivities and fellowship before going back to the house for the big party later that night.

As soon as she and I showed up to the party, we realized what we'd created. The thing was huge. Hundreds of people showed up to wish us well and to celebrate the wedding. The two kegs of beer I'd ordered had already been tapped. Sasha's sister, brother-in-law and father cooked enormous amounts of food within hours. They just kept churning it out to the masses of people who gobbled it up as quickly as they could prepare it. Wine was on every table and booze was being chilled in the coolers outside. By ten o'clock, the house was jumping with people, bumped with music and percolated with plenty of laughter.

It was the greatest party that neighborhood had seen in some time. Throughout the night, neighbors stopped by with flowers, pies, cakes, cookies and cards. It was better than I could have ever imagined. Happiness and celebration was in the air.

The day and night zoomed by relatively quickly, and before we knew it, it was just Sasha and I in our bed, falling asleep together with the pug between us. The day had completely exhausted us.

Early the next morning, we jumped a plane to Colorado for our honeymoon. We were going to spend two full weeks exploring the state. We both had an affinity for Colorado and wanted to experience it together. We stayed in the Stanley Hotel, the Hotel Colorado, and the Hotel Boulderado, all well known for being haunted. We checked out Pike's Peak, the Garden of the Gods, and the active mountain towns of Vail, Aspen and Breckenridge. We had a wonderful time hiking, rafting, eating and enjoying all the scenery. I couldn't have asked for a better honeymoon. Sasha and I were closer than ever, and I was so incredibly excited to be on the journey with her.

When we finally got back to work a couple of weeks later, the practice picked up right where it had left off. There were absolutely no gaps in treatment or payments. A different feeling was in the air around the clinic. A residual joy surrounded our lives. The party kept going, and I was eternally grateful.

On the home front, Sasha and I started actively creating our future together by creating a Code of Conduct. It was a mutual agreement and protocol for how to proceed when emotions inevitably fired up. We always wanted to continue to respect each other and actively to support, and be accountable for, the goals we had created and the actions between us within our marriage. We wrote down our goals for the relationship and did a daily focused meditation to begin to resonate at the frequency of each of those situations. We got deep into the sensation of each of our goals, which drew us closer together and allowed us mutually to focus our intentions for our future.

## *Point Of Responsibility*

*88. Create your own personal Code of Conduct. The Code of Conduct is a necessary component to one's arsenal of self-awareness. From a technical standpoint, it is comprised of the rules by which you have chosen to live. But it ends up being so much more. Your personal Code of Conduct represents the essence of you, the type of force you exert upon your environment. One technique to help create such a Code is to envision the person you love most on earth giving your eulogy. This is a powerful way to precipitate and crystallize your thoughts of how you will be remembered. This is NOT the time to think about your past, but to envision your future in the present. Think about the very essence of YOU. Declare the person you are! What are the top twenty things your eulogizer will say? If you have any immediate negative thoughts, give yourself a snap on the wrist with your rubber band. Then think of the positive ways you project yourself, how you resolve issues, how you interact with people, how you deal with stress. As you write, envision yourself living your Code of Conduct. Use all five senses. Write about all the good things you do and create, such as working hard, being a good listener, being loving, purpose-driven, humble, fun, or always laughing. The eulogy should be one to two pages. It is the synopsis of your Code of Conduct. When the eulogy is complete, expand upon each of those points with the exact vision of you physically and mentally doing each one. Take your time with your Code, and sign and date it when you've finished. Revise it as needed, but at least yearly. It's also a great idea to create a mutual Code of Conduct with your partner. It will certainly help you both to be on a level playing field. Detail exactly the Plan for Defusing for when arguments arise. The best time to create such a document is when things are going well in your relationship. You'll be more rational and honest. Creating a Code of Conduct in your relationship will also create confidence, good will and a deeper connection. For an example of a Code of Conduct, visit www.responsibilitymovement.com. You might also be interested in downloading the Universal Covenant of Responsibility for you and your family.*

A few days after returning home from our honeymoon, I ran into my long lost friend Chloe. I was in the village picking up some dinner when I bumped into her. We hadn't seen each other since I showed her our new house back in April. After that, she had basically fallen off the face of the Earth, at least to me. Since she had learned Sasha and I were to be married, she hadn't contacted me in any way. She didn't even show up to the wedding, which stung a little. Up until that point, I had thought Chloe was one of those "kindred spirit" kinds of friends.

I didn't exactly know what to say to her. So we stood for what seemed like an eternity, face to face. Finally, I said, "Hey there."

The situation clearly caught her by surprise. "Oh…hi to you too," she replied.

"How have you been? I missed you at my wedding. I really wanted you to be there."

"Oh, well," she said, "I had signed up for a yoga retreat at the last minute that I didn't want to miss." I looked her in the eyes. I knew there was more to it, but she wasn't going there.

"I want you to know I really miss our friendship. You're one of the greatest people I've ever known."

Chloe looked away. She didn't say anything. Our eyes were never to meet again. The meeting was over and I knew my friend was gone. I gave her a hug and walked to my car. My eyes welled up as I quietly grieved the loss of our friendship. She was the only one in the whole city of Seattle with whom I genuinely connected before I met Sasha. I loved her deeply, but only as a friend. I wanted to be her friend deep into old age, but it wasn't meant to be. In effect, she had released me.

## *Point Of Responsibility*

*89. Like Mick Jagger said, "You don't always get what you want. But if you try real hard, you get what you need." We all know this to be true. Life is an undulating energy that flows wherever there is no resistance. When things don't go the way you like, or the way you've envisioned them, know that they've happened that way for a reason. Relax and honestly ask yourself whether you could have done something differently with the same knowledge you had at the time. Don't beat yourself up if something could have changed things. Your will is not the only force in your life. There are many different energies out there. Take what you've learned and use it if and when such a situation appears in the future. Then let it go. There is an old Native American story about a warrior that is relevant to this situation:*

*There was a great warrior who had a fine stallion. Everyone said how lucky he was to have such a horse. "Maybe," he said. One day, the stallion ran off. Many said how unlucky the warrior was. "Maybe," he said. The next day, the stallion returned leading a string of five ponies. Everyone said how very lucky the warrior was. "Maybe," he said. Later, the warrior's son was thrown from one of the ponies and broke his leg. People said it was very unlucky. "Maybe," the warrior said. The next week, the chief ordered a war party against another tribe. Many men were killed. But because of the broken leg, the warrior's son was left behind, and his life spared.*

I went home and felt ill for days. I'd lost a good friend, so I actively grieved to let it go. I realized that with new growth, perceptions and relationships would necessarily need to change. Letting go of someone with no strings attached was difficult, but it was one of the caveats of living consciously and responsibly. My life had no room for women in my back pocket, or for any confusion or lack of clarity.

Only two days after my conversation with Chloe, I started receiving "Private Caller" phone calls on my cell. The first five or six times I received them, I assumed they were some solicitor because the caller never left voicemails. Then they became incessant, and at all hours of the day and night. I had immediate visions of Esther. She was notorious for being a "Private Caller."

When I told Sasha about the calls, she said the same thing had been happening to her for a few days, but she just ignored them.

One night after dinner, Sasha and I were watching a flaming red sunset and sharing a great glass of wine when my phone rang; it was the "Private Caller" again. I couldn't take it anymore, so I quickly scooted the pug outside to go potty and answered the phone as I walked down the porch stairs.

When I asked who it was, I heard the worst sound in the world—the raspy, sickening voice of Esther. "Mark?"

"Why are you calling me?" I demanded.

She had obviously already worked herself into frenzy. "I need you to be completely honest with me, Mark."

"What are you talking about, Esther?"

"It's about Derek Jones," she said.

I felt like I had just been hit on the back of the head with a shovel. The names Esther and Derek Jones had absolutely no connection within my brain. I searched but couldn't locate any common thread.

"I don't understand. What are you talking about, Esther?"

"Didn't you get my emails?" Her voice was like a comedy skit I'd seen years ago about a family that whines all the time.

I hadn't checked my personal email since returning from Colorado. "No, I haven't. Why do you ask, Esther? And what do you know about Derek Jones?"

She confusingly ranted on. "This is all so terrible, but there's another doctor that I dated before you who had a lawsuit brought against him for sexual misconduct, and even though it wasn't true, he lost everything and had to move to a different state. His life was ruined for a long time. I just don't want that to happen to you, so you have to tell me the truth, Mark."

I got the distinctly putrid feeling in my gut that I shouldn't trust her at all. It was too extraordinary that she could possibly be part of the whole thing. I was still confused about how she played into all of it. I quietly replied to her, "I have no idea what you're talking about Esther."

"Did you cheat on me Mark?"

"Are you serious Esther? Our relationship has been over for a long time. But no, I didn't cheat on you," I said honestly. "What's this all about? Why are you calling me about Derek Jones?"

"You really didn't cheat on me? Are you telling me the truth?"

"Esther, what are you doing? What do you want?"

"Did you cheat on me, Mark? You did, didn't you?"

I couldn't care less whether she thought I cheated on her. I wanted to know how she knew Derek Jones. But she wouldn't divulge anything. All my questions were replied to with her asking me whether I had cheated on her. Finally, after listening to her babble on for a minute or so, I realized I wasn't going to get anything from her. "Okay, Esther, I'm hanging up now. You're still just a little too off-the-wall for me. And for the record, again, I didn't cheat on you. That's the end of the story."

"Wait!" she screamed as I hung up the phone.

For five minutes after our phone call, my heart pounded hard within my chest. The pug was finished, so I let him back inside. Not surprisingly, as I was on the front porch, the phone rang again. I didn't have to wonder whom it could be. I walked back down to the sidewalk and answered it.

"What do you want from me, Esther?" I firmly said into the phone.

"Did you cheat on me, Mark?"

"You're being ridiculous, Esther. Please just get out of my life."

Before I could hang up the phone for the second time, she set the hook. "Derek Jones is going to file a formal complaint against you with the Board of Health in two days. And I just don't want to see it happen to you too."

I was stunned. I didn't know what to say except, "How do you know him?"

"Did you cheat on me?" she asked for the hundredth time.

We were getting nowhere. So I said, "Okay, Esther. Goodbye," but I waited for her to continue talking.

"Okay, okay, okay," she said. "We went on a date earlier this year." ("The serial dater lives," I thought to myself.)

"So?"

"He told me he lived in Atherton, so I told him my ex-boyfriend was a chiropractor there. When he asked whether it was you, I told him, "Yes." Then he told me you were a sexual predator and he was going to bring you down. So I'm just calling to get to the truth. Did you cheat on me with those women?"

I began to suspect she was working with Mr. Jones, and her calls might be recorded. So I chose my words very wisely. "What are you talking about, Esther?"

"He claims you slept with a bunch of women. So did you cheat on me?"

"Esther, I never cheated on you, and what women are you talking about?" I thought if I could get names out of her, I would better understand the situation.

"You never slept with a woman named Betsy, or Chloe, or Derek Jones' fiancée? Come on, Mark. Tell me the truth." She was looking for details. I wanted to scream out that she should get a life, but I wanted as much information as I could glean from her.

"Esther, I never slept with anyone other than you while we were dating. But why are you bringing up those women specifically? What are you not telling me?"

"Are you sure you never cheated on me?"

"Give me a break! What are you not telling me Esther?"

"He has a copy of your diary!"

I was completely thrown off. My diary? I didn't keep a diary…was she talking about…the scribblings I put in the book that my sister gave to me? I thought back and remembered writing a few names in there, but I certainly didn't remember which names. And I couldn't go back and look. I'd thrown the notebook away when we moved to the new house. I was at her mercy with regard to the information in it. It had been almost a year since I'd written those things. And then I wondered how he knew what was in the diary. And how did Esther know about it?

"How do you know what was in my diary, Esther? And how did he get it?" I suddenly remembered how my diary had mysteriously shown up in the back of my car, moved by someone else's hand.

"I don't know how he got it. I just know he has it." Did he really have it? Did he search through my garbage to get the thing? She knew more. I was sure she knew more.

"Don't lie to me Esther. Where did he get it?"

"I don't know!" I could tell she was holding back.

"Do you know you're messing with my life right now, Esther? Does that make you feel good? To mess with somebody's life? I'm hanging up now."

"No! Wait!"

I waited silently.

"Are you there?" she asked, still whining.

"Yes. You better talk quickly. I'm losing patience. Where did he get it?"

"Oh God. Oh God. He got it from me!"

"What are you talking about?" I asked.

"When I was over at your place once, during that week we spent together last year, I took it and read it. And then on our date, I told him about the diary and what was in it because I didn't think what you were doing was right. Is that who you cheated on me with? All those women in the diary?"

I was angry, so I twisted the dagger just a little so she would spill some names. "That depends; which women are you talking about?"

"Betsy and Chloe, and his girlfriend! Were you sleeping with all of them behind my back?"

I felt somewhat relieved there wasn't an all-inclusive list in the diary. But the information was still damning, at least with regard to Erin. One encounter was enough to file a complaint. But did Jones actually have the diary? Did he have the physical diary? Did she make a copy of it for him? Or was hers an empty allegation to get me to spill my guts over the phone? I had no idea what was going on. It was all so incredibly confusing. On the one hand, I certainly had no desire to lie about anything. On the other, I didn't want to self-incriminate. I'd already changed my life, and I had a wife and a future family to protect.

"Esther, look. I never cheated on you. While we dated, it was just you and I. That's the truth. I don't understand why you would try to hurt me, when all I did throughout our whole relationship was try to make it work. I loved you, but you just jerked me around. And if that wasn't bad enough, you're jerking me around some more now. Why do you want to keep hurting me? What did I ever do to you, Esther?"

"Did you sleep with his girlfriend? And what about Betsy and Chloe?"

"Esther, you don't have to say anything to anybody. This guy just wants to destroy me at any cost. He doesn't understand what really happened. For some reason, he thinks I was the only one involved. He's completely demonized me."

"What do you mean?"

"I'm not going to explain it to you over the phone. All I'm saying is there's more than one side to the story." Yes, I had slept with his fiancée, and although Erin had pursued it, it never should have happened, but I wasn't completely at fault.

"If I'm subpoenaed by the Board of Health, then I'm going to have to talk about what I know, Mark, so you better be telling me the truth."

"Don't threaten me, Esther. You don't even know the truth. You have no idea what you're in the middle of. Mr. Jones is using you as a pawn to get to me. Can't you see that?"

I had nothing more to say. When she went back to asking whether I had cheated on her, I hung up.

I went back inside. Sasha could tell something was wrong. I immediately told her the whole conversation. We checked my personal email and found Esther had sent me a message at lunchtime that day. It casually detailed everything she'd said, but it was too organized and well thought out—it was calculating; she wasn't concerned about me—she wanted something.

The next night, Esther sent me two text messages. She was still messing with me. She said Mr. Jones knew about a few of the women I'd had sex with, and I had until nine a.m. the next morning to make it right.

Mr. Jones was obviously employing as many people as he could in his battle to bring me down. I knew Chloe and Betsy would want nothing to do with him. They certainly wouldn't indulge him in his delusion. All that aside, the last thing Esther wrote was what piqued my interest most. How could I possibly make it right? What did they want?

Only minutes later, she texted me again to say it was already too late; he was going to contact all the women he suspected.

Why was it too late? Had he already sent in the formal complaint? What women did he really know about? The only ones Esther had mentioned were Betsy and Chloe. I racked my brain to come up with the exact names in the diary passage, but to no avail. It was too long ago to recall. And I hadn't been thinking clearly when I wrote in the diary. I would just have to sit and wait for his or her next move.

The next day I received even more text messages from Esther. The first, around six in the evening, said she would share her information if I shared mine. She wanted to meet A.S.A.P.

She was really pushing for something. Her sense of urgency stabbed me a little. Why did she want to meet so badly? I'd already told her repeatedly that I had never cheated on her. Why was she so invested? I could only think she wanted revenge for my discontinuing our relationship, and she was working with Mr. Jones to get it. Esther thrived on the chaos, so she would be in it to the end. Absolutely no way would I meet with her. I could just see her being wired and recorded by Mr. Jones. I wouldn't give them the sword.

Text messages and phone calls continued into the early evening, but I ignored them. After dinner, we listened to one of the messages she left on the voicemail. In the sweetest, most caring fake voice I'd ever heard, Esther said, "It's raining and God is sad. Give me the truth, and I'll do whatever I can." She was completely delusional.

Esther continued to barrage me with texts late into the night, stating Mr. Jones was back in town, and everyone was going to pay the price. She warned me this was my only chance to tell the truth; she said I would need a great malpractice lawyer. She and Jones were probably sitting side by side as they created and sent the messages.

Mr. Jones was obviously ready to move forward on his claim. But I didn't understand when I got a text stating that Chloe was going down? She had no interest in the matter at all. And Betsy could care less about his claim. I was the only one who could potentially pay for everything and everyone involved.

Another message came the next day informing me that Mr. Jones had just faxed the formal complaint, and that the investigation was to begin the following week.

All I could do was wait. If the complaint had been faxed in, an investigation would cause all the names to come out anyway. Mr. Jones had planned all along to send in the complaint; he had just used Esther to try gleaning more details from me. When she had been unsuccessful, he had sent in the complaint. Esther was clearly not in it to help me, so I continued to ignore her.

The next day at the office, Julie came back to where I was working and placed a single sheet of paper in front of me before quickly exiting. I turned it over and picked it up. It was an email from Mr. Jones. He was informing me that he was going to come for me. What I didn't understand was that he still wanted me to contact him; he was pretending he still might not expose me, which according to Esther's text message, he had already been done.

The guy obviously wasn't going away, and I knew he didn't want money. He wanted me to feel pain, emotionally, physically, and by any other means. He probably would file a complaint with the Department of Health; it was just a matter of time. Meanwhile, he wanted me to incriminate myself further, but I wasn't going to bite.

Derek Jones was a major threat to my well-being, but I didn't know to what degree—that was the difficult part for me. I didn't know where he was coming from, and he was cunningly calculating each of his moves. It was terrorism at its finest. I wondered how long the torment would last, and what he ultimately hoped to achieve. Was he waiting to take the case live, or had he, in fact, already done so? Did he have the legal capacity to sue me civilly?

All Sasha and I could do was prepare ourselves mentally for the impending uncertainty. We had to remain solid within our relationship and ourselves. We wondered what was next. The answer wasn't far away.

Chapter Nineteen:

# Wheels In Motion

The morning was cool and the sun just about to come up over the ridge. A couple of older race car drivers and I surveyed and inspected the track as we walked and shared stories about nothing in particular. I had recently begun to appreciate more such times of camaraderie, quiet understanding and humility of self, as well as the combination of passion and healthy competition.

We quickly walked back to our cars and finished our cups of coffee. With few words spoken, we all took to visualizing the course. I put on my helmet and got into Natasha. Within minutes, we roared around the track at speeds above one hundred forty miles per hour. Natasha belted out scream after scream as I went through the gears and in and out of the turns.

The course, where I had learned how to drive so meticulously, had been professionally built decades before, but it was still considered one of the most challenging in the country. There were tight and long turns, hills and banks, and lengthy straight-aways for a driver to test the upper limits of his or her vehicle while surging adrenaline into the arteries at lightning speed.

Racing was seldom about being the best, or beating one's opponents. When drivers bested themselves through technically sound interpretation, then the game was won. It was a culmination of many events, planned, intuited and executed with precision. Racing, to me, was much like life itself. The course was always an internal one. Whether a driver achieved a successful finish was always in direct correlation to how unclouded was his internal environment. Racing was pure—an uncompromising ability to shed emotions like fear and anger manifested itself directly into a successful finish.

Hours later, I was back at the office treating patients when Julie brought back another email that instructed me to prepare for litigation. I didn't have to wonder who it was from.

Sasha was beside herself. While she and I discussed the possible effects, she said to me, "All he wants is to place blame somewhere so he doesn't have to accept that his fiancée dumped him. He doesn't care about the collateral damage, just his own pain. It's like the pain just keeps switching hands, from one person to the next. Isn't someone going to stop it?"

"I am, honey. I'm going to make sure we don't pass the buck. I guarantee the pain of this situation is going to be turned into something positive. No matter what happens, I'll see to that."

The next morning, we finally received a fax of a formal complaint, written on DOH letterhead, and signed by a Mr. Jones. It gave all the details Erin had told him. He told the Department of Health to act quickly because he had hired a civil attorney, and he had media contacts in place, among other things.

At first, I thought it highly unprofessional for the DOH to fax the complaint to my general office fax number, but then I realized it was Mr. Jones who had faxed it over, for everyone to see. It was now obvious the situation would have to be met head-on.

Julie, Sasha and I immediately had a conversation about how we were going to handle everything. I told them I had no idea what was going to happen, but business had to go on as usual. We owed it to our patients. As we finished up our limited talk on logistics and possible actions, Julie asked, "So this whole thing is about consensual sex between adults?"

"Yes," I confirmed.

"Doesn't he have anything better to do, like blame his ex-girlfriend?" she asked.

"The fact is that I shouldn't have played any part in it, Julie."

Once they went back to work. I immediately started thinking about what I should do next. Unfortunately, there weren't exactly consultants who could handle that sort of thing. I was on my own.

I wondered how much hard evidence Derek Jones really had. Did he really have a copy of the diary? And how much had I written in it? I just hoped I hadn't been so stupid as to detail everything in that silly little book.

Thinking in such confusing patterns was difficult for me. It had been some time since I'd lived that way. I wasn't able to draw clear conclusions about how I acted or thought back then. I was living a different life, and no longer being in that type of chaos, I couldn't think on the same distorted level I once had. Because I had decided to live my life with integrity, I wasn't going to be elusive about anything. Honesty was the best policy.

## *Point Of Responsibility*

*90. Honesty is ALWAYS the best policy, in all situations. Our level of honesty with regard to our outside world is a direct reflection of our honesty within ourselves. If you're grossly dishonest, meaning you tell bold-faced lies often, your ego is seeking to keep hidden from you your true nature, which is honesty. If you find you tell little white lies to shield either yourself or others from pain, think if you would appreciate someone doing that to you. It's important that we hold ourselves, and each other, accountable for our actions. If you condone or make excuses for bad behavior in yourself or others, what are you really saying? You're declaring that unserving, negative conduct is okay. Such behavior will then continue. But that's the most vital time to stand up and do the right thing. When we see something that is not okay, we must say something, rather than simply pretend it is okay. It is not polite to lie, and it takes a ton of energy to keep all your lies straight. You're worthy enough to have a voice and to stick up for truth. So the next time someone asks you something and you get the urge to pad his or her ego, or to tell a white lie, or to lie plainly, don't do it. Figure out a way to state the truth with tact, compassion and without judgment. Don't forget, when you're honest, you're authentic. And when you're honest, you'll have self-respect, and the respect of others.*

I had patients coming in about an hour, so I took a quick walk to clear my head. I had to stay present to create some damage control. What was the best thing I could do to salvage as much as I could? I knew for sure I was going to be investigated. I started thinking in terms of worst-case scenario. Mine was the kind of case that caused a doctor to lose his or her license. If the Board decided to yank my license, the practice would immediately fold. Everyone involved, including the bank that owned the loan, would be completely screwed. That would be the beginning of the end for everything.

Selling one or two of the houses might have been an option a year prior. But with the depressed real estate market, I couldn't sell any of the homes quickly, and I would never get what I paid for them. Since the purchases were so recent, I would undoubtedly have to inject money into such a transaction. And that wasn't a possibility. I needed to keep as much liquid cash as possible to pay for potential legal costs.

I started thinking about the practice figures. If I sold the practice on the open market, I might be able to liberate enough cash to keep the mortgages afloat for a couple of years, or until I was able to sell the houses. I had built up quite a bit of equity with the increased business, the beautiful remodel and newly computerized and virtually paperless office. The place would be a dream office for most doctors. It took only a couple of minutes to decide to call the broker who listed the practice only three years earlier. It was time to sell.

As the phone rang, I couldn't believe how quickly things were changing. Just hours before, I was living the charmed life. And now, I was actually allowing myself to put up for sale the very vehicle of my accumulation. Strangely, I didn't have much emotion around it. I wasn't even in a state of shock. The process was eerily uncomplicated within me. I simply followed my internal flow chart. If A happened, then do B. If C happened, then follow with D. I didn't necessarily have everything all figured out. I just wanted to get to the end of it as quickly as I could. I wanted to know how it was all going to fall out.

Dr. Moseley picked up the phone. After the cordialities, I told him I wanted to sell my practice. He immediately knew something wasn't quite right. After all, it wasn't normal for a young doctor with a huge, successful practice just to wake up one morning with the inclination to sell. He quickly probed with some very direct questions. From the first time I'd talked with him years before, I liked Dr. Moseley's direct nature. He was calm, confident and concise. He asked me whether I was in trouble. I said yes. He asked me to explain so I did. After he understood the basics, he decided we should go ahead and sell it quickly; when everything was over, I could just buy another practice. But first we needed to erase the practice from the equation. We decided to list it for full price. I voiced my concern about the timing of everything, as it could take up to a year to sell such a practice. But he reassured me that the Board wouldn't make a rash decision. It wouldn't immediately yank my license. The Board's specific protocol would allow us a bit of time to sell, although he couldn't give me a specific time line. Until the Board decided how it wanted to proceed, things were going to be uncertain.

I next asked Dr. Mosely whether he could recommend an attorney experienced in cases similar to mine. He referred me to a fellow in downtown Seattle. I thanked Dr. Mosely, and then called the attorney. After listening to my story, the attorney understood the gravity of the situation and scheduled an appointment for me on Saturday morning. His urgency instilled a sense of fear within me.

Sasha and I tried to make it through the next couple of nights with some semblance of normal, but neither of us slept well. We just lay together, wondering what was next.

When Saturday finally arrived, my body was achy and stiff. I had an emotional hangover. Sasha and I slowly and silently got ready and headed downtown for the early appointment.

The attorney's office was clean and comfortable, as inviting as it could be. We walked in and were promptly greeted by a nice young lady who got us some water and showed us into the conference room. As we took our pick of the many executive chairs, I wondered how many other doctors had sat at that very table, and how they had reacted to their situations.

Sasha sat next to the head of the table, where it was assumed the attorney would sit. I sat directly opposite his chair on the other end of the table. We sat in silence as I looked out the window to the bay. The orange sun shimmered off the cool blue water and illuminated the mountains facing east. Regardless of my present situation, Seattle was still a wonderfully beautiful place.

A large, jovial bald man who had way too much energy for that particular hour interrupted my daydream. He bounded into the room and introduced himself as Henry. He was my attorney. After shaking my hand, Henry turned and introduced a tiny little woman who stood in his big shadow. Her name was Aimee, and she was his sidekick. I shook her hand and we all sat down.

We quickly got into the meat of the issue. Henry asked me to explain the basics of the situation. I proceeded to tell him that we had received a fax the day before from a complainant regarding sexual misconduct with his fiancée, and that the same guy had sent me a letter in the mail back in April, some four months prior. Sasha passed both letters to him. I awaited his response.

When he was finished reading them, Henry looked at me over his glasses. He was no longer smiling. He quickly cut to the chase and asked me to share my side of the story.

I told him it had been over two years since I'd been with the complainant's fiancée, but that there had been other patients with whom I'd had consensual sex. I didn't think it necessary to divulge my whole sexual history, so I told him about the women whom I considered relevant, the ones Mr. Jones could possibly know about from the diary. I included Atia, Summer, Erika, Chloe, and of course, Esther and Erin. I had no idea who Erin knew about, but since I thought Esther was involved, I included those I thought she might know about. I was very honest and straightforward as I talked. I just wanted to get everything out into the open.

Henry informed me that the Board took such complaints very seriously. I figured, from the hurried nature of his conversation, that the Board would probably suspend my license first, and ask questions later.

I had no time to stall. Hiring Henry and Aimee was a foregone conclusion. They both had experience in cases like mine, and their office had a good relationship with the Board from years of working together, albeit on opposite sides. So I gave them the green light to get the ball rolling.

We immediately got into the particulars of my case. As our meeting continued, I started to notice that all too familiar out-of-body feeling. My voice didn't even feel like mine. I was definitely sliding into shock mode.

Henry must have seen the look of vague horror on my face and quickly kept things moving. He told me to cease contact with all of the women, which I'd already done. I explained that all of it had happened before Sasha and I met, and that she already knew everything there was to know. I informed him we intended to tell the truth about everything.

Sasha included, "We just want to deal with this and move on with our lives together."

I spent the next hour detailing the specific events with regard to each of the women.

### *Point Of Responsibility*

*91. At various times in all of our lives, we're confronted with extremely stressful situations. These are the times that define our character. How you react to such inevitable occasions is a direct reflection of your internal environment. As Henry and I talked on that day, I wanted to tell the whole truth, but there was an uncomfortable hesitation within me. I was unable to break completely free from the protectionistic maneuvers of my ego. I didn't lie, but I didn't divulge everything either. I kept the numbers and details to myself as if to pretend the actions I discussed were less egregious than in reality. Even though I had the sincere urge to tell all, I hadn't found the courage to do so yet. Unfortunately, by hanging on to some of the details, I also held onto the guilt and shame associated with those actions. In your notebook, detail the three most relevant interactions in your life where you haven't necessarily lied, but neither did you divulge the whole truth, simply to make yourself appear better, or to give the sense that you were the victim.*

When I was finished, Henry began to discuss with me the likely impending events. The process was more complex than I'd imagined. The first thing the Board had to do was determine whether I was a direct threat to the public. The mere thought of his statement made me slink down into my chair. I was completely deflated that people could possibly think me a direct threat to anyone, let alone the people I'd been treating with care for years. I was getting increasingly lightheaded and nauseous.

The Board would probably bring up the case at the next monthly meeting, within two weeks. If it thought I was a threat, it would immediately suspend my license. Then the investigation would begin. However, if we handled things proactively by initiating the dialogue, the Board might give me the benefit of the doubt by letting my keep my license until the investigation was completed and it handed down its judgment. Basically, if we didn't reassure the Board's attorney that I wasn't an immediate threat to the public, my practice would be doomed and bankruptcy would soon follow. My days of practicing could be over within a couple of weeks.

Henry said he would contact the Board and attempt to set up an interview with an investigator at his office. If I weren't in shock before, I certainly was now. The room began to spin around me; I couldn't focus; my breathing was shallow and my chest tight.

Henry gave me some proactive things to do as my acknowledgement that my situation was of a serious nature. I had to create a chaperone policy in my clinic, even though none of the events ever took place at my office. In effect, a staff member would have to join me in the presence of all female patients. I felt like a complete delinquent, but I understood I deserved such treatment. Henry then went on to prep me for the interview. Basically, I was instructed to tell the truth. If they caught me in a lie, or if other women came out of the woodwork during the investigation, my suspension would be for my lifetime.

Things were going from bad to worse. I'd done a little research into past rulings for such cases around the country. Some doctors had initiated nonconsensual sex with patients under anesthesia, while only receiving minimal suspensions and therapy. Other doctors, who hadn't even had intercourse with patients, were never able to practice again. There was no rhyme or reason to any of it. When I asked Henry for his best guess, he wouldn't reply. He just told me to prepare for the worst and hope we'd be pleasantly surprised.

The whole thing could turn into an ugly situation very quickly, all depending on how many complainants came forward, who wanted to go through the interview process, the Board members' personal opinions, and which complainants might enter a civil suit against me for ruining their lives.

As if that weren't enough, cases like mine were highly publicized by the American media, and once the Board made a decision about the length of my suspension, it was protocol for them to send out a press release.

I could understand alerting the media in a criminal case, but actively to sabotage my future by putting it all over the Internet made me incredibly angry. If my license were suspended, how would I support my family? No one would take my resume seriously. I hoped the Board was more concerned about its appearance than potentially ruining people's lives; after all, my family's lives hung in the balance of its decision as well. All I could do was hope it would act responsibly.

The bottom line was we just had to wait; that was the worst part. The uncertainty of the whole situation was what was killing me slowly. I just wanted to see my enemy, fight him, and move on. But that wasn't possible.

When I was finished signing all the legal paperwork so Henry could get started, I peeled my sweaty hands from the glass-topped conference table and we said our goodbyes.

As Sasha and I rode down in the elevator, the anger had receded. I was spent. The purging of information relieved me. And I was exhausted after all the emotion. No, I didn't name everyone with whom I had slept, but I really didn't think it mattered. If one incident could get me a suspension, so could ten. So I just let it go.

That afternoon, I got a call from Dr. Moseley. He had just talked with Henry, and they agreed we should list the practice at a much-reduced rate to inspire a buyer. He wanted to create a fire sale situation because after talking to Henry, he had no doubt everything could quickly change for the worst. So I agreed to sell the practice for what I owed. It was going to be a huge hit to my financial stability not to recoup the equity in the business, but I had no other options, unless two buyers wanted the practice and got into a bidding war, which was highly unlikely.

After hanging up the phone, I tried to remain strong by going down to the office to take care of some odds and ends.

When I got there, I checked the mail as usual. There was an envelope from the State of Washington. Those were never good. Was this "the envelope" that would end my practice?

I opened it up and read it. It was from the tax department. I was being audited. All I could do was shake my head in disbelief. I couldn't believe all the crap that had just popped up in my life. I must have been an evil son of a gun in a previous incarnation because I was definitely being paid back for something much worse than anything I thought I'd done in my present lifetime.

I asked my accountant to handle everything, as he knew all the particulars. After our phone call, I did some research to shed some light on some of the reasons for being audited by the state. It was apparently a random process, but I also heard from another business owners that the state apparently gave bonuses to employees who could suck more personal property tax money out of a business. I didn't know that to be true, but if it were, I wouldn't necessarily be shocked. My books were completely clean, so if an underpayment were made, it would be due to a legitimate mistake.

Two weeks later, I was told I owed thousands of dollars more for unpaid personal property tax associated with my business. I was blown away. I asked my accountant how the State calculated such an amount. She explained that in Washington, when someone took over or started a business, one must record all the assets of the business, including things like chairs, tables, and any equipment. I'd done that. Further, a business owner was taxed a certain percentage on all the equipment in the office. But the kicker was this: it didn't include only new equipment, but all equipment, year after year after year. Business owners basically had to pay the government to have equipment, whether they used it or not.

When I moved to Seattle and bought the clinic, I had also brought some equipment I'd previously leased in Colorado. I didn't own it, but I'd already paid the sales tax, which was included in the overall lease value. But that didn't matter to the State of Washington. It was equipment on which I still had to pay more taxes. And three years worth of accrued taxes and penalties added up to thousands. I envisioned a little bean counter sitting at his cubicle enjoying his new pair of Converse sneakers that I'd just bought for him.

During that two week period, I became much more introspective and began to pull away from my patients as the uncertainty around my life mounted. The office felt like a scream muffled by a snowdrift. There were plenty of patients, but the place was quiet. Patients started asking me what was wrong, but I just deferred back to their care.

During each break, I kept my eyes peeled for a car with the State of Washington crest to pull up outside. I assumed the State would be along at any moment to pull my license and chain up my doors. It was a horrible time. And to compound the issues, I kept receiving threatening emails from both an anonymous person and from Esther.

In one passage, Esther wrote, "I want to do the right thing and now I am getting calls from the investigator and the surgeon general. Mark, this is off the record. Please cooperate with me…I would like my closure and I have some questions…I asked the man (investigator) on the phone how long you could lose your license for and he said it could be for a very long time…I want to tell the truth and I would like the truth from you. I don't want to testify, but it's looking like it's going that way."

I still had no idea how Esther was involved. How and why was she still in my life?

Those times were tough. I constantly had to refocus my mind and clear my head of all the junk. Unfortunately, I was usually consumed with contemplating the big picture. In fact, it was all I could think about. How were things going to affect my wife, my ability to practice in the future, my family and my long-term reputation? Had I been more proactive about it in the first place, I might not have been in my present position. But there I stood, preparing to pay for the past. It certainly wasn't a drill, and it wasn't a time to alter behavior for the future. I was at the mercy of everyone, my broker, my attorney, my wife, the Board of Health, my accountant and even Mr. Jones. I was in a position I'd always vehemently despised. I was being pushed into a corner with no way out.

I couldn't talk to the women with whom I'd had dalliances to figure out who knew what. I couldn't talk to my friend Bobby because gossip came and went around him like the rain in Seattle. I didn't want to worry my family. And Sasha already knew everything. Talking with her about it just made the cloud around us darker and thicker. I was stuck within my own head every day as I waited for some type of news. It was the single worst feeling I'd ever experienced up to that point in my life.

## *Point Of Responsibility*

*92. Do you often find yourself living inside your head, in constant thought, worry and/or preparation? Do you replay the reels of tape of past negative experiences? Does your ego keep recreating the situation, interjecting different things to say in an attempt to "win" a confrontation, or to be right, or heard? Can such behavior last for hours, days, and even for weeks, or months or years? This is called the Cascade of Insanity. Many of us have suffered with such behavior from as early as childhood. It becomes habit, and quickly spirals into compulsive and, ultimately, addictive behavior. (If you get emotional when you talk or think about the confrontations and emotions, you're addicted to them.) The Cascade of Insanity can come out of nowhere. You may be living in the moment, with things going very well. Then, all of a sudden, your mind switches gears. You wander, and that all-to-familiar, self-critical voice begins to take hold of your consciousness. You begin to focus on needless, garbled thought and/or negative situations. That's when the focus turns to "what-if's" and "yeah-but's." You start to fabricate fictional outcomes that will probably never happen; this leads to emotional and internal stress almost immediately. The fight or flight mechanism begins to take hold; your chest tightens, breath becomes shallow, body rigid, jaw immobile, and palms sweaty. When the fight or flight mechanism is elicited, reason is thrown out the window, and unfocused thoughts quickly lead to reliance on bad habits, feelings of dread and a shrinking of posture, both figuratively and literally. This activity becomes manifested in a negative feedback loop, which repeats and builds upon itself until you decide to stop it. There are moments within this negative feedback loop, however, where you can choose to jump out. A split second always occurs where you objectively observe your behavior and can see that your thoughts are not rational. Within that moment you can choose whether you desire to fall back into the loop, or snap out of it. Take advantage of that split second the moment you notice what you're doing. Immediately say aloud, "STOP!" Take seven long, deep, slow breaths and clear your mind. A good visual to focus on is small waves lapping on the beach. Calm yourself, and then move into action. Focus on the task at hand; become aware of your physical body; twist your spine gently; stretch your neck and shoulders. If you're among others, start a conversation with someone. It is absolutely imperative to reaffirm your connections to physical reality. Get out of your head if at all possible. If it's not possible, then actively change your thoughts. Get involved with something other than what you were doing. Stay out of the sea of self. Fill the very next thought with things for which you're grateful, or with your visions of your life, or go for a walking meditation.*

As the days trudged on, I was increasingly consumed with how the financial side of things would play out. If I didn't sell the practice, I would most certainly go bankrupt. And even if I were able to sell the practice, without the income, I would also lose the three houses in less than a year. I'd already cut my net worth in half by deciding to sell the practice at half its value.

Everything I'd worked so hard to achieve was in jeopardy. It should have been a wonderful time in our lives. Sasha and I had been married for only a couple of months, and we'd been in our new home for about five months. Unfortunately, I felt like a renter in my own home. Even if I were up for a minimal two-year suspension, I would have to sell the place. And because of that, I never felt comfortable there. The stress was compounded by the fact that the real estate market in Seattle was leveling off significantly. The timing couldn't be any worse. I had dropped the price on the smaller home twice, and the foot traffic was dwindling. Even if I sold the place, it was to the point that I wouldn't make any money on it. And I had thrown down a hefty down payment for the big house, which depleted my cash reserves significantly. The whole thing was slowly beginning to swirl into the perfect storm.

Then in a flash, as Sasha and I shared a bottle of wine at the house, I reclaimed my spirit. In a moment of clarity, I began to inspect the grand nature of it all. The issues were so all-encompassing that they actually allowed me to step away from the details. I understood that I would endure and move past whatever happened in the near future. I might not like the process, and I certainly wasn't going to pretend it wasn't happening, but I would definitely live through it and ultimately thrive. Because the amount of loss had the potential to be so great, it was actually easier to become detached from all the toys, status and prestige. I had never really identified with it anyway. What set me apart from most doctors was my down-to-earth, practical approach to life and healthcare. Never did I have a holier-than-thou ego stature. Sure, I enjoyed the things money and prestige provided, but those things had never defined me; they were only the manifestations of my hard work and dedication.

I wondered whether I was simply justifying and rationalizing. But I had already dealt with my demons. I truly wasn't that person anymore. I knew that. Sasha knew that. And my life reflected it.

I wondered why it was all happening. Three years earlier, my business life couldn't have been any better, and my personal life left a lot to be desired. Now, it was the complete opposite. Just when I'd finally figured things out and started living within a loving, healthy relationship, the crap hit the fan. Did the Universe require me to learn yet another lesson? Did I have to prove myself further? I'd been through so much already. The writing was on the wall, but I was just beginning to understand its meaning.

Chapter Twenty:

# Lawyers, Brokers and Investigators

After being listed for two weeks, we finally had a serious bite on the practice. Dr. Patel was a middle-aged chiropractor who owned a number of clinics in Washington. And after talking with Dr. Moseley, he wanted to meet me to discuss the details. I immediately set up a meeting with him for that evening.

At lunch, I checked my phone for messages. Atia had sent a series of text messages saying, "Meet me outside at twelve-thirty." It was already ten after twelve. I told the girls I was going for a walk and would be back around one.

I hadn't talked to or seen Atia for months. I was quite happy with that; my life was much less chaotic without her in it. I wasn't supposed to talk with her, per Henry's instructions, but I knew Atia wasn't exactly the type who would just go away. She would force an impromptu meeting if I didn't allow her to talk. I found her sitting on a park bench under a shade tree, thirty feet from my office.

I was already on edge from everything I was going through when I asked her what was so important that she had to come down to the office and demand my presence.

She answered in a loud whisper, "I've been contacted by some investigator who wants me to come in and talk with him. Are you going to tell them about us?"

"I'm telling the truth about all of it, Atia. I'm not out to hurt anyone, but I can't keep all this inside of me any longer. I need to get it all off my chest, so it doesn't come back to haunt me in some way. I need it to be done. Listen, when they call you, just tell them the truth."

"I'm not talking to anyone," she declared.

"Well, then don't talk with them. It's my understanding that they're here for your protection. So they can't make you do anything you don't want to do. Just do what you need to do. Don't worry about me. I've made my bed. Look, I'm not supposed to be talking with you at all, so you need to go, okay?"

She gave me a hug and said, "What's going to happen to you if this continues?"

"I have no idea."

"Are you going to be able to practice?"

"Probably not in the state of Washington."

"But that's not fair! You're a great doctor, and your patients love you! Everyone in this whole community loves you!"

"Not everyone," I said.

"But she's the one who pursued you. Doesn't that count for something?"

"That doesn't matter, especially since she's not the only one. I haven't exactly been a saint."

"What about that you're married, and that your life is, like, completely clean and that all that stuff is so far in the past?"

"Atia, I don't know anything except that the Board needs to take the situation seriously because there's a vindictive, scorned ex-boyfriend who's threatening media coverage. He wants my head on a platter, and the Board is obligated to do something. This probably won't end well for me. So you should probably just be happy that you get to live your cozy little life here in Atherton while I pay for our indiscretions."

She started crying again and tried to hug me, but I walked away. Tears filled my eyes as my emotions flared up. I really was paying for all of our indiscretions.

After my walk, I went back to the office. There was a small pile of mail sitting on my desk. One of the envelopes had the DOH stamp on it. I took a deep breath and opened it slowly. I unfolded the pages and started to read. It was a formal letter stating I was being investigated for sexual misconduct. It stated the code that had allegedly been violated and listed the name and number of the investigator. I was to call him to set up an interview. I was already beaten down and felt like heck. I couldn't get any more emotional than I already was, so I filed the letter and went for another walk.

After work that day, I received a few more messages on my phone. Two of them were from Chloe and Betsy. Both had called to inform me a woman had called them numerous times over the past week to ask whether they wanted to file a civil suit against me for having sex with patients. Betsy told me she would never do anything to hurt me, so she told the woman to stop calling, and to leave us both alone. Chloe apparently told the woman to go to hell. She also said she'd been contacted by the Department of Health; when they asked her to come in for an interview, she told them she wasn't interested. She said to my voicemail, "I don't know what they want, but I'm a busy person, and I could really care less. I just wanted to give you a heads up." That's all she said. She didn't ask for an explanation. I wanted more than anything to call her back and explain the situation, but I couldn't. I just had to let it go.

I had another message from Henry. My interview was scheduled for later that week. I called him back immediately to get the details.

I told him I'd received the letter from the Department of Health. He told me to expect quite a few more in the coming months; that it was just the beginning. He said the Board's next meeting was scheduled out a couple of weeks. We needed to get our interview in before then to show we would be up front and honorable about everything. For this reason, we decided to do it sooner than later.

Then Henry switched gears. He said it would go far, in the Board's eyes, if I started to see a therapist to help me deal with my issues rather than waiting for the Board to instruct me to do so. Even though I felt I'd already done the work, I agreed.

As it stood, if they suspended my license on the day of the Board meeting, I had only two or three weeks to find a buyer for the practice. If I at least got a commitment from someone, the business transition could begin. The only thing I could do was hope for the best.

That evening I met with Dr. Patel. He was a clean-cut, smiling fellow. We shook hands and started talking right away. He said he had talked with Dr. Moseley at great length about the practice, and that he was quite excited to learn more. He understood my dilemma and knew time was of the essence. I showed him around the office, and I shared statistical reports with him in great detail. He was definitely impressed with my practice, from its efficient operations, to its significant collections and patient retention.

When we finished discussing the practice, he started asking me questions about my future. I hadn't thought about what I was going to do because I was so focused on getting through the present and trying not to lose everything I owned. Then he shared with me his terms. After his due diligence, and if everything worked out with the numbers, he wanted me to sign a three year contract to run the office for him. I replied by letting him know my license would probably be pulled, and I couldn't run the office alone, which was why I was selling it. He told me he understood that; he wanted me to manage the clinic while an associate saw the patients. I tried to tell him it was in the best interest of both the clinic and the new doctor that I not be on the premises once my license was suspended. But that didn't faze him one iota.

I wasn't exactly excited about his proposition, but if that were what it took for him to buy the practice, I'd probably do it; at least I would to continue getting a paycheck. I told him I'd certainly consider it.

Dr. Patel told me he'd look through the financials and call me later in the week to set up a second meeting. As we shook hands, he told me that my situation would pass; that the transition in my life would end up being a good thing. I smiled and thanked him for his kind words as I locked up and went home for the night. The sale looked promising.

When I talked to Dr. Moseley the next day, I informed him things had gone well the night before. He immediately said that if the deal didn't go through, we'd be up against a wall. We wouldn't have any time to find another doctor, so he wanted to start looking for an associate to run the practice if my license was pulled before we could sell it. It was obviously a good idea, so I agreed. But I still wanted to believe Dr. Patel would take care of things.

When Dr. Patel and I met two days later, my goal was to get him to sign the Letter Of Intent (LOI) to purchase the practice. Once he signed that, I would know he was serious, and I'd be much more inclined to work with him on the terms of the deal. It wasn't like I had much leverage anyway. I answered a few of his lingering questions and casually asked him to sign the LOI. He looked at me and took my pen. Then he got up from his chair, walked over to the counter where the LOI was, and scribbled his name on the line while saying, "I'll sign Dr. Moseley's little paper." I could care less about his condescending attitude. I just needed him to sign the thing so we could move forward with the terms of the deal.

When he handed it to me, I noticed he'd completely crossed out a number of lines and initialed them. As I read the finer points, I realized the things he crossed out absolved him of all liability. He wasn't even willing to put forth a nominal earnest money deposit. It was all in his favor, and I really had no choice, so I signed and initialed where indicated.

When I was finished, he said to me, "I'd like for you to continue carrying the loan on the practice." I was momentarily confused and thought that maybe he didn't understand that, as a soon-to-be unlicensed doctor, I couldn't legally own a medical office, and that the bank would immediately call the loan due because of that. I thought he already knew the rules. But I took a deep breath and explained everything to him again.

"Oh yes, I know that," he said. "But I need to know that this practice is a good deal before buying it fully."

I wondered what the heck he was trying to pull. The practice wasn't like a used car. He couldn't test drive it to determine whether or not it was good for him. The tax paperwork and my copious amounts of positively trended statistics proved it was a great opportunity.

So I said, “We both know this is a stellar practice, and that whoever takes it over is going to walk into it with about three-hundred thousand dollars of equity, if not more. This practice is a steal.”

“Yes, that may be. But I don’t know that without seeing how it operates for a few months.”

“Dr. Patel, I thought you understood the situation. We don’t have months.”

“And that’s why I would like for you to stay on as manager.”

“I would be more than willing to stay on as manager, if you purchase the practice.”

“I will purchase the practice under my own terms. And those terms are for you to carry the loan for no fewer than three months.”

“I would probably do that, except the bank is going to call the loan due in full when my license is suspended. That’s potentially two weeks away.”

“Those are my terms,” he said.

It was then I realized what he was trying to do. He just wanted to reduce his risk. Carrying the loan worked for me in no way. If I bent to his demand, I would still be carrying all the risk. Hypothetically, after my license was suspended while running the office as a manager, he could still walk away at any moment with zero responsibility. And on top of that, he’d be making all the money in the interim. I felt a tinge of anger, but pulled it back.

“Your terms are unreasonable, and further, they’re illegal. I can’t own a practice without a license. Quite soon, I will not have a license. The bank will call the loan due.”

“We’ll worry about that when the time comes,” he said.

"Hypothetically, under your terms, if we were to sign a purchase and sale agreement right now, you would begin receiving all payments made into the clinic immediately, right?" I confirmed.

"That is correct."

"And if I lost my license in, let's say two or three weeks, you could simply just walk away from the deal if you found it a little too stressful for you. Is that right?"

"I could do that, but I wouldn't."

"And how do I know that?"

"You don't. But I'm telling you I wouldn't."

"Unfortunately, I don't know you very well at this point, Dr. Patel. I'd love to believe you have my best interest in mind, but that you're unwilling to budge on these unreasonable terms tells me you don't."

"I just want to make sure this is going to be a good investment for me."

"How could you possibly lose?" I asked. "This is a dream practice for any doctor. You're paying half of what it's worth. Even taking into account a worst-case scenario, there's nowhere for all my patients to go. They all like and identify with this particular clinic. And as far as numbers go, you'd be getting one hundred and fifty thousand dollars in clean receivables. This is a winning situation. If I were in your position, I'd be thanking whatever deity lined up the stars to create this event for you."

He smiled and said, "You have my offer. I'll be awaiting your phone call. As per the LOI, we have a week or so to discuss the terms. If we can come to an agreement, then we'll move on together. If we can't, we'll move on in separate directions."

As I showed him to the door, I figured out what he was doing. Since we both signed the binding LOI agreement, he had me locked into discussions with only him for a full week. If something else came down the pipe, such as another doctor, I couldn't begin negotiations with him or her. And since time was of the essence for me, every day that went by drew me closer to a suspension. I was being strong-armed and had no recourse. Dr. Patel wanted me to hand over the reins to him completely. He wanted the money the clinic brought in, but he wasn't interested in accepting any of the liability. He expected me to retain that. Of course, the whole point for me was to shed that liability so I wasn't forced into bankruptcy. On one level, I admired Dr. Patel's cunning; on another level, I wanted to knock his teeth down his throat.

The next day Dr. Patel called me during lunch.

"What if I replace your name on the loan with mine?" he asked.

"I have no idea whether the bank would do that," I replied.

"Why don't you call the bank and ask them?"

I agreed. Unfortunately, the bank was less than interested. They told me Dr. Patel would have to apply for the loan as anyone else would. He couldn't just be added to it.

I quickly called him back and told him what I'd discovered. I hoped he'd just make everything easy and apply for the damn loan. I knew he could afford it. Getting the loan wasn't an issue. He was just trying to be in the right position. If I defaulted on the loan, when he was running the practice, the bank would probably take a considerable loss and sell it to him for a significantly discounted price.

"Okay, well that's unfortunate," he said. "You have my terms. I'd like to have you manage the clinic with an associate doctor. That's the only way I will sign a Purchase and Sale agreement."

"The bank won't allow me to continue owning the practice without a license, Dr. Patel."

"We can deal with that when the time comes," he said for the hundredth time.

I was feeling pretty beaten down by that point. I asked him to apply for the loan, but he just reiterated his terms yet again. Then we hung up. All I could do was wait, either for him to make a more reasonable offer, or for the LOI to run out.

I didn't have time to worry about Dr. Patel anymore. The next morning was my interview with the DOH investigators. That night was a tough one. Henry's instructions to "tell the whole truth" kept rolling around in my head. He knew about some of the women, but not all of them. And I wanted to take the opportunity to cleanse myself of everything negative that remained within my grasp.

Sasha and I awakened the next morning to another beautiful orange and purple sunrise. I made breakfast and we ate facing the Sound. I opened the doors and windows to let in the maritime warmth. The white Seattle ferries quietly passed one another in the distance. The mountains jutted sharply up into the sky. Sasha and I sat in total comfort with each other until it was time to get ready.

On the way to the appointment, we held hands and didn't say much. I really loved the time we spent together, regardless of the circumstances. I was so thankful to be with such a wonderful woman.

We parked the car and went up to the tenth floor. When we walked into Henry's office, the receptionist greeted us. She showed us into the glass-walled conference room, and within minutes, Henry bounced into the room. I was already in a state of shock. My hands were sweaty and I could feel my body temperature rise by the second. As Henry briefed me on the interview protocol, all I could think about was the extended list of women I hadn't mentioned to him. What if women I hadn't talked about came forward during the investigation? I'd lose my license forever.

## Point Of Responsibility

*93. Denial is an interesting concept. It is defined as the assertion that something is not true, or a refusal to acknowledge. Technically speaking, at the very moment something is acknowledged, it can no longer be denied. In my particular situation, I certainly didn't deny anything that I'd done. But it was time to move past those events in my life. I took the lessons to heart. I changed my own self-perception and subsequently altered my lifestyle to reflect the person I knew I wanted to be, the person I was all along. Studies show that to move forward, one must create new patterns of thought in his or her life. You don't need to wallow in the past, believing that's what defines you. At any point in life, you can change your perception of who and what you are. Many people get stuck in the thoughts and actions of their past, hopelessly reliving that same existence with no hope of getting out of it. Once you acknowledge that you want something different, the next step is to forget about all that other negativity. Don't let anyone control your thoughts, or guilt you into believing that the only way to enlightenment is to live in your past. It's not true. Stand up, lift your head up, and then focus on the milliseconds in front of you.*

As Henry talked about the interview particulars, I interrupted forcefully, "There's something else we need to discuss, Henry." He stopped talking for a moment before saying, "Okay, what's that?"

"I have more to tell you."

No sooner did I say it than into the reception area walked the two investigators. The receptionist greeted them as we all took notice of their entrance. I'd put him in quite a spot. Unsure what to do, Henry told me he would greet the investigators, and then return to talk about what I wanted to discuss.

I was so tired of carrying all those names around with me. I just wanted it all out in the open. Only the complete truth would make the process easier. I couldn't even imagine trying to keep up with all the lies upon lies that could potentially be fabricated. I simply wanted to surrender, knowing I had the strength from within to deal with everything that came my way.

When Henry came back in, he looked a little nervous. "Okay, what do you want to discuss?"

I told him there were more names and events I needed to share with him. I told him I'd originally held them back because I didn't think they were relevant to the Erin Jones case. Now I realized I was the case, and all participants must be handed over. I told him it was important for me to be completely honest about everything. I didn't want to have to lie when asked whether I'd slept with any other patients. I'd be screwed if one of those women came out into the open after the media was alerted.

I could see the wheels turning in Henry's head. I knew he needed to hear what I had to say before the interview, and he didn't want the investigators to wait. So I asked whether he could help me to postpone the interview until the following week. He gave it his best shot. Luckily, they graciously agreed to give me another two weeks to prepare, which was much more than I thought I'd get.

I sat tight as Henry escorted the gentlemen into the elevator. When he came back in, I went through every single detail I could remember. I told him that many of the women I'd had sex with were either girlfriends or employees. But I had adjusted all of them at some point. I talked about all the women. I talked about all the encounters. I told him how I had rationalized my behavior by believing that just because they pursued me, or that it wasn't in the office, it was less wrong. I described how I had completely changed my life since. I felt relieved to get it all out into the open, and Henry finally had all the variables at his disposal. All this new information would make my case almost impossible to defend, but divulging the truth was the right thing to do. I simply had to hope that my honesty and good will would breed some kind of mercy from the Board.

Henry and I finished our conversation with talk about the sale. The lawyers had prepared the purchase and sale documentation on two days notice. I informed them that Dr. Patel was trying to strong-arm me into selling the practice to him and detailed his ridiculous terms.

Henry sunk into his chair as he realized the deal probably wasn't going to go through. We needed more time. It was good we had a couple of more weeks, because once the Board reviewed my interview, they would probably act quickly to suspend my license. Every day was vital, and we were all feeling the heat.

That weekend, Sasha and I went back to the cabin to get out of town. We decided to do some hiking before the snow season began. Every time we went to the cabin was like a mini vacation. We loved the mountains and the sleepy little country towns. Sasha and I cooked, talked and meditated our way through the weekend. We didn't discuss the upcoming interview; we'd already talked it to death the whole week before. We just enjoyed our time together and mentally prepared for what was to come.

The next week, the lawyers revised the purchase and sale agreement and created a promissory note just in case Dr. Patel decided to make the move to purchase. On the last day of the binding LOI agreement, I received a call from Dr. Moseley. He'd found another buyer. Just as I thought the whole situation was hopeless, we had a new lifeline, and I was so incredibly thankful.

A day after the LOI ran out with Dr. Patel, I talked with Dr. Michaels over the phone. He was a doctor younger than myself and had been practicing at one of the local high-volume clinics north of the city. Dr. Michaels was a soft-spoken gentleman whose manner was completely in contrast to my more extroverted and high-energy nature. My patients would certainly have to get used to a change in personality. But Dr. Michaels had a solid background in treatment. He'd picked up a number of tools and techniques along the way and was more than competent.

My only concern was his ability to run a business of that magnitude successfully. He had minimal experience. But he did have a plan to hire a consulting firm to help where he was deficient. As we spoke, I made sure he was fully aware of the situation around the clinic. I had no desire to hide anything from him since he was my only option at that point. Again, honesty was the best policy. Dr. Michaels didn't want the details, quickly informed me he'd already talked about everything with Dr. Moseley, and that the sale price reflected the issues generously.

Dr. Michaels explained he'd been looking for a clinic to buy for about a year, but he hadn't had any luck on the financing side of things. The clinics he tried to purchase didn't have a wide enough profit margin for the banks to call the deals a good risk, and he didn't have much experience running a business. The ground was shaky, but I had little choice in the matter. I had to take a chance on him. I had until my interview with the Board at the end of the month to get someone into the office. After that, all bets were off.

Dr. Michaels and I had many conversations about the clinic over that week. We talked everything through and he was quite excited to have the opportunity to own a million-dollar clinic for so little. It was an unbelievable opportunity for any doctor. We just had to jump that major hurdle of getting him financed. But if there were ever a person who could get that job done, it was Dr. Moseley. The guy had connections all over the place. Within three days, he'd contacted several lending institutions and forwarded them Dr. Michaels' information.

Things were finally in motion. Henry's office created the LOI and associate paperwork to move things forward. But the only way Dr. Michaels would sign them was if I matched his exorbitant weekly fee and allowed him to put in a minimal financial injection when we signed the binding Purchase and Sale Agreement (PSA.) My bank account was feeling the pain by that point. Checks were going out much quicker than they were coming in. But again, I had little choice, so I signed on the dotted line. I took a little solace in knowing the payments would only be until we closed the loan. As for the minimal down payment, I just took what I could get. If the deal fell through, I'd at least have a little cash to pay for the accruing legal bills.

The next week, Dr. Michaels' loan had been accepted by only one bank, ironically, the same bank I'd used to get my first loan. But it wasn't a slam-dunk. We needed to prove to the bank that Dr. Michaels was qualified to run the practice, and we only had about thirty days to do it. They wanted an unbelievable amount of paperwork from many different people. They wanted guarantees, certifications and all kinds of things. The process would be far more difficult than when I first bought the clinic. But again, it was our only option. No other banks were interested in the loan. We were already hanging on by our fingernails.

After Dr. Michaels and I signed the associate paperwork and the LOI, he was set to start on September 10th. I was very happy I had someone to cover for me within weeks if my license were immediately suspended following the interview. The next step was to get Dr. Michaels to sign the binding PSA, which couldn't be created until we were further along in the process.

Those next two weeks before the interview went by like molasses. Sasha was wonderful, but I was usually cranky and tired. The practice had leveled off a bit because I hadn't been as focused on it. I wasn't necessarily just going through the motions, but I felt like I was half asleep the whole time. Sasha and I tried to do the best we could with our home life, but every time we got home, I felt it wasn't really my house.

On yet another of those quicksand days, Julie came into my office and quietly handed me a letter that had come in the mail. It was a note from Heather, the girl who used to do my books. Julie had accidentally sent an invoice to Heather stating she owed quite a bit of money to the clinic. Per our agreement, Heather's balance had been paid in full by her accounting work, but I had forgotten to zero her account in the computer. Heather had written on the invoice that there was no way she was paying the total. But the note didn't stop there. She continued on to say that I shouldn't sleep with patients, which made me wonder whether she was somehow involved in everything. I didn't remember writing her name in the diary. Did she know Esther? It was an unbelievable mess I'd created.

I was disgusted with myself. My life had been so out of control when I had thought I was just having some fun.

The day before my interview, I got another call from Aimee. She had finally completed the new PSA for Dr. Michaels and I to sign. She said it was in my best interest for us to sign the document that day, before the interview occurred. By signing that document, Dr. Michaels would be bound to the clinic legally. She informed me my bank wasn't exactly excited about the deal because there wasn't solid financing on Dr. Michaels' side. But they understood the situation was fragile, so if Dr. Michaels signed the PSA, it would improve their chances of getting paid back on the loan because the practice would remain intact and productive, regardless of what happened to me. And with the relative uncertainty of my case and the possibility of everything hitting the media sometime soon, the bank needed to secure all opportunities to cover its assets. Allowing the private sale was a necessary move on the bank's part. Simply adding Dr. Michaels to the loan would have been best for everyone, but for some reason, the bank was less than interested in that. In my supposition, they just wanted to weather the immediate storm and depend on Dr. Michaels to get a different loan, in which case my bank would be paid in full.

I called Dr. Michaels and we met for lunch to sign the PSA. I was quite nervous he might turn and run since he really had nothing to lose at that point, but the transaction went smoothly and I finally had his check in my hand. I felt like I could breathe just a little more deeply.

The interview date was August 30th. When it finally came, it was none too soon. I wasn't nervous at all on the second go around. In fact, I was lighthearted when I walked into Henry's office. It was finally time to let all the insanity out into the open. Within minutes, everyone was in the conference room and the lead investigator offered up some encouragement by telling me the whole thing was sure to pass, so I should just relax and get it all off my chest.

Before long, the tape recorder was running, and we were going back and forth with questions and answers. I spoke with calm reassurance. We went through the whole timeline, all the relationships, the basics with regard to all the encounters, and my personal state of being at each time. In addition to all the patient files, the investigator also wanted the diary my sister had given to me. I truthfully told him I'd thrown it away when I moved. I told him everything. At the interview's end, he asked me whether I'd like to say anything directly to the Board. I reminded them again that those times in my life had ended over a year ago, that I was happily married, I was presently in therapy to work out any lingering issues, and I was completely willing to cooperate with them.

The investigator asked me whether any other women might possibly come forward. I reassured him by saying, "I'm certainly not hiding anything at this point."

And just as quickly as it began, it was over. Sasha and I quickly went back to Atherton to finish the workday. We didn't talk much about the interview. I replayed some of it over in my head the rest of that day. I hoped the Board heard the sorrow and mea culpa tone in my voice because I was being genuine. Henry had told me I was doing the right thing by just telling the truth, and it felt right. The only variable was how the Board was going to take it all. I wanted to believe I had presented a favorable picture to the Board of my present life, but all I could do now was wait for the Board's judgment.

When Henry called the next day, I asked him whether he knew if any other women had come forward at that point. As far as he knew, there was only Summer and Esther. That came as both a surprise and a relief. I thought about all the phone calls to Betsy and Chloe, about the way Esther tried to manipulate me with the diary, and how she was probably in cahoots with Mr. Jones; they were apparently the only two people involved. Both of their egos were hurt so badly by me that they were going to do anything and everything within their power to hurt me back. They, just like me, didn't take into consideration the people they were hurting while they got back at me. It was an endless sea of blame, and nobody was exempt or blameless. All that was certain was I was going to pay the biggest price of everyone.

## *Point Of Responsibility*

*94. When acting irrationally, do you think of those you might indirectly affect by such inconsiderate behavior? The answer is probably no, because irrational behavior comes from the ego, and the ego does NOT think of other people. We all have irrational moments. That's part of being human. But it's our responsibility quickly to step away from emotional events and determine whether such ego-based actions are the best way to achieve positive results; i.e. are they going to cause more harm than good? When I was caught up in compulsive activity, the last thing on my mind was how it could potentially affect the lives of those indirectly involved. There is a responsible way to act when emotions flood your mind. When confronted with an emotional decision, take the emotion and seal it in a jar for evaluation. Take a look at the jar from the outside. Watch the emotions dissipate into nothing. When the emotions have receded, then rational behavior can prevail. Take yourself out of the emotional situation and be ACTIVE, not REACTIVE. Think of the most responsible way to proceed. Don't be tricked by your ego's desire to be right. If after you've thought about how to progress, you still feel emotionally charged, you're still acting from ego. Take more time before making a decision. Envision acceptance, and take responsibility for your part. With practice, such emotional flare-ups and even negative self-talk will diminish from days and weeks to mere milliseconds. Practice makes better, so actively work on it.*

Chapter Twenty-One:

# Therapy, Transitions and the Opportunistic, Shark-Like Media

I was happy to be done with the interview, but thoughts of the potential destruction of my life kept creeping into my consciousness. The days that followed were dreadful; and the mornings were the worst part of it. I would awaken late almost every day with the sense that I could sleep another seven hours if given the chance. I'd get out of bed and feel pains I'd never had before. My body was stiff and tight. My mind was cloudier than it had ever been. When I'd pull myself off the bed and drag my body into the shower, I was insidiously welcomed by dread and impending doom. I fought to shake off the feelings with stretching and meditation, but their tentacles were wrapped deeply within my body. They had insidiously become part of me again. I recognized them as shallow breathing, as slightly hunched-over shoulders, as a tight and expressionless face, and as a less than bright disposition.

I felt like a caged animal with no teeth or claws, at the mercy of everyone on the outside. I felt the distinct sensation that I'd gone back in time, and I was living with my mother again. I was increasingly anxious and my bodyweight was dropping by the day. I was going through a lot, but that was no excuse for the way I was treating my loved ones with indifference and disrespecting them with snippy comments. I acknowledged that a shift needed to happen if I were going to push through with my relationships intact. After all, I still had complete power over my mind and immediate environment. I needed to get away for the weekend to recalibrate. I had to remain strong.

## Point Of Responsibility

*95. How do you treat others while going through difficult times? Understand that there are no excuses for disrespecting others with indifference, anger and snippy comments. Your character during the difficult times is what defines you. It can be difficult, but it doesn't have to be. Diffuse situations by asking others for help or support as you process your issues. When you're in your little cloud of misery, try your hardest to step from underneath it and into the light. Use the techniques you've already learned to jump out of the negative feedback loop. Breathe into your gut a few times. Gently twist your spine and swing your arms. Get the blood flowing. Actively think about the things for which you're grateful. Call or talk with someone about something constructive. People will respect and trust you more if you show your vulnerable side and act responsibly with their emotions in such times. Be strong, be honorable and challenge yourself to do the right thing. Above all, don't play victim. You're much more powerful than that.*

That first weekend in September, I went to the cabin alone to regroup. I left the pug at home with Sasha and took off immediately after work on Friday. As I pulled my car onto the freeway, I aggressively started fighting the hoards of traffic until I realized what I was doing. I was just fighting the flow, or the lack of flow, as it were. If I were fighting it on the freeway, I was sure I was also fighting it in every part of my subconscious. I slowed down to focus my intention. As I drove with more control, the fighting sensation let up and my fear and uncertainty seemed to melt away.

## Point Of Responsibility

*96. When you're stuck in traffic, how do you typically deal with it? Do you tend to act aggressively, scream at other drivers, ride the bumper of the driver in front of you, or constantly switch lanes in order to get to your destination faster? Do you "space out"? Are you aware of those around you? When people are riding your bumper, do you move to the right to let them pass, or do you go slower to anger them? Take a few minutes to write in your notebook your natural tendencies as a driver. Describe five separate occurrences where you have intentionally cut off another driver, sped up when passed, refused to move to the right, screamed at others, or any other situations that have elicited emotions while driving. Understand there are many different types of drivers, with an infinite number of skill levels and personalities. Everyone thinks he or she is a good driver, and no one likes to be challenged. When emotions are elicited while driving, they are directly related to our internal environment at that time. It's no surprise that road rage is greater in the afternoon when people are tired and less tolerant. The next time another driver annoys you, slow down a little and put a smile on your face, even if it's a fake one at first. Do the right thing. It's more important that you arrive at your destination, even if it's two minutes late, than wind up in the hospital.*

In that moment, I had subconsciously refocused my attention to living in the present. I realized absolutely nothing was wrong in my life. I had a wonderful relationship with an incredible woman, with whom I connected on every level. And I still had myself. I had led quite an interesting life. I had knowledge and experience that very few people did. I'd developed myself into a success story. Even if the worst-case scenario followed me around until it consumed everything in its path, I was going to endure by living with refocused intention in the present. I put the train back on its tracks. From that moment forward, I would not allow myself to brood or worry. I knew such thoughts were sure to present themselves from time to time, but when they did, I would thank them for sharing and shoo them away. Then I would fill my mind with grateful thoughts for everything I had, my relationship, my ability to adapt, and my abundance in all its forms.

I spent the weekend writing down the things for which I was grateful. I wrote up a basic code of conduct for myself to get me through the tough times. It was more relevant to do it while I was going through this difficult situation because new points of light and different avenues of thought were being experienced.

I went hiking deep into the mountains on both Saturday and Sunday. I worked my body to exhaustion before coming home to a light meal and rest. My sleep patterns were erratic, as the quiet time allowed my mind to process all the things happening around it. I sat in silence and sipped coffee as I listened to music, cried and wrote.

For the first time, I was fully able to detach myself from the chaos. I began to appreciate the process by which everything was unfolding. I was amazed at how Esther was still so deeply involved in my life. If she weren't in the picture, my battle would have been one-dimensional. It would have involved only Mr. Jones and Erin. Esther knew I had slept with other women, but she had no idea who they were. Without Esther's involvement, I would have known exactly what to expect and how to combat it. But with her involvement, and the whole diary fiasco, I had no idea who knew what. Because of that uncertainty and fear of losing my license forever, I had no other choice but to divulge all the details.

But that process of complete disclosure, of verbalizing it all to others had also seemed to complete the task of coming to grips with the shame and guilt associated with my previous lifestyle. Would I have done so if I'd had only one claim to fight? In a backhanded approach to destroy me, the people who were attempting to bring me down were actually allowing me to become stronger than I'd ever been. Although I still had to go through all the crap on a human level, spiritually, I felt clearer and more powerful than ever.

When Sunday evening came, I felt I wasn't even close to being finished. I wanted to stay and continue the process, but I had to get back to Seattle.

On Tuesday, I started therapy. I was excited to start processing everything with someone objective. When I met Dr. Cunningham, I informed him I wanted to become healthy in the eyes of the Department of Health, but more importantly, I wanted to do it for my family and myself, and I was willing to do whatever it took. I talked quickly and confidently as I brought him up to speed with regard to my past. I included everything I could think of—the molestation, boundary issues and my tumultuous relationship with my mother. I discussed how all those things had affected my life in the recent past, and how I thought they were at the forefront of my problems and the events that escalated into the complaint with the Department of Health.

Eventually, Dr. Cunningham and I discussed how I had changed my life the year before and had made no missteps since. I shared with him the basics of my program, which included focused meditation, nutrition, exercise and the complete changing of my neuronet with focus on living in the present moment only. I explained that my perception of life was completely different, and that as soon as I took responsibility for everything in my life, I was changed forever. Because I'd chosen not to be that person anymore, a relapse was highly improbable. Literally within weeks of making that choice to live actively instead of passively, I had met my wife and we had worked actively on having a solid relationship.

Dr. Cunningham was less than enthusiastic about anything I said. He was most definitely a staunch psychotherapist, who believed that people with problems had to be subjected to significant amounts of therapy. I could tell by his reaction, or lack of it, that he would never believe someone could change his or her life the way I did. I knew, whatever he thought, I had changed my life, but Dr. Cunningham's standards were what the Board would base its decision upon.

## *Point Of Responsibility*

*97. In my past, I had used traditional psychotherapy as an objective voice. Unfortunately, the treatment I received was substandard. The therapists I chose never offered structurally based steps to help me to get out of my particular negative thought patterns. After utilizing such methods for three different events in my life, and with the same ineffectual, talk-based counsel, I decided never to go back. This was certainly not the best way to handle things. In hindsight, as issues came up in my life that I needed to resolve, I should have taken responsibility and sought the counsel of a good therapist, no matter how long it took to find the right one. When you seek the counsel of others, it is of paramount importance to ask yourself one question: Is this person offering me solid steps so I can lift myself out of my present patterns? If the answer is no, then choose someone else. If the therapy is geared toward thought only, it's not enough. If the therapist does not hold you accountable, it's not enough. Keep in mind that you don't necessarily have to like your therapist. In fact, it typically works better if the therapist keeps you on point, or even guessing. The therapist shouldn't be your friend, but should stimulate your individual thought. And just as importantly, he or she must give you homework for each session and hold you accountable for doing it. It may take time to find the right person to help you, but when you do, the search will have been worth it.*

During that first session, I was focused on getting everything out as quickly as I could. I didn't like the idea of paying someone hundreds and thousands of dollars to sit there and listen to me talk about something that wasn't a part of me anymore. I didn't want to use psychotherapy as a crutch, as so many people did. In my experience, people too often let their problems tend to define their lives, and therapists tended to get stuck in the issues by constantly talking about them rather than creating ways for people to get out of their dysfunctional thought patterns.

People could benefit greatly from simple, action-based therapy, as opposed to the incessant need to dive ever deeper into the psyche. Life doesn't have to be that difficult! Most people do have control over their actions and emotions, but they relinquish control of their own lives by choosing, either actively or passively, not to change. Such a concept may be easy to deny, but at the deepest depths of our being, we know it to be true.

As I ended my first session with Dr. Cunningham, I realized I'd talked for almost two hours. He hadn't said more than twenty words, which was fine with me. I was invigorated to get everything out for his understanding. He had his cards to play however he wanted in the next week.

The following Monday, Dr. Michaels started at the clinic. I introduced him to patients, told them he was the new owner, and explained their individual situations to him. Most of the clients were surprised by the sale. I answered their questions about it by just telling them it was time for me to move on. My patients knew I wore my heart on my sleeve, so many suspected something was amiss, but I had to keep up appearances.

Meanwhile, I still carried a huge financial burden at the clinic. I had salaries and mounting bills to pay, and the monthly profits became deficits. Sasha and I stopped taking paychecks to keep a little money in reserve, but that couldn't last forever since we still had three monthly mortgages to pay. The money had to come from somewhere. I could only hope the sale would be as quick and painless as possible.

## Point Of Responsibility

*98. In your life, are your finances out of control? Are you in debt? Are you being financially responsible for your family? Your view of money is a direct representation of how you view life in general. Determine where you came up with your view of what money represents. How did your parents look at money? Is your money blueprint inherited from them? Is it from a significant other? Where did you get your ideas of what money represents? Write everything in your notebook, including common sayings that you've heard spoken about money (for example, Money is the root of all evil). If you live with no respect for money, it's probably not the only area where you lack respect. If you were wealthy, or if you are wealthy, would you, or do you, feel guilty for having money? If you live in fear that you'll never have enough money, or if you give all of your money away, those are also representations of your general life philosophy. Do you think in terms of abundance? Does money come easily and freely and from many different sources? If you seek more money, then view that within your meditations. Declare that money has always come easily to you, for as long as you can remember. It's a manifestation of your abundance to have money, if that's what you desire. Just make sure you're responsible with how you receive it. If you don't seek money, that's fine as well, as long as you have a means to take care of your responsibilities. Don't judge those who choose to be financially abundant. If you feel such emotions, you're not being true to self. Other people's prosperity or lack of it should have absolutely no bearing on your emotions. Remember there's nothing noble about being poor and living with no money. It's simply a manifestation of imbalance. There's plenty of abundance to go around. We don't all want the same things, which is a wonderful thing about life, and it's true that money does not buy happiness. I had tons of it and I still self-destructed. Money does, however, buy you freedom. Begin to expand your view of money and what it represents. Money comes and goes in direct proportion to the achievement of your life's passions. The closer you are to living your life's passions, the happier you'll be. You'll be more confident, more truthful, friendlier, more believable, happier, and less stressed and anxious. Money will come into your life more freely as you obliterate all the restrictive obstacles and take responsibility for your life. Money is simply the end manifestation of your creation. It is the essence of human morality. In fact, money is the root of all good! Build a simple budget and stick to it. Cut up your credit cards and use only debit cards. Prepare for your riches! For easy steps to take control of your finances, visit www.responsibilitymovement.com.*

To expedite the lending process, I made sure that Dr. Michaels stayed on target with regard to the bank's requests. We worked diligently to get all the necessary paperwork to them so the process wasn't delayed. We were still scheduled to close by the end of September.

Billing was the other major issue we were combating. We could bill Dr. Michaels' services under my insurance contract numbers while I owned the clinic, but once the sale became final at the month's end, he would no longer be able to continue that. He would, in effect, be on his own. That, of course, could easily translate into losing patients. If people didn't have insurance coverage, they were much less likely to come to the doctor's office. To add insult to injury, the process to get credentialed with most insurance companies took about ninety days. That left sixty days in the interim. That uncertainty had been a primary factor in lowering the clinic's price. But we were doing what we could to minimize the possible loss of income by quickly getting the ball rolling.

On Tuesday, I received a voicemail from Betsy letting me know someone had contacted her, who wanted to involve her in a civil suit against me. She reassured me she wasn't interested, but I wondered who had contacted her.

I called Henry, who had a cease and desist letter sent to the parties involved. He let the investigators know other suspected "victims" were being contacted, and I was possibly being slandered. All the DOH could do was tell them to stop. I had no rights. I just had to suck it up.

My second psychotherapy treatment was on Thursday. Dr. Cunningham and I discussed how I was dealing with everything. I quickly realized he wouldn't let me justify or rationalize my behavior. Like me, he had a hard edge about my incorrect behavior. He gave me some action steps to bring to light how my actions affected my relationships, and vice versa. I didn't like the idea of reliving those things for yet a third time, but I agreed to show my good will toward the process.

On Friday after work, Sasha and I went to the cabin. We spent the weekend together licking our wounds. The past two months had been surreal, but neither of us were the type to get stuck by such things. We constantly reassured one another and made the best of our situation. The worst thing we could do was break under the stress. So we agreed to put on our flak jackets and take the pounding together.

### *Point Of Responsibility*

*99. Sasha and I were going through things to the best of our abilities. But within every relationship, there can be times of mistrust, uncertainty and confusion. If both partners don't actively work to remain connected, such times can lead to serious disharmony, and ultimately, separation. Sasha and I knew we wanted to be together, but the very nature of the discussions that swirled around us caused us an unspoken uncertainty. As things began to crumble, it was almost impossible not to wonder whether even our relationship was forever. As we sat next to each other in front of the fire one night at the cabin, we shared a couple of glasses of wine, and I held my gaze into her eyes. She then reciprocated. I put down the glass, sat up tall and faced her; she did the same. We spent the next fifteen minutes or so in unspoken, non-physical, intimate contact. Tears of sorrow, of grief, of sadness, and of happiness, flowed from our eyes. This exercise was one of the most meaningful, most powerful, techniques I'd ever used to connect, or reconnect, with another person. Sasha and I decided we would repeat this every morning and night for five minutes each time. What we found was simply amazing. As the months passed, we held steadfast in our aim. The few nights we missed due to my being out of town I would call Sasha and we would visualize the same act together. Almost immediately, we found we were inseparable on the most emotional and spiritual levels. We both smiled more, and shared a deeper knowing that we were going to be all right, no matter what happened. I encourage you to follow through with this exercise. Do this with family members, children, and, of course, your partner. You will be amazed by how much it will change both of you.*

*In our fast and busy times, it is extremely important to nurture our most cherished relationships. One of the simplest things you can do to take care of the relationship with your partner is to go to bed at the same time. It may not seem like much, but the act of coming back together at the end of every day is perpetuating the "team" dynamic. Nothing you're doing at night cannot wait until the morning. Go to sleep with your partner, and wake earlier in the morning to attack the next day. You'll feel more rested, have more energy, and your partner will appreciate the renewed connection. You only need to decide what time you go to bed. We'll talk more about time management and Circadian rhythms later. You can also find more information at www.responsibilitymovement.com.*

On that next Monday, I was called into Henry's office to sign the interview I'd given seventeen days before. If my license were to be suspended, it would be very soon thereafter.

Between patients and on breaks, Dr. Michaels and I diligently spent our time working on the transition. He picked things up quickly as the office basically ran itself. He was on the receiving end of much hard work and an incredibly efficient office. I was thankful the process was so smooth.

In moments of clear introspection, I realized the events of the past couple of months were way beyond chance. It was like the Gods had decided I wasn't in the right place and quickly swooped down to direct me where I was meant to go. My overriding sense was one of disconnection from all things material. Life was becoming much more internal, as I was forced to analyze myself further under a microscope.

On Friday, after two weeks of training Dr. Michaels, I decided to let him treat all patients exclusively. He was more than capable, and it was better to rip the Band-Aid off than slowly to tear it. It would be less confusing to patients, and he could start doctoring them with his own advice. It was a good move because I was getting tired of making up stories about my future plans.

Sasha and I spent another nice weekend at the cabin meditating and hiking and returned to Seattle for her workweek to begin. I dropped her off at the office and went to the house. Around ten in the morning, someone called me, but I didn't pick up. I didn't recognize the number. I promptly checked my voicemail and heard the ever-familiar nasal voice of Mr. Jones as he giggled into the phone, "Hey, uh, just heard that you've lost, uh, your license. Uh, yeah. Uh, there you go."

How could he know that? I didn't even know the outcome yet. As I deleted the call, I wondered who leaked the information to him. Obviously someone in a position of power, someone in the know, had befriended him and leaked the Board's decision to him before notifying even me.

Immediately after that phone call, Sasha called me with the news. On the five-year anniversary of my graduation from doctor school, my license had been summarily suspended, effective immediately. She'd received a call from Aimee detailing the instructions on how to surrender my license.

I asked Sasha to get my license from a file at the office, and I told her I'd be down to pick it up shortly. As I hung up the phone, my primary feeling was relief. Of course, I was sad I could no longer see my patients or create my business. But I was relieved that I no longer had to worry about my clinic because I could no longer actively create its existence. For better or worse, I had to move forward, and moving forward had always been a good habit of mine. I finally knew, without a doubt, that my license was gone. I could do nothing about it until many months later at a possible hearing with the Board. I had two options, either sulk and worry, or continue living responsibly as I had for over a year with my wife.

I mounted the Harley and rode down to the office to pick up my license. Sasha greeted me outside and handed it over. I tucked it away in my pocket before giving her a kiss. Sasha didn't really know what to do next. It was obvious that my facial expression wasn't exactly clear. She couldn't read me, which was understandable. I pulled her into me and gave her a big hug. Quickly enough, I was on my way downtown to surrender my license to Henry's office.

On the way downtown, I thought about how, for the first time in my life, I no longer had a job. I had no vehicle for accumulation. I had no plan for the future. It was strange, and I felt a little empty.

But it wasn't time to start crumbling. I still had many things to live for. I knew the present situation was just a bump in life's road, a big bump, but not insurmountable by any means. I had to keep my head up high, and my focus on the bright side of things.

### *Point Of Responsibility*

*100. By that point in my life, I surrendered to Trusting the Universe. Most things were out of my hands. In my experience, a person can only go one of two ways at that juncture: up or down. I could either complete the self-sabotage and ruin my marriage, or step onto that pedestal and take my lumps like a man. I had to trust in the ebb and flow of life and stop trying to control everything. I finally understood other forces were at work, and sometimes, the best I could do was influence those forces. I could never control anything or anyone. I had to trust that my path was necessary for my evolution. But until I owned up to everything, became honest with myself, and cleared the slate once and for all, I wouldn't be living my ideal life. I had done the work. Now I had to trust in that process. Anais Nin once said, "Life shrinks or expands in proportion to one's courage" and Mark Twain said, "Courage is resistance to fear, mastery of fear—not absence of fear." Be courageous in your own life. When things aren't going well, acknowledge it. Write down why things aren't going well. Follow that with what you're going to do about it. You're powerful! Be the hero of your life!*

The only thing holding up the closing of the sale was the lease assignment. It needed to be signed by the landlord to transfer liability from myself to Dr. Michaels, and the bank we were working with required it. Everything had been completed and reviewed a week earlier, but that one sheet of paper was the lynchpin for the whole deal.

Unfortunately, the landlord's attorney didn't see the urgency of the situation and had put it on the backburner for the last two weeks. We had wanted to close the loan before my license was suspended, but now we could only hope that Dr. Michaels' bank would be all right with the negative press surrounding the clinic it was about to finance.

Thoughts about the sale were replaced by downtown traffic as I made my way to Henry's office. His secretary met me in front of his office and I handed over my license. As she ran back inside, there I sat, freshly unburdened, at the curb on my motorcycle. The whole event played out like a floating dream.

My phone ringing quickly brought me back to reality. It was Sasha. I sat down on the bike, took off my helmet and took a deep breath before picking up. I had a feeling the next wave of horror was just a few breaths away. When I answered the phone, Sasha shared with me that she'd just fielded a phone call from a local TV news reporter. The Board had wasted no time in sending out the press release and the media was calling for our comments. We were previously instructed by Henry simply to reply "No comment," which is what Sasha did, but she wanted me to know the story would be the headline in that night's news, at both five and eleven o'clock.

I hung up the phone and stuffed it into my jacket pocket. My mind was completely empty. The only thing I could do was put my flak jacket back on and wait for whatever came next. I donned my helmet and rode away from downtown toward the mountains.

Six hours later, after a slow, scenic ride, I pulled up to our home. The garage door was open; Sasha had just arrived a few minutes earlier. We hadn't talked all day, so I went inside to let her know I was okay.

I heated up some leftovers as we hugged in the kitchen. After a few minutes, I took the pug outside. The mountains across the Sound were alive with light. I wondered how many more nights I would have to watch the sun go down over the Olympics from our dream home.

I took the pug back inside and the three of us retired to the media room. Sasha turned on the TV. There was my mug front and center. We timed the broadcast to the second. I had absolutely no interest in watching it, so I just got up and quickly left the room. Luckily, the TV was muted, so I didn't have to hear anything, but I did see that they used my own picture from my website as the primary graphic for the introduction to the news that night. They had used the worst photo and manipulated it to make it look really weird. As if the photo weren't bad enough, my head was surrounded by golden sunshine-like graphics. As I left the room, Sasha turned on the audio, and I heard the reporter say, "Do you recognize this man?"

I jumped back on my bike and went down to the dive bar, the one with no TV's, for a couple of beers. After a while, I went over to see Mike, who had gotten his own place after Sasha and I married. He heard me coming and greeted me at the door with a huge grin.

"Looks like you've seen the newscast," I said.

"I bet you could use a drink," he said as he shoved a beer in my face. "Now I know why you're selling the practice! It all makes sense now! All this because of sex?"

"Seriously, Mike. It's kind of a tough time, in case you haven't noticed."

"I'm sorry, but I'm here to keep your spirits up, buddy. I can't really imagine what you're going through right now. So which chick had the jealous fiancé?" He continued to laugh and badger me.

"No comment," I said with a forced smile.

He continued, "As per the TV interview, the guy apparently thinks you're to blame for the demise of his engagement. I'm sure it had nothing to do with him or his girlfriend."

"He seems to think it's all me," I said.

"Well, he's living in a delusion then. If she was out sleeping around, she probably got bored or frustrated waiting for him to marry her or be a real man, so she moved on, you know?"

"The bottom line is I never should have slept with her in the first place. But potentially to lose everything in my life because of it is tough to swallow." I took a big, long swig of brew.

"Hey man, people love this kind of dirt. Everybody knows what the story is. They see this guy crying out, playing victim, and they feel sorry for him. He'll never agree that he has any fault in the matter or that he just chose the wrong woman for his prospective wife. It's easier to blame you. There's no logic in any of it. But people feel better when they have someone to blame. It keeps their sense of self intact. Just blame it on someone else, and they won't have to be wrong. It's the American way, buddy!"

It was good to get out of my head and talk with someone else for a change. Mike and I talked for a couple of hours that night before I made my way back home. Sasha greeted me as I came into the bedroom. She gave me a big kiss and a hug. She told me that her mom had called after seeing the news. For a split second, I was mortified. Sasha quickly continued by saying that her mom and dad fully supported us, and that her mom actually instructed her to support her husband completely. That woman never ceased to amaze me. She had taken the high road. How many people actually do that? She'd remembered that all humans have their battles to fight, and no one is above anyone else.

My eyes welled up a little. The day had been a long one, and I was starting to feel severely beaten down. Sasha squeezed me and lovingly talked into my ear. "Listen.

You're the most dynamic and loving man I've ever met! You just went through a hard time and made some really bad choices. But then you completely overhauled yourself. I've never heard of anyone doing the things you did to make yourself better. How many people actually do that for real? Most people just take an anti-anxiety pill or cover up their issues with more addictive behavior." I loved her so much. We were so different in many ways, but so much alike in others.

The next day was sure to be a doozy, so we climbed into bed and I attempted to get some sleep.

I meandered my way in and out of the dream world that night and repeatedly thought about how amazingly quickly everything had culminated. At about three in the morning, the witching hour, I rolled out of bed and went down to the media room to put in a movie. There was no more sleep to be had that night.

As I watched the story of an up-and-coming Italian boxer from Philadelphia for the hundredth time, the mental chaos came full circle. How was I going to make payments on three mortgages with no income? What if the practice sale fell through? Would my relationship with Sasha survive through this? How could I face Sasha's Mom and Dad? How was I going to bring this up to my closest friends and my own family? Was I doomed to lose everything? I only had enough funds for nine months, and legal costs were mounting very quickly. I even felt like the people on my side weren't really on my side. Except for my wife, I was alone, more alone than I'd ever been. It would be a long time before I slept peacefully again.

## *Point Of Responsibility*

*101. Do you have trouble falling asleep? First of all, make sure you plan your night of sleep in 1 ½ hour increments, as each cycle of sleep takes that long to be completed. For example, sleep for six, seven and a half, or nine hours. Try your best not to awaken in the middle of a cycle. Next, there is an easy technique that is sure to put you into the dream world. (Before you get into bed, cover any lights that tend to keep you awake). As you lay in bed, close your eyes and begin taking slow, full breaths into your gut. Your lower abdomen should rise and fall, while your chest remains relatively still. Focus on your breath only. When thoughts come into your mind, simply let them keep moving to the other side of your field of vision. The mind may continue to flood your vision with such holograms, especially when you're more stressed. Simply keep bringing your focus back to your breathing, and don't get angry. Anger is an addiction to the chemicals that create it. As you continue the process, begin to focus your attention on your physical body. Visualize each breath that you inhale going into a very specific part of your body. Upon exhalation, envision that air picking up all toxins and stressful residue from the tissues as it leaves your body. Literally see and feel the process. Start with the first breath cleaning out the left arm, and the next breath going into your left hand, and the breath after that going into the left side of the chest. Keep moving around the body and keep focus on the breath. You might find certain areas of your body more difficult than others. Give them more time. When you finish this process, you should feel at one within yourself. You are a part of your body. It is a part of you. Anxiety will be significantly decreased. If you fall asleep during the process, that's all right. Your body is simply telling you what it needs most at that time. If you're still awake, it's time to put your visions of life into the Universe. Envision a small sailboat sailing off into the sunset. On the main sail, project a vision of you living your wonderful life. See yourself with abundance, surrounded by wonderful people, living in the house of your dreams with family all around. And then allow that vision into the Universe by watching the sailboat with your vision upon it slowly roll into the sunset.*

Chapter Twenty-Two:

# The Sieve

"A twenty-year revocation?" I screamed into the phone. Henry had just informed me that the Board was going to hit us as hard as they could. "What about precedence?" I asked. "Aren't there cases like this elsewhere?"

I believed what the Board was trying to do was literally unconstitutional. But the Board felt it necessary to make a statement that sex with clients, in any form, consensual or not, was unacceptable.

## *Point Of Responsibility*

*102. When confronted with issues, remain present at all times. Don't allow your body to go into shock or into the fight or flight response, especially in times of stress and heightened emotion. Calm yourself down and act rationally using the techniques you've already learned. Become aware of your physical body, slow your breathing, and focus on the things for which you're grateful. Stay present and in the moment until the confrontation is complete. Let the emotions recede, whether it takes seconds, minutes or days. Then responsibly move forward with active decision-making. Think critically and consequentially. When issues aren't dealt with, they accumulate. That is the cause of most anxiety.*

We continued our talk for a few minutes before I was interrupted by a call from my bank. I told Henry I'd talk with him later, and I picked up the other line. Within seconds, I understood the bank was doing exactly what I had feared—calling the loan on my practice due. The Bank's board of directors was aware of the situation from the news and had decided the loan was at risk, so it was time to take a formal position. If Dr. Michaels couldn't secure financing, I would have to come up with the amount due. I didn't have those kinds of funds, but I reassured the bank that the sale was only days from being final.

I immediately called Dr. Michaels. As soon as he picked up, I knew something was wrong. He told me the bank we were working with to secure his financing dropped the loan outright only minutes before.

But Dr. Moseley, anticipating the turn of events, had already sent Dr. Michaels' financial packet to a second round of lenders. Again, only one bank didn't balk at it. It was far from a sure thing, but this bank knew the story with the clinic and was still willing to move forward with the loan process. The bank saw enough value in the clinic to offset any negative effects. It was daunting that we had to start the whole process over, but I was grateful for the opportunity.

Since it was only eight in the morning, I went across town to get some coffee; I wasn't going to any establishment in Atherton. I didn't want to talk to or see anyone.

As I sipped my coffee, I took a gander at all the newspaper headlines. Sure enough, I was on many of the front pages. The whole thing was quite amazing to me. Two days before, I was just a regular guy. Now the media was depicting me as a criminal. It wasn't until I jumped online that I realized how big the story was. It was so big the Associated Press picked it up. TV newscasts carried the story as far away as California, Montana, and Colorado. I was a superstar for all the wrong reasons.

At lunchtime, the mailman brought the biggest envelope I'd ever seen. Its contents stunned me. Within three inches of paperwork were formal allegations, arguments, charges and notice of summary action. At the end were signed interviews by both Esther and Erin. They were the only women who had come forward. They hadn't filed a complaint, but had supported the claims of Mr. Jones.

As I read through all the legalese, I started to feel that out-of-body experience again. The pages described the "perpetrator" of such events as a malicious, evil being.

But that wasn't me. I wasn't malicious. I wasn't a bad person. I'd just made some bad decisions. I had not directly hurt anyone. I'd been hurt just as much by others as they'd been hurt by me. The anger and pain within me bubbled to the surface. The whole thing literally made me vomit into the toilet.

That day I received nearly a hundred phone calls from patients and friends within the community. People were disappointed, but not as judgmental as I expected. Everyone agreed I had made stupid mistakes, but none that warranted my losing my license for so long, or everything I owned. Without talking about the case, I thanked them for their support and understanding. Even Bobby sent me a text message letting me know he was there for me, but I couldn't talk to him—I couldn't afford anything I said to be leaked to the public. I heard nothing from Chloe.

The last thing I received that day was an email from a creative username that read, "was it worth it THANKS [expletive, expletive expletive]." I didn't have to wonder who had sent it. It was so completely inconsequential next to all the loss I'd suffered that I just deleted it.

That night, I reviewed the testimony within Esther and Erin's interviews. As I read through their erratic, mostly pointless, testimony, I realized how lost and confused those women were. I became cynical about the whole process and the unlikeliness that there would be any objectivism in my case. I felt an undulating ebb and flow between acceptance and emotion, but by the end of the evening, I leaned toward the former.

The next day, to add insult to injury, my landlord's attorney said I owed another six thousand dollars in back rent, and the landlord wouldn't sign off on the lease assignment to Dr. Michaels until I paid it. I was getting good at taking in bad news and just dealing with it so I tried my darnedest not to get emotional.

After getting off the phone, I immediately reviewed the lease agreement. There it was in black and white. The lease amount went up every year, but I had kept paying the same amount. Unbeknownst to me, the escalating lease rates were written in the document when I first bought the practice. But when I signed it, I had no idea what to look for. The attorneys had known I was a green horn, just focused on buying my first big practice. Ultimately, they legally had a right to go after the arrears.

I didn't have that kind of money. I would still collect the payments from the clinic until we closed with Dr. Michaels, but no profits existed anymore. The bills were mounting significantly. Besides the cost of legal representation and Dr. Michaels' salary, I still had to pay all the traditional expenses associated with the business, as well as the three mortgages and the upkeep on three homes and vehicles. And I needed to conserve enough cash to pay taxes for the next year. So ridiculous issues like the lease assignment were especially aggravating. Again, I had no leverage. I just had to figure out a way to make it work. I just hoped the landlord and I could come to some agreement so the sale could go through.

Overall, the clinic seemed to be doing well. Dr. Michaels seldom called me for anything, as things were relatively self-sufficient. Sasha continued working the front desk and was the glue that held the whole transaction together. She worked hard for Dr. Michaels and made sure patients were happy. Daily, she would come home and tell me it wasn't the same around there; the patients missed me and thought it quite ridiculous I was being forced out of practice. They offered their support and love to us, which was deeply felt and appreciated.

Sasha told me a few funny stories that happened at the clinic. One patient I'd treated for years didn't know Sasha was my wife. After being adjusted by Dr. Michaels, he made a wisecrack to Sasha about fishing off the company pier and how I really got around. Sasha promptly squashed his humor by telling him, "Yeah, Mark's my husband. I'll be sure to tell him he shouldn't do that next time. But I kind of think he already knows it." The look on his face was apparently priceless. I just laughed when she told me. I gave him a phone call to razz him a bit. I thought it important to keep the humor on an upswing, and not to take myself so seriously.

### *Point Of Responsibility*

*103. Do you take yourself too seriously? Understanding that you're only a spoke in the wheel of life can be an incredibly recalibrating opportunity. Know that you are wonderfully important, but also, that you are a piece of everything and everyone else. When we focus only on ourselves, we aren't living to our fullest capacity. We become lost within that sea of self, and forget about the bigger picture of life. Think for a moment about your self-imposed anxieties. Are you pushing too hard? Are you trying to control, instead of creating? Step back, laugh it off, and understand it's your ego pushing you, trying to make you important. Realize you're already inherently powerful, with or without your ego's influence.*

Sasha was also amused at the number of random individuals who would stop their cars out in front of the clinic to gawk at the posting on the door. Some would actually park and run up to read it. They assumed it was some dirt on the good doctor, but it was really just a welcome note to patients from Dr. Michaels. People were shameless.

That Thursday in treatment was quite a big day. We had many things to discuss with all the events of the week. I felt like I was sitting at the bottom of a big vat that was quickly filling with water while an anchor was tied to my foot. It was all I could do to keep my head above water.

Dr. Cunningham and I talked about all the confusion around the clinic's sale. We talked about how I felt when I had to turn in my license. We talked about how Sasha was taking everything. That's when he said something that really hit home. He told me it was very rare that a relationship would make it through such a case. I cried. Sasha was the love of my life, and the thought of losing her struck me deeply.

That statement from Dr. Cunningham again made me shift. Over the previous few days, I had been living completely inside my head about how things were affecting me. I was definitely concerned for Sasha, but it was difficult for me to internalize, and have compassion for, the things she had to go through everyday. But, at that moment, I vowed I would force myself continually and actively to recreate my relationship with Sasha. I wasn't the only person in my life anymore, and I wanted it to work between us. I had to help her cope as I healed myself.

Through tears, I told Dr. Cunningham that Sasha and I were strong together; that we had a great understanding of the situation, and a healthy sense of independence from it. This thing we were going through was horrible by any standard, but it didn't define us. Yes, issues of trust, fidelity, and self-esteem would have to be dealt with, but if any couple could pull through this situation, it was we.

Even though I was emotional, I was still being pragmatic. As Dr. Cunningham continued to share with me how I should prepare for the worst, I noticed a gnawing pang of anger in my gut. To allow the worst as a scenario for my own life was unacceptable to me. I became more irritable, sat up taller in my chair, and held a fixed gaze on him. I perceived him as a threat. In his small interjections, he was spurring me on to act irrationally. His semantics were precise and seemed put forth in an attacking manner. At one point, he asked me when I was going to stop my womanizing ways. I told him for the hundredth time that I wasn't that person anymore. I was different. And I didn't say it in a manner like I was trying to convince myself. I was self-assured at the roots of my being.

Dr. Cunningham continued on with the more aggressive approach for a few minutes before finally backing down. He obviously saw I wasn't going to bite. I had no interest in verbally sparring with him. I understood he was trying to figure out whether I was just smart enough to know the right things to say, or whether I had truly made long-lasting and powerful changes in my life. I didn't have that familiar sense of needing to fight. Dr. Cunningham was going to form his own opinion of my mental health. His job was to evaluate me, to determine whether I was truly capable of change, and to offer solid advice for my further growth. The best thing I could do was to follow his instructions and complete the homework he gave me to show I was willing to work on myself.

That weekend at the cabin, Sasha and I spent time reconnecting and revisiting our goals and dreams. On Monday, Sasha drove back to Seattle while I stayed at the cabin to work on myself. I thought it was imperative that I continue processing things. It was the perfect time for isolated evolution, as long as I stayed present and focused. I had been dealt a series of major blows in succession that week, and the biggest player in my survival was myself. I couldn't blame or pass the buck. I didn't want any of the negativity that surrounded my life in Seattle to stay buried within me. I wasn't going to allow that sense of separation from myself, that "out of body" sensation to creep back into my life. I wanted to feel all the emotions as they happened, so there would be none left to store. I meditated, beat pillows, screamed and cried before repeating it all over and over. I reintroduced many of the techniques I'd created the year before to help further the process. It was a wonderful week of release. And by the time Thursday rolled around, I was ready to drive into town and continue with Dr. Cunningham.

### *Point Of Responsibility*

*104. Few things are more empowering in life than getting closer to the truest representation of egoless self. By first being strong and responsible within yourself, you lead by example and inspire others to trust in the process of creating a purpose-driven life. Stop looking elsewhere for reassurance, or for a way to live your life. Becoming a leader means standing on your own two feet. Lead your life; don't be led.*

Our next session was quite different from the last. Dr. Cunningham offered advice I could use and we talked in greater detail about the issues at hand. The conversation flowed and I found it very helpful.

After I left Dr. Cunningham's office, I went to a coffee shop to check my email. As I scanned the numerous emails from attorneys, accountants, brokers and everyone else, I noticed yet another email that Sasha forwarded me from the clinic's inbox. It was from someone with another creative username, and it was absolutely disgusting. By that point, there weren't many people in the know with regard to what was happening, so I figured I knew who it was. Again, all I could do was suck it up.

I talked with Henry about everything the next day. He said there probably wouldn't be a civil case because nothing would be left for anyone to take. My assets were drying up quickly, and any such case would simply drive me into bankruptcy, which was already a distinct probability.

As for my case with the Board, we were waiting to see when we could arrange the hearing. I just had to sit and wait patiently for the Board to decide my fate as my physical world crumbled around me.

Henry let me know he'd sent in my formal "Answer to the Stated Charges" and "Request for a Prompt Hearing." He suspected the hearing could be in February if we pushed hard enough.

As for the lease assignment, if I wanted the sale to close, I had to pay the six grand by the end of the month. Had I known I owed it before I listed the practice, I could have included it in the sale price, but now it had to come from my ever-diminishing savings.

The first week of October, I had beers with a friend who showed me some of the blogs he had run across. They were written by various members of the public and were listed after the articles written about my case in the newspapers and on the web.

-"Since when was 'consensual sexual relations' a crime?"

-"So what if he did? Not a rapist and not a pedophile equals no 'imminent danger to the public.' I hope he's reinstated."

-"This article didn't indicate he raped them. Now did it? From the tiny bit of information that it did provide it didn't state that. And not to assume, but from what I think might have happened is that some of the female patients found out about some of the others and called "dirt" on him. Now look! If it was consensual, he'll get off. He might still lose his license. Not at all professional to fish off the company pier. That's usually lesson number one in the employee handbook. Regardless whether you own the pier or not. Pretty bad judgment. In my opinion...they're all guilty. And they all have some explaining to do."

-“It’s not like he’s a ‘real’ doctor. He’s a back-cracker, for heaven’s sake—just a glorified physical therapist. It’s not like he’s a psychiatrist where he can take advantage of a vulnerable patient, or a dentist groping the patients while they’re under anesthesia, or an OB/GYN taking the pelvic exam too far. Besides, this is Atherton. I’m sure there are plenty of bored and under-sexed rich housewives who just loved the attention the attractive ‘doctor’ provided in spades.”

-“‘Those who play, must pay’ does not apply here, unless maybe he’s married? If I am a male lesbian, it does not make me a bad quackapractor.”

-“It sounds like he was really good with his hands in all sorts of ways! Let me guess what happened. Eight of his female patients hit it off with him really, really well. The ninth one turned out to be a bit crazy, so he ended it with her and she turned him in to the State. If there was an inappropriate touching issue, I might have a problem with this. But it sounds like someone got vindictive and is using the law for revenge. That really sucks.”

-“Why name him if he hasn’t been charged with a crime? Remember not long ago when the [newspaper] wouldn’t print photos of people the FBI wanted to talk to because they weren’t charged with a crime? Seems inconsistent to me.”

-“It does seem unfair that he gets his name mentioned, but…the other eight patients do not.”

-“This is scary. Thank God there are grown up men in our State Government who understand the seriousness of the problem and have suspended his license. This is called…’sin’ and the man needs some help. And contrary to assertions in other comments, women are vulnerable when they trust a doctor and are recovering from serious injury. I hope this man can now admit his problem, seek some help and accountability and be released from his shame.”

-“I am a female patient of Dr. Mark. He is a really nice guy and very good-looking not to mention he was single and so very nice. He was new to the city and looking for friends. I imagine it would be difficult meeting a female that seems compatible to you and both looking for someone and not dating them!…He got married in June and that is when this all started. I believe there were some unhappy gals wanting to snatch him up for themselves. I hope he gets his license back and I can see him again…as he was a great doctor."

-"This does not surprise me in the least. This is Karma in its truest form."

-"He was a friend of mine. I miss him."

-"Quite a novel way to adjust a spine."

-"What's next, no tipping the waitress?"

-"This guy is a stud. So what if the ladies like him? As long as it wasn't rape there should be no problems."

-"Maybe he was billing insurance for it, and that's how he got caught, LOL."

-"So what if he did?"

Some of the comments were funny, some were highly judgmental, but all had merit in one way or another. The common thread was that if my case were left up to the court of public opinion, I'd have received a suspension, but been able to keep the practice. People didn't understand how the Board could take my whole life away, including my right to earn a living, for such an incredibly long period of time. Regardless of what others thought, I had to move forward.

## *Point Of Responsibility*

*105. In my case, I was completely guilty for not following the rules I'd agreed to when I received my license to practice. But in the cases of others, do you keep an open mind? Do you tend to judge others without knowing the facts, or do you accept them? There is no in-between. Judgment comes purely from the ego. It's an attempt to create the belief that you are better than another. When you find yourself in a state of judgment over another person, take a deep breath and act from your higher self. Learn from his or her mistakes and actions. Don't simply jump on the bandwagon. Doing so takes the focus off the lessons that might be learned and puts it on emotion and degradation.*

That week, I lowered the price of the remodeled house again. The Seattle market was definitely stagnant, and I hadn't priced it right at the beginning. Plenty of people looked at it, but nobody liked dark cherry cabinets, black granite and stainless appliances anymore. I actually had complaints that the gardens were too plush, even though they were completely low maintenance. I didn't understand what the heck was going on, but I had bigger issues. I just hoped it would sell sometime soon.

By that time, the reality of the situation had set in with Sasha. She was becoming aware of how grand all of the destruction was. She decided to see a counselor every week, which allowed her the opportunity to bring up issues from her past, as well as to discuss the obvious events at the present. She and I began to process the negative side of things together.

For me, those were logical discussions. I'd become quite adept at making the transition from emotion to analysis. Sasha, on the other hand, processed the events much more emotionally. She would dive deeply into questions and concerns I thought irrelevant to our relationship. She was forced into the situation by my past actions, and I felt horrible; how my past indiscretions hurt her was one of the most difficult things with which I had to deal.

I owed it to our relationship to talk about everything, to help her understand where I was at that time in my life, and how I could have let myself spiral out of control. Even though we had the same conversation over and over, I continued to share my thoughts whenever Sasha wanted reassurance. At times I felt downright horrible over these discussions, but I wanted her in my life, so it was the only way. I just hoped that all the conversations and even our fights would ultimately bring clarity to her mind. I appreciated that she was still there at all, and that she never threatened to leave. She just needed to process things in her own way.

## *Point Of Responsibility*

*106. We all deal with things differently. Allow others to process their own lives without offering unsolicited advice. The last thing emotional people want to hear is how they should be acting. Don't poke a raging bull. Stay unemotional. Don't get caught up in their fury. Keep your thoughts to yourself, and support the other person in any positive way you possibly can. Don't forget, when someone is going through something emotionally, no matter what they say, they really want support. Be strong and support them.*

When Dr. Cunningham and I next met, we discussed the issues with Sasha. He informed me yet again that our relationship might not work out, and I just had to hang on for the ride. Again, I wasn't just going to get what I wanted, which was a perfectly functioning relationship. My wants and needs had to take a back seat to Sasha's. All I could do was wait.

Before the session concluded, I realized that in every part of my life, I just had to wait humbly and see how things would turn out. I'd never lived my life in such a way; it was completely foreign to me. I was always the guy who had everything planned with very little left to chance. I abhorred the "wait and see" philosophy. I had always been a big fan of creating my own destiny. I'd created everything I'd ever wanted. But now, in this time of turmoil and destruction, all I could do was wait and see. The whole idea of leaving one hundred percent of my life up to chance churned my stomach. It created anxiety and frustration that constantly had to be cleared from my mind.

That weekend at the cabin was another of self-discovery. I pondered the gray area between leaving my life up to chance and being completely controlling of it. A balance between the two had to be achieved.

On one end of the spectrum, the ego tried to control all in its presence. It wanted everything "just so." But there's a bit of inherent dysfunction in believing one can control the finer points of life. One can control if a house is clean or messy. One can control one's own moral constitution. One can control self-responsibility. But as soon as others enter the picture, control becomes dysfunctional. We cannot, in a healthy way, control another person. We cannot control his or her actions on the world or us. We cannot control another's emotional state. The best we can do is to determine whether we want to allow such bundles or packages within our own existence. Do we want such agents in our lives? If so, we work mutually to agree on a code of conduct to resolve any disputes. If we don't want such agents in our lives, we part ways, regardless of the emotional ties.

On the other end of the spectrum, from ego's control, we have a complete "letting go" of everything.

The balance between the letting go and ego's control is where we allow a properly functioning and responsible ego to create a clear plan to bring abundance into the world; we let that plan go into the Universe to mingle with the powers that be so it will be manifested. The next step, however, is the most crucial in the process. We must reinforce our plan with actions that will allow its manifestation. We must be confident that it already exists. For if we are not, the dysfunctional ego takes over and manipulates to try to make things happen faster, not allowing for the proper timing of things. The balance shifts, which destroys the system of abundance that was being created, and was leading to manifestation of the ego's initial plan.

The bottom line was that I was done trying irresponsibly to control my life by focusing on accumulation. But I certainly wasn't going to give it all up to chance or a Higher Power; that also led to irresponsibility, in my experience. Most of my issues were of a humanistic origin, not spiritual. I had to strike a balance between the two extremes. It was my aim to create a life of responsibility, abundance and manifestation of all the things I wanted by aligning myself with the natural balance of things. I didn't focus on getting or wanting, but on already having such abundance. And it took the present situation to allow me to understand greater things were at work than just me. There was my soul, and there were the souls of many others who lived within our world. A very specific timing to things existed that I hadn't taken into account until I thought about how the recent events in my life had played out. The whole process was quite poetic, and I had very little control of it. One could easily call it a Higher Power, or a plan, but to my understanding, all things on earth were created by humans. And all those things that we chose to manifest were ultimately brought into being by the balance of our egos and the ability to release those manifestations into the spiritual realm for contemplation and creation.

That weekend at the cabin was truly enlightening. I revisited and updated my goals and personal code of conduct to reflect my most recent positive alterations.

On Monday, however, one foot stayed rooted in chaos. I received a letter from a large insurance company formally letting me know all payments due my clinic were to be withheld due to my investigation by the DOH. Basically, the insurance company didn't want to pay any money out, even if payments were legitimately owed, and any time it could postpone payments, even if only for thirty days, it made money on the interest earned. It was a wonderfully corrupt system, but that's how insurance companies worked. When I let Henry know what was up, he promptly sent a letter informing the insurance company of the consequences of nonpayment.

On Tuesday, Aimee informed me that my malpractice insurance carrier wasn't going to cover any part of my case regarding sexual misconduct, as my case was about my own negligence. It wasn't much of a shock; in fact, it was expected. Henry sent the company a letter pleading our case, but we certainly didn't expect it to change its tune. To get coverage, I would literally have to sue for it, which would cost me even more money.

As for the sale of the practice, things seemed to be going along smoothly. My bank finally came to its senses by securing its interest in the practice. The bank told me what I already knew; since I wasn't legally practicing, it was illegal for Dr. Michaels to bill insurance under my name and contract numbers. The loan officers were going to push hard for its Board of Directors to allow Dr. Michaels to be added onto the loan with me, which would significantly reduce the bank's risk. I didn't understand why it took so long for them to come to that conclusion, but I wasn't the owner of a bank. The loan officers told us they would know something from their Board by the end of November. At that point, Dr. Michaels and I could sign the Purchase and Sale document, whereby he'd be the full owner of the clinic. Of course, until the other institution refinanced him, I would still be on the hook. But it was much better than the alternative.

Around Halloween, ironically, I became haunted by a recurring nightmare where Dr. Michaels just up and left the whole situation, foregoing only his minimal down payment. It was the only thing I truly dreaded. If that happened for real, I might as well take a long walk off a short pier.

Meanwhile, the landlord wasn't going to budge from the amount owed. I was informed officially that they wanted the full six grand. I closed my eyes and thought happy thoughts about rainbows and puppies and such.

Throughout November, the lawyers, brokers and all other interested parties battled back and forth to bring the financing issues to a hopeful conclusion. Impromptu emergency meetings were followed by emergency phone calls, followed by me freaking out about the next insurmountable issue at hand. But the way it finally ended up, after thousands of dollars of accumulated legal fees, was exactly the way my bank first drafted it up. Dr. Michaels would be allowed to sign the PSA, and he would be added to the loan. That would make everything legal. The only caveat was that he continually needed to seek financing for the loan. Until that unknown day, I was still the primary person on that loan, with the bulk of the liability. It was the best-case scenario with all variables taken into account. We just had to hope that the other bank was going to come through for us.

I now spent most of my time at the cabin alone. It became my sanctuary. That month contained some of the most transformative moments of my life. I continued the God-awful, however enlightening, process of cleaning out my closet. I started meditating, in various forms, three to five times each day. In the morning, before my mind got a chance to think of all the things I had to worry about and to do, I'd imagine my day. I would imagine it exactly as I wanted it to occur. I would visualize Sasha and I together, laughing, with children, and needing nothing. I lived it with all five senses. I envisioned myself following my passion of being a highly successful, world-class, international speaker, consultant and coach. I was happy, healthy and vibrant. I went through my whole day in my mind. The process allowed me to stay focused on my ideals throughout each day. If I were confronted with a decision, that decision came to an easy conclusion because it had to fall in line with my ideals.

## *Point Of Responsibility*

*107. Are you chaotic in the morning? Do you jump right out of bed and attack your day without a blueprint to build it? Take a more proactive approach to living. Before you get out of bed in the morning, before you start thinking of all the things you have to get done, before your heartbeat starts to increase, Imagine Your Ideal Life. Lay still with your eyes closed. Like you did the night before, begin to focus on your breathing. Take a few long, deep breaths. Then imagine your day, envision how things are going to go. As you do, FEEL the power and confidence shine from within you, held within every thought, action and conversation. Feel your actions and thoughts on every level of your body and mind. This is where you begin to manifest the process of achieving the goals you've already created.*

*Project positive outcomes to the situations you know you're going to deal with that day, and in the days ahead. See yourself disallowing compulsions, addictive behaviors and negative thoughts as others try to test your resolve. You simply say, "No, thank you," to such things and move your thoughts to the next activity that will further create your purpose-driven life. Know there will be change-ups, but the way you react to them is different than in the past. Your actions are calm, creative and responsible, regardless of how emotional others may be. You are a pillar of strength. See yourself smiling, shaking hands with people, and being a part of the community, surrounded by great people with whom you have mutually beneficial relationships. Envision yourself in wonderful shape, eating good foods, and laughing. See yourself with all the abundance you've ever thought about and being passionate about the work you do. Be as specific as you can. This is your life. Do this as long as you can every morning.*

On most days, I would awaken with the sun. After I imagined my ideal day, I would walk outside and sit on the ground, watching the sun come up. I would sit there for about ten to fifteen minutes to recapture my connection to the earth. On sunny days, dew glistened on the plant leaves as the sun burned away the morning mist. I took in deep breaths of fresh, mountain air and smelled the dark, volcanic dirt beneath me. The slight chill in the air was invigorating; life-giving. On rainy days, the smells of the forest were deeper, stronger. It was darker and cooler, but much more vibrant with energy. Even in the rain, I still took advantage of my opportunity to connect to Mother Nature. I came to have a much deeper appreciation for my place in the world. Spending time in nature, away from people, allowed me to forget the less important, inconsequential things in my life, and desire more the things that I already had.

### *Point Of Responsibility*

*108. Each morning, after you Imagine Your Ideal Day, don't immediately talk to anyone or think about anything. Keep your mind free and clear. Change into the necessary clothing, and go outside for five to ten minutes alone. Take deep breaths. Relax. Take notice of the sights, smells and sounds of nature. Feel the Earth, the grass and the bark on trees. Know that you're part of it all. And your connection with nature must not be broken, ever. Fend off all thoughts and sit in silence. Allow the visions in your mind to walk right through your field of vision, and right out of the picture. Do this every morning and every evening.*

When I was finished sitting in silence, I would then get up and do a walking meditation for about twenty minutes. I would say my goals aloud as I walked along the one-lane logging road that led to Heliotrope. I forcefully declared to the world who I was, and what I was all about. I'd read about such meditation in a biography about Alexander Hamilton. Every morning, he would awaken and walk outside to do his walking meditation. He visualized all the expected interactions for that upcoming day going exactly as he planned. I'd done this from time to time for a couple of years, but not with any repetition. Now I thought it a useful tool because it involved using visual, auditory, kinesthetic and sensory input, which is how we create our brain's connections. Adding my own story and goals proactively into my life using this technique every day would, theoretically and practically, create the connections in my brain that would eventually manifest exactly what I'd cultivated.

When finished with my walking meditation, I felt unbeatable. It took a week or so to figure out exactly what I wanted to manifest, and how to say it. But I actively worked on talking about my life and who I was. Once I crystallized my thoughts into words, and then used them in the meditation, each day became easier, and the physiological response more powerful. I'd never felt such a high in my entire life.

After the walking meditations, I would stretch using the techniques I'd learned in various places throughout my years as a doctor and student of yoga. I synthesized a wonderfully simple stretching program that loosened up the low back, neck, torso and extremities. I focused on the stabilizing muscles that typically give people issues later in life: the psoas, multifidus, adductors, piriformis, the rhomboids, SCM and suboccipitals. After a few weeks of stretching alone, I added a gently invigorating strengthening program to the same groups of muscles. Once in a while I'd use bands, an exercise ball, and light weights. But for most exercises, it was body weight alone that did the trick, at least for my purposes.

When stretching time was through, I began to retrain the physical connections in my brain through physical exercise. I'd recently become a student of cross-crawl research. Studies showed that by doing simple, cross-crawl activities for fifteen minutes every day, within months, you will show objective improvement in coordination, and more interestingly, in your ability to act rationally and make better decisions. A cross-crawl activity is one where you move contralateral (right and left) sides of your body simultaneously, such as lifting your left leg while also lifting your right arm. Such activities reintegrate both the left and right sides of the brain. They improve the connection between the logical and the creative. Such activities were once thought to affect only the physical aspects of the brain-body connection. But when objective testing also showed an improvement in one's own emotional self-evaluation and subsequent response, cross-crawl exercises became much more functional and all-encompassing.

One study involved two groups of about 1500 prisoners who volunteered for the study. They were all repeat offenders of the worst kind, basically lifetime criminals. All of them were slated to be let out of prison about six months after the study's projected conclusion. Half of the prisoners were asked to do nothing. The other half were given supervised cross-crawl exercise to do for fifteen minutes, three times each day. Study results showed that two years later, a whopping percentage of the prisoners who did no cross-crawl exercises were back in prison. I don't recall the exact percentage, but it was around 95%. Interestingly, of the prisoners, who did the cross-crawl exercise, only 5% were back in prison.

Somewhere in my education, I happened upon another study that was a basic investigation into the possible causes of dysfunctions like Attention Deficit (Hyperactive) Disorder, adolescent addiction, and various learning disabilities. There were two groups of mothers with children who were in their adolescent years. Half of the children had, at some point, been diagnosed with one or more of said dysfunctions. The other half were perceived as being normal, happy kids suffering from none of the diagnoses that their counterparts had. The mothers were asked a series of questions regarding the rearing of their children. The investigators were looking for deviations on any front: social interactions, nutrition, household income, education of the parents, etc. One of the most interesting questions posed was: At what age had the child stopped crawling, and started walking? In popular culture, your baby is stronger and healthier the sooner he or she walks. But what the study found was the complete opposite. Those children who were helped to their feet quicker, typically under twenty-two months, had actually stunted the growth of the projections of the brain responsible for integration between the two halves; incidentally, those were the same projections responsible for emotional self-evaluation and response. The crawling was of paramount importance to brain integration on many different levels. The study also determined a direct correlation between time spent crawling as an infant and incidence of ADD and similar dysfunctions. The incidence of ADD dropped significantly and directly with relationship to the number of months spent crawling before finally walking. Basically, those kids who crawled longer were healthier, and much less emotional.

From that point forward, I knew cross-crawl exercise was powerful, and I designed a series of such exercises to enhance and rebuild my brain.

Each day I also went for a vigorous hike to build up my cardiovascular system. After years of doing just enough exercise to look good, I realized I had a long way to go to be truly healthy. I never liked doing cardio training, but since I liked to hike, that became my cardio workout.

## *Point Of Responsibility*

*109. Exercise is important because it allows us the opportunity to integrate our visions of a wonderful life into our physical reality. We learn to become one with our body. (Powerful, focused exercise routines, cross-crawl techniques and stretching plans can be found online at www.responsibilitymovement.com. There are exercises that specifically target problem areas like low back pain, sciatica, general inflexibility, poor posture and neck pain). Due to our often sedentary lifestyles, disease has become rampant within the average American's body. It's our responsibility to take care of ourselves, to make our hearts beat and to flush our tissues with life-giving blood, oxygen and nutrients. Exercise does this for us, and it introduces endorphins into the bloodstream; over time, we become positively reinforced by the behavior. Take time to stretch every morning and evening for at least ten minutes. Walk every day for at least thirty minutes. Walk fast enough to be just on the verge of breathing hard, but slow enough so you can still carry a conversation.*

By that time, I was usually incredibly hungry. I'd started weaning myself off of things I knew I was allergic to: wheat, dairy, sugar and alcohol. I ate only whole foods, and cut out anything processed. I took the time to take care of myself for a change. As my gut slowly healed, I had so much more energy. My skin became vibrant. And my thoughts even became more pure.

## *Point Of Responsibility*

*110. Proper nutrition is paramount to living a focused and healthy life. (A detailed nutritional plan, as well as various truthful, nutritionally-related concepts, motivations and ideas can be found online at www.responsibilitymovement.com.) There are some specific rules to follow that will maximize the efficiency of your brain and body. Cut out foods that have processed sugar and wheat. Eat between four and six smaller portions throughout your day. Take a daily multivitamin. Don't eat carbohydrates less than three hours before you go to bed. When you need to snack, make it a protein. A boiled egg will do the trick. When you eat, eat slowly. The body's reflex for a full stomach takes fifteen minutes. So the less you eat over that fifteen minute period, the less food will be in your gut when you're full. Drink no fewer than eight glasses of water each day. If you feel tired or fuzzy during the day, you're probably dehydrated. Coffee and soda should be eliminated from the diet. When you wake up in the morning, make sure you have at least a little bit of protein. Your brain needs it to break the fast it's endured overnight. Yogurt is fine. Eggs are great. Meat will work as well, as long as it's lean. Bacon, ham and sausage don't count. Eating healthy fat, avocado, olives, olive oil, flax, helps your body to burn additional fat. If you have more fat than you'd like on your body, start every morning off with a spoonful of flax seed oil or an omega-3 fatty acid pill of some type to kick start the burning of fat within your body. Fat is good, when it's taken in moderation. And it's essential to a properly functioning nervous system. Fat's not the bad guy, complex carbohydrates and processed and/or refined foods are. Understand that we're not all meant to look like Adonis. Bodies come in different shapes and sizes. Millions of people are considered overweight by the standards of others, but they are actually quite healthy. Unfortunately, even more people truly are unhealthy. Their weight is a direct manifestation of their inability to make good decisions, of escapism, of compulsion, and of lacking responsibility to self, community and Earth. Only you know which type of person you are. So be yourself and do the right thing. Make the changes necessary. There's a simple way to wean yourself from poor eating habits. Start off by allowing yourself to indulge in whatever you want to eat every other day. On the days between, mind your foods and control portions properly. You'll go through some tough days, but it's your responsibility to push through. If you must, keep focus on the day that follows, the day when you can eat anything and everything in sight. Do that for a month. By the end of the month, the process will become much easier. At the beginning of the second month, give yourself only two days within each week in which you can eat however you choose. In the third month, you will have only one day each week to do so. After that, you will have gained the control to make conscious decisions about your eating habits. Your gut will be much healthier, and you'll feel okay about occasionally having some ice cream or a hot dog. You've done the work. You've changed your habits. It's okay.*

Recreating myself became my life. I had been living the typical American life for so long, and it took a massive amount of effort to move from my ego-based mindset to a healthy mindset. I knew I was lucky to have had the training in my past to create such a system. And I took full advantage of it.

I focused my attention and intention on healing my body and mind. In the beginning, I still had a lot of negative emotions to work out: anger, frustration, rage, shame and guilt. The process of changing one's life doesn't simply happen overnight, but over years of conscious, diligent action. I wanted to come out of my turmoil as a wild success story. So creating a new, healthier life was the only option.

Until my dying day, I will be grateful for the opportunity to change my life, and that Sasha gave me the space I needed to do so. We mutually agreed she would stay in town during the workweeks and live at the big house on the hill. She came up to the cabin on the weekends. My buddy Mike rented a room downstairs and took care of the home maintenance over the next few months.

I came home twice that month for treatment, and I spent only a couple of nights at the big house. I really disliked it there. The house was physically wonderful, but it represented so much pain for me. It was a huge burden financially, and I couldn't bring myself to become invested in it emotionally. Every time I walked through the door, I had the feeling it wasn't mine and would soon be gone. I was hurting on many different levels. But I was also doing the internal work to make myself better.

At the month's end, it was time for Dr. Michaels and I to sign the paperwork to add him to my practice loan. His bank was still processing his loan application. At the escrow agent's office, I signed everything. The last paper was an invoice that showed a thousand dollars due immediately to the escrow office. When I asked what it was about, the escrow agent said a mistake had been made in the pre-sale calculations. I had to write a check for that amount to close the deal. On top of that, I also had to get a check over to the landlord's attorney's office by the end of business to allow the lease assignment to be binding, which meant seven thousand dollars more out of my pocket.

Just when I was about to walk out, the escrow agent asked me whether she could copy my driver's license to have confirmation for the deal. I checked my pockets and realized I'd forgotten it at home on the kitchen table. She told me the only way the deal would close properly was to have a copy of it by the end of the day. So I had to drive all the way back home, pick up my license, copy it, and then fax it to her. It was all quite a fiasco, but it was finally over. The deal was closed. Dr. Michaels and I were partners.

As I left town toward the cabin, I stopped by the landlord's attorney's office to drop off the six thousand dollar check. As I sat in my truck and wrote it out, I began to seethe with anger. I wrote on the back of the check that by signing it, they would also basically leave me alone with regard to all liability with the office. I was so incredibly angered at them for all the shady things they'd done to me over the three and a half years I occupied their overpriced building. They were, without a doubt, the worst landlords I'd ever run across, and I was letting them know it with the writing on the check. After I composed myself, I quickly took the check in and set it on the secretary's desk. I told her who to give it to and walked out.

Unfortunately, when the attorney saw the writing on the back, he called up Aimee and told her that they wouldn't accept the terms I'd written on the back of the check. Even though the lease had been assigned to Dr. Michaels, I was still legally on it, as was Dr. Michaels and the doctor before me. I was about twenty miles north of Seattle when Aimee called me up to give me the news. Poor Aimee was on the wrong end of another screaming outburst. It was the angriest moment I'd lived in some time. I hung up and chucked my phone across the cab of the truck, smashing it to bits. My rage had gotten the best of me, and I had no one to blame but myself.

I had to swallow my pride yet again and go back to that lawyer's office to write them another check. But of course, I had no more checks with me. I had to drive all the way home to pick one up, and then I had to drive to the other side of town to drop it off. Every little thing was working against me, including my own judgment.

### *Point Of Responsibility*

*111. Sometimes in life, things simply don't go our way. And the more we push to correct, trying to force our own outcome, the worse things get. The acknowledgement of such situations, energies and people is what sets us apart from all other animals. Most of us get caught in the endless spiral of anger and frustration. When you are met with friction, when conversations aren't going well, when you find yourself being completely bogged down by everyone and everything, know that you are the only common denominator. It's your perception that must be altered to get past all of it. And it's an active choice to live with anger, or with acceptance. This is the exact moment at which you can practice trusting in the process. Take a few deep breaths, gently twist your spine from side to side, and then begin and complete the action steps associated with the tasks at hand. In effect, they are the only things you have any control over. The rest is needless worry and unnecessary emotion. Accept the rest as the way it's meant to be. When you've completed your action steps, go for a walking meditation, focusing on the joy the outcome will provide.*

I couldn't get out of that city fast enough. I jumped back in the truck and made my way toward the lumberyard on my way to the cabin. I had to build the rest of my deck before the snow halted construction for the season. I picked up the necessary lumber and hardware required to finish the job and carefully rolled down the curvy, two-lane road in the big diesel.

As usual, I started to think about everything ad infinitum. I had no more income. The sale was final, and I was completely out of a job. Sasha would only work at the clinic for an additional two weeks after closing, and then she would also be out of work. I had two weeks to make my internal environment something that others could bear.

On that drive and into the night, I couldn't stop the waves of emotion that consumed me. They were fierce and relentless. I would be out of resources very quickly, and I needed to stop the sieve. The smaller house wasn't selling at all. I loved it, but no one else wanted it. I finally came to the conclusion that I had to let go of our dream house. It had the high-end appeal, and it was the type of home people with money would want, regardless of a depressed sales market; the place had everything, and was certainly the most desirable of the three. And, of course, it accounted for more than half of my mortgage payments.

Just thinking about it brought on emotions of defeat and depression. Things had changed so rapidly the past two months that it took everything I had just to hang on to my sanity. The last thing I wanted was to lose it all, but I pondered the possibility that maybe things were supposed to happen the way they had. Maybe I had to lose everything to make everything right. Could it be that's what it was all about? I had to lose it all to realize what was really important in my life. And Mozart couldn't have better orchestrated the way everything went down. The Universe was obviously telling me things were changing, and I had little control over it.

I was deeply conflicted. I fought within myself from both ends of the spectrum. On one end, I had my ego fighting to hang on for all I was worth. It was represented by my hate, anger and frustration. It needed to fight and prove I was right. On the other end were thoughts of constant abundance that surrounded my life. That abundance wasn't just in the form of things, but in self-assurance, wisdom, love and positive adaptation. No amount of destruction could take away that abundance.

I'd always thought punishment for crimes should be in accordance with the crime committed. The punishment should fit the crime. But I'd committed no crime. I was being ostracized and stripped of everything for improper behavior, for having bad morals. To my ego, my punishment didn't fit the "crime." I was being judged based on whom I used to be, not whom I'd become. And that was truly frustrating.

As I drove on, I realized the only way I could truly break free from my past was just to let it all go. How I reacted played a huge role in how I would perceive the world for the rest of my life. I was literally laying the groundwork for my life and habits in my future, and just as importantly, how I dealt with conflict. I didn't want to think of people as bad or vindictive. I also didn't want to play the victim. Even though I was literally paying for all my indiscretions with my assets, that didn't give me permission to cower in the corner and say "poor me."

During that conversation of self-discovery, I realized the ego does serve a good purpose. It helps us dig ourselves out of the holes we create in life. It has a positive, functional purpose, as long as it remains in balance. And as for abundance, it is always there, and always will be there.

After I pulled into the cabin's driveway and shut down the truck, I sat in silence, caught in a moment of introspection. I was gaining vast amounts of knowledge, wisdom and clarity while losing everything fear and anxiety had created in my life. I was gaining abundance by losing "things."

While my losses needed to be grieved, I was humbly excited to see what was to come.

As I brushed my teeth that night, I looked at my face in the mirror. I was tired. My eyes were red and puffy. My head was down, and my mouth in the shape of a frown. As I looked at myself, it was evident I'd changed. I leaned in, closer to the mirror. As I consciously peered into my own pupils, my eyes gave way to tears, slowly at first; then quickly they ran down my cheeks. I blew my nose and continued for another ten minutes or so. I didn't say anything, or ask questions. I just stood there, looking at myself. I couldn't remember the last time I looked myself in the eye. But when I was done, I felt calm. My body wasn't as rigid; my head was up and my shoulders were back. I felt better. I decided to do that exercise for at least five minutes each morning and evening, taking notice of my own appearance, reaffirming that connection to my soul.

## Points Of Responsibility

*112. That first time I looked into the mirror, I took notice of my appearance. I was depressed. My hair was a mess; I was unshaven; I needed a shower; my clothes were frumpy and my posture was poor. Understand that personal care is of paramount importance to keeping a positive mind. By showering daily, you literally recalibrate your body's polarity. You infuse your immediate environment with negative ions, which is good. Incidentally, that is why you feel that same way when a thunderstorm rolls through. And that's why you always feel better after taking a shower. If need be, write into your weekly calendar a specific time for you to take care of yourself, a time you can attend to the necessary grooming of your nails, teeth, skin and hair. Take time daily to floss, to apply lotion and to clean yourself. It's not just good for everyone else, but for you too. Studies show that those who wash daily are objectively happier and more productive.*

*113. Doing the mirror work was an important part of acknowledging my particular relationship to the outside world. As I looked into the mirror, I saw both my appearance as it related to others, and I saw my own judgment of myself. As time went by, the simple awareness of both helped me to process my feelings more productively by adding a new form of understanding and interpretation of my emotions and presence. I highly recommend doing mirror work to stimulate and bring to the surface the harbored shame, guilt and love we all have for ourselves. It's quite an enlightening experience.*

Sasha came up to the cabin the next day after work. On Saturday, we built the remainder of the deck and glued my phone back together.

At lunch, Sasha brought up that she thought we should sell the big house. The woman was amazing. I knew how much she loved the place, and it broke my heart even to discuss selling it. But she knew we had no other options at that moment. I was overcome with gratitude to her. We decided to list it after the holidays.

Then she pulled out the mail that had come on Friday. Of course, another letter had come from the DOH, stating it had scheduled my hearing for June 2008. I laughed. No way did I want to wait another nine months of my life for a conclusion to this horrible existence. I just wanted it to be over. I had to let it go and move on with my life.

On Monday, I called Henry to see whether he could get the hearing scheduled sooner. He explained to me how everything was structured, from a system of depositions, to discussions with attorneys and panel members, and several hearings, with the final hearing in June.

If we weren't happy with the outcome of that hearing, we had the option to bring our case in front of a second panel. The system was set up well, if one had the financial capacity to last that long. Since the first hearing wasn't tentatively scheduled until the middle of next year, the whole process would undoubtedly go into 2009. I definitely didn't have the staying power for that. By dragging out the process, the system basically created a situation that deterred one from fighting. One couldn't really move on in life without having such an event in the rearview mirror. It was just an accepted evil.

On the surface, the system seemed to lend itself toward objectivity. I'd always been an idealist, so I could appreciate that, but beneath the surface was a whole different world all about the art of practicing law; it was calculating, cold, reactionary, and in my opinion, consumed by a high-stakes game of one-upmanship and of beating the bad guy into submission, not to mention, a system of half-truths and hidden agendas. It was a battle to see who could beat his or her chest the hardest. It was no longer about me and what I'd done, but about precedence, the way others felt about what I'd done, and about control. My case was quickly becoming "us versus them," rather than about doing the right thing.

I asked Henry whether I had any other options. He said the only one was to have a settlement conference where I would meet with the primary representative from the assigned panel and the staff attorney, and we would hammer out a settlement on the spot. We could possibly schedule a settlement conference by year's end. It sounded more appealing to me because it would expedite the process.

I asked Henry, if we went the route of a full-blown hearing, how much it would cost; he estimated it would cost anywhere from fifty to a hundred and fifty thousand dollars because of the amount of work involved. I already knew which way I wanted to go, but he argued that he wanted to fight hard, to use all the idiosyncratic facts about the process and the Board to bring to light how everything was so subjective. He called the twenty-year revocation literally unconstitutional, and that a precedent had previously been set.

But when it came down to it, two major things outweighed for me the benefit of fighting. First, I didn't have that kind of money. Second, there was no guarantee we would win. What I did was wrong, and that warranted a suspension of some length, which meant I couldn't practice for some time. After spending a hundred grand, I might be suspended for ten years instead of twenty. To me, they were about the same. Either way, it felt like a lifetime revocation. The Board had seen to that. I told Henry I wanted to schedule a settlement conference. So he put the wheels in motion.

My next phone call was to a real estate agent I'd met in social circles. Nick had a great reputation for being a hard-nosed negotiator, a no-frills, straight shooter kind of guy. We discussed the particulars of the situation and set up a meeting at the house for the next day. Through the rest of the morning, I finished the work on the deck, packed up my bags and headed back to Seattle.

On the way down, I talked to another buddy of mine named Tom. Tom offered me a job doing some quick remodeling work to offset some of the bills and give me some dough for the holidays. I quickly agreed to help him out.

At our meeting, Nick was up front about the depressed sales market in the region, which meant he felt the house was a great buy for the next owner. I had done well when I purchased it eight months before. We determined we should list the house for the same price I bought it, which would show we were motivated to sell, and hopefully, it would bring prospects quickly. I wasn't exactly happy about it since it chipped away significantly at my net worth, but it was either list it at a good price, or get hit during negotiations. Unless the house was caught up in a bidding war, and those days had long passed, I was going to lose a minimum of a hundred grand in equity. But I had no other options. I had no other professional training to fall back on to make hundreds of thousands of dollars a year. I had to agree to sell at that price. I had to let it all go. We agreed to list the house at the beginning of the year. At least we could enjoy it through the holidays.

The next day I had another session with Dr. Cunningham before I started working with my friend Tom. We discussed in great detail my extreme stress and all the loss that had surrounded me. I told him I was more stressed than I'd ever been, but I also had a resolve I'd never experienced before. I was understandably angry and sad, but I still retained a deeper knowing that everything would be all right in the end. He asked me whether I felt the urge to go drink and "hook up" with people. I was happy to report that I didn't drink anymore, and I had no desire to be with anyone other than my wife. In the middle of the most trying moment of my life, I was genuinely happy. I loved my wife and our life together.

Dr. Cunningham asked what would happen if Sasha left. I told him I'd be devastated; it would hit me incredibly hard. I loved her more than anything. But if she wanted to quit on us, it was her prerogative and I could do nothing about it. I had no control over anyone else, and I wasn't going to force someone to be with me. If she did leave, I knew from my recent experiences that I'd find a healthy way to deal with it.

I saw a comfortable radiance of light within my mind telling me I would be okay. I told Dr. Cunningham that nothing was going to make me stop moving forward. Nothing would impede my evolution.

I had this sense that everything we were going through was like practice. I remembered back to all those years of hockey practice I'd endured. It was brutal; and so were our present events. But if we could make it to the other side of practice, we'd be rewarded with a sense of accomplishment, of achievement, and experience.

Dr. Cunningham poked around those statements for a few minutes, but I was unshakable. I really meant them. Although I cried as I talked, I was filled with self-assurance and self-reliability. They were my new gifts to myself; the only things no one could ever take away.

Then he discussed the possibility of Sasha enabling my behavior. I told him I didn't allow Sasha to enable me. I had told her I knew what I did was wrong, and no one else was to blame, no matter how much she thought the others were getting off easy. I was the common thread, and I'd already changed my life for the better. I no longer resonated with my "illness."

## *Point Of Responsibility*

*114. Do you enable the poor behavior of others? Allowing those around you repeatedly to act badly shows a serious lack of self-worth on your part. You deserve to be surrounded by good people. This old adage is all-powerful, "Surround yourself with the people you want to be like." This doesn't mean you should seek to be like others. It means you should first determine the characteristics you want to represent. Then seek out people who are a model of those characteristics. Always hold others accountable for their poor behavior. Discuss with them why such behavior is not acceptable, and let them know that if it continues, you will not be a part of their lives. If it ultimately comes to that, accept that person for who he or she is; then focus on the type of people you want surrounding you, no matter how much guilt that poorly acting individual doles out onto you.*

During our next session, Dr. Cunningham wanted me get into a frame of mind where I found it comfortable for my sexual compulsions to exist. He told me to focus on the stress of my life, write down how it felt, and then write down how it felt to be within that compulsive state. I looked at him for a few seconds before I told him I simply didn't live there anymore; those connections no longer existed within my brain, and I didn't want to recreate them. I had to take a stand right then and there. It would have been easy to fall back into allowing that type of thought, but I'd worked so hard up to that point to eliminate it. To me, it was like telling an alcoholic to focus intently on what it's like to hold, smell, and sip an alcoholic beverage, even though that person had already successfully changed his or her environment.

Dr. Cunningham forced the issue hard. As I continued to tell him I wouldn't go through all that again, I noticed I felt very little emotion as I talked; I carried little, if any baggage, with me. I was proud of myself for being strong, and for forgiving all those people in my past, including myself. I told Dr. Cunningham I was ten times more stressed now than I'd ever been in my life, and stress had formerly caused my negative behavior to surface. That I was so unbelievably stressed and had absolutely no desire to "womanize," as he had put it, spoke volumes about my internal environment.

At the end of our session, I thanked him for helping me, but I let him know, logistically, it would be too difficult for me to continue care. The holidays were right around the corner, he was going on vacation, and I was moving north to the cabin at the beginning of the year. He agreed to help me find someone to talk with regularly near the cabin. I got up, shook his hand, and left his office for the last time. It was my birthday, and I was done with psychotherapy.

As I walked from the office, my father called to wish me a happy birthday. He told me I had his support in everything, which was interesting since I hadn't told him anything about it. I was extremely ashamed to talk about such things with the people closest to me, including my father, sister, and good friends. I'd always commanded a certain amount of respect from those people. I'd been a super achiever, a pillar of strength for them. My present situation was a hard hit against my ability to provide such strength, not to mention it would kill my reputation. I couldn't bear to think about how they would all react. So I thought it best to wait until I had a clearer picture of how things were going to end up before I discussed it.

I was humbled finally to discuss things with my father in full detail. He offered some advice, but more importantly, he listened. He listened more than I'd ever known him to listen to anything in his life. I continually had to wipe tears of relief and grief from my cheeks as we talked.

After talking with my dad, I called my best friend Erik. He wished me a happy birthday and brought up the same issue. I noticed the obvious trend. Everyone already knew, but they didn't know how to discuss it with me. They all apparently chose the same day to offer their support from afar. Erik and I didn't get into the details, but having his support helped me to gain some strength. For the first time in my adult life, others were supporting me.

After I hung up the phone, I sat on the secluded park bench in the cold drizzle and broke down. Tears flowed heavily as I let go of the continued need to control. After connecting with my father and Erik, I felt a sense of release. I continued to release the guilt, shame and anger from within. I must have been there for a good twenty minutes before the sobbing abated. I felt cleaner, more upright. I jumped up, wiped my face on my sleeves and went to work.

The house remodeling went well for a few weeks. It felt good to work with my hands again. And being around people was nice as well. Tom had enough work to last up to the holidays, but then I'd be a free agent again.

Meanwhile, things went well at the clinic. For obvious reasons, I hadn't been involved within the community much.

Sasha's last day at the clinic was on the fourteenth. Over the past few months, she had continually told me how the patients missed and supported me. We'd received a pile of patient testimonials regarding me as "an upstanding individual within the community," a "good person, and a great doctor." Once her work there ended, she spent the next couple of weeks in the well-deserved vacation mode.

I worked up until Christmas Eve, and later that night we went to Sasha's sister's house for the festivities. Times were good. The evening was full of cheer and laughter. I was so very thankful to be a part of their family and to have their support. They all took me in and made me feel at home, even when my mood swings made me clearly disconnected from everything and everyone. They just let me be. They allowed me to process things my way. I seriously had never seen that kind of support in my life.

The day after it was first listed, we got a reasonable offer on the big house from a local businessman, so we moved all our belongings back into the small house. It was nice to be in the place again, but all of our nice furniture was used to stage the other house. A few days later, Nick called to inform me the buyer had done an inspection on the house, and now he wanted a hundred thousand dollars dropped off the price. I just laughed; there was no way I could do that. As it stood, I was going to lose all the equity in the place to brokerage fees and taxes. I couldn't go any lower. After a few days of trying to negotiate, the deal was dead. Back on the market it went.

As February began, chaos returned. Aimee called to inform me the six thousand dollar check to the landlord had bounced. I wondered why, after almost two and a half months since closing on that deal, we were even having that conversation. I knew I had the money in the account when I paid it. But because they had waited to cash the check, I had used the funds in the account to pay other bills. So when they finally got around to cashing the "desperately needed" check, there wasn't enough money in the account to cover it. I thought the landlord didn't have any leverage over me since the lease assignment had already been completed. I told Aimee I didn't have the funds to cover the check so we'd have to work something else out. She didn't really say much, so I just dropped it, and asked her to call me when she figured out what we should do.

After a ridiculously low offer on the house I refused, Nick finally called to tell me an older couple was interested in the house; they were going to put a third down, and wanted to close within thirty days. I had to pinch myself. Nick explained the offer was solid. It wouldn't leave me with anything in my pocket, but I just needed the house to be gone. The payments were killing me, and I couldn't afford one more month. I asked him to email the offer so I could sign it and get it back to him.

I didn't have a computer or printer at the cabin, so Sasha and I stopped at a small place where we could process the paperwork. It took longer and cost more than it should have, but the offer was signed and official. The next step was the inspection, which they'd already scheduled for a week out. Things looked good, but we just had to wait and see.

Sasha and I were finally beginning to slow down together. Our day-to-day lives were completely different than we'd ever expected. We lived in a cabin in the middle of nowhere. There were no gas stations. There were no food stores. There were no hardware shops. There was nothing but snow, trees, rivers and solitude. It took some getting used to, but we quickly learned to enjoy it. After the recent months, we didn't mind being away from people.

Our days consisted of activities we felt we needed to become healthy again. We skied, hiked and snow-shoed along logging trails and rivers. We actively worked on ourselves, both together and separately. We played games and laughed a lot. We devoured books and created some wonderful, and some not-so-wonderful, recipes.

We still had major issues to attend to, with the hearings and houses, but those things would all work out in one way or another. The most important thing was we were together, and we were successfully making it through.

Two weeks went by before we heard anything about the house. When we finally did, Nick's voice was less than calm. He told me the other agent still hadn't done an inspection. They were dragging their feet, and Nick didn't know why until that very day; the other agent had done a background check on me and knew exactly who I was. She understood fully the urgency of the situation, so she told Nick I should sell to them at a lower price before my assets dried up. She'd waited as long as she possibly could to drag out the process, knowing every day counted against me.

That was certainly enough to cause a spike in my adrenaline level. I asked Nick whether we could use her extortion attempts against her as leverage. He told me we could go that way; he had the complete string of emails to confirm what she was trying to do, but we would possibly lose the sale altogether if we pursued such action. To me, negotiating with such opportunistic, shady characters was revolting. I wanted to fight her, but I was in no such position. We couldn't lose sight of the forest through the trees, so we agreed we would try to make it work first. Only, I couldn't afford to go any lower than their original offer. I had no wiggle room because I didn't have the cash to come out of pocket, no matter how hard they negotiated.

Nick tried to convince her to ease the noose a little, but she wouldn't; when we rejected the offer, she told him straight away their offer wouldn't change, and they'd be back in a couple of months with an even lower offer. She assured him we'd get nothing better from anyone else.

I was so disgusted with her. I wondered whether the people she represented knew how she acted. Clearly, money was the only thing that mattered. I understood that since it was a business transaction, but the way she attacked me was disgraceful. And the ugly truth was that if the house were still for sale in two months, I'd need her even more. The whole thing literally made me ill.

But we weren't quite done for the week. Not only did we not have a buyer for the house, but I got a brand new formal notice from my landlord's attorney demanding immediate payment. After several question and answer sessions, my attorney's office determined the landlord had a legitimate claim to the funds, and if I didn't pay, I would definitely be sued. When I asked what would happen if I didn't contest it in court, Aimee said the landlord would get the judgment, and I would have a criminal claim on my permanent record; even if I were ultimately forced into bankruptcy, the claim wouldn't be discharged. They had me from every angle. But if there was one thing that I was not, it was a criminal. I asked how much it would cost to fight it in court; I thought maybe a judge would agree that, because the landlord waited more than two years to say anything about the incorrect rent payments, I wouldn't be liable for the whole amount. I had a chance, especially since I'd never done anything criminally wrong in my whole life. She replied it would probably cost me twelve to fifteen thousand dollars. I obviously had to find a way to pay them the six thousand.

For the next week, the attorneys went back and forth, until out of nowhere, I received a phone call from the landlord herself. She told me she didn't want to use the attorneys anymore, and she was tired of them racking up the bill. Within minutes we came to an agreement. I would pay her one third down on a credit card, and I'd pay the balance off in monthly installments over the next year. It was the best-case scenario for me. I gave her my credit card information and hung up the phone. The fiasco was finally over.

It was one heck of a week. The chaos seemed to chase me down everywhere I went. I felt like there was no escaping it. I reaffirmed it was necessary to see it all through to the end. The last thing I was going to do at that point was avoid anything.

Sasha and I decided to drive into town to bum around on Sunday. In the evening, we went out to dinner and had a great time. Our relationship was deeper than ever. We were living proof that if couples focused on the bigger picture, they could make it through to the other side with a more meaningful and less judgmental relationship.

After we finished eating, the server gave us the bill, and I handed her my credit card. Within minutes, she came back to say it had been declined. I hadn't been in that position since college. At first, I thought it must be an error. That card should have had plenty of room on it. She told me she had tried it three times, but it obviously didn't work. We paid in cash and walked back to the car. En route, I called up the credit card company. I was astounded at what they told me.

The customer service person said there had been a charge against the card for six thousand dollars two days before. I was enraged. I took my hockey stick out of the car and beat it on the ground like I'd never beat anything in my life. I must have looked like a lunatic basket case, but I needed to get the anger out of me right there on the spot. I couldn't believe the gall of that landlord. Our agreement meant absolutely nothing to her.

When I was finished with my ridiculous tantrum, I picked up the shards of my stick that littered the sidewalk and joined Sasha in the car. I apologized for my behavior and we went home.

The next day I woke up and had a cup of coffee before I made the call. When I mustered the energy, I grabbed the phone and walked outside to call up the landlord. I hoped the charge was just a mistake on her part. But within seconds, I realized it wasn't. In the most condescending and arrogant voice humanly possible, she said she had spoken to her attorney after our phone conversation a couple of days before. He had told her our agreement wasn't favorable to her, so she had reneged on the deal and simply billed the full amount to my credit card. Her cavalier attitude shook me to my core.

I calmly told her she was the most cunningly evil person I'd ever met, and the only true measure of a person was his or her word. I told her she should genuinely be ashamed of herself for treating another human the way she had throughout her tenure as my landlord, and if her ancestors knew the kind of person she'd become, they'd probably be so completely disgusted with her that they would take back everything she had inherited and leave her in ruin. Unfortunately, when I hung up the phone, I didn't really feel a whole lot better.

## *Points Of Responsibility*

*115. Dealing with toxic people can be some of the most difficult situations in our lives. When I had this confrontation with the landlord, the anger was a natural part of the process. It's okay to be angry. The conversation I had with her was also warranted. But I went wrong when I irresponsibly aired my dirty laundry in front of anyone who could see me on the sidewalk that day. We must deal with our emotions alone. I should have let it go until I was back home where I could burn off the energy physically by running, chopping wood, or beating that same hockey stick against a tree.*

*Another good point here is learning how to live with unconditional tolerance. Tolerance matters most in those highly emotional times. Getting caught up in an emotional reaction to a situation dooms you, and your relationships, to failure. When things get emotional, removing yourself inherently puts you in a position of reason, and it is a representation of tolerance. Let people be who they are. Let them live their lives without judgment. Don't forget that judgment comes from the ego, and the ego is all about proliferating itself, and it is NOT interested in tolerance whatsoever. If another person is harming him or herself or others, it's your responsibility to make sure you don't enable the behavior, and to discuss lovingly with the person the consequences of his or her actions. But you mustn't judge or be self-righteous. That's holding power over another, and you don't do that. You have tolerance.*

I went back inside the cabin, asked Archie whether he wanted to go on a hike, and gave Sasha a kiss goodbye. He and I hiked around for hours that day. We scoped out the river and various trails that coursed the mountains. When we finally got back later that night, I felt much better. The walk had done me good, and Sasha had made a wonderful dinner. We sat and talked about things as we ate. Afterward, we curled up on the couch and fell asleep with the pug.

Three weeks later, our favorite real estate agent sent us another offer on the big house. True to her word, the offer was lower than the original. The situation hadn't changed from our standpoint. We had a hard number that had to be collected to pay off the note, and her offer wasn't enough. Nick told her we couldn't go any lower than just under asking price. So we just let it go, assuming the deal was dead.

Lo and behold, hours before the offer sheet was to expire, Nick called me back with good news. He decided he would forego more than half of his commission to make the sale happen, and he had gotten the other agent to do the same! I was absolutely amazed. Things really were on the upward trend. We had a deal on our hands!

The last hurdle was for the buyers to do an inspection. Days later, the new deal again went south.

Nick called and told me to sit down. As I did so, he said the inspector had found numerous issues with the house. They said the Spanish tile roof needed to be replaced at fifty thousand dollars. The structure needed to be rebricked at seventy-five thousand dollars. And other ridiculous odds and ends added up to another twenty-five thousand dollars. Everyone involved knew the house was solid. They were just messing with us again.

As Nick talked, I played out my financial situation in my mind. It was the first week of March and our cash was almost fully depleted. If I didn't sell the house to those people, it would be forced into foreclosure. That's when I had a flash of brilliance. I had bought the house less than a year earlier, and of course, I'd had my own inspection done before I closed on it. It showed absolutely nothing wrong, other than a crack in one of the sidewalk tiles. I also had boxes full of paperwork listing all the home repairs that had been done on the place since it was built in 1949. I told Nick I would get everything together and send it to him that afternoon. When finished, I met with Nick and he took the bundle off my hands. He went directly over to the other agent's office to dump it in her lap.

Two days later, the prospective buyers backed down. We were able to come to an agreement that included me losing all the equity in the house to taxes and the remaining brokerage fees. But at least I didn't have to come out of pocket.

Sasha and I had acclimated nicely to the slower pace of mountain life. Oftentimes, as I worked on the property, I would test myself with the question, "Did I miss all the things I've lost?" As the days became slower and more focused on quiet, the answers became clearer. I certainly missed the money and helping people to change their lives. I missed great conversations with wonderful patients. I missed building my business. But if I had the chance to go back into practice, I wouldn't. Happily, I no longer had to deal with the constant battling with insurance companies to get paid on legitimate claims, the huge tax payments with no benefits, the incessant and constant influx of various fees and premiums, nor the very real fear of being frivolously sued. And I definitely didn't miss the constant buzzing of "more, more, more" from within my own head. Things were different. I was much more in line with the natural laws of the universe. I was quiet, comfortable and more grounded. Whatever we decided to do in the future would come from that same place. I dedicated my future not just to accumulating money, but also to helping others and to thriving in abundance.

During this time, I came up with the idea of the Responsibility Movement. After everything I had experienced, I decided I could use what I had learned to help people—I had done that as a chiropractor, but now it would be in a different, new and exciting way. I began by trying to pull together practical ideas and actions that would help people to become more of whom they truly desired to be. The program quickly became all encompassing, a proactive approach to creating a life from the inside out. I came up with The Seven Pillars of Responsibility, which became an easy, step-by-step process to creating balance. The Seven Pillars were Wellness of the Mind, Love and Relationships, Success and Leadership, Finance, Physical Wellness, Codes of Living and Spirituality. I designed the whole program to educate people on life topics that are too often neglected, but absolutely necessary to a good life and the evolution of our souls.

In the meantime, I did some menial labor jobs and Sasha did some temporary work at a few places. Unfortunately, the job market north of Seattle was relatively stagnant. Sasha and I were living month to month; we still had mortgage payments on the houses, mounting legal bills and regular monthly expenses, which included a hundred and fifty thousand dollars in student loans. Our meager income wasn't even close to enough to cover it all, so we had to sell almost everything we owned just to get by. Bankruptcy was still a very real possibility.

Money and possessions had created a false sense of stability within me. Now as I watched it all being erased, I noticed a much stronger underlying sense of stability bubbling up from within. I wasn't anxious about the losses we'd sustained, and I didn't fear losing more. Although the money and toys were gone, I knew if I wanted them back, I'd find a way.

## *Point Of Responsibility*

*116. Do you have a false sense of stability or security when you have money and possessions surrounding you? Do the things you own or have define you? Are you in fear of potentially losing your material things? If so, your intention around them is misplaced. They are not a definition of you, but a manifestation of hard work and proof you can create things in your life. Begin only to appreciate those things as positive manifestations, and not the most important things in your life. They are only materials. The greatest things in your life are your relationships and your ability to manifest positivity. When those two areas are creatively working together, material items show up regularly.*

At that point in time, our focus was on truly slowing down and allowing our goals and dreams to show themselves; that was more important than anything else. We were going to do it right this time around. We didn't focus on the lack, or any impending doom, but on the things for which we had to be grateful, which were plentiful. We focused on our relationships with others, our families, for still having a beautiful cabin in the woods, for the opportunities to change our ways of being, for our minds, intellect and vision, our work ethics, responsibility and love. We changed our neuronets together hour by hour. When we stumbled, we'd get back up and continue moving forward. When we faltered, we'd talk about how great our lives truly were, how much we appreciated everyone and everything. We were extremely thankful we'd kept our agreement to be married. Either one of us could have easily decided it was all too much. But we didn't. We took solace in how everything had worked in our favor to get us to that point. Slowly, we came back in line with what it meant to be human, at the most fundamental level. We came closer to organized, unemotional reason, and floated further from the need to accumulate and control. It was an eye-opening time, and positively life-altering.

### Point Of Responsibility

*117. Keep your agreements. Do you follow the rules relative to the situations in your life? When you make an agreement, whether with a person, an employer, or a group, it is imperative you keep that agreement. If you choose not to, for any reason, you will house guilt and shame within yourself, knowing you could have handled the situation better. You'll have a diminished sense of self. And on top of that, the other party will trust you less. Don't make excuses. Push through them and get into action. Think in terms of how good it will feel when you do so. Think of the long run. Live up to your end of every agreement. It's the right thing to do, and you'll have a renewed sense of confidence.*

Four days before the sale on the big house was to close, Sasha and I went down to Seattle for a few days to do a little cleaning. She dropped me off at the small house and went to the big one. What happened next was unbelievable.

Not fifteen minutes after I dropped her off, Sasha called me. She said that when she had walked into the big house, a woman was sitting in my chair looking out over the Sound at the beautiful view. Obviously startled to have someone in her home uninvited, Sasha asked her what she was doing there. The other woman told her that she was the buyers' agent, and she was taking some measurements for them. As the woman walked across the living room, Sasha realized she was completely drunk. She slurred her words and wobbled as she walked. Her paperwork was scattered all over, and it looked like she might have been living there. Sasha told her to get out of the house; the house wasn't sold yet, and she had no right to be there without her clients. The woman pled her case and apologized as she stumbled down the front steps and got into her car. She drove off speedily, running over the freshly-cut grass on the way.

I couldn't believe what Sasha was telling me, but at least she wasn't harmed in any way. It just showed us how truly messed up the other agent was. It disgusted me that she was going to get paid tens of thousands of dollars out of my pocket for such behavior.

When I called Nick to let him know what had just happened, he was horrified. He really wanted to pursue some kind of legal action, but that would take some cash and affect the deal negatively, so we just let it go.

A couple of days later, I was at the big house loading some of my furniture into a truck when I got a call from the State of Washington regarding personal property tax. Surprise, surprise, they wanted more money. I couldn't say I was shocked. Apparently, the fifty thousand dollars of Business and Operations tax I'd paid, along with the thousands of dollars I'd paid after the recent audit, with absolutely nothing in return I might add, wasn't quite enough.

The agent said I owed personal property taxes associated with the business for the year 2007. I had no idea what he was talking about. I explained to him that I'd sold the practice, and any taxes should have been paid from escrow. He said the escrow company must have messed up, and I still owed the tax to the State of Washington. I said I would do some research before I just sent a check in the mail.

When I called the escrow company that had closed the sale of the practice, I was told, upon inspection, that it had paid off only one of the two tax accounts associated with the practice. The other was not paid. I assumed it was the escrow company's mistake, but unless I wanted to pursue legal action against it, which I couldn't afford, I'd have to pay personal property taxes. 2007 was a monumentally financially draining year, by any standard.

As I drove the truck back to the cabin, my stomach churned anxiously over the seemingly never-ending negativity associated with my past indiscretions. I just wondered when it would all end.

After a few minutes of stewing in anger as I drove north into the snow, I remembered some of my buddies were playing hockey around that time, and they had asked me to join them. Since my equipment was lying in the cab of the truck, that's exactly what I did. I burned that anger off in a flurry of skating and reaffirmed positive relationships with guys I hadn't seen for some time. By the end of the session, I was a new man. I felt relieved, happy and free. My body was loose and my mind was clear, if only for a little while.

## *Point Of Responsibility*

*118. As I went through this monumentally tough time, it became obvious I'd forgotten a few of my passions. Life had become monotonous and unfulfilling. I hadn't played hockey, lifted weights, picked up new hobbies or continued reading motivational and inspiring books. I only focused on work and accumulation. When I was in practice, I would often ask others whether they were being passionate in life. Unfortunately, most people would tell me they weren't. Time has a way of insidiously flying by without so much as a whisper. It is your responsibility to recapture that time. Think back into your past and write in your notebook some of the passions and hobbies you've let slip into nothingness. Do they still excite you? From now on, add a new passion or hobby every two months or so. Learn how to do something new. This process will keep you young by keeping your brain active and dynamic. Get out of the rut and become more passionate about life. Forget the television, video games and planning your next meal. Get out of the house and/or the office and do it.*

The next day, I reluctantly wrote a check for almost a thousand dollars to Washington State's Department of Revenue. I tried to envision my thousand dollars being used to improve Washington's schools from their ranking of forty-eighth in the nation.

Two days after moving the staged furniture out of the big house, we closed on it. The sale brought a mild sense of relief by dissolving half of my monthly mortgage payments. With it also went the one hundred and fifty thousand dollars I'd put into the place in the form of a down payment. I didn't get any cash out of the deal. But it was just another step in the process to become leaner.

Sasha and I talked that night about our next move. Our net worth had been obliterated. In nine months, we'd gone from being near millionaires to being about a million dollars in debt. We lost the biggest part of our equity in the sale of the practice. And the timing of the bursting real estate bubble had worked to reduce our home values to almost exactly what we owed. No equity was left in the other two houses. In fact, if we were presented with the opportunity to sell them, we'd have to pay out of pocket the taxes and brokerage fees. Things were more than grim on the real estate front.

The only option we had was to trim the fat by unloading more debt. The remodeled Atherton house represented about two-thirds of it. Unfortunately, we didn't have the resources and we weren't bringing in enough money to continue making payments on it, as well as payments on all the other obligations. So we made the unbelievable decision to stop making payments on the house. I never thought I'd be in such a position.

We kept it listed, but with little hope someone would buy it since it had been on the market for over a year with very little action. All the work I had done on that house, all the hopes and dreams I had when I first bought it were all being squashed. The party was over. I'd done everything I possibly could. I had to admit defeat. It would soon be in the hands of the bank that owned it.

We had been living at the cabin for a few months full-time, so we decided it was time to move up there for good, or until another great working opportunity presented itself. It was the least expensive option for us, and we genuinely liked it there. Being away from people was also helping us to recalibrate. We didn't look at the time we spent at the cabin as getting away or escaping, but as a welcome sanctuary to re-create. We worked out hard, ate healthy foods, learned to communicate with one another, and focused our intentions on living our lives in a balanced way. As we lived in the present, it seemed that time was slowing down. We both looked and felt years younger. As we got back to basics, we gained a better understanding of how to live more responsibly, and how to be purpose-based, as opposed to floating from one action to the next. And in the process, we found ourselves being much less emotional.

Being at the cabin in the middle of the mountains offered us the opportunity to shed social norms, get away from gossip and entertainment, as well as separate ourselves from the constant management of peoples' egos and aggressive behavior. We had the space to practice being non-reactionary, simply because there weren't many people where we lived. Purely and simply, being at the cabin decreased the stimuli and the overall noise in our lives. When the noise was gone, the self shined through; like a groundhog in springtime.

Chapter Twenty-Three:

# The Awakening

The first week in April, the weather started to break at the cabin. The sun seemed to become brighter overnight and quickly began to melt the snow and ice. Winter hibernation was finally coming to a close, and spring was just ahead.

The winter had been a tough one, but we had made it through. We looked to the near future with a positive vision and a revitalized hope. The worst was behind us, both emotionally and financially. Our new minimalist lifestyle had become overwhelmingly invigorating. Sasha and I were both becoming recharged and ready to move forward with our lives together. We made it through all the uncertainty and destruction, remaining strong for one another along the way. In fact, we were alive and thriving.

In the beginning, my case was one of sex, adultery, blame and devastation. But it had quickly transgressed into something much more powerfully life changing. It became about learning how to live with complete honesty and self-responsibility. Once I finally came to that precipice, it was easier to understand and correlate the recent sequence of events into something clearly created by a process higher than, or more involved than, the self. At the very least, the subsequent events that followed my negative behavior years before were not just retribution, but Karma in its fullest sense. It was a violent swing that quickly and without opposition brought things back into balance. There was no way that Karma would be denied.

## *Point Of Responsibility*

*119. Is your life in balance? Are you more dedicated to work than play, or vice versa? Are you waiting for a day in the future to start taking care of your body? Are you healthy, or are you tired? Do you eat processed foods? Are you confused about the type of workouts you should do? Are you on medications for imbalanced hormones and/or organ dysfunction? Are you emotional, or are you objective in your decisions? Do you plan your days, or do you play it by ear? The typical American is so unbalanced, that he or she doesn't take the time to take care of him or herself until the body, or mind, begins to break down. The Seven Pillars of Balance provide an easy, proactive approach to living responsibly for the self, and then for all of those around you. In your notebook, create two action steps from each of The Seven Pillars that you will work toward achieving from this point forward. The Seven Pillars are Wellness of the Mind, Love and Relationships, Success and Leadership, Finance, Physical Wellness, Codes of Living, and Spirituality. For example, within the realm of Wellness of the Mind, an action step might be to focus intently on Not Blaming Others, or to do a walking meditation with your goals in mind three times each day. An action step within the realm of Finance might be to create an active budget, bringing into balance the money spent on entertainment, education, food, utilities, etc. At www.responsibilitymovement.com, you'll find many tools to help you to balance your life, and to become more powerful from the inside out, which will allow you to create yourself into an asset for the human race.*

Thinking in terms of balance and Karma melted most of the anxiety associated with recent events. I realized other forces were at work, and if I didn't completely align myself with truth, I'd always be working against it. The thing with ultimate, egoless truth is that people either live it, or they don't. There is no in between. Of that I was certain, and that was what drove the shift within myself.

Personally, I felt gratitude for having dealt with my demons successfully. Had I not gone through such measures a year and a half prior, there was no telling where I might be. Now there was no way I would revert back to the negative types of behavior that had littered my past.

As I was chopping wood one afternoon at the cabin, I thought about the times when I had lived unconsciously. I had to laugh at how ridiculous I had been. I had played the role of the high society doctor in an affluent neighborhood. I'd done things I saw others do, and made decisions based on nothing other than the want at hand. There was very little consequential thinking.

### *Point Of Responsibility*

*120. Do you play a role in your life? Early in our childhoods, with the help of those around us, we passively choose to follow a certain path. The easiest way to think about role-playing is to remember back to high school. There were definitive groups, or cliques, of individuals. In my school, there were the nerds, the jocks, the burnouts, etc. Most people continue to live within their high school roles for their whole lives, unless there is a life-altering event that may allow someone the opportunity to drop the shroud of his or her role. One interesting thing about playing a role is that it's a complete manifestation of the ego. The ego put us into a box, and seeks to organize not only others, but ourselves as well, into this box. It becomes our comfort zone. And since we become similar to the people who surround us, we think in terms of what those people would do in our situation. In order to fit in and to be liked, we continue with this behavior. It becomes its own negative feedback loop. We seldom reach outside of that clique for advice, or anything else, for that matter. We close our brains off to input from anyone other than those with whom we typically surround ourselves. What we don't realize is that in reality we are much more than those people in cliques. At any point, we have the ability to be whomever we want. The only thing that defines us is the next moment of choice; that's it. If you find yourself playing a less than desirable role that you have unconsciously allowed yourself to slip into, change it immediately. You must alter the way you think about life. Visualize the type of people with whom you like to surround yourself. Envision everything perfectly, as you wish to live. This can be an incredibly scary step, but it's also a necessary one. You truly deserve to be on a path that makes you happy. Never let anyone tell you how to be, or guilt you into remaining in your place of unhappiness. Change it; no one else will do it for you.*

Everything that had happened had worked to raise Sasha and I up to a level of consciousness I'd never experienced. We had separated ourselves from the more typical forms of thought and living and viewed our lives with much wider eyes. We had a fuller picture of our place in the world and how the world related to us. The noise and chaos from ego-based living was gone. Self-responsibility allowed for the obliteration of blame in our own lives. We felt that blaming others for all the devastation we'd endured took away our own power. And without our own captured empowerment, humans were led to irresponsibility and sustaining negative feedback loops. The only thing that broke such a loop was to reclaim our power and self-responsibility.

Of course, allowing blame to become a thing of the past was difficult on many levels. There were pangs of hate, anger and rage focused on other people. Blaming others was, after all, how most people dealt with pain, loss and grief. At some point within our culture, self-responsibility had gained the mystique of being on par with an unreachable sense of nobility, instead of a true representation of self, manifested by each person's inherent way of being. But just because that was how others acted, that didn't give us the right to do the same. Yes, it would have satiated the ego to place blame on others. But no one had forced me to have sex with anyone. I had done it on my own volition.

Blame kills self-evolution. That's the bottom line.

Friends and family members, trying to console me, enabled the blame train. Within such conversations, I had many opportunities to avoid taking responsibility. Many acquaintances tried to convince me I couldn't be responsible for everything in my life because there were just too many variables. But I never believed that line of thought. While living irresponsibly, I never once thought I was getting away with something. I had just hoped I would never have to pay the price for those acts.

My understanding of life had always been that it's not random in any way. By the thoughts we carry and the acts we live, so our futures are created. I understood that friends and family wanted to protect their own. But again, it just passed the buck.

It would have also been easy just to lie down and play the victim. But choosing introspectively to seek out the ultimate truth within the events in question could serve as a powerful catalyst to raise one up to a place never before achieved. It is simple fact that tumultuous times create an opportunity for a person to go one way or another. They bring forth either repetitive negative occurrences, or they bring forth a situation of growth. I had the power to make the choice, and I chose to evaluate, adapt and move forward in a healthy way. Almost every other person involved in my specific case went the other way. And he or she continued to move forward with harbored guilt, shame, fear and anger.

So then, the next step was to move forward into the future. Sasha and I had done many things to live with purpose. We actively read thought-stimulating books, actively recreated our existence and watched various documentaries and films about doing so. One film that caught my interest was called What The Bleep Do We Know? It sought to bridge the gap between spirituality and physics, two of the most interesting topics that weaved threads of repetition throughout my own life on many occasions. It discussed, among other things, how Quantum Theory related our ideas and habits to physical and spiritual manifestation; how thoughts became things. The speakers described in plain detail how, as humans, we have the power to create our existence. Whether we choose to utilize that power constructively or destructively is always up to us.

On one hand, to realize such a thing appeared enlightening and incredibly exciting, like we could do absolutely anything. We have within us the same innate power of life and creation as the mustard seed. On the other hand, with that power comes tremendous responsibility. Scientists understand there is one inherent law within all existence, and that law is one of balance. So Quantum theory allows us to create anything we want, good or bad, happy or sad, active or passive. If, however, our creations become too far out of balance, both as individuals and as a species, we will, with time, inevitably have to come back to balance, either by our own power, or by the power of another influence.

One of the speakers in the film interested me more than the others. While online one afternoon, I noticed she had an educational school in our area, so I signed up for one of her courses.

While at the retreat, I was astonished by the similarity between the teachings and my own previous writings and ideas with regard to physics and its real-life relationship to each one of us. The ideas were so similar that, oftentimes, throughout the teachings, I caught myself wondering whether it was possible someone had read my writings from many years ago and run with the ball, so to speak, while I simply put them aside.

For example, within the teachings was the postulation that the microtubules within each human cell were the actual conductors of particular resonating frequencies of specific thoughts. I had written that exact idea many years before when I learned, while being taught in an undergraduate class, that the actual functional purpose of those same microtubules was simply structural in nature. At that time, scientists also knew that the basic material of the microtubules was similar to that of superconductors used in inorganic communications devices throughout the world. On a gut level, I knew it wasn't a coincidence. There was much more to it, but exactly what it was, I didn't know. I was just a naïve kid at the time.

Weeks after that class, however, as I studied organic chemistry in a rowdy coffee shop where they played loud, alternative music, I pulled from the ether an interesting theory of my own that related an individual's thoughts with physiology, Quantum theory, Eastern medical theory and emotion and behavior. It was a basic theory of everything with regard to humans' internal and inter-relational habits. I had no idea where it came from, but as I fine-tuned the theory and discussed it with people, there was very little obstruction or resistance on the part of others. The theory made sense on every level, and it was clear.

There truly was no starting or ending point, as all of life is circular. But if we had to assign a beginning, it would be in the form of a thought within the brain.

That thought traverses a series of nerves within our body at the speed of about 500 Hz, which had been proven by science. Those impulses of energy ultimately affect a muscle, organ or gland to do things like move a leg, secrete a hormone or to digest and assimilate a turkey sandwich. They also control all emotional states, whether consciously or subconsciously. Those are the processes that regulate the internal environment of the body. All of that information has been understood and well documented by science for decades.

But things get much more interesting when we add to the mixture our relationship to our external environment. For example, when we think of a friend, and then that friend calls us "completely out of the blue," is that coincidence? How about when it happens over and over consistently? It's actually a principle called synchrodestiny. We resonate at a particular frequency for various things within different cells of our body. Whatever I think about or habituate the most is what I draw into my life, whether positive or negative.

The easiest way to explain such a thing is first to describe our actual reality. We are not "things," but space. Elementary physics describes all components of the Universe, including humans, in terms of particles. The basic atom of any substance, including flesh, has a tiny nucleus that accounts for over ninety-nine percent of the mass of the whole atom. Around that nucleus is a little "cloud" of electrons that circle it. The interesting thing is that ninety-five percent of the space taken up by that atom resides in that cloud. So what makes up all that space? Quite literally, it's just non-stuff. To take it even further, the electron cloud is only a probability that one could actually find an electron encircling the nucleus at a certain distance from that nucleus. At a very specific point from that nucleus, it can no longer hold onto the electrons that encircle it. That is the point at which the outer envelope of that atom is determined physically, meaning the actual size of the atom.

Again, the electron cloud is the "space" within an atom. When there are other atoms present nearby, they might collide with one another. When this happens, they might share electrons, they might not. The one thing certain is that those two atoms don't compress one another. Ultimately, things in our visible world are collections of atoms in one way or another. When I pick up my coffee cup, what I'm feeling is a solid collection of various ceramic atoms. I never actually touch that coffee cup, even when I'm sipping from it because, since the outer part of every atom is mostly non-stuff, i.e. an electron cloud or space, the space of the coffee cup's atoms is bumping up against the space of my finger's atoms creating a buffering zone between the two. Because we are both solid, there is no mixing of the two. If we were liquids, the coffee cup and I, our atoms would mix to form another solution. But that's not the case. As I lift the cup to my lips, the feelings of weight and heat I perceive are certainly real, at least to me. But that's all they are, just perceptions. And those perceptions have absolutely nothing to do with the fact that neither one of us, the coffee cup or myself, is real or not real, because all things are real. But our perception of them is what reinforces and creates an object we actually can perceive. The bottom line is that everything in the Universe is non-stuff. Without perception, we are all collections of atoms reacting to one another. And this brings us back full circle to how humans perceive their external environment.

When we have a thought, we put that thought out into the Universe in the form of energy. When those thoughts are higher in frequency, around ten thousand Hz, they are propagated by the super conducting materials of the microtubules that line up along the meridian systems understood and explained in Eastern medicine. These propagations flow along the meridians within the body, utilizing the Chakra system as junction points by which to alter course when necessary. That, however, is not where the story ends. The propagations continue through the meridian system while inside the body, and then exit the physical body into the immediate environment around us. Along each meridian, we have exit and entrance points for this high frequency energy to propagate. The energy flows into the body carrying information from the immediate environment, picks up our reaction to it, and then flows back out into the environment. These propagations are extremely fast, and they are, quite literally, the aura, or the "sixth sense" that helps us to relate to our outer environment in a much quicker and meaningful way than the slower, more humanistic nervous system, which operates at about five hundred Hertz. It's how we know, with no other perception, that someone is approaching us from behind. It's how we manifest everything external in our lives, including things and relationships.

There are also spiritual implications to this type of thought. It is the way to begin living spiritually within every minute of life, and the means by which we can bring our ideals from a place of "wishing and hoping" them into existence, into a place within our everyday reality. As more and more of us begin to think in a similar fashion, Gestalt's theory of Universal Mind becomes even more realized. The more we think about good, the more good happens because the "collective mind" is focusing on it ever more often. It is a self-actualizing event caused by all of us.

An experiment was done where a group of terminal cancer patients were split into two groups for experimentation. One of the groups had people actively pray for them, from across the country, every day for a certain amount of time. The other group did not. After five years, the group that had prayers sent to them from a distance had a much higher rate of living than the ones who did not. The positive intention of the people sending the thoughts of health became part of the "collective mind" of the group of supposedly terminal cancer patients, and it helped them to survive.

Physiologically, as impulses of thought literally buzz with energy through the microtubules within all of us, they are resonating at the frequency of whatever that thought means to you. If it's a happy thought, you will resonate and reciprocate happy things while you hold it. If you think a destructive thought, you will draw negative things into your life. Since all things, on the most fundamental level, are just a bundle of frequencies, there is no choice but to resonate with the frequencies around us. Birds of a feather flock together.

An easy way to understand the fundamentals is to allow the vision of a guitar in your mind. Imagine you have three guitar strings of the same gauge pulled to the same tension. If you strum only one of them, within a short amount of time, the other two also begin to resonate. The reason is they share a common frequency, so they come into harmony with one another.

The same thing happens within our own microtubule system in every cell of our body. The main difference between inanimate objects and us is our ability to deduce our situations, and to make choices to, or not to, evolve our consciousness. Simply knowing this is how things are created and destroyed is our inherent capability to change our surroundings. It is our free will to choose whether we like our environment or not, and then change it accordingly. We all make choices every day. Some of us are responsible with those choices. Others are not. But have no doubt, when we impart our frequencies into the Universe, they are mirrored back to us. Our thoughts become things, in one way or another.

Manifestations are specific and the Universe is literal. If we "want," then we keep getting "want" in our lives. If we envision ourselves living that perfect life, truly living it, there is no other possibility than for it to be manifested. The human brain knows not the difference between the physical world and its internal world. Actually, there is no difference, since everything is non-stuff, and it's all made up of the same non-stuff.

As the retreat continued, every day brought some new validation to me that I was on the right track not just with theory, but also with action. We were taught some new forms of active meditation and utilized breathing techniques to heighten our focus and to retrain the brain to live in the present. We reviewed anatomy and physiology, and learned how to train various parts of the brain to work in unison to create our daily environment. The whole event was truly surreal. I'd never experienced anything like it.

I liked that the whole philosophy around the retreat was to improve the efficiency of the underdeveloped human brain. The retreat leaders used physiologically sound techniques combined with the understanding of the latest brain-related research to change thought patterns and to live in the present at every waking moment. The best thing about all of it was the onus was put back on each of us as humans to change our environment. There was a definite sense of spirituality within the group, but not of religion, per se. The determination was made very quickly within the first day that it was every human's responsibility to live a life connected to the infinite, to break free of polarity (i.e. good vs. bad, light vs. dark, sick vs. healthy) and to bridge the gap between being humans versus humans being. Focus was on how we needed to get back to balance, and break free of the extreme ways of life we'd been living in recent times with endless entertainment and escapism.

The retreat made me realize how I had changed my life forever in the weeks just before I met Sasha. I had literally chosen not to live with all the negativity in my life. And I meant it on every level of my body and mind. I envisioned a life with my dream partner, with children, with abundance and balance in every way possible. I envisioned joy in every part of my life and surrounded myself with great people who shared common ideals. I changed my neuronet (the connections within the brain) from one of habitual confusion, chaos and ego, to one of joy, abundance and clarity. I even had numerous chances to test myself, and I had passed with flying colors. Of course, I didn't have as much money or the cool toys I once did, but those things were part of the old system. Everything from that point forward was sure to happen again. I would have the money, because I was finally living with passion, not with scarcity. And that was an interesting point, because if I could create all the things I had in my past on the shaky grounds of scarcity, it was going to be so much more powerful to create that abundance, and more, with passion, balance and responsibility. I was excited!

The afternoon I came home from the retreat, Sasha greeted me at the door. I embraced her like I never had before. As we walked inside and I put down my things, she told me how much younger I looked. All the focused meditation, exercise, learning and breathing techniques had done me some good. I felt like a new man. I had tons of energy and was raring to go.

## *Point Of Responsibility*

*121. Utilize time-tested breathing techniques to create a rush of oxygenation and endorphins into the bloodstream and into the brain. Do this as many times as possible throughout each day. First, sit cross-legged on your floor. Use a pillow if you like. In the West, we typically have poorly developed lower back musculature. So if necessary, put your back against a couch or chair for support. But over time, work toward using no support. Put your palms down on your knees and straighten your back as you close your eyes. Begin by taking deep breaths in through your nose and out through your mouth, filling both your chest and abdomen. After a couple of minutes, fill only your abdomen with air. Then fill only your chest with air. When you've completed those tasks, start breathing much shallower through your mouth only. Pull the air deep into your abdomen, and on the exhalation, make a constant "shhhhhh" sound. Squeeze your diaphragm forcefully to push every molecule of air out of your lungs. Do that for about twenty or thirty seconds; then go back to breathing slowly. Repeat the breathing for as long as time allows. Fifteen to twenty minutes in the morning and at lunch will give your body a wonderful rush of energy. Do slow, deep breathing to relax at the end of the day. If, at any point, you feel light-headed, stop. Only do the deep breathing portion.*

Sasha made a wonderful dinner that we lazily picked at as I shared all the things I'd learned about and thought up over the previous five days. The conversation went deep into the night. When we finally decided to hit the hay, it was three in the morning. I could have talked for hours more, but it was time for a little sleep.

We spent the next couple of days at the cabin. I got the motorcycle fired up and ready to go, gave the yard a nice cleanup, and built a small barn for storage and a workshop. Mike called to see whether I wanted to take a road trip for a few days over to Idaho. He was thinking about working there at some summer resort. Sasha gave me the green light to go have some fun. It had been a long time since he and I had hung out. It would also help if he had an extra set of eyes on moose patrol, as Mike was prone to hitting random things on the sides of the road, like cars and campers.

So he and I did our thing. We ate, we drank, and we listened to the locals tell stories. I tried to impart some of my new knowledge to Mike, but every time something blonde passed him, he lost focus and I had to start over. So I gave up after a few tries. It was fun just to hang out with no big-brain activity for a few days. We were just dudes, and it was refreshing.

On the night I returned, I got some of the greatest news of my life. Sasha informed me she was pregnant! I couldn't believe I was finally going to be a father! I was so proud, so full of warmth and a joy I'd never felt before!

We immediately started preparing for the baby to arrive. My father and his long-time girlfriend started buying up baby clothes, and we started looking for cribs and strollers. It was a whole new world to me. I started to think in terms of safety and protection. How would I baby-proof my home? How was the car seat supposed to be placed again? How would I know whether the baby was warm enough in the winter? I had no idea what the hell I was supposed to do! All I knew was that the baby was going to be the most loved baby I'd ever laid my eyes upon.

In the middle of May, Henry called to say the settlement conference with the DOH would be the first week of June. I told him that would be fine and just to let me know exactly when. It wasn't like I had a job or anything.

Afterward, I called my dad to give him the news. Then I asked him what was new on his end. He told me our family reunion was going to be the last week of June. He'd rented eight cabins for about thirty of us in Southern Indiana. The place sounded great. I told him I didn't know whether we'd make it, but we would certainly give it our best shot.

As the days dragged on until the settlement hearing, we stayed focused on our new little prize. We planted a tree for him or her and started to arrange things in the house to accommodate the baby's furniture. After tons of research, we decided to work with a midwife throughout the pregnancy. Things moved along very quickly, and before we knew it, we were coming up on the end of the first trimester.

On one random night, I was awakened by the toilet flushing. As I lay in bed, something didn't feel right. I jumped up and went toward the bathroom. Sasha was crying and was obviously distraught. I asked her what was up, trying to calm her down. I didn't want to add to the already palpable emotion in the room. She told me she was spotting, and it was bright red, not a good thing. But all we could do was wait.

The next few days were horrible. She continued to spot, and then the cramps started. I was torn between hoping for the best and preparing for the worst. I couldn't even imagine how Sasha must have felt. All I could do was lie by her and talk with her as she began to process all the emotions that flooded her bloodstream.

Two days before my settlement conference, our initial fears were confirmed with an ultrasound. Sasha had had a miscarriage. It was absolutely devastating. We both wanted our new little baby to thrive. But it wasn't meant to be. The emotions we rode over the next couple of days were so unbelievably extreme. On one hand, I was very sad and disappointed with the obvious. On the other, I knew her body had rejected the fetus for a reason. I also knew we'd have many more opportunities for children. Many first-time mothers had miscarriages before popping out a whole slew of kids. Sasha wasn't with me on that one.

I tried to keep Sasha's spirits high, but the constant rushes of emotion were enough to drive us both insane. One minute, she clung to me for support; the next, she'd pushed me away. I couldn't say anything right. I annoyed her by simply looking in her direction, and then annoyed her by not looking at her. She was like four different people in one little body. Like everything else we'd been through, we just had to ride it out until its completion.

On June 6, I woke up after sleeping for only a couple of hours. I showered, put on my suit and headed off for the settlement conference in Olympia.

As I drove down the highway toward my inevitable fate, I had mixed feelings about the conference. I was a little sad at the way things had turned out, and I was very much ashamed, but I was also grateful to have lived through it all, and for becoming balanced and responsible. I was also relieved that the process was coming to a close. I even felt a little sorry for those who were so active in my judgment. It was clearly beyond their understanding that my life was different than it had been in the past. I'd done my part to change my life, well before I was ever instructed to do so. Unfortunately, that didn't make much difference.

In my opinion, my case ended up being more about punishment and retribution than healing. The primary claim was that I was a threat to the public, yet no one asked how I was doing, either emotionally or therapeutically, through any of the proceedings up to this point. Not one person had made sure I was getting healthy.

I pulled into the parking lot and turned off the car. I looked in the mirror and smiled at myself. I really loved the person I'd become. I was going to be okay. I was detached from outcome and had an overwhelming sense of peace.

### *Points Of Responsibility*

*122. Detach from outcome. Enter into every conversation and situation confidently and be solid in your self. Spend the necessary time before the event to educate yourself, to prepare for it, to think about ways to be responsible. When you prepare diligently, you inherently erase most of the anxiety you might have originally felt. You become more confident in you and your product, whether that product is a physical product, a service, or yourself. To be prepared is the best we can do. When you think in such terms, the outcome becomes quite ineffectual. You truly have no control over it. From this point forward, visualize and prepare for your scheduled conversations and events (and even the unscheduled ones) in advance. Do the work. Practice doing this in both your business and personal life. Smile and do your best.*

*123. Smile. When you put a half-smile on your face, whether you mean it or not, it activates receptors in the nerve endings in your face that send signals to your brain to release endorphins, the feel-good chemicals in your body. When endorphins course through your arteries and veins, you feel more balanced and even elated. And you're almost instantly in a better mood. When you're depressed, or caught in the middle of a negative feedback loop of destructive thought, put a smile on your face, no matter how ridiculous it may seem at the time. Just do it. You'll feel better.*

I met Henry and Aimee on the way into the building. After a few minutes, the Department of Health's attorney and the Board's representative came over and introduced themselves. We all quickly walked back to a sterile little conference room to get started.

I'd done little to prepare for the event. It was the kind of thing where one just sits and takes his lumps. I just hoped my attorneys were prepared. I knew Aimee was going to be there alongside Henry. I wanted to believe she'd practiced her speech all night. I wanted to see a dramatic courtroom battle.

We all sat down and the representative began to read through the allegations. Everyone already knew the charges, but he wanted slowly to go through them, one by one, to reintroduce the grand, evil nature of the case at hand. He even added a little scowl, and an occasional shaking of the head for effect. When he was finished, he waited for one of my attorneys to reply.

Henry was the first to speak on my behalf. He brought up many great points, like how I had chaperoned women patients, had sought successful psychotherapy before being required to do so, how I had to sell my practice and didn't make any money on it, and that nothing sexual with regard to any former patient had occurred for almost two years. He told them I was happily married, that I had to sell one of our homes, and that the other was going into foreclosure. He explained I had to move out of town, was forced to sell almost everything I owned, and I was nearly bankrupt. He added that I was untrained to do anything other than be a chiropractor, and I would be financially ruined for a long time. Because of the negative press, I was basically not hirable. Not only would I be unable to practice chiropractic, but I also wouldn't be able to secure any other type of respectable position. My reputation had been forever tarnished, regardless that I had not committed any crimes. He described how I had paid quite a hefty price for the things I'd done. He even brought up that the Board's own investigator had said I was the most honest and upright individual he'd ever investigated. Henry concluded by requesting a minimal suspension; he humbly stated that a twenty-year revocation, which was what they were still pursuing, was basically the same as a lifetime ban, which was exactly true. I liked his approach. It was clear and concise.

When it was my turn, I explained that, from day one, I had always been completely truthful. I knew everything was my fault, and I had taken full responsibility. I had hoped that telling the absolute truth, getting counseling and completely changing my life would work in my favor. After all, everyone is guilty of something. I hoped the Board members could find within themselves the ability to forgive some of my past mistakes due to my positive actions. And as I talked, I felt comfortable because I had taken complete responsibility for everything. I didn't blame others or justify anything. The whole event left me clean and pure.

When I finished, the negotiations were in full effect, and they weren't pretty. The Board was still pushing for a twenty-year revocation, and Henry humbly worked for a reduction. As they went back and forth, all I could do was sit there and watch the chess match unfold. They discussed the new standards and precedence. There were mild to moderate theatrics, and plenty of awkward silences. After a couple of hours, I simply wanted the conference to end.

Henry was more than willing to continue negotiating, and I was inspired that he was at least trying to put up a fight. But it wasn't like there was a judge or an arbitrator involved at that point. The bottom line was that I was at the mercy of the Board. Since that was the hearing where I wanted things to end completely, we didn't have much leverage. There was no guarantee a formal hearing would provide me with a shorter sentence, and if I went that route, the media would be in frenzy over such a case. It would be a no-win situation. Since absolutely no good would come out of it for anyone, I agreed it was going to end at that conference, for better or worse. I hadn't the will or the financial capability to go on fighting. So we ultimately agreed to a ten-year revocation. I was instructed to continue counseling, and at the end of the ten years, I had to prove I was healed. I wasn't guaranteed I'd get my license back. That was the best we could do.

In the end, it was the Board's position to make sure I wasn't a threat to the public. The Board members repeatedly declared it was not in their interest, in any way, to punish me for the things I'd done. They just wanted to make sure I wasn't going to harm anyone else, but after being through the process, I knew there was more to it.

I sincerely hoped that regaining my health wouldn't take ten long years of my life to achieve, especially since it had basically already happened. I'd already done the work. And more importantly, I took all the responsibility, even for the others who were part of the activity. I blamed no one but myself.

And I certainly wasn't a threat to the public anymore, no matter how much the Board wanted me to be that monster. In my opinion, the hearing was all about punishment. If it weren't, someone would have asked me how therapy was going at some point through the proceedings. But interestingly enough, it never came up. They were too busy focusing on the terms of my "not punishment."

No one but myself had a clear understanding of the gravity of the decisions they were making. They could have been part of the rebuilding of a person rather than the further destruction of a family. I felt like a pawn. I agreed a suspension was necessary, as was functional therapy. But ten years was a long time when no crime had been committed. It was decisions like theirs that tended to reinforce the blame mentality of our wonderful country. But nobody seemed to care. There was absolutely no regard for anything positive I'd done, or for the truth that lay within everything I'd been through.

I didn't want to believe it, but in my opinion, there was very little objectivity or justice within the process. It was all so ego-based. In no way was it geared toward actually helping anyone, but focused more on power, control and blame. Of course, I was the one who was being forced into ten years of exile. I had very little credibility, and no leverage whatsoever. But that didn't diminish that out of all those individuals on the Board, and of the three people who submitted interviews and blamed me for the demise of their lives, I was possibly the least egoistic, most responsible and consciously purpose-driven person involved. I didn't blame anyone other than myself. But I gave them the sword to cut me down. I had a flashback to when I used to be one of those people, constantly fighting to be more right, to be heard, and to accumulate wealth and prestige. I grew ever more thankful that I'd crystallized a completely different life than the one I'd suffered in the past. I wasn't better than anyone, and none of them were better than me. I simply allowed for consciousness, tolerance and for the perfusion of passion and joy in my life. I'd never been wealthier. I'd never been happier. And I was finally starting to follow my passion to help others break the unnecessary chains responsible for keeping us bound to the ground.

At the conclusion of the conference, I pushed my chair away from the table, stood up and asked whether that was all. They all just looked at me as if they had no idea when I entered the room. Someone said the proceedings were complete, so without another word, I pushed in my chair, shook their hands and left.

I felt freer than I remembered feeling in years. I got in my car, opened all the windows and took off toward the freeway. I called up Sasha to give her the news. I told her the Board had gotten its way with a ten-year revocation. She asked me whether I was all right. I smiled and told her I was great. I actually felt great. It was getting a little noisy to talk with the windows open, so I told her I'd just see her at the cabin in a few hours.

The drive was nice, the weather perfect. I felt I had a new lease on life. I could finally do anything and go anywhere I wanted.

Later that night, as Sasha and I talked over dinner, we discussed how nice it was finally to be able to move forward. In the moments between words, I thought about how my life had been before I met Sasha. I had all the toys, cars, houses, and plenty of money, but I was always exhausted. I never saw my family, and my life was confused. I was, quite literally, sleepwalking through life. If I had never been forced to go through all of the recent devastation, I might never have awakened. I now had a full life, the life for which I'd always searched. I owed it to that process. And I was grateful. I was finally living a life of consciousness and purpose.

It was time to forget the turmoil that had once surrounded me. I'd taken the lessons and actively formed them into a new program that helped me to become more confident and tolerant. My lifestyle was completely different than it had been, and I wanted it to continue.

## *Point Of Responsibility*

*124. Studies show that people who welcome new experiences have stronger connections between their hippocampus (the memory center), the frontal lobe and reward centers within the brain. Basically, if you think it's time for a change, your attitude can go a long way to influence that change. When you actively seek new things, your brain releases chemicals that lead to positive feelings. Also, when you desire to be recognized within your environment, those actions and intentions create stronger connections to the reward centers. So decide what you want in your life, create those visions in your mind as having already taken place. Revisit those visions many times each day; live them from your memory, and from your constructive thoughts created in the frontal lobe. These will integrate and become stronger within the reward centers, allowing for a positive feedback loop to be created. Soon enough, you will manifest your life in the physical realm.*

The next day Sasha and I woke up and I made some coffee. She looked at me, gave me a hug, and told me that it was time for me to take a cross-country motorcycle trip. It was time to venture out into the world in a way I'd never known. She'd previously called my father to plan my arrival for our family reunion in Indiana in three weeks, and she planned for us to meet in Lake Tahoe a couple of weeks after that, to celebrate our one-year anniversary and the Fourth of July. I couldn't have asked for a better ending, and subsequent beginning. I had the love and support of my life partner, my family and my friends. And that is what I hold within me as I continue to create my new life every day.

Chapter Twenty-Four:

# The Essence of Change and Leadership

As I made my two-wheeled trek across the great lands of America, inspirational and motivational thoughts wriggled and writhed in and out of my mind. The ride illuminated many obvious analogies to which I could easily compare my life. While I rode, some days were markedly better than others. They were filled with sun, good people, vivid scenery and a want for nothing. Others were filled with angry drivers, split fuel lines, wild animals and killer storms. All were a necessary part of my journey, and all were navigated more proactively by simply relaxing and taking everything in stride.

All of our lives contain events we've designed, consciously or unconsciously, to evolve each respective soul. One might declare that my situation was an extreme case, that it holds very little fodder for the molding of another's life. But therein lies the crux of the issue. That would be the ego separating you from everything else, trying to put you above everyone, including me. Our lives are not a comparison, and one life is not more important, better, or more extreme, than another. A relative place exists for every thought and action that takes place on Earth. It is true we are all separate, but we are also equal. There is no place for any view that works to separate us. For me, my life's events were extreme. For another, they might not be. But rest assured, the events that make up my life have the same relative importance to me as do the events that make up each person's life. Find the lessons in every person's story and make the necessary adjustments in your own life. Don't focus on the story itself. That is certainly not the point of life.

The last statement begs that the question be asked: What is the most important point of this book, and possibly of our earthly lives? It is that we all have within us the power and the abilities to live and to love with responsibility, to live and to love consciously, and to live and to love without blame. Once understood and agreed to, these are the principles that will lead us further into the evolution of self, family, community, country, and of the Earth.

Although the principles and action steps contained within the pages of this book could certainly help the most addicted individuals, it is primarily aimed at changing the lives of those who can most definitely CHOOSE their fates on a daily basis, but who are too consumed with ego-based living, which, in fact, is an enormous number of people. So we're not talking about the most extreme cases, but YOUR case. This book is designed to stimulate creative thought to overcome YOUR life's most difficult obstacles.

The most profound changes in life are the ones inherently contained within the small paradigm shifts. Life, after all, is a series of small corrections. Each correction is first a decision followed by a small, manageable action step. Take a more anamorphic view of your life. View it from a bird's eye. Take it all into account.

There is no easy way to do the work on yourself. And, of course, there is no one-size-fits-all blueprint to self-creation. We all have our own lessons to learn. That is the point of this book. The principles herein uncover and stimulate that self-creation. When doing the steps, think about what YOU require to evolve, and then do it. It's not enough simply to follow the steps. You must take your power and use it to create the life you have been afraid to live. THAT is where emotions are functional.

Understand that YOU are in control of your Earthly life, no one else. You control your emotions. You have your perceptions. You control your experiences. And you can change all of it. When you work through the steps, you will begin to gain confidence in yourself as a human on this Earth. Having that confidence allows you to create, to manifest something unique. Once you complete the steps, your perceptions will be more wide-eyed than you ever could have imagined. Each and every experience will be so much more meaningful, while anxiety and compulsions will become a thing of the past.

You can choose to do the steps, knowing you are changing your life for the better because you inherently and intentionally are. Or you can continue to make excuses for why the steps here won't work for you. Either way, you'll get exactly what you want. Anything that can create such empowerment and clarity in a human's life is absolutely worth whatever it takes to achieve. And besides, how much longer can you put it off? Would you put it off again if you knew you only had months left in your life to clean up the messes you've created? The urgency is important to the process. Procrastination and blame kill self-evolution. So get to work.

Once you've made the choice, go for it. Don't turn back because you've already changed. There is no going back to that old life, unless that's really what you want.

When faced with adversity, many people declare they are going to change their lives with a newfound vigor. Change may happen for a time, but most fail because there are self-imposed expectations around the hopeful outcome. There is also no framework by which to create such an existence. Instead, focus must be lent toward the small action steps that allow for a new and healthy neuronet to develop. Mind your thoughts. Mind your actions. Make active decisions. Smile. Work. Enjoy your relationships. Accept and appreciate people for who they are, not for what you think they should be or have the ability to be. Learn to laugh at your faults, and be more understanding of the faults of others. Create abundance and joy everywhere you go. Make tons of money, but have balance within the rest of your life. Balance is the natural state of the Universe. Rid yourself of harm. Catapult blame out of your way of being. Take responsibility. And live your life the way it was meant to be lived! Anything different is less than the fulfilled human experience.

A staggering number of people know themselves to be good, but they walk around blindly, take more than they give, are irresponsible in one way or another, or place blame on others for their misery. There are people who spend countless hours every day within the endless realm of entertainment or other forms of escapism. This book is a call to action for the human species to challenge each day of life with consciousness, to spend time creating, to help each other, to decrease anxiety by dealing with and learning from issues instead of escaping from them. It presents a proactive approach to bridge the gap between our spiritual ideals, whatever they may be, and life on the physical plane. For if we don't make the necessary changes, we will be destined to repeat the same ego-based patterns that keep us where we are in life. The only way to make this happen is to lead, by example, a purpose-driven, blame-free life with self-responsibility.

## *Points Of Responsibility*

*125. Remain present in every second of your life, no matter how vehemently opposed to that action your ego might be.*

*126. Avoid passive daydreaming at all cost. It steals your life by the second.*

*127. Work diligently to interpret and understand emotions, but don't live by them.*

*128. Disengage self-doubt immediately by refocusing your intention on the new format of your goal sheet.*

*129. Blame kills self-evolution. Take responsibility.*

BECOME PART OF THE RESPONSIBILITY MOVEMENT NOW!

WWW.RESPONSIBILITYMOVEMENT.COM

Appendix:

# Points of Responsibility

# About the Author

Dr. Mark J. Svetcos is a renowned speaker, educator and consultant to individuals, corporations and organizations that are seeking clarity of purpose, motivation and efficiency. He is widely viewed as America's new-world pioneer in the field of personal responsibility and integrity.

Dr. Svetcos is the founder of The Responsibility Movement™, The 7 Pillars of Balance™, and the creator of the CSE (Common Sense Evolution) System™, a series of diagnostics, awareness techniques, and easy to follow action steps that focus primarily on recreating a powerful, new America through individual self-responsibility. He spends much of his time speaking and coaching on the principles of The 7 Pillars.

Dr. Svetcos has been a frequent guest on numerous radio and television programs. He has been recognized in various newspapers, including the Seattle Post-Intelligencer, and has been featured on "Inside Edition" and in the Associated Press.

As a highly successful doctor, teacher and small business owner, Dr. Svetcos' concise, real-world expertise and methodology has helped to improve the lives of thousands of his patients and clients. His challenging new mission is to spearhead a revolution of blame-free, self-responsible people across the globe. He believes we truly can change the world, but that change must begin within each of us. Once we become balanced within the self, across all 7 Pillars, we may then begin to give to humanity from a healthy, enlightened place. We become purpose-driven and more balanced for our family, our friends, our community, our state, our government, and our earth. We become people of intentional action.

Originally from Michigan, Dr. Svetcos graduated from Western Michigan University in 1998 with a Bachelor of Arts in Biomedical Science, heavily weighted in chemistry. He completed his doctorate at Life University in Marietta, Georgia, in 2002. He has been the owner and clinic director of private practices in Colorado and Washington State. He and his wife, Denise, currently reside in the North Cascade mountains, in the town of Glacier, Washington.

# About the Responsibility Movement™

Responsibility is the common thread that binds us as humans. It is the basis of morality, religion, and widely accepted codes of conduct. The Responsibility Movement ™ is a free system of practical education, articles, introspective diagnostics, and powerful action steps to help you begin proactively to bridge the gap between your conscious ideals and your everyday real life. Primary access to this information is in the free monthly newsletter and the free pages at responsibilitymovement.com. The Responsibility Movement™ is for anyone who desires to create a powerful, purpose-driven, conscious life.

The fundamental components of the Responsibility Movement™ are The 7 Pillars of Balance™, which include: Wellness of the Mind, Love and Relationships, Success and Leadership, Finance, Physical Wellness, Codes of Living, and Spirituality. In order for a life to be truly enlightened, conscious and responsible, balance must be achieved across The 7 Pillars.

When you sign up to become part of the Responsibility Movement™, you will begin to learn how to recapture your power and self-esteem from the inside out. The program has been designed to help you to create the life you know you are meant to live, and to recapture the priceless moments between thoughts. You will learn easy, functional steps to resolve needless conflict quickly and efficiently, to deal with internal and external emotions, and to live more objectively. When you become strong in the awareness and understanding of your self, and begin to live your purpose-driven life, you will be more balanced for your family, friends, community, state, country and earth. Your decisions will be based solely on your own thought. You will be living from the place you've always desired to live, without fear and apathy. When these things are achieved, you will finally be able to give to humanity from a healthy, enlightened place. You'll begin to live your passions, and have a newfound zest for life.

In addition to basic Responsibility Movement™ membership, other products and services are offered to evolve your life. The CSE (Common Sense Evolution)™ System is a collection of books, writings, CD's and DVD's relative to each of The 7 Pillars, including exercise and weight loss programs, personalized nutritional programs, Active Thought Creation™ techniques, and efficiency training.

For those who desire a more personalized, or face to face approach to their whole-life evolution, there is the CSE™ Speaking, Coaching, and Workshop division of the Responsibility Movement™, within which Dr. Mark J. Svetcos coaches and speaks to elite professionals, athletes, mothers, fathers, and children to better balance The 7 Pillars. His approach is highly motivational, and more importantly, he provides an easy to follow, step-by-step program by which to recreate your life within each of The 7 Pillars.

The most functional and most powerful way to change the world is to change your self. The Responsibility Movement™ has been specifically created to help you disengage from the stressful, unbalanced, entertainment-based, day to day life you've created, and transform it into what you envision it to be: conscious, happy and purpose-driven.

Join the next wave of human enlightenment now. Join the Responsibility Movement™. And don't forget to sign up for the action-packed monthly newsletter!

# About the CSE™ System

The CSE (Common Sense Evolution)™ System is a newly released collection of revolutionary writings, techniques and products that will help you and your family facilitate health, wellness, objectivity and purpose within each of The 7 Pillars of Balance™. The system is organized into each of the 7 Pillars to create clarity, and maximum efficiency and assimilation.

The CSE System was developed by Dr. Mark J. Svetcos over many years of education, research and experience in the medical field. After seeing countless dysfunctional fad diets, programs and systems that narrowly focus on either the physical, the emotional, or the spiritual, Dr. Svetcos decided to create an easy-to-follow, whole-life evolution program that focuses on the whole person. At its core, the CSE System teaches you how to understand and live your ideals within each second of your day. You will learn how to be self-responsible and balanced in all situations. As you work the system, a new level of clarity will enter your life. You will become healthier in body, mind and soul. The physical exercises and breathing techniques will rejuvenate your body, increasing flexibility, strength and stamina. The emotional exercises facilitate self-awareness, and will lead to eradication of shame, fear and anxiety once and for all. Your thoughts will become clearer and more focused. The Active Thought Creation™ techniques will help you to create every moment of your life. You will be more focused and will stop living by the whims of others. You will learn to understand and manage your ego, uncovering your truest self. You will garner respect and admiration from others as you systematically begin to live your One True Life. The financial exercises will allow you successfully to manage and create your wealth. You will learn how to find and keep the most meaningful relationships in your life. You will learn the fundamental characteristics of all spiritual practice, and learn to be more tolerant of everyone and everything around you. Specific action steps will guide you along the path to success and how to be a powerful and responsible leader. Within the CSE System are techniques for you to create your own Codes of Living. You can either construct your own Codes or use the ones provided within the program as a template.

When you purchase the CSE System, you will receive: all the awareness techniques, action steps, forms, exercises, nutrition and weight loss programs, breathing and meditation techniques, success and leadership techniques, Active Thought Creation™ techniques, time management and efficiency training, stress and anxiety management techniques, the Universal Code of Responsibility™ methods that show you how to deal with change, training on how to diffuse emotional situations, and much more.

Check out the Products section at www.responsibilitymovement.com for more information on writings, CD's and DVD's, physical therapy devices, and for speaking, consulting, coaching and workshop products from the CSE Speaking and Coaching division.

# About CSE™ Speaking, Coaching and Workshops

For those who desire a more personalized, or face to face approach to their whole-life evolution, there is the CSE™ Speaking, Coaching and Workshop division of the Responsibility Movement™, within which Dr. Mark J. Svetcos coaches and speaks to elite professionals, corporations, organizations, athletes, mothers, fathers, and children on the principles of The 7 Pillars of Balance™. His approach is highly motivational, and more importantly, he provides you with an easy to follow, step-by-step program to recreate your life within each of The 7 Pillars.

## Speaking:

Dr. Svetcos spends much of his time as a successful international speaker. Three of his most sought after talks are:

1) Aspire to Inspire,

2) Lead by Example, and

3) Manage Change Successfully.

He has many talks from which to choose, and he will customize his message to accommodate the meeting planner's objectives. Contact Dr. Svetcos at www.marksvetcos.com today to discuss availability and content for your next event.

## Coaching:

Dr. Svetcos has successfully coached thousands of patients and clients into lives of profound enlightenment and physical wellness. His unique system will change your life. Dr. Svetcos offers personal and business coaching to those who sincerely desire to achieve success and balance in every part of their lives. When you sign up for coaching with Dr. Svetcos, you will receive the complete CSE System at no charge.

For a free 30-minute, complimentary coaching session, contact Dr. Svetcos at www.marksvetcos.com.

## Workshops:

Dr. Svetcos offers CSE workshops that focus on The 7 Pillars of Balance at various times and locations throughout the year. When you sign up for a workshop, Dr. Svetcos personally guarantees that you will learn the necessary components to achieving health, wellness, and success in all parts of your life. The workshops often sell out quickly as Dr. Svetcos limits the number of attendees to allow for maximum efficiency and assimilation of information. So be sure to sign up quickly.

You can find more information on the CSE™ Speaking, Coaching, and Workshop program at www.marksvetcos.com.

To purchase and/or sign up for a speaking engagement, coaching, and/or workshop, go to www.marksvetcos.com.

# Disclaimer

**Literary Disclaimer:**

Although this book is based on true events, all names, places and events have been fictionalized, modified or changed completely to protect the innocent and the guilty, without implying either. Characters, institutions, corporations, and organizations are either products of the imagination or, if real, used fictitiously without any intent to describe their actual conduct, thoughts, physical characteristics, intentions, backgrounds, or medical conditions. Any similarity to actual people, events or location is not intentional.

**Age of Intended Audience:**

The Content of this book is intended for adults and should not be used by children under the age of 18.

**Governing Laws and Jurisdiction:**

These Terms and Conditions of Use shall be governed by and interpreted in accordance with United States law and the laws of the Owner's (Responsible Life, Inc.) State and County of residence, whose courts shall have sole jurisdiction over any dispute.

**Medical Disclaimer:**

This book is solely intended for educational purposes. Any medical description or what may appear to be medical advice is not meant to be represented as accurate, safe, or, in some cases, even remotely possible. If you need medical or psychological care, please seek the help of a competent health care practitioner. It is never safe to self-diagnose. Any recommendations are the personal opinion of the author and do not necessarily reflect the views of Responsible Life, Inc.